Multimedia
Information Extraction and
Digital Heritage Preservation

T0350144

Statistical Science and Interdisciplinary Research

Series Editor: Sankar K. Pal *(Indian Statistical Institute)*

Description:
In conjunction with the Platinum Jubilee celebrations of the Indian Statistical Institute, a series of books will be produced to cover various topics, such as Statistics and Mathematics, Computer Science, Machine Intelligence, Econometrics, other Physical Sciences, and Social and Natural Sciences. This series of edited volumes in the mentioned disciplines culminate mostly out of significant events — conferences, workshops and lectures — held at the ten branches and centers of ISI to commemorate the long history of the institute.

Vol. 4   Advances in Multivariate Statistical Methods
          edited by A. SenGupta (Indian Statistical Institute, India)

Vol. 5   New and Enduring Themes in Development Economics
          edited by B. Dutta, T. Ray & E. Somanathan
          (Indian Statistical Institute, India)

Vol. 6   Modeling, Computation and Optimization
          edited by S. K. Neogy, A. K. Das and R. B. Bapat
          (Indian Statistical Institute, India)

Vol. 7   Perspectives in Mathematical Sciences I: Probability and Statistics
          edited by N. S. N. Sastry, T. S. S. R. K. Rao, M. Delampady and
          B. Rajeev (Indian Statistical Institute, India)

Vol. 8   Perspectives in Mathematical Sciences II: Pure Mathematics
          edited by N. S. N. Sastry, T. S. S. R. K. Rao, M. Delampady and
          B. Rajeev (Indian Statistical Institute, India)

Vol. 9   Recent Developments in Theoretical Physics
          edited by S. Ghosh and G. Kar (Indian Statistical Institute, India)

Vol. 10   Multimedia Information Extraction and Digital Heritage Preservation
          edited by U. M. Munshi (Indian Institute of Public Administration,
          India) & B. B. Chaudhuri (Indian Statistical Institute, India)

Vol. 11   Machine Interpretation of Patterns: Image Analysis and Data Mining
          edited by R. K. De, D. P. Mandal and A. Ghosh
          (Indian Statistical Institute, India)

Vol. 12   Recent Trends in Surface and Colloid Science
          edited by Bidyut K. Paul (Indian Statistical Institute, India)

Platinum Jubilee Series

Statistical Science and
Interdisciplinary Research — Vol. 10

Multimedia
Information Extraction and
Digital Heritage Preservation

Editors

Usha Mujoo Munshi

Indian Institute of Public Administration, India

Bidyut Baran Chaudhuri

Indian Statistical Institute, India

Series Editor: **Sankar K. Pal**

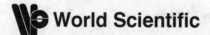

NEW JERSEY · LONDON · SINGAPORE · BEIJING · SHANGHAI · HONG KONG · TAIPEI · CHENNAI

Published by

World Scientific Publishing Co. Pte. Ltd.
5 Toh Tuck Link, Singapore 596224
USA office: 27 Warren Street, Suite 401-402, Hackensack, NJ 07601
UK office: 57 Shelton Street, Covent Garden, London WC2H 9HE

British Library Cataloguing-in-Publication Data
A catalogue record for this book is available from the British Library.

MULTIMEDIA INFORMATION EXTRACTION AND DIGITAL HERITAGE PRESERVATION
Statistical Science and Interdisciplinary Research — Vol. 10

Copyright © 2011 by World Scientific Publishing Co. Pte. Ltd.

All rights reserved. This book, or parts thereof, may not be reproduced in any form or by any means, electronic or mechanical, including photocopying, recording or any information storage and retrieval system now known or to be invented, without written permission from the Publisher.

For photocopying of material in this volume, please pay a copying fee through the Copyright Clearance Center, Inc., 222 Rosewood Drive, Danvers, MA 01923, USA. In this case permission to photocopy is not required from the publisher.

Desk Editor: Tjan Kwang Wei

ISBN-13 978-981-4307-25-3
ISBN-10 981-4307-25-4

Printed in Singapore by World Scientific Printers.

Foreword

The Indian Statistical Institute (ISI) was established on 17th December, 1931 by a great visionary Prof. Prasanta Chandra Mahalanobis to promote research in the theory and applications of statistics as a new scientific discipline in India. In 1959, Pandit Jawaharlal Nehru, the then Prime Minister of India introduced the ISI Act in the parliament and designated it as an Institution of National Importance because of its remarkable achievements in statistical work as well as its contribution to economic planning.

Today, the Indian Statistical Institute occupies a prestigious position in the academic firmament. It has been a haven for bright and talented academics working in a number of disciplines. Its research faculty has done India proud in the arenas of Statistics, Mathematics, Economics, Computer Science, among others. Over seventy five years, it has grown into a massive banyan tree, like the institute emblem. The Institute now serves the nation as a unified and monolithic organization from different places, namely Kolkata, the Headquarters, Delhi, Bangalore, and Chennai, three centers, a network of five SQC-OR Units located at Mumbai, Pune, Baroda, Hyderabad and Coimbatore, and a branch (field station) at Giridih. The platinum jubilee celebrations of ISI have been launched by Honorable Prime Minister Prof. Manmohan Singh on December 24, 2006, and the Govt. of India has declared 29th June as the "Statistics Day" to commemorate the birthday of Prof. Mahalanobis nationally.

Prof. Mahalanobis, was a great believer in interdisciplinary research, because he thought that this will promote the development of not only Statistics, but also the other natural and social sciences. To promote interdisciplinary research, major strides were made in the areas of computer science, statistical quality control, economics, biological and social sciences, physical and earth sciences.

The Institute's motto of 'unity in diversity' has been the guiding principle of all its activities since its inception. It highlights the unifying role of statistics in relation to various scientific activities.

In tune with this hallowed tradition , a comprehensive academic programme, involving Nobel Laureates, Fellows of the Royal Society, Abel prize winner and other dignitaries, has been implemented throughout the Platinum Jubilee year, highlighting the emerging areas of ongoing frontline research in its various scientific divisions, centers, and outlying units. It includes international and national-level seminars, symposia, conferences and workshops, as well as series of special lectures. As an outcome of these events, the Institute is bringing out a series of comprehensive volumes in different subjects under the title Statistical Science and Interdisciplinary Research, published by the World Scientific Press, Singapore.

The present volume titled "Multimedia Information Extraction and Digital Heritage Preservation" is the tenth one in the series. The volume consists of twenty chapters, written by eminent scientists from different parts of the world. These chapters provide a current perspective of different areas of research and development, emphasizing the major challenging issues. Subject areas covered include: use of ontology for access and extraction of information, role of semantics in information archiving and retrieval, types of heritage documents in different parts of the world for digitization and storing, problems of storage devices, and issues in Indian document processing. I believe the state-of-the art studies presented in this book will be very useful to researchers as well as practioners.

Thanks to the contributors for their excellent research contributions and to the volume editors Dr. Usha Mujoo Munshi and Prof. Bidyut Baran Chaudhuri for their sincere effort in bringing out the volume nicely. Initial design of the cover by Mr. Indranil Dutta is acknowledged. Sincere efforts by Prof. Dilip Saha and Dr. Barun Mukhopadhyay for editorial assistance are appreciated. Thanks are also due to World Scientific for their initiative in publishing the series and being a part of the Platinum Jubilee endeavor of the Institute.

August 2009
Kolkata

Sankar K. Pal
Series Editor and Director

Preface

Preserved knowledge is the most precious treasure of humanity. The process started with the discovery of writing systems for natural languages. Libraries, museums and archives were established and scope of preservation extended over drawing and painting, sculpture and other matters of arts and science. Invention of phonograph opened up vistas for sound and music preservation. Photography cinema and video started multimedia storage. However, digital technology and its miniaturization revolutionized the whole process, bringing us to a new era of digital preservation, which was accentuated by the ultra-fast World Wide Web technology.

There are two aspects of digital preservation. One is the electronic conversion of the heritage documents by a suitable mechanism and format so that they can be accessed by interested users. The other is the adequate preservation of these electronic documents, so that they cannot be lost in future. Digital files can be destroyed in quickest time and they are vulnerable to fast pace of hardware and software change. Unlike books, a digital archive requires content and access tools that need be upgraded continuously. Also, there should be foolproof way of protection from tampering of documents.

A large number of initiatives have been taken up for digital preservation of knowledge. Among those who have started Large-scale digital preservation initiatives are big commercial houses like Google, Microsoft and many cultural institutions as well as non-profit groups like Open Content Alliance (OCA) and Million Book Project (MBP). Important libraries like British library are responsible for several initiatives on digital preservation. Digital Preservation Europe (DPE) is an EU funded project to co-ordinate the digital preservation activities across Europe. Also, to aid any person put his/her work in the Web archive, open source software (OSS) such as DSpace, EPrints, and others have been generated. These take data in multiple formats like text, video, audio and numerals, index them for easy retrieval, and preserves them over time.

The present edited volume deals with various aspects of multimedia information extraction and digital heritage preservation in twenty chapters written by eminent researchers in the field. It starts with finding approaches for access and extraction of information using ontology. Ontology is the explicit specification of shared concepts and hence ontology-driven approach can improve efficiency of access and extraction of information from multimedia resource involving text, graphics, audio, image and video. The first two chapters are devoted to this aspect. The third chapter also considers semantic integration between classical and digital library using resource ontology.

Semantics play an important role in information archiving and retrieval. The next two chapters look at the problem of image retrieval from semantics angle. The first of them combines fuzzy features for color, Bayesian distance estimator for texture and Lie descriptors for shape features and train a self-organizing map to obtain an indexing scheme for images. In the second paper, a multi-modal approach has been used to combine low level image features with text annotation, audio annotation and other metadata.

Next two chapters deal with a specific area, namely Indian document processing. Little research has been done on the Indian languages, though these languages have very large number of users. Of the two chapters, the first one deals with the difficulty of processing the Indian scripts and then proposes a solution by looking for techniques of direct word spotting from the script images. The second one reports the construction of a big electronic text corpus in Bangla, the second most popular script in India and presents some primary statistics on the corpus that may be useful in the information retrieval in this language.

The following few chapters mainly report digitization of materials at different regions of the world and a few focus on information retrieval techniques. For example, chapter 8 discussed the digitization work of cultural heritage of India, while chapter 9 deals with digitization of European heritage documents and text retrieval. A review of some information retrieval techniques that have been found to be useful for measuring the similarity between documents is the focus of chapter 10. A learning content management system is reported in chapter 11. Chapter 12 is on representation an access of medical (radiological) information. An interesting conceptual model metadata of old palm leaf manuscript of Thailand is the subject of chapter 13, while Chapters 14 and 15 deals with the metadata extraction techniques and information access to heritage documents respectively. An African perspective on digital preservation is described in chapter 16. Next two chapters deal with digitization of cultural heritage in Germany.

The last two chapters consider some different issues. In the first of them, it is pointed that the creators of digital heritage materials cannot physically examine the way traditional heritage creators could do. So, the question is how to establish trust of the creators and potential depositors of digital data to an electronic archive. The next and the last chapter of the book raises issues about failure of the system and storage devices, since the material is huge in size. The chapter tries to set strategies and measures to cope with the situation.

Thus, the volume covers interests of a wide range of readers including students, teachers, software professionals, library science experts as well as intellectuals interested in preserving heritage documents. Efforts have been made to minimize typo and other types of error.

Finally, it is our duty to acknowledge the technical committee of *International Workshop on Digital Preservation of Heritage and Research Issues in Archiving & Retrieval* (*IWDPH 2007*) from where the idea of bringing this volume bloomed. We are grateful to Professor Sankar K. Pal, Director of the Indian Statistical Institute for the encouragement and support in preparing this volume. We express our heartfelt gratitude to all the contributors of the chapters for their precious work that made it possible to bring out this volume.

Usha Mujoo Munshi
Bidyut Baran Chaudhuri
Editors

Contents

Foreword   v

Preface   vii

1. Motivating Ontology-Driven Information Extraction   1
   Burcu Yildiz and Silvia Miksch

2. Ontology Based Access of Heritage Artifacts on the Web   21
   Santanu Chaudhury and Hiranmay Ghosh

3. Semantic Integration of Classical and Digital Libraries   51
   S. Thaddeus, A. Jeganathan, Gracy T. Leema

4. Low-level Visual Features with Semantics-based
   Image Retrieval   67
   V.P. Subramanyam Rallabandi

5. Narrowing the Semantic Gap in Image Retrieval:
   A Multimodal Approach   89
   William I. Grosky and Rajeev Agrawal

6. Challenges in the Recognition and Searching of Printed
   Books in Indian Languages and Scripts   119
   R. Manmatha and C.V. Jawahar

7. Construction and Statistical Analysis of an Indic Language
   Corpus for Applied Language Research   137
   Prasenjit Majumder, Mandar Mitra and B.B. Chaudhuri

8. Heritage Preservation in Digital Way — A Contemporary
   Research Issue   155
   A. Chatterjee and S.G. Dhande

9. Digitising European Renaissance Prints — A 3-year
   Experiment on Image and Text Retrieval   169
   Marie-Luce Demonet

10. Measuring Document Similarity with Information
    Retrieval Techniques   187
    Sudip Sanyal

11. Intinno: A Web Integrated Digital Library and Learning
    Content Management System   205
    Udit Sajjanhar, Mayank Jain, Arpit Jain and Pabitra Mitra

12. A Radiologist's Digital Workbench: Balancing
    Representation and Access Challenges for Medical Images   217
    Mayank Agarwal and Javed Mostafa

13. A Conceptual Model Metadata of Thai Palm Leaf
    Manuscripts   243
    Nisachol Chamnongsri, Lampang Manmart,
    Vilas Wuwongse and Elin K. Jacob

14. Techniques for Extraction of Metadata from Heritage
    Documents   261
    Ratna Sanyal

15. Adaptable Records: Making Heritage Information
    Accessible to All   281
    Liddy Nevile

16. An African Perspective on Digital Preservation   295
    Hussein Suleman

17. nestor and kopal – Co-operative Approaches to Digital
    Long-term Preservation in Germany   307
    Thomas Wollschläger

18. Preserving the Past — Towards the Digitization of German
    Cultural Heritage   321
    Thomas Stäcker

19. Establishing Trust in Digital Repositories   341
    Bruce Ambacher

20. Issues of Scale and Storage in Digital Preservation   361
    Richard Wright

Index   381

Chapter 1

Motivating Ontology-Driven Information Extraction

Burcu Yildiz[1] and Silvia Miksch[1,2]

[1]*Institute for Software Engineering and Interactive Systems*
Vienna University of Technology
Vienna, Austria
{yildiz,silvia}@ifs.tuwien.ac.at

[2]*Department of Information and Knowledge Engineering*
Danube University Krems, Krems, Austria
silvia.miksch@donau-uni.ac.at

Abstract

Ontologies, being explicit specifications of shared conceptualisations, can provide Information Extraction Systems (IESs) with much needed domain and task knowledge. Yet, it has to be analysed to what extent and in which form ontologies can be utilised to enhance the overall performance of an IES. An important issue is that the use of ontologies requires an accurate management, where the most substantial aspect is to keep the ontology up-to-date, because the domain it represents will change inevitably. In this paper we motivate the use of ontologies within IES, especially for automating the extraction-rule generation process, which currently is the main obstacle on the way to portable and scalable IESs.

Keywords: Information Extraction, Ontology, Ontology-driven Information Extraction, Ontology-based Information Extraction, Ontology Management.

1

1.1 Introduction

Knowledge Representation tackles the problem of developing technologies to capture knowledge about the world in a computer-understandable way and thus, is substantial for Artificial Intelligence (AI) on its quest to make intelligent computer systems. Such representations are important, as any information system that does something meaningful relies to some extent on knowledge about the task it has to perform and about its application domain. Probably the most obvious examples for that are object-oriented programs, where one can get an insight on how the programmer sees the domain on which the program is going to work, by looking at the class structure of the program[1].

Information Extraction Systems (IESs), which have the meaningful task of recognising and extracting relevant information from mainly text documents, i.e. Information Extraction (IE), are not an exception here. In IESs, task knowledge is needed for the system to know what 'relevant' information actually means, whereas the domain knowledge represents parts of the conceptualisation of the domain and is needed for the system to perform its task accurately. Ontologies, being explicit specifications of conceptualisations[2], can be used in that context to provide IESs with a formal definition of relevant information and with domain knowledge.

In this paper, we will motivate the development of ontology-driven IESs, where the ontology is utilised to automate the rule generation process. Further, we will motivate the integration of ontology management services to keep the underlying ontology up-to-date.

1.2 Information Extraction

Information Extraction (IE) is defined as a form of natural language processing in which certain types of information have to be recognised and extracted from text[3, 4]. It is a task that gained a lot of importance in the last three decades, mainly fostered by the Message Understanding Conferences (MUCs) started in 1987[5], which provided a platform for system developers to present and evaluate their work.

One of the main contributions of the MUCs to IE research has been the definition of concrete extraction tasks. The main tasks, which became more complex over the years, can be listed as follows[6]:

- *Named-Entity Recognition Task (NE):* This task represents the lowest level of IE tasks and is domain independent. It involves the identification and categorisation of proper names (i.e., organisations, persons, and locations), temporal data (i.e., dates and times), or numbers (i.e., currency, percentage).
- *Template Element Task (TE):* In this task an output template is given, which has slots for basic information related to organisations, persons, and artifact entities. The IES has to draw evidence from anywhere in the text to fill these slots.
- *Template Relation Task (TR):* This task is about extracting relational information among entities. Examples for such relations are employee-of, manufacturer-of, or location-of relations.
- *Scenario Template Task (ST):* This task represents the top-level of IE tasks. In this task the focus is on the extraction of pre-specified events, where the system has to relate the event information to particular organisation, person, or artifact entities involved in the event.
- *Co-reference Task (CO):* This task is about capturing information on co-referring expressions (i.e. different mentions of a given entity).

These tasks were usually represented using frames[7] and were called templates or forms. Wilks and Catizone[8] describe a template as a linguistic pattern, usually a set of attribute-value pairs, created by experts to capture the structure of the task. The participating systems at the MUCs had to fill the slots of these templates using extraction rules, to be later evaluated against hand-filled templates.

The work presented at the MUCs showed that it is very hard to generate extraction rules that are general enough to extract relevant information from unseen documents, yet specific enough to perform well for the given task specification. Further, rule generation turned out to be an iterative process, where an initial set of rules are applied on the data and according to the results are updated, until the system yields a reasonable performance. This kind of rule generation, where a knowledge engineer is generating the rules manually is called the knowledge engineering approach. It is clear that the generation of extraction-rules by hand represents the main obstacle on the way to portable and scalable IESs, because for the IES to be applied on a different domain or task often the generation of a whole new set of extraction rules is required. Therefore, the (semi-) automatic training approach has been introduced[9], where the human intervention is reduced to perform annotations on a given data corpus indicating relevant information using which the IES can learn extraction patterns. However, this approach requires the annotation of a large number of files, so substantial human intervention is still required.

Appelt and Israel[10] suggest to use the knowledge engineering approach when resources like lexicons and rule writers are available, training data is scarce or expensive to obtain, extraction specifications are likely to change, and highest possible performance is critical; and to use the automatic training approach when resources and rule writers are not available, training data is cheap and plentiful, extraction specifications are stable, and good performance is adequate for the task.

The overall architecture of IESs may vary from system to system, but there are three main knowledge resources used by all systems: a template, a lexicon, and a rule set. As previously mentioned, templates contain the task definition of the system and are mostly represented using frames. Lexicons contain domain specific words and are usually annotated with part of speech tags. Rule sets contain task specific rules to extract information from text in order to fill the slots of the templates and may vary in complexity as the task complexity changes. An example case frame can be seen in Fig. 1.1[11].

The description of these structures resulted in considering template generation from the perspective of identifying the following elements in the context of the task[12]:

- objects which interact in the domain,
- relationships representing the interaction between the objects,

Name:	%MURDERED%
Event Type:	MURDER
Trigger Word:	murdered
Activating Conditions:	passive-verb
Slots:	VICTIM < subject> (human)
	PERPETRATOR <prep-phrase, by> (human)
	INSTRUMENT < prep-phrase, with> (weapon)

Fig. 1.1: An example case frame for IE (Riloff, 2002, p.3).

- features that are specific to the objects/relationships.

Obviously these structures can be formulated in any common ontology representation language, as all of them provide the means to represent these elements. Similarly, Nedellec and Nazarenko[13] argue that IE is an ontology-driven process, even in the simplest cases. It goes beyond text filtering based on simple pattern matching and key words, because the extracted pieces are interpreted with respect to a predefined partial domain model.

Since Berners-Lee proposed and started to endorse ontologies as the backbone of the Semantic Web in the nineties, a whole research field evolved around the fundamental engineering aspects of ontologies, such as the generation, evaluation, and management of ontologies. However, it has to be stated that most of the available research regarding ontologies had the Semantic Web as their application field in mind. We know that the Semantic Web is an extended form of the current Web, where machine readable semantics are added to the content available on the Web[14]. As such, it represents a largely distributed and heterogeneous application field. However, these properties are not shared by many application fields where ontologies can be useful as well.

In the following, we will take a look at related work where ontologies are a part of the IE process, either as knowledge bearing artifacts to be referred to by the user, or as yet another component within the system that interacts with other system components.

1.3 Related Work

To use ontologies within the context of 'ordinary' IESs is a relatively new research field. We have to state beforehand that to our knowledge only the work of Embley[15] can be considered to be ontology-driven, whereas the other works represent ontology-based systems.

Embley[16] presents an approach for extracting and structuring information from data-rich unstructured documents using extraction ontologies. With "data-rich" he means data that has a number of identifiable constants such as dates, names, times, and so forth. He proposes the use of the Object-oriented Systems Model (OSM)[17] to represent extraction ontologies, because it allows regular expressions as descriptors for constants and context keywords. Both, the generation of the ontology and the generation of the regular expressions are being done manually. The ontology is then parsed to build a database schema and to generate extraction rules for matching constants and keywords. After that, recognisers are invoked which use the extraction rules to identify potential constant data values and context keywords. Finally, the generated database is populated using heuristics to determine which constants populate which records in the database.

For the extraction of relevant information from car advertisements, the presented approach achieved recall ratios in the range of 90% and precision ratios near 98%. For domains with more complex content and where the relevant records (e.g., car advertisements) are not clearly separated from one another, the performance decreases, though.

Aitken[18] presents an approach to learn information extraction rules from natural language data using Inductive Logic Programming (ILP). He proposes the use of an ontology as a knowledge bearing artifact as a reference to which an annotator can commit to while annotating the data with ontological terms. The supervised induction algorithm then uses those annotations to generate extraction rules.

McDowell and Cafarella[19] present an automatic and domain-independent ontology-driven IES called OntoSyphon. Their system takes an ontology as input and uses its content to specify web searches in order to identify possible semantic instances, relations, and taxonomic information. For instance, for a concept "Mammal" in an ontology, the system specifies web searches using the phrase patterns introduced by Hearst[20], like "mammals such as", etc. The system then searches the web for occurrences of these phrases and extracts candidate instances.

Maedche, Neumann and Staab[21] present a semi-automatic bootstrapping approach that allows a fast generation of ontology-based IESs relying on several basic components: a core IES, an ontology engineering environment, and an inference engine. They start with a shallow IE model that specifies domain-specific lexical knowledge, extraction rules, and an ontology. A domain specific corpus is then processed with the core IES. Based on this processed data, the IE model is extended using different learning approaches. Finally, the human modeler reviews the learning decisions and decides whether to stop the learning process or not.

However, our focus is on the analysis of ontology usage within IESs to develop unsupervised and adaptive ontology-driven IESs, that are able to generate extraction rules automatically from a given input ontology and are also able to react to changes in the domain.

1.4 Ontology-driven Information Extraction Systems

We have seen that there are two approaches to IE, namely the knowledge engineering approach and the (semi-) automatic training approach. We think that ontologies can be used in conjunction with both approaches as a specification of the conceptualisation of the current domain. With the knowledge engineering approach, the knowledge engineer provides the system with extraction rules that cover the domain and task of the IES. Using an existing ontology, the developer can commit to the ontology while generating the rules (compare Fig. 1.2), and does not have to perform a domain analysis by his own, unless he has to develop the ontology by

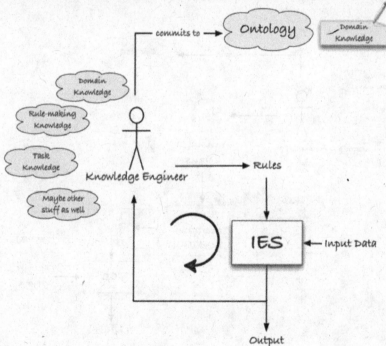

Fig. 1.2: Knowledge engineering approach to IE using an ontology.

himself as well. Using an ontology in combination with this approach can increase interoperability between systems by committing to the same ontology.

With the (semi-) automatic training approach the goal is to automate some or all parts of the rule generation process to decrease human intervention and thus, to decrease the development time of an IES. For this approach, one or more human annotators have to mark relevant pieces of data in a large document set, from which the system can learn extraction rules to extract information from unseen data. However, annotators often do not agree among themselves about the relevancy of pieces of data. Ontologies can be used here (compare Fig. 1.3) to achieve a consensus about relevant data by specifying the task knowledge in an unambiguous way. It is clear that neither the time needed to do the annotations, nor the time to adapt the annotations when the specification or the domain changes is reduced just because using an ontology.

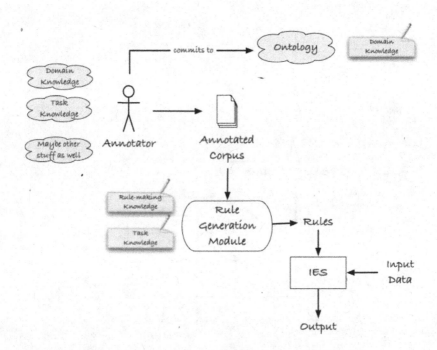

Fig. 1.3: Automatic training approach to IE using an ontology.

1.4.1 System Architecture

Besides the two mentioned scenarios where either the knowledge engineer or the annotator can commit to an ontology, one more scenario could be of interest. Namely, to automate the rule generation process fully by using an ontology as a source of domain knowledge and task specification. In Fig. 1.4, the general architecture of an ontology-driven IES is depicted. The required task and domain knowledge is captured in an ontology. The required rule-making knowledge and task knowledge are implicitly coded in the Rule Generation Module (RGM).

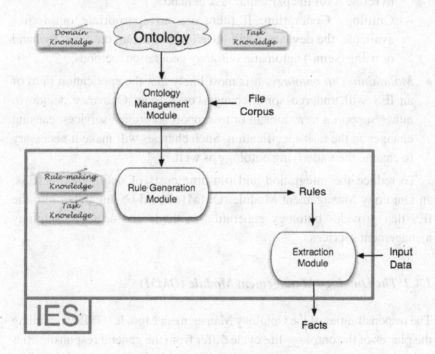

Fig. 1.4: System architecture of an ontology-driven IES.

Despite the benefits ontologies apparently can offer, it is not yet a common approach amongst IS developers to integrate and use ontologies in their systems. The main reason for that is perhaps that it still takes more time for a developer to build an ontology-driven application than a usual application.

There are several factors related to the ontology life cycle that cause the additional time and costs required to build an ontology-driven IS:

- *Obtaining an ontology:* The first thing that has to be clarified before developing an ontology-driven IS, is how to obtain the ontology. Either, the developer will have to look for already existing ontologies in that domain or to generate a new ontology.

  - Ontology Import and Reuse: Although a large set of ontologies have been developed and made publicly available for many domains by now, the developer still has to understand the ontology in order to refine it for the particular task at hand.
  - Ontology Generation: If there are no appropriate ontologies available, the developer will have to generate an ontology by hand or using (semi-) automatic ontology generation methods.

- *Maintaining an ontology:* It is most likely that the application field of an IES will undergo some changes over time. One may decide to either support a new domain or to support additional services, causing changes in the task specification. Such changes will make it necessary to change the underlying ontology as well.

To reduce the integration and run-time costs of ontologies in IESs, an Ontology Management Module (OMM) should be integrated into the IES that provides ontology generation methods and accurate ontology management services.

1.4.2 The Ontology Management Module (OMM)

The responsibilities of the Ontology Management Module (OMM) regarding the phases of the ontology life cycle differ from the general responsibilities for ontology management in conjunction with the Semantic Web. In a scenario where an ontology is used to capture the domain knowledge needed for an IES and where the focus is on portability and scalability, the requirements that the OMM has to reconcile are different.

By examining existing work in that field, one can observe that in many cases additional knowledge about components in the ontology is needed to perform the task at hand more accurately. Often researchers use an abstract ontology model to integrate existing ontologies and to enrich the encapsulated knowledge with their proposed additional knowledge.

For the case of ontology learning from text documents, for instance, Cimiano and Völker[22] argue in a similar way and attach a probability (*confidence level*) to ontological components learned by their system. Doing this, they aim to enhance the interaction with the user by presenting him the learned structures ranked according to their confidence level or by presenting him only results above a certain confidence threshold.

Tamma and Bench-Capon[23] also motivate an extended ontology model to characterise precisely the concepts' properties and expected ambiguities, including which properties are prototypical of a concept and which are exceptional, as well as the expected behaviour of properties over time, and the degree of applicability of properties to sub-concepts. Since we are dealing with IESs, not all of their proposed meta-properties are of interest for us. However, we may use the property describing the properties' expected behaviour over time, for it can help during the ontology management phase when the ontology has to be adapted according to changes in the domain.

In the following we will give an overview of the responsibilities of an OMM for enabling portable, scalable, and adaptive IESs.

1.4.2.1 Ontology Learning and Population

It should not be hard to generate an ontology for a particular task specification if the ontology is not that large. However, changes in the task specification would require the adaptation of the ontology if not the generation of a whole new ontology. For an IES to be fully portable and scalable the generation process of an ontology should be automated. No matter how an ontology for an IES has been build, it is necessary to mark the ontological components with additional semantic knowledge indicating the level of confidence the generator has in a particular ontological component. If the ontology is being generated by hand, the ontology developer has to model this kind of knowledge into the ontology. Whereas, if the ontology has been generated automatically, the generation module has to compute the level of confidence. Other modules of the system will likely use this kind of knowledge for further decision-making.

1.4.2.2 Ontology Integration

To provide maximum flexibility, an IES should be able to react to new-coming standards. Further, it certainly should be able to combine different ontologies in different representation languages. To ease this procedure, the OMM should be based on an abstract ontology model, rather than on a particular representation language. In cases where the system is provided only with a corpus of relevant documents as input, an ontology model has to be generated using that file corpus. For that purpose several ontology learning algorithms presented by Maedche[24] can be used.

1.4.2.3 Ontology Evolution

An ontology used in conjunction with an IES should not be considered as a static artifact, because changes in the task specification or the domain have to be reflected by the ontology as well.

Therefore, an OMM should provide data-driven and perhaps also usage-driven change discovery[25]. Data-driven change discovery ensures the detection of changes in the file corpus attached to the OMM, whereas usage-driven change discovery reflects the changes in the users' interests.

Data-driven change detection, for instance, can be achieved by providing the OMM with a file corpus of relevant documents to the domain. Two components are needed to allow automatic change detection from a file corpus: source-link components and change components. *Source-link components* represent links between the ontological structures in the ontology and their respective occurrences in the file corpus. If documents are added to or removed from the file corpus, these links can be used to detect which components in the ontology are affected by the change. *Change components* represent actual changes in the ontology. Every addition, deletion, or edition can be represented in form of additional change instances, with appropriate properties about the kind of change, the date of change, etc. These change components also allow to keep track of the evolution of the ontology over time.

This process would be further eased by marking components of the ontology with additional semantic knowledge indicating their estimated behaviour over time. In their proposed extended ontology model, Tamma and Bench-Capon[26] propose an attribute that indicates whether a component is allowed to change its value over time or not by marking them with a value like 'final', 'frequent', etc.

Change management of ontologies is responsible for keeping the ontology model consistent during processes such as generation or adaptation. During these two processes, components are going to be removed or added to the ontology model. It is essential to decide what to do in cases where a change can cause an inconsistency in the ontology. Stojanovic[27] propose the use of so called "evolution strategies" to define the course of action when facing critical changes in advance. A case captured by such an evolution strategy is for example "what to do with orphaned sub-concepts?"; where the course of action could be to delete it together with its parent concept or to relate it with the super-concept of its parent. These strategies might need to be adapted with respect to the needs of a particular IES, because we think that changes themselves can be of interest for some IESs too. In such cases, ontology components should not be removed from the ontology, rather their valid times should be changed.

For providing these functionalities a developer may build on the work of Cimiano and Völker[28]. They present a framework for data-driven change discovery with several integrated ontology learning approaches. They represent the learned knowledge at a meta-level, using an abstract ontology model, which they call Probabilistic Ontology Model (POM). For each learned component they calculate a value indicating the confidence level of the system, which allows the design of visualisations of the POM. The integrated learning approaches in the ontology are able to learn is-a, instance-of, part-whole, and equivalence relations, and restrictions on the domain and range of relations. Further, they claim that a particular application that wants to support data-driven change discovery has to meet several requirements. The most important one is to keep track of all changes to the data. Such a system should also allow for defining various change strategies, which specify the degree of influence changes to the data have on the ontology or the POM respectively.

Further, we aim to develop unsupervised IESs and therefore concentrate on automatic rule generation. For that purpose we propose the use of a Rule Generation Module (RGM) as part of an IES (compare Fig. 1.4), which is able to produce extraction rules from a given ontology automatically.

1.4.3 Rule Generation Module

The rule generation module (RGM) is responsible for automatically generating extraction rules for the IES. It takes an ontology as input and generates extraction rules exploiting all kinds of knowledge in the ontology.

Let us assume that someone who has no information about digital cameras is given a set of camera reviews and the job to mark information about several relevant properties of the reviewed cameras. The only domain knowledge that is provided to this person is in form of an ontology that represents only the relevant properties of the digital camera domain (see Fig. 1.5), whereas it is also assumed that the person knows the semantics of

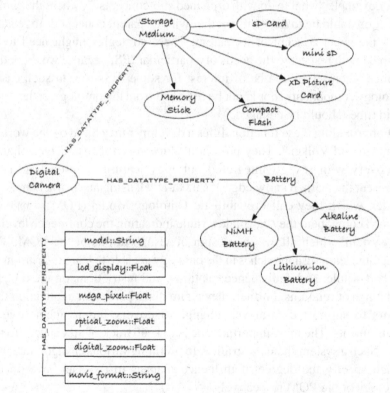

Fig. 1.5: An example ontology of task relevant information about digital cameras.

the given ontology representation, that is, he knows that arrowed lines indicate subclasses and that labeled lines indicate data type properties. How would this person proceed?

First of all he would look for words that are similar to the concepts names, for example 'storage', 'zoom', etc. Then he would look for words or numbers that fit the constraints of the concepts. For example, a float that appears in conjunction with the word 'optical zoom' would be an indicator for him that he is on the right track.

The following algorithm gives a general outline of one possible way in which the RGM of an IES could proceed:

Algorithm 1:

Rule Set R = Ø
Bag-of-words B = Ø
for each concept c in the ontology {
    B □ trigger words of concept c

for each property p of concept c {
    R □ regular expression to capture the data type of property p
    B □ trigger words of property p
}
}
for each word w in B {
    Look for word w in input text
    if (found) {
    apply rules in R to the neighbourhood of w to find appropriate values
    }
    else {
    go on with next word
    }
}

So, we can say that the more constraints ontology components have the more specific the generated extraction-rules would be, because the constraints enable to narrow the range of possible values for particular properties. Else, sophisticated heuristics would have to be developed that are able to choose amongst different possible values.

1.4.4 The Extraction Module

The Extraction Module (EM) is responsible for applying the rules generated by the RGM and using them to identify candidate values for properties in the ontology. The tasks that an EM should undertake can be considered in two main steps: the preprocessing step and the extraction step.

Preprocessing is needed to transform the input data into a format that can be processed more easily by successive modules (i.e., eliminating noisy data that could affect the performance of the system, removing stop words, etc.).

The extraction phase is the actual phase where the text is going to be scanned for trigger words of properties in the ontology. Having found trigger words, the surrounding text has to be analysed to find candidate values that are conform with the predefined data type of the properties. While collecting candidate values, they should be marked with confidence levels computed by using various heuristics, such as the inverse distance function to favour candidate values that are nearer to the keywords, etc.

1.5 Conclusion and Future Work

In this paper we motivated the use of ontologies in IES to develop ontology-driven IESs, which are unsupervised, portable, scalable, and adaptive. For that purpose we proposed the integration of an Ontology Management Module (OMM) into the system that is able to generate and integrate ontological knowledge and can detect changes in the domain represented by a file corpus. Further we proposed the development of a Rule Generation Module (RGM) as part of an IES, which is able to automatically generate extraction rules from an ontology.

We think that such a system would be useful for people with light-weight extraction demands and people who are not familiar with generating all kinds of knowledge resources (e.g., gazetteer lists, extraction rules, etc.) or do not have access to linguistic processing resources (e.g., part-of-speech tagger, etc.) that other state-of-the-art IESs require to yield feasible results.

The system as it is, can be seen as a scalable and portable IES, because to adopt the system to a changed specification or a new domain, only the ontology has to be changed. Some domains require better performing IESs and therefore, it is likely that some IES developers will tailor their systems for only a particular domain at hand. But although this would cause a decrease in the portability of the system, it remains easier to scale than with other approaches to IE.

It should also be stated that generating ontologies today is much more easier then generating extraction rules or making annotations on large data corpora. Whereas the generation of extraction rules requires a knowledge engineer who is familiar with the particular rule representation language, ontologies can be generated using ontology editing tools which require no knowledge about the underlying syntax of the ontology representation languages. As such, ontologies can be generated by a larger community of people, widening the application field of ontology-driven IESs.

We think that there are several possible directions for future work in the field of ontology-based and ontology-driven IE, because a lot of work has still to be done in this field in order to convince developers that it is indeed beneficial to use ontologies in conjunction with IESs. The following directions represent some of those.

- *Developing extensions to ontology representation languages:* We already mentioned that it is common to augment ontologies with additional knowledge in order to enhance the performance of the system that uses them. It could be interesting to develop extensions to common ontology representation languages, such as OWL, that provide the means to represent linguistic information, temporal properties, quality related properties, etc.
- *Incorporating linguistics:* For that, the ontological components could be enriched with linguistic information, such as their part-of-speech tags. Of course, the IESs would have to be developed in a way that it can process this kind of knowledge. Further, it would be necessary to pre-process the input files of the system linguistically, to at least assign part-of-speech tags to the words in the input files as well. Such an attempt would especially be useful for domains where the data types of the relevant information are mainly strings.
- *Utilising intentional knowledge:* For better extraction results the ontology could also contain intentional knowledge, that is instances, because they could be used to compare identified candidate values for properties with existing values of instances to make decisions based on various similarity measures.

References

1 Chandrasekaran, B., Josephson, J.R. and Benjamins, V. R. (1999), What Are Ontologies, and Why Do We Need Them?, *IEEE Intelligent Systems*, **14**(1), pp.20-26.

2 Gruber, T.R. (1993), A Translation Approach to Portable Ontology Specifications, *Knowledge Acquisition*, **5**(2), pp.199-220.

3 Appelt, D.E. (1999), Introduction to Information Extraction, *AI Communications* **12**(3), pp.161-172.

4 Riloff, E. (2002), Information Extraction as a Stepping Stone Toward Story Understanding, In *Understanding Language Understanding: Computational models of Reading*, pp.435-460, Cambridge: MIT Press, p.499.

5 Marsh, E. and Perzanowski, D. (1998), MUC-7 Evaluation of Information Extraction Technology: Overview of Results, In *Proceedings of the Seventh Message Understanding Conference (MUC-7)*.

6 *Ibid.*

7 Minsky M. (1974), A Framework for Representing Knowledge, In *The Psychology of Computer Vision*, pp.211-277, New York: McGraw-Hill, p.282.

8 Wilks Y. and Catizone R. (1999), Can We Make Information Extraction More Adaptive?, In *Information Extraction: Towards Scalable, Adaptable Systems*, pp.1-16, London: Springer-Verlag, p.165.

9 Kushmerick, N. and Thomas, B. (2002), Adaptive Information Extraction: Core Technologies for Information Agents, In *Intelligent Information Agents*, pp.79-103, Berlin/Heidelberg: Springer, p.273.

10 Appelt, D.E. and Israel, D.J. (1999), Introduction to Information Extraction Technology, In *Proceedings of the 16th International Joint Conference on Artiûcial Intelligence (IJCAI)*.

11 Riloff, *op.cit.*

12 Collier, R. (1998), Automatic Template Creation for Information Extraction, Ph.D. thesis, University of Sheffield, UK.

13 Nédellec C. and Nazarenko A. (2005), Ontology and Information Extraction: A Necessary Symbiosis, In *Ontology Learning from Text: Methods, Evaluation and Applications*, pp.155-170, Amsterdam: IOS Press, p.180.

14 Berners-Lee, T. (1999), *Weaving the Web: The Original Design and Ultimate Destiny of the World Wide Web by Its Inventor,* San Francisco: Harper San Francisco, p.240.

15 Embley, D.W. (2004), Toward Semantic Understanding: An Approach Based on Information Extraction Ontologies, In *Proceedings of the 15th Australasian Database Conference,* pp.3-12.

16 *Ibid.*

17 Embley, D.W., Kurtz, B.D. and Woodfield, S.N. (1992), *Object-oriented Systems Analysis: A Model-Driven Approach,* New Jersey: Yourdon Press, p.302.

18 Aitken, J.S. (2002), Learning Information Extraction Rules: An Inductive Logic Programming Approach, In *Proceedings of the 15th European Conference on Artificial Intelligence (ECAI'02),* pp.355-359.

19 McDowell, L.K. and Cafarella, M.J. (2006), Ontology-driven Information Extraction with OntoSyphon, In *Proceedings of the 5th International Semantic Web Conference (ISWC 2006),* pp.428-444.

20 Hearst, M. (1992), Automatic Acquisition of Hyponyms from Large Text Corpora, In *Proceedings of the 14th International Conference on Computational Linguistics,* pp.539-545

21 Maedche, A., Neumann, G. and Staab, S. (2002), Bootstrapping an Ontology-based Information Extraction System, In *Intelligent Exploration of the Web,* pp.345-359, Heidelberg: Physica-Verlag GmbH, p.417.

22 Cimiano, P. & Völker, J. (2005), Text2Onto – A Framework for Ontology Learning and Data-driven Change Discovery, In *Proceedings of the 10th International Conference on Applications of Natural Language to Information Systems (NLDB'2005),* pp.227-238.

23 Tamma V. and Bench-Capon T. (2002), An Ontology Model to Facilitate Knowledge-Sharing in Multi-Agent Systems, *The Knowledge Engineering Review,* **17**(1), pp.41-60.

24 Maedche, A. (2002), *Ontology Learning for the Semantic Web,* Massachusetts: Kluwer Academic Publishers, p.272.

25 Stojanovic, L. and Motik, B. (2002), Ontology Evolution within Ontology Editors, In *Proceedings of the OntoWeb-SIG3 Workshop at the 13th International Conference on Knowledge Engineering and Knowledge Management,* pp.53-62.

26 Tamma, *op.cit.*

27 Stojanovic, L. (2004), Methods and Tools for Ontology Evolution, Germany: University of Karlsruhe, PhD Thesis.

28 Cimiano, *op.cit.*

Chapter 2
Ontology Based Access of Heritage Artifacts on the Web

Santanu Chaudhury[1] and Hiranmay Ghosh[2]

[1]*Department of Electrical Engineering*
Indian Institute of Technology (IIT)
Delhi, India
santanuc@ee.iitd.ernet.in
[2]*TCS Innovation Labs Delhi, India*
hiranmay.ghosh@tcs.com

Abstract

Experiencing tangible and intangible cultural resources on the web is an emerging way of knowing about cultures and heritage. These resources are primarily in multimedia – text, image, audio, video, graphics, etc. Developing user friendly modalities for accessing these resources is a challenging problem. In this chapter we explore use of ontology for designing intelligent ways for accessing multimedia heritage resources. We show that a new model of ontology representation scheme for multimedia: M-OWL provides mechanisms for implementing interfaces for thematic access, intelligent navigation and personalized searching of heritage resources. We describe some example systems as illustration of our proposed approach.

Keywords: Ontology based Access, Heritage Artifacts, Multimedia Resources, Distributed Digital Library, Agent based Systems.

2.1 Introduction

Cultural heritage information of the humankind is distributed in various forms, such as paintings, scriptures, architecture and audiovisual records of performing arts. In recent times, the economics of computing and networking resources have created an opportunity for large-scale digitization of the heritage artifacts for their broader dissemination over the Internet and for preservation. Several renowned museums such as the Louvre[1] and the British Museum[2] have announced their presence on the cyberspace. The Web Gallery of Art[3] is a virtual museum and searchable database of European painting and sculpture from 12th to mid-19th centuries. Back in India, Kalasampada[4] is a rich web-portal of Indian cultural heritage resources. ASI has set up a portal[5] portraying Indian heritage monuments and pre-historic arts. Don Bosco Centre for Indigenous Culture has come up with a portal[6] for disseminating information on heritage arts and craft of North-East India. Osian's web-site[7] combines portrayal of information on art- films with business. These portals provide access to the digitized heritage artifacts in different media forms, e.g. photographs (still images), document images, music, and video. Moreover, they provide several value-added presentations such as self-guided tours, virtual galleries and walk-throughs, virtual exhibitions and research resources to the on-line visitors. These presentations embed digital heritage objects in a stream of narration and interactive guidance tools comprising text, speech, animation and interactive 2D/3D graphics. Currently, most of such presentations available on these portals are hand-crafted and static. With the increase of collection sizes on the web, correlating different heritage artifacts and accessing the desired ones in a specific use-case context creates a significant cognitive load on the user. The virtual environment in cyberspace offers agility to create dynamic presentations to suit the specific needs and interests of a visitor, a potential which has not been fully utilized. Of late, there has been some research efforts to facilitate semantic access in large heritage collections. For example, Global Memory Net[8] intends to create large volume of annotated visual contents and to facilitate their access through traditional metadata based as well as content based retrieval techniques. The research initiatives under *MultimediaN*[9] project aims at use of domain ontology in correlating the media artifacts for their semantic access.

It is pragmatic to consider that digital heritage collections are likely to be built on the Internet by multiple agencies in a distributed fashion, with each agency focusing on a specific area of interest. For example, some agency may specialize on heritage manuscripts while another may focus on performing arts. There is, in general, a strong thematic overlap across such distributed collections. Thus, there is a need to correlate multiple collections and present an integrated semantic view to the user in a specific usage context. The existing approaches rely on creating centralized metadata store and indexing scheme to address this issue. These approaches assume significant coordination between the central agency building the metadata and the different agencies developing their individual collections, which may not be sustainable in the long run. In this context, we present a new ontology assisted scheme for accessing digital heritage collections at thematic level. The technology presented in this chapter can be used for seamless semantic synthesis of several independent collections distributed over the Internet. Our approach is based on logical separation of knowledge-based sub-tasks required for multimedia data interpretation, which enables their distribution over the Internet resulting in scalable and sustainable solutions. In particular, our approach relies on peer-to-peer coordination across several intelligent agents encapsulating the different knowledge-based functions and do not require any central metadata creation.

Several research groups[10-13] have proposed use of ontology in semantic interpretation of multimedia data in collaborative multimedia and digital library projects. While ontology is a useful tool for modeling a conceptual domain, it has not been designed to model multimedia data that is perceptual in nature. In the current approaches, specific computer vision algorithms are used to recognize pre-defined objects or events of interest in the media documents to generate automatic annotations. Domain ontology is used to interpret these conceptual annotations in specific query contexts. Thus, the ontology needs to be customized for the specific annotation scheme followed in the collection. The ontology and the metadata schemes are tightly coupled in these approaches, which necessitates creation of a central metadata scheme for the entire collection and prevents integration of data from heritage collections developed in a decentralized manner.

In order to separate concept interpretation and media feature recognition tasks, we have developed a new scheme for ontology representation that enables perceptual feature based modeling of concepts. This ontology representation scheme is embodied with Multimedia Web Ontology Language (MOWL), which is an extension of OWL, the ontology language for the web standardized by W3C forum. A software agent that is independent of any specific collection encapsulates and reasons with multimedia ontology to interpret a semantic query. The resultant Observation Model comprises a set of media features that are expected to materialize in media instances depicting the concept(s) expressed in the query. Concept recognition task involves observation of these media features in specific media instances in the collections, and is independent of query interpretation. The Observation Model contains a redundant set of features and a specific subset is chosen for concept recognition in a specific collection depending on its characteristics. The flexibility in choice of concept recognition strategies provides the key to integration of distributed *independent* multimedia collections. In contrast to the deductive Descriptions Logic based reasoning model with contemporary ontology schemes, we have developed an evidential reasoning system that can produce robust results with limited observations or pattern detection. We follow a probabilistic approach for evidential reasoning with Bayesian Networks to cope up with the inherent uncertainties of the multimedia information processing. We propose a Service Oriented Architecture (SOA) involving several independent service elements as a convenient tool for building flexible and scalable digital heritage library with many independent collections. Each service element in the system has been modeled as an intelligent information agent and performs specific knowledge-based multimedia information processing task.

2.2 Ontology for Multimedia

Information professionals have traditionally relied on several tools, e.g. thesauri, subject taxonomies, established classification systems and specialized classification schedules, for knowledge classification. More recent Dublin Core metadata initiative[14] aims at developing an interoperable metadata standard that can be used by the different libraries to share the information about their collections. Ontology is a further generalization of these tools. It is a formal representation of conceptualization of a domain in terms of concepts, their properties and their interrelations. Ontology establishes a common vocabulary, meaning and relations for the concepts in a domain. Carlyle[15] provides a critical review of application of ontology for knowledge organization in libraries.

At the other end of the spectrum, AI professionals have been exploring tools for representing and reasoning with explicit domain knowledge for use in knowledge based systems. A number of knowledge representation techniques, such as Cyc[16], Ontolingua[17], KL-1[18], Classic[19] and LOOM[20] have evolved over the logical formalism of Description Logics (DL)[21]. The last decade saw a rapid proliferation of intelligent web-based applications, prompting the need for sharable knowledge resources. W3C community stepped in at that juncture to standardize Web Ontology Language (OWL)[22] as the standard ontology representation language for the web. The domain model in OWL essentially consists of a class hierarchy of concepts together with definition of their properties as RDF triplets[23]. In addition, it is possible to define property constraints for the classes in OWL. However, the crisp DL based reasoning has been found to be unsuitable for many domains in the real world. This has led to development of adaptations of OWL for incorporating uncertain reasoning[24-25].

All the knowledge representation tools explored so far, including OWL, enable conceptual modeling of domains and the concepts and their properties are expressed with linguistic structures. This makes these tools convenient for textual information processing. However, concepts are expressed in multimedia documents in perceptual media forms. Present knowledge processing tools make no efforts for perceptual modeling of the domain. Most of the knowledge based media processing applications apply ontology tools on textual annotations for media instances, which are created either manually or using computer vision techniques. This approach restricts semantic processing of media to *a-priori* created annotations only. True semantic processing of multimedia data requires in-context machine interpretation of the information encoded in the media instance itself. Bertini et al.[26] have used ontology extended with visual examples of events to detect specific events in sports video towards achieving this goal.

We have developed a new ontology scheme for multimedia applications that enables perceptual modeling of a domain using media property descriptions and media examples of the concepts. In this context, it is interesting to note that the concepts are refinements of perceptual experience of humankind[27]. Observing many monuments leads to discovery of some common visual properties, which is an abstraction of the concept and which is labeled with a linguistic construct such as "monument". Further observation of subtle differences in such visual properties leads to further refinement of the concept and formation of concept taxonomy. Thus, a concept leads to expectation of some visual properties in the multimedia documents, which when observed leads to a belief in the realization of the concept. Fig. 2.1 illustrates the idea of perceptual modeling for a concept, labeled as "Indian Medieval Monuments". The same idea is applicable to audile properties as well.

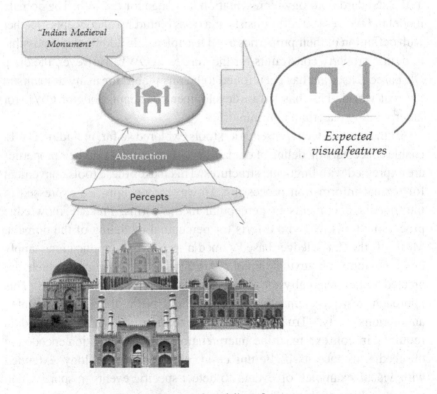

Fig. 2.1: Perceptual modeling of concepts.

Our model of multimedia ontology and reasoning with media properties for concept recognition is founded on this basic premise. We have extended OWL to include media property descriptions and example media instances of the concepts and to *reason with them*. The resulting ontology language "Multimedia Web Ontology Language" or MOWL in short, is described in more details in Ghosh, *et al.*[28] Fig. 2.2 illustrates a small ontology segment that depicts the relationship between a few concepts in the domain of medieval architecture and their media properties. The oval nodes and edges of the graph depict the concepts and their relations as expressed in a traditional ontology representation and the square nodes and edges depict our extensions to include media properties of concepts. Another interesting aspect of multimedia ontology is that the textual annotations associated with a media artifact can also be used as a feature and utilized in the same way as audio-visual feature descriptors.

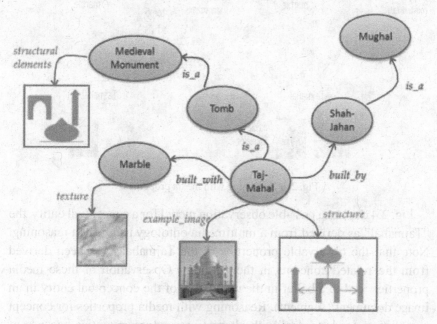

Fig. 2.2: A section of multimedia ontology.

While OWL can be used to assign media properties for concepts, reasoning with media properties requires attribution of specific semantics to the media properties and examples, which is not supported with OWL.

Fig. 2.3 illustrates such reasoning process. The figure in the left depicts the monument "Tajmahal" to be an instance of a tomb and to be made of marble. A tomb is typically characterized with a dome, which is in turn characterized by some shape parameters. Thus, an image instance of the Tajmahal is likely to depict those shape parameters. Similarly, since the Tajmahal is built with marble, we may expect the color and texture properties of the stone to be depicted in an image instance of Tajmahal. The picture in the right illustrates that the example images of Tajmahal can be used as example images for the generic concept class "tomb" for visual comparisons. Such property propagation across a knowledge graph is quite unique to multimedia ontology. We have built a reasoning scheme around MOWL that uses such media property propagation to build an observation model for a concept.

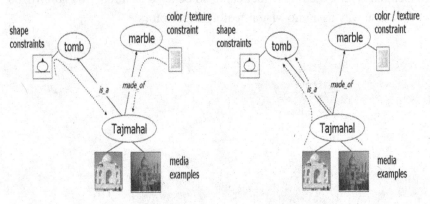

Fig. 2.3: Reasoning with media properties.

Fig. 2.4 depicts a possible observation model for a conceptual entity, the "Tajmahal" as derived from a multimedia ontology using such reasoning. Note that the observable properties of the Tajmahal have been derived from the related concepts in the ontology. Observation of these media properties lead to a belief in the realization of the conceptual entity in an image document (segment). Reasoning with media properties for concept recognition needs to deal with alternatives and uncertainties because of various factors, e.g. inherent differences across the instances of the concepts, audio-visual aberrations arising out of lighting condition, viewpoint and occlusions, and imperfections of media feature recognition algorithms. We have provisioned specifications for such conditional probabilities in MOWL (motivated by[29]), modeled the observation model as a Bayesian Network and applied abductive reasoning principles for concept recognition.

The media properties of the concepts can be expressed in MOWL at different levels of abstractions. We use a descriptive scheme following MPEG-7 data model to ensure interoperability across various independent knowledge resources. At the lowest level, statistical properties, e.g. MPEG-7 tools, can be used to characterize the media properties. At a higher level, the media properties of concepts need to be correlated with spatial and temporal relations. For example, the Tajmahal is characterized by a dome above an arch and between a pair of minarets (see Figs. 2.2 and 2.4). Similarly, a "goal scored" event in a football (soccer) match is typically characterized by ball *within* goal-box *followed-by cheer*. While, the ball, the goal-box and cheer in this example are characterized by their respective visual and audile properties, these properties need to be connected with spatial and temporal relations "within" and "followed-by". MPEG-7 data model supports use of such relations to interconnect media descriptions. However, formal specification of the semantics of such relations is beyond the scope of MPEG-7. Moreover, like the media properties of concepts, such spatio-temporal relations are also subject to uncertainties. We have formulated a scheme for formal definition of spatio-temporal relations with fuzzy membership functions[30]. This is an extension of the classical work by

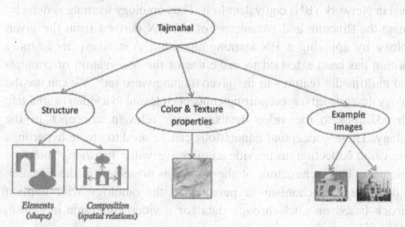

Fig. 2.4: An observation model.

Papadias[31] in creating a computational model for the Allen's relations.

2.3 Construction of Multimedia Ontology

Multimedia Ontology typically encodes highly specialized domain knowledge and association of domain concepts with perceptual features. Construction of ontology, therefore, involves a process of knowledge acquisition through interaction with domain experts. In this process, there exist possibilities of missing out some concepts and relations which may exist in the real-world, while coding some extra knowledge which might be irrelevant. It is possible to fine-tune the knowledge obtained from the experts by applying learning from real-world examples belonging to the domain. An ontology refined in this manner is a better structured and more realistic model of the domain that it represents.

The input expert knowledge is typically encoded in M-OWL. A set of media examples like video is also conceptually annotated by experts. This annotation step helps associate conceptual annotation to low-level observables in the video. This data set is used for refining and retraining the base ontology provided by the experts. The ontology learning module refines and fine- tunes the ontology by learning from the training set of annotated videos. MOWL encoding of the ontology allows us to construct a Bayesian Network (BN) equivalent to it. Thus ontology learning is done by learning the structure and parameters of the BN derived from the given ontology by applying a BN learning algorithm. A standard BN learning algorithm has been extended to make use of the observation of content-based multimedia features in the given training video set[32]. We can use the ontology thus refined for recognizing concepts relevant to a video to annotate fresh additions to the video database with relevant concepts in the ontology. These conceptual annotations can be used to create hyperlinks in the video collection, to provide an effective video browsing interface to the user. The architecture of the system is presented in the Fig. 2.5. We describe a mechanism to personalize the ontology with implicit feedback based on click-through data for a video collection in Ghosh, *et al.*[33]

2.4 Concept Recognition using Multimedia Ontology

Our concept recognition scheme is based on the premises that the conceptual entities result is some expected media patterns, which when observed leads to belief in the concept. We model the concept recognition problem as an evidential reasoning problem, which can be formalized as:

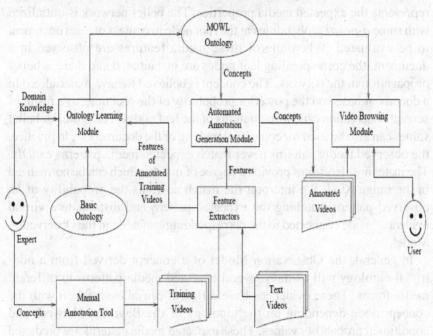

Fig. 2.5: Architecture for learning ontology.

If a concept c manifests in a set of patterns M, a set of observed patterns $M' \subseteq M$ leads to the belief in concept c with a suitable set of assumptions A., i.e.

if $c \rightarrow M$ and $M' \subseteq M$, then $M' \wedge A \Rightarrow c$.

As explained in the earlier sections, multimedia ontology includes the knowledge about the expected media properties of the concepts. We reason with the knowledge to derive an Observation Model of the concept which comprises several media properties. A document D is modeled as a set of observed media features M'. The characteristics of the closed domain for which the ontology has been built provide the necessary contextual assumptions required for the evidential reasoning system. In other words, the media features observed in a document provides an explanation for a concept in context of a specific domain. We use a probabilistic model to cater to the uncertainties inherent in the multimedia information processing.

The Observation Model is encoded as a Bayesian Network to reflect the causal relations between the concept and the media properties. The root node of the network (see Fig. 2.4) represents a concept and the leaf nodes represents the expected media properties. The belief network is initialized with some *a-priori* probabilities at the root node in context of each document to be evaluated. When any of these media features are observed in a document, the corresponding leaf nodes are instantiated and there is belief propagation in the network. The concept is believed to have materialized in a document based on the posterior probability of the root note, as a result of several observations and instantiations of the leaf nodes. The posterior belief values can also be used for contextual ranking of the documents[34]. In practice, the observed media patterns never match expected media patterns *exactly*. The matching algorithms provide a degree of match, which can be normalized in the range [0,1]. We interpret the match score as the probability of an observed pattern matching the expected pattern and instantiate a virtual evidence[35] node connected to the corresponding leaf node in the Observation Model.

In general, the Observation Model of a concept derived from a non-trivial ontology will contain several expected media patterns in different media forms. These evidences have different causal association with the concept node depending on the topology of the Bayesian Network and conditional probability values. These expected media patterns are predicted by virtue of domain knowledge without any consideration of the collection characteristics. As a result, it may not be possible to evaluate every media pattern in a particular media instance. As a trivial example, the domain model for Indian classical dance may suggest the characteristic audio pattern of accompanying music as evidence. However, it is not possible to use that evidence in a still photograph depicting a dance form. Even when it is possible, on-line evaluation of many such media patterns can be extremely expensive in terms of computation. Fortunately, the evidences generally follow a law of diminishing returns in an evidential reasoning system. It is possible to achieve sufficient confidence in the inference with a few observations only – subsequent observations do not significantly improve the belief in the concept. Thus, a practical information system using an evidential model needs an optimal selection of observations, considering their evidential weights as well as the cost of observation. A distributed planning algorithm for deriving an observation plan from an Observation Model has been described in Ghosh, *et al.*[36]

The contemporary ontology schemes employ deductive reasoning systems. Our scheme of evidential reasoning is weaker than the deductive reasoning, but is essential for dealing with multimedia artifacts due the inherent uncertainties that they are associated with. The major advantage of the evidential reasoning system is that it can produce robust results with fewer and uncertain observations. Another advantage of our concept recognition scheme is the separation of the domain ontology from the underlying collection characteristics. This separation enables integration of multiple distributed collections under a common conceptual framework.

2.5 Distributed Architecture for Digital Heritage Library

Heritage artifacts are distributed in various museums of the world. Different institutions generally focus on specific themes of their interest to build a specialized collection, e.g. paintings, music, performing arts, architecture, manuscripts, and so on. Digitization drives are often localized to the institutions to administrative convenience and content ownership issues. Thus, digitized artifacts representing heritage information are generally distributed over several web-sites. There may be significant thematic overlaps across these collections. In general, each collection provides some browsing and/or search interface for the user to explore the collection. In order to facilitate such action, the repository designer may create a data-model for content description and indexing scheme for the digital artifacts in the collection. MPEG-7 provides a standard extensible data-model for multimedia content description[37] using feature based as well as textual descriptions. It has been widely used to create multimedia content description in recent times to enhance interoperability across multimedia information systems. While standardizing on MPEG-7, the developers of these web-sites may however choose to use different repository organizations, different feature set, different indexing and annotation schemes and implementation technologies to realize these web-sites. A researcher exploring the heritage information would like to have an integrated view of these distributed collections. It is therefore necessary that the systems design should offer a seamless integration of a large number of independent collections, despite their heterogeneity.

The separation of domain knowledge from the collection architecture in our approach facilitates semantic integration of distributed heterogeneous repositories. The access mechanism for media artifacts in response to a semantic query is broken down to several independent knowledge-based sub-tasks as illustrated in Fig. 2.6. As the first step, a semantic query, which in general comprises free text, parameter specifications and example media instances, is interpreted using domain knowledge to determine a set of expected media features that need to be explored. As explained in the previous section, the domain knowledge is encoded in MOWL and the expected media features are organized as a Bayesian Network. The next stage involves selection of the media patterns to be observed for concept recognition at a heritage repository. This step requires an analysis of causal strengths of the media patterns and knowledge of the repository characteristics, e.g. the features used in describing the media artifacts and the indexing scheme used. The output of this stage is an observation plan for a repository, which is a sub-graph of the Observation Model. Note that, the different repositories in the system can, in general, have different characteristics and a unique plan is required for each of them. The third step involves matching of the audio-visual patterns in an observation plan. This stage requires media-specific knowledge-based pattern matching algorithms.

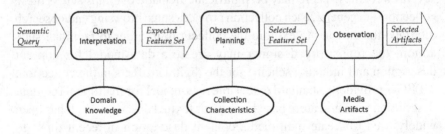

Fig. 2.6: Data flow for conceptual access.

Agent based systems offer a suitable framework to design and develop massively distributed knowledge based systems. We envisage an agent class for each of the knowledge based tasks. Fig. 2.7 shows generic agent based architecture for digital heritage libraries. In this architecture, each of the individual and independently developed heritage collections is encapsulated as a *Repository Agent* in the figure. These agents are assumed to create some feature-based and textual description of the artifacts following MPEG-7 data model, which can be used for indexing and retrieval. Semantic integration of these individual collections is achieved through the ontology and the coordination agents. *Ontology Agents* encapsulate multimedia ontology and interprets abstract user queries to produce an Observation Model as described in the previous sections.

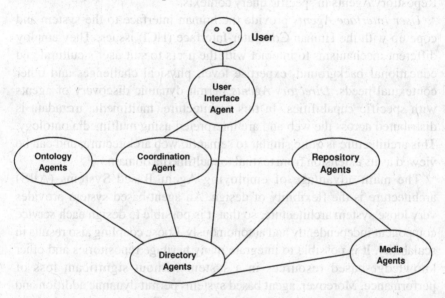

Fig. 2.7: Agent based architecture for distributed digital library.

A *Coordination Agent* assumes the overall responsibility of query processing in the system. It engages appropriate Ontology Agents for query interpretation in a specific query context. Further, it analyzes the causal strengths of the evidences and the characteristics of the Repository Agents and collaboratively develops their respective observation plans. It engages a subset of available Repository Agents for execution of the observation plan depending on their characteristics. The interaction between the knowledge elements encoded in the *Ontology Agents* and the *Repository*

Agents poses an interesting research issue on multimedia ontology integration[38]. Finally, it combines the partial results returned by the individual repositories.

During the execution phase, the Repository Agents rely on their native retrieval capabilities to evaluate the media artifacts according to the observation plan. There is also a provision for the Repository Agents to engage third party *Media Agents* for specific intelligent media processing tasks, such as face recognition, either during indexing or query processing phase. The architecture makes it possible to deploy such specialized third party pattern recognition services on the Internet to be utilized by the Repository Agents in specific query contexts.

User Interface Agents provide the human interface to the system and cope up with the Human-Computer-Interface (HCI) issues. They employ different mechanisms to interact with the users to suit user's cultural and educational background, expertise level, physical challenges and other contextual needs. *Directory Agents* permit dynamic discovery of agents with specific capabilities. In this architecture, multimedia metadata is distributed across the web and are interpreted using multimedia ontology. This architecture is quite similar to semantic web architecture, and can be viewed as its extension from textual to multimedia domain.

The main advantage of employing Agent Based Systems (ABS) architecture is the flexibility of design. An agent-based system provides very loose system architecture, so that it is possible to design each service component independently and autonomously. Loose coupling also results in scalability. It is possible to integrate many heritage repositories and other knowledge-based resources in a system without significant loss of performance. Moreover, agent based systems permit dynamic addition and deletion of agents without disruption of services. This feature is particularly useful to cope up with the situation where the collections are dynamically reconfigured without global knowledge. It is quite possible that new heritage collections be built are released on the web and some older ones merged with others or go out of service. The agents in the system automatically regroup on such occasions to provide uninterrupted system functionality. Moreover, the agent based architecture provides robustness against temporary unavailability of independent repositories and other knowledge services. The system sustains itself through a peer-level message exchange, rather than being controlled in a centralized fashion.

Since the different agents in the system are independently developed and deployed on a variety of hardware platform and software framework, they need a common framework for communication. Web Services Architecture (WSA)[39] provides a standard means of interoperating between such heterogeneous agents. In this architecture, each agent is modeled to have realized a set of 'services', which can be accessed by the other agents by exchanging messages following a definite set of protocols. Simple Object Oriented Protocol (SOAP) defined as a part of this architecture standardizes the method of exchanging XML messages between two agents. However, WSA does not specify the interpretation of the XML message contents and an agent's action on receiving a message. FIPA[40] defines a set of protocols that guide such interactions between the agents. We have defined a few generic service types over these protocols for each of the agent classes to access their respective services. These service types are extended to individual service requests with specific media types, media features and such other parameters depending on the specific agents involved.

The overall retrieval scheme in this agent based distributed digital library

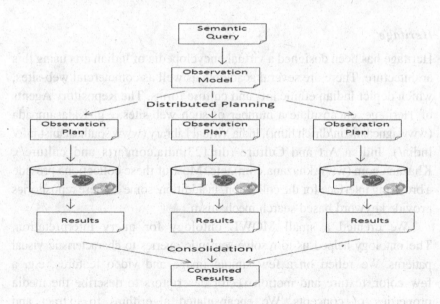

Fig. 2.8: Retrieval in distributed digital library.

architecture is summarized in Fig. 2.8. A semantic user query is interpreted to extract the conceptual specification by the Ontology Agents, and an Observation Model is created. Observation plans for the individual repositories in the form of Bayesian Networks are derived from the observation model with a distributed planning process participated by the Coordination and the Repository Agents with due considerations to the repository capabilities. The observation plans are executed at the repositories with support from Media Agents, wherever necessary. The resultant belief revision in the Bayesian Network results in a ranked set of media artifacts. Finally, the result sets from the different repositories are combined. Combining of results from multiple independent repositories are generally considered to be an issue. In our approach, since the observation plans for the different repositories are derived from a common Observation Model, the retrieval scores for the results from the different repositories are comparable and can be used for overall ranking.

2.6 Application Examples

Heritage

Heritage has been designed a virtual encyclopedia of Indian arts using this architecture. There are several academic as well as commercial web-sites, which depict Indian ethnic arts and culture forms. The Repository Agents of Heritage encapsulate a number of such web-sites, e.g. Kalasampada (www.ignca.nic.in/dlrich.html), India Virtual Library (www.southasianist.info/india/), Indian Art and Culture (dir.123india.com/arts_and_culture/), Khazana.com (www.khazana.com), etc. Most of these collections provide a browsing interface for the collection. In addition, some of these repositories provide keyword based search mechanism.

We created a small MOWL ontology for query interpretation. The ontology helped us to resolve semantic queries to characteristic visual patterns. We relied on a few simple image and video features, e.g. a few color, texture and motion vector descriptors to describe the media properties of concepts. We encapsulated algorithms to extract and compare these media features in a few media agents. To increase the reliability of the system, we used the textual annotations surrounding a media artifact as a feature and implemented a few Media Agents incorporating some probabilistic text matching algorithms. For example, *Madhubani paintings*, a school of ethnic East Indian painting has been characterized in our ontology with its characteristic color usage and distinctive color correlograms[41]. The themes depicted in the paintings and their place of origin, determined by analyzing the textual annotations, can provide additional evidences.

Heritage employed a specific User Interface that permitted query specification using a set of pull-down menus, free text specifications and example images. These specifications were combined to form a semantic query. The conceptual entities are resolved through domain knowledge. Any additional parameters and the example images were annexed to the Observation Model with some default conditional probabilities.

We provide a few query examples and retrieval results in Figs. 2.9, 2.10 and 2.11. In the first query example (Fig. 2.9), we seek information on *Vocal Carnatic music* (a style of classical music nurtured in Southern India). The system produced a number of artifacts, including still images and videos depicting recital of the music form, biography of some renowned artists and some upcoming music events from the different encapsulated repositories. In query examples 2 and 3 (Figs. 2.10 and 2.11) depict retrieval of paintings with different styles and themes. While in query 2, the theme has been specified textually, an example image had been specified in query 3. In all the cases, there have been several media property specifications in the Observation Models, subsets of which (typically 2-5 in cardinality) have been used in specific collection contexts. While it has been difficult to ascertain recall, we have observed an average precision of more than 75% over more than 50 distinct queries, which has been substantially higher than image retrieval engines on the Internet. Notably, these image retrieval engines miserably fail for most of these thematic queries as illustrated in these examples.

Heritage+

Currently, large collections of scanned images of document pages are becoming important component of digital libraries. This has created a demand for development of techniques for indexing and efficient access to document image collections. Many of the earlier document image management systems transform document images to XML format by exploiting the document layout model or the logical structure, together with OCR techniques. Such techniques cannot be used for legacy documents in those Indian scripts for which reliable OCR technology is not available. In case of those documents, word-image based document image indexing, i.e. searching for keywords in document images using image properties, can only be used. However,

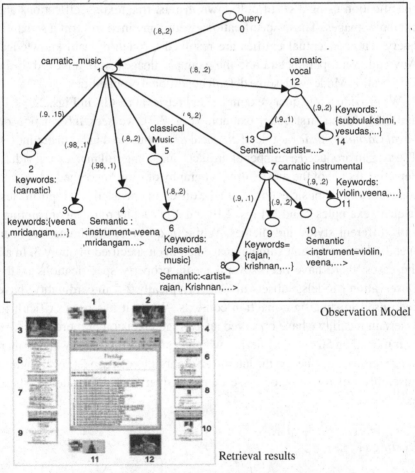

Fig. 2.9: Heritage query example 1: Vocal Carnatic Music.

conceptual access to document pages requires modeling the domain (pertaining to the document category) specific concepts in terms of the document layout, features extracted from picture components, and word image characteristics. The domain knowledge is required to process, analyze,

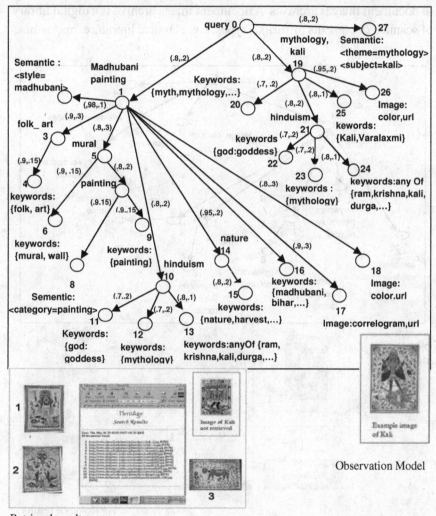

Fig. 2.10: Heritage query example 2: Goddess Kali depicted in Eastern Indian folk-painting.

identify, and label the logical components in a document image. In addition to the component properties, we also include relations between components as part of domain knowledge. This facilitates access to document pages as a set of logically related components.

Heritage+ extends HeritAge to include conceptual search and navigation in document images archives. A document image archive is a digital library of scanned documents of various types, e.g. classical literature, magazines,

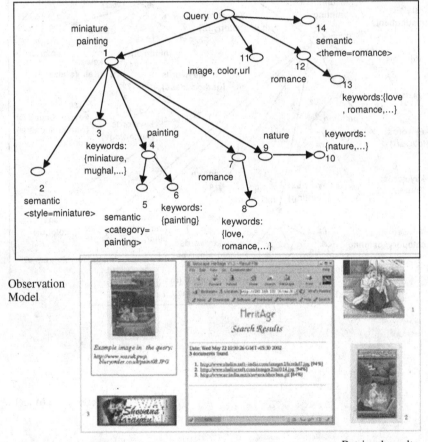

Observation Model

Retrieval results

Fig. 2.11: Heritage query example 3: Mughal miniature painting depicting romance.

newspapers, pictures, and other miscellaneous documents, in several Indian languages. M-OWL can represent a document image structure in terms of the spatial layout and the image characteristics of its components. We use M-OWL to encode the domain knowledge, which includes abstract concepts and relations, a set of keywords related to the concepts and their observable forms (image based features of words) in document images in a number of Indian languages. M-OWL is also used to model the document features, e.g. the layout and compositional structure together with the observable image properties. Fig. 2.12 depicts the logical decomposition of a typical newspaper page. It is also possible to model the words in native languages as concepts and define their media properties in terms of spatial and sequential relation of some shape primitives (Geometric Feature Graph) using M-OWL, as shown in Fig. 2.13. Observation of the connected shape primitives with some confidence, is used in robust recognition of the words in the native language[42]. The structural properties of the identified components in the document page can be used to classify document images into generic categories.

Fig. 2.12: Logical decomposition of document image: The Hindu crossword puzzle.

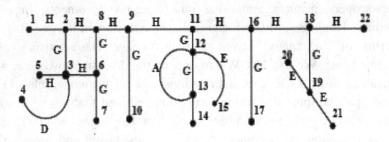

Fig. 2.13: Modeling of words as a sequence of shape primitives.

Query processing in Heritage+ involves identification of document class (e.g. sport news) followed by concept spotting (e.g. Tendulkar). Document images in a collection are segmented into pages, labeled with semantic descriptors using document ontology. These pages are hyperlinked based on the relations between the page descriptors, to facilitate navigation. Concept spotting in documents uses domain ontology to expand the query concept into expected media features of the alternative keywords that signify the

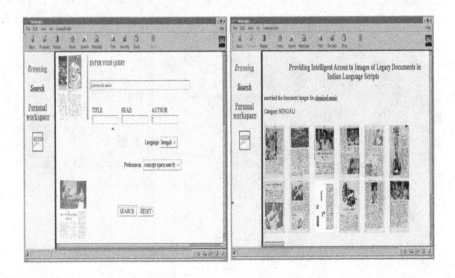

Fig. 2.14: HeritAge+ document image archive.

concept. These media features are then searched in the document images to identify the keywords and hence results in concept recognition. Fig. 2.14 shows the query interface and the search results for 'Classical Music' with Heritage+.

2.7 Contextual Advertising in Heritage Libraries

The sustainability of heritage portals often depends on the business model supporting such portals. Contextual advertising on free information portals is considered to be a source of revenue to support maintenance of the portals[43]. It refers to recommending products and services that can be of users' interest in context of his current activities. For example, an advertisement for a DVD containing examples of Indian folk-dance forms or replica of rare manuscripts can be of interest to the researchers on these subjects. Efforts have so far been focused on thematic analysis of the text artifacts, e.g. search results and mail threads and click-through data[44-45], to relate user interests with product advertisement. However, products related to cultural heritage artifacts, e.g. paintings, music, video recordings, handicrafts and ethnic garments, are strongly characterized by their audio-visual appeal and aesthetics, which generally cannot be described in words. Advertisements for such media-rich commodities generally comprise image, graphic depictions, audio/video excerpts and such other media artifacts. ImageSense[46] uses a few image properties to embed an advertisement at an appropriate unpopulated place of an image. However, low level visual properties cannot establish conceptual similarity. Effective product recommendation on heritage portals requires perceptual reasoning to complement conceptual reasoning in establishing similarity of an advertised product with user's interest.

WindowShopper[47] is an application for product recommendation based on the architecture proposed in this chapter. The system uses multimedia ontology to analyze user interactions with the system and to create an observation model of user's interest. The observation model is used to search the audio-visual components of the advertisements to complement traditional text based and metadata based search. The semantic reasoning with the media components of the advertisements result in better product recommendations. Fig. 2.15 shows an example of recommendations for paintings by contemporary artists that are similar to a popular painting by VanGogh, shown as the inset. The observation model in this example comprised color combination of the painting and color correlogram features characterizing VanGogh's style. While the observation model may appear naïve, more features can be introduced in the multimedia ontology by domain experts and the resulting observation model can be further enriched to achieve better results.

Fig. 2.15: Paintings recommendations similar to a Van Gogh's work.

2.8 Conclusion

With the growing interest for traditional arts and crafts forms, cultural heritage portals are likely to become a major source for infotainment as well as serious resource for research. In this paper, we have described a new ontology based method for accessing such portals to enhance the user experience by way of semantic interpretation of media artifacts and creation of flexible and personalized presentations. The core of the system is based on a new multimedia ontology description scheme that enables media-feature based perceptual modeling of concepts. We have presented a method to create such ontology and its adaptation to user's world-view. We have also presented a new approach to use of such ontology for contextual advertising which is essential for economic sustenance of such heritage portals.

References

1 Louvre Museum Official Website, URL: *http://www.louvre.fr/llv/commun/ home.jsp?bmLocale=en*

2 British Museum – Welcome to the British Museum, URL: *http://www.britishmuseum.org/*

3 Web Gallery of Art, image collection, virtual museum, searchable database of European fine arts (1100-1850), URL: *http://www.wga.hu/*

4 Kalasampada – Digital Library: Resources of Indian Cultural Heritage, URL: *http://ww.ignca.nic.in/dlrich.html*

5 Archaeological Survey of India – Home, URL: *http://asi.nic.in/index.asp*

6 Don Bosco Center for Indigenous Arts – Home, URL: *http://dbcic.org/*

7 Osian's – Home, URL: *http://220.226.203.134/home.html*

8 Global Memory Net – Home, URL: *http://www.memorynet.org/home.php*

9 Multimedia N: Multimedia is the message, URL: *http://www.multimedian.nl/ en/home.php*

10 Hunter, J. (2003), Enhancing the semantic interoperability of multimedia through a core ontology, *IEEE Transactions on Circuits and Systems for Video Technology*, **13**(1), pp.49-58.

11 Hammiche, S. et al. (2004), Semantic Retrieval of Multimedia Data, In *Proceedings of the 2nd ACM international workshop on Multimedia databases*, pp.36-44.

12 Tsinaraki, C. et al. (2005) Ontology-based Semantic Indexing for MPEG-7 and TV-Anytime Audiovisual Content, Special issue of Multimedia Tools and Application, *Journal on Video Segmentation for Semantic Annotation and Transcoding*, **26**, pp.299-325.

13 Petridis, K. et al. (2005), Knowledge representation and semantic annotation for multimedia analysis and reasoning, *IEE Proceedings on Vision, Image and Signal Processing*, **153**(3), pp.255-262.

14 Dublin Core Metadata Initiative (DCMI), URL: *http://dublincore.org/*

15 Carlyle, A. (2002), Document Ontologies in Library and Information Science: An Introduction and Critical Analysis, *Knowledge Technologies Conference 2002*, Seattle (USA).

16 Lenat, D.B. and Guha, R.V. (1990), Building Large Knowledge Based Systems: Representation and Interface in the *Cyc Project*, Addison-Wesley.

17 Farquhar, A. et al. (1997), The Ontolingua Server: A tool for collaborative ontology construction, *International Journal of Human-Computer Studies*, **46**(6), pp.707-727.

18 Brachman, R.J. and Schmolze, J.G. (1985), An overview of KL-ONE knowledge representation system, *Cognitive Sciences*, **9**(2), pp.171-216.

19 Borgida, A. et al. (1989), CLASSIC: A structural data model for objects, In *Proc. ACM SIGMOD International Conference on the Management of Data*, pp.58-67.

20 MacGregor, R. (1991), Inside the LOOM classifier, *SIGART Bulletin*, **2**(3), pp.70-76.

21 Badder, F. et al. (2003), *The Description Logics Handbook*, Cambridge University Press.

22 McGuinness, D.L. and Hermelen F. van (2004), OWL Web ontology language overview, W3C Recommendation, URL: *http://www.w3c.org/TR/owl-features*

23 Lassila, O. and Swick, R. (1999), Resource description framework (RDF) model and syntax specification, W3C Recommendation, URL: *http://www.w3c.org/TR/REC-rdf-syntax/*

24 Ding, Z. and Peng, Y. (2004), A probabilistic extension to ontology languages, In *Proc. of the 37th Hawaii International Conference on System Sciences*.

25 Stoilos, G. et al. (2005), Fuzzy owl: Uncertainty and the semantic web, In *Proc. of the International Workshop on OWL: Experiences and Directions*.

26 Bertini, M. et al. (2007), Dynamic Pictorial Ontologies for Video Digital Libraries Annotation, In *Proceedings of, ACM Multimedia Conference* (MS Workshop).

27 Kangassalo, H. (1991), Conceptual level user interfaces to databases and information systems, In *Advances in Information Modeling and Knowledge Bases*, IOS Press.

28 Ghosh, H. et al. (2007), Ontology specification and integration for multimedia applications, *In Ontologies: A Handbook of Principles, Concepts and Applications in Information Systems*, Springer.

29 Ding, *op.cit.*

30 Wattamwar, S. and Ghosh, H. (2008), Spatio-temporal query for multimedia databases, In *Proc. ACM Multimedia Conference* (MS Workshop).

31 Papadias, D. (2001), Approximate spatio-temporal retrieval, *ACM Transactions on Information Systems*, **19**, pp.53-96.

32 Mallik, A. et al. (2008), Multimedia ontology learning for automatic annotation and video browsing, *Proceedings of the 1st ACM international conference on Multimedia information retrieval*, October.

33 Ghosh, H. et al. (2007), Learning Ontology for Personalized Video Retrieval, *International Workshop on Many Faces of Multimedia Semantics (WMS07)*, ACM Multimedia, Augsberg (Germany) September.

34 Harit, G. et al. (2006), Using multimedia ontology for generating conceptual annotations and hyperlinks in video collections, *International conference on Web Intelligence*.

35 Neapolitan, R.E. (1999), *Probabilistic reasoning in expert systems: Theory and algorithms*, John-Wiley and sons Inc. pp.226-228.

36 Ghosh, H. and Chaudhury, S. (2004), Distributed and reactive query planning in R-MAGIC: An agent based multimedia retrieval system, *IEEE Trans KDE*, **16**(9), September.

37 Manjunath, B.S. et al. (2003), *Introduction to MPEG-7: Multimedia Content Description Interface*, John Wiley and Sons.

38 Maiti, B. et al. (2004), A Framework for Ontology Specification and Integration for Multimedia Applications, *Knowledge Based Computer System (KBCS),* Hyderabad, December.

39 Web Services Architecture: W3C Working Group Note, URL: *http://www.w3.org/TR/ws-arch/*

40 Welcome to the Foundation for Intelligent Physical Agents, URL: *http://www.fipa.org*

41 Huang, Jing et al. (1997), Image indexing using color correlogram, *Proceedings of Computer Vision and Pattern Recognition.*

42 Harit, Gaurav, Chaudhury, Santanu and Pranjpe, Jagriti (2005), Ontology guided access to document Images, *Eighth International Conference on Document Analysis & Recognition*, 29th August – 1st September 2005, **1**, pp.421-425.

43 Kenny, D. and Marshall, J. (2000), Contextual Marketing: The Real Business of the Internet, *Harvard Business Review*, November-December.

44 Jang, Y. et al. (2007), Keyword Management System Based on Ontology for Contextual Advertising, ALPIT '07, *Proceedings of the Sixth International Conference on Advanced Language Processing and Web Information Technology*, August.

45 Chakrabarti, D. et al. (2008), Contextual advertising by combining relevance with click feedback, WWW '08, *Proceeding of the 17th international conference on World Wide Web*, April.

46 Mei, Tao et al. (2008), Contextual in-image advertising, MM'08, *Proceeding of the 16th ACM international conference on Multimedia*, October.

47 Ghosh, H. and Chaudhury, S. (2002), WindowShopper: Guided Shopping in e-market, *Knowledge Based Computer Systems (KBCS)*, Mumbai, December.

Chapter 3

Semantic Integration of Classical and Digital Libraries

S. Thaddeus[1], A. Jeganathan[2], Gracy T. Leema[2]

[1]*Sacred Heart College (Autonomous)*
Tirupattur, Vellore Dt. Tamil Nadu, India
[2]*Bosco Info Tech Services, BICS InfoTech,*
Yelagiri Hills, Vellore Dt. Tamil Nadu, India
{thad, jegan, leema}@boscoits. com

Abstract

The automation of bibliographic catalog and house-keeping operations in a library and/or the introduction of digital library system have seldom delivered context-specific or personalized information for the end user. In addition, the availability of the information is restricted to specific libraries. The existing cataloging and classification rules do not provide intelligent mechanism to store and retrieve ever-expanding information resources. Adopting semantic technology with ontology as the formalism to represent all resources can provide a better system for information storage and retrieval, irrespective of the cataloging standard. A Resource Ontology based on the cataloging rule to provide semantic description of the resources that leads to integration of both printed and digital libraries is demonstrated. Further, a technical solution architecture to provide semantic library services triggered by an ontology management infrastructure and software agents is proposed.

Keywords: Ontology, Semantic Technology, Digital Library, Print Library, Classical Library.

3.1 Introduction

There is a paradigm shift in the way library collections are handled since World War II. It was *collection development* era from 1950 to 1975 when most of the libraries concentrated on acquiring resources. Greater impetus to *collection management* than collection development emerged with the application of information technology for library management from the year 1975 to 2000[1]. Library operations namely cataloguing, acquisitions, circulation, serial control, bibliographic services and likewise were computerized. Most of the universities and research centers began to reap the benefits of automation. The dynamic growth of digital content and the demand to supply just-in-time resources to the end users precipitated the need for digital library. Today, the information explosion through Internet is reaching saturation. Information retrieval from billions of web documents using conventional search engines is inadequate to cope with the demands of the end users.

Tim-Berners Lee envisioned the Semantic Web as an extension of the World Wide Web, which adds semantics (meaning) to web documents and make them machine-processable so that computers can process the required resources based on user's preference[2]. This opens a new digital era in library science called *semantic digital library* incorporating semantics in the management of library resources.

This paper presents a schema to integrate semantic enabled digital library application with the existing legacy applications so that the gamut of library resources is available to the end user through a single interface. The semantic description of resources, users and the services using appropriate ontologies will make information retrieval personal, contextual and relevant, independent of a particular library cataloging or classification scheme. Solution architecture is proposed to add semantics and provide intelligent, information retrieval services. While the proposed architecture provides an approach to link a classical library with a digital library, the role of legacy library information system in the context of library automation remains the same.

Section 2 presents the need for integration of classical and digital library applications due to the paradigm shift in library science from collection management to knowledge management. Section 3 is an overview of semantic technology and ontology as a knowledge model for digital libraries.

In section 4, ontology for library resources is developed using Anglo-American Cataloguing Rule (AACR2) as the source. The solution architecture to implement the integration of classical and digital libraries using the Resource ontology is proposed in section 5.

3.2 Motivation

Most of the libraries are built on a cataloging scheme of their preference like AACR2, an international cataloging standard. Classification of the resources of a library is done using Dewey Decimal Classification (DDC), Library of Congress Classification (LCC), Colon Classification (CC) or any other scheme[3]. These cataloging and classification rules provide a static structure for organization of the resources. They are not flexible to adapt and expand the services of growing digital resources in a library. This leads to a chasm between the digital and classical systems. Libraries that opted for automation in collection management era view digital library as a separate entity. Those who opted for digitization in knowledge management era combine both digital and classical library systems as a single fold. Moreover, there is a strong urge to share the resources with other libraries. These challenges can be effectively handled with semantic technologies and web services. Libraries that intend to share information can choose to share the digital services or classical services or both. The libraries are in a two-tier system for classical and digital library services with differing approaches for cataloging and classification and lacking intelligent dissemination services. However, at the organization level, the content and services of a library (be it classical or digital) can be grouped together and addressed via a single interface. Fig. 3.1 depicts the numerous forms of library resources as digital and physical and the services that can be provided and combined. It is expected that legacy application for library management with its huge repository of bibliographic cataloging records cannot be ruled out. The application of semantic technology with ontology as the formalism to define library resources, users and environment can lead to a binding of digital and classical library services.

Acquisition	OPAC	Search / Browse	Personalizer Ports
Cataloging	Circulation	Resource View	SMS Services
Binding	SDI	Path Finder	User Profile
Classical Library Services		**Digital Library Services**	

Classical and Digital Library System			

Monograph	CD / Cassetes	Lbrary Catalog	Digital Collection
Articles	Serials / Journals	Web Documents	Multimedia Files
Cartographs	Other Printed Materials	Electronic Journal	Eectronic Monograph
Physical Resources		**Digital Resources**	

Fig. 3.1: Resources and services of classical and digital library systems.

3.3 Overview of Semantic Technology

Semantic Technology is the software technology that allows the meaning of and associations between information to be known and processed at execution time. The backbone of any semantic technology application is a knowledge model, defined formally as an ontology that provides executable knowledge during run time[4]. Ontology provides a framework to represent any domain knowledge as 'explicit, formal specification of shared conceptualization'[5]. Ontology enables shared knowledge and reuse where information resources can be communicated between human or software agents. Semantic relationships in ontologies are machine readable, which enable automatic representation of facts and rules, and querying in a subject domain. Web Ontology Language (OWL) is adopted as ontology representation language in this system as it has matured to become an accepted standard by World Wide Web Consortium. OWL is a consolidation of its preceding languages namely SHOE, OIL, DAML+OIL[6]. OWL provides a rich set of constructs to define classes as named or anonymous using property restrictions, logical operations or axioms[7]. OWL-DL is a version of OWL, based on Description Logic, a derivative of First Order Predicate Logic, which enables sound and decidable reasoning facility[8].

Any semantic application is built on an ontology whose data is maintained in a persistent store with information transaction processing and access enabled through SOAP and software agents. A software agent is an artificial agent, which operates in a software environment that includes operating systems, computer applications, databases, networks and virtual domains. Delegacy for software agents centers on persistence. By making decisions and acting on the environment independently, software agents reduce the human workload by interacting with their end-clients when it is time to deliver results.

3.4 Resource Ontology

In simple terms, ontology is seen as a controlled vocabulary, glossary or taxonomy. In the context of semantic technology applications, ontology is much more a complex structure, which provides sharable and executable knowledge of the addressed domain. A common cataloguing structure for all information resources of both classical and digital library systems can be devised as Resource ontology. This ontology can grow as the knowledge base of a library accommodating every aspect of bibliographic description about the resources. Resource ontology is defined for any existing cataloging rule to incorporate the experience of the community and is updated to include bibliographic requirements of the future. This ontology can be agreed upon for all library resources and shared by various user communities. In this article, the development of resource ontology based on AACR2, an internationally accepted cataloging standard is shown in Fig. 3.2. It gives a schematic view of the main concepts of the ontology with relationship of various bibliographic elements linked to a resource item. Table 3.1 in appendix presents the complete scheme for ontology with its classes, data properties and object properties for representation in OWL-DL. Each bibliographic area of AACR2 is considered as a separate concept with its own hierarchy of sub-concepts. A resource is annotated and defined by linking various related concepts using object or data properties.

Developing this ontology, we have realized that the entire AACR2 definition can be brought under a single, consistent schema. This can expand the

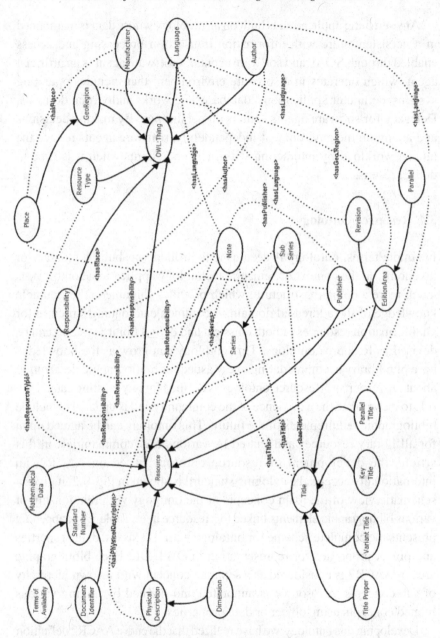

Fig. 3.2: Resource ontology based on AACR2.

Asserted Conditions for the Note Area in OWL

```
<owl:Class rdf:about="#Note">
    <rdfs:subClassOf rdf:resource="http://www.w3.org/2002/07/owl#Thing"/>
    <owl:disjointWith rdf:resource="#Publisher"/>

    <rdfs:subClassOf>
        <owl:Restriction>
            <owl:onProperty>
                <owl:ObjectProperty rdf:ID="hasTitle"/>
            </owl:onProperty>
            <owl:someValuesFrom>
                <owl:Class rdf:about="#Title"/>
            </owl:someValuesFrom>
        </owl:Restriction>
    </rdfs:subClassOf>

    <rdfs:subClassOf>
        <owl:Restriction>
            <owl:onProperty>
                <owl:ObjectProperty rdf:ID="hasSeries"/>
            </owl:onProperty>
            <owl:someValuesFrom>
                <owl:Class rdf:about="#Series"/>
            </owl:someValuesFrom>
        </owl:Restriction>
    </rdfs:subClassOf>
</owl:Class>
```

Asserted Conditions for the Class Mathematical Data in OWL

```
<owl:Class rdf:about="#MathematicalDataArea">
    <owl:disjointWith rdf:resource="#StandardNumber"/>
        <owl:equivalentClass>
            <owl:Restriction>
                <owl:onProperty>
                    <owl:ObjectProperty rdf:ID="hasResourceType"/>
                </owl:onProperty>
                <owl:hasValue>
                    <ResourceType rdf:ID="Cartographical_Material"/>
                </owl:hasValue>
            </owl:Restriction>

        </owl:equivalentClass>
</owl:Class>
```

existing cataloging standard of a library, taking it beyond its limitations. In the first version of ontology, trivial details are ignored. However, all main concepts are covered. Different types of resources such as books, pamphlets, cartographic materials, manuscripts, music, computer files and likewise defined in the cataloging rule are considered as individuals of <Resource Type> class and mapped to a resource through object property <hasResourceType>.

Common specification rules of AACR are not explicitly defined for each resource type. This is facilitated in ontology definition from the perspective of machine-processing. For instance, AACR2 differentiates many types of a title namely title proper, variant title, key title and parallel title. These options are also mentioned for bibliographic areas of Series and Note but not explicitly linked. Using an object property <has Title>, the classes of title are mapped to these as shown in Asserted conditions for Note Area.

Similarly, Statement of Responsibility for a Resource has to be included for Edition, Series and Note. This is very well taken care by the object property <hasResponsibility>. Mathematical Data area is used only for cartographic materials. This rule is incorporated into the definition of the class Mathematical Data by OWL asserted condition with the property <hasResourceType as Cartographical_Material> so that Cartographs alone be members of this class as shown in Asserted Conditions for the Note Area. The ontology definition need not be restricted to AACR2. There can be ontology for other cataloging standards too and mapping can be provided to ensure the interoperability. Semantic searching into different library will choose other library's native classification standard to search the resources and again will convert the results to the requesting library's cataloging standard.

3.5 Solution Architecture

The proposed solution (Fig. 3.3) provides two levels of services namely Digital Library services and Classical Library services. Classical library services are routed through the legacy library information systems (LIS). Digital Services are implemented as semantic technology applications coupled with an ontology management server, which directs and controls the required ontologies, the data stores and functional agents. The existing bibliographic catalogue records from LIS must be annotated with semantic descriptions compatible with Resource ontology and this process is called as data harvesting. Resource details needs to be exported to common interchangeable standard like MARC21 for data interchange between the LIS and Data Harvesting Agent. LIS should have the capability to export the resource details as MARC21 standard. Data harvesting agent which runs periodically senses changes made to the resources and notifies the ontology server to update the ontology repository. For example, whenever a new resource is added or modified LIS periodically exports those details as MARC21 format which in turn sensed by data harvesting agent and notifies the ontology server to update the ontology repository with the required resource details. It is difficult for the potential users to make the semantic description of all physical resources of a library, which are already in electronic format. This task can be automated if the required information can be extracted in one of popular legacy bibliographic formats such as MARC21. Annotation agent bridges the gap between LIS and Ontology Server and does the annotation of semantic descriptions for physical resources. Whenever a new resource is added or modified, the agent reads

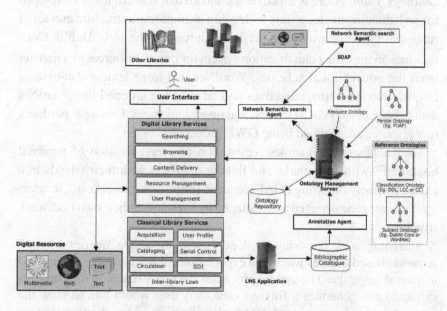

Fig. 3.3: Semantic bound digital and classical library systems.

the change (say in MARC21 format) in LIS bibliographic catalog, and notifies Ontology Server to update the ontology repository with the required annotation and resource details.

This proposal is deployed using an Open Source solution based on Joseki and Jena APIs[9]. It provides multiple functionalities to create, store, retrieve, maintain and apply ontologies. Semantic-based applications for the digital services are engineered and plugged into the Server. Each digital service with its distinct functionality is implemented via APIs. Jena API handles all transactions, modularisation, ontology evolution, metamodeling, lexica management and querying.

Crawling through library resources and collecting data will lead to manageability issues and a good network infrastructure will replace the need of collecting data from other libraries. Network Semantic Search Agent can take the responsibility of getting the search results from other libraries. Any resource can be classified under different retrieval categories. This is facilitated by mapping every annotated resource with a Subject Ontology. Any popularly used ontology such as Dublin Core (http://dublincore.org) or WordNet (http://wordnet.princeton.edu) can be selected as the Subject Ontology. Dublin Core is a metadata standard that was originally developed for web documents. Its goal is to develop a simple data structure and set of rules that could be used to describe resources on the web. Dublin Core becomes an important classification system for library resources as a transfer from the conventional schemes. WordNet is a large lexical database of English. Nouns, verbs, adjectives and adverbs are grouped into WordNet data to be accessed via RDF APIs and query languages. Concepts pertinent to a resource are mapped using OWL properties.

User management handles registration of users, creation of personal bookshelf[10] with bookmarks and linking the users with their friends in a closed user network using FOAF metadata (http://foaf-project.org). Readers can link categories created and managed by friends into their own bookmark structure.

Searching and browsing is done based on simple queries as well semantic-based queries where the expectations of the viewer are expressed in natural language. The system processes the query based on the concepts extracted and generates a filtered view. Any user would like to view the resources based on a predefined classification. The existing library classification schemes such as DCC, LCC or CC based on disciplines will continue to be relevant to provide a general classification schema. A user can opt for any classification scheme if each scheme is represented as ontology and mapped with Subject ontology. While Subject ontology defines the categorization of a resource, Classification ontologies facilitate the viewing of the resources according to the choice of the end user. Any classification scheme can be transformed to a relating ontology and linked to the system.

Network semantic search agent is connected with library participating in the network. The users search request is notified to Search Agent and the Search Agent communicates to the other search agent of the network library. Search Agent running in other libraries converts the request to the library specific classification and searches the result and converts the results back to requested libraries classification. Communication among the Search Agent is based on SOAP and so interoperability with solutions is quite feasible.

3.6 Related Works

The basic notions for the developed Resource ontology and the related solution architecture have emerged from the works of two research communities namely Digital Library and Semantic Web. Although there are many digital library systems that have proven successful like DSpace (http://dspace.org), Fedora (http://fedora.info), and Greenstone (http://greenstone.org/cgi-bin/library), most of them do not include semantic functionalities. JeromeDL is one of the first open source digital library solution using Semantic Web technology that provides browsing and searching based on semantic description of resources and context-specific user management[11]. The concept of personalized profile management using FOAF is adopted from this implementation. The MarcOnt Initiative[12] of JeromeDL provides ontology for bibliographic purposes combining MARC21, BIBTex and Dublin Core.

The BT digital library is based on the 5-layer approach of SEKT (http://sekt-project.com) project to build any semantic enabled knowledge technology application[13]. SIMILE extends DSpace (http://www.dspace. org/)[14], enhancing its support for arbitrary schemata and metadata, primarily though the application of RDF and semantic web (http://www.w3.org/2001/ sw/) techniques DOGMA is a project of STAR LAB (http://starlab.vub.ac.be), which has developed a semantic application to convert WordNet ontology to build a category system to be incorporated into the digital library.

In the past three years, many semantic applications have been developed as part of Semantic Web Challenges of the International Conference on Semantic Web. Study of these applications show many techniques that can be incorporated in the development of semantic digital libraries[15]. CS AKTive Space (CAS) is an integrated Semantic Web application, which provides a way to explore the UK Computer Science Research domain across multiple dimensions for multiple stakeholders, from funding agencies to individual researchers[16]. Bibster (http://bibster.semanticweb.org/) is a Java-based system, which assists researchers in managing, searching, and sharing bibliographic metadata in a peer-to-peer network.

3.7 Conclusion

The special contribution of this article is that the existing cataloging and classification rules can be enhanced with a distinct ontology (named as Resource ontology) to accommodate all kinds of resources providing personalized, simple and semantic-based access. Towards this end, a Resource ontology based on AACR2 is developed. The ontology presents the details of the rules concerning various resource types addressed in AACR2 in a machine-processable manner. This ontology can be further refined based on experimental results of implementation.

As further work, we need to test the performance of Resource ontology and develop ontologies for various classification schemes like DDC or CC. Experimenting the ontology with the semantic application built on Joseki server for digital services will throw light on the performance and scalability of the system.

References

1 Branin, Joseph J. (2003). Knowledge Management in Academic Libraries: Building the Knowledge Bank at the Ohio State University, *http://www.lib.ohio-state.edu/*

2 Berners-Lee, Tim, Hendler, James and Lassila, Ora (2001), The Semantic Web, *Scientific American*, **284**(5), pp.35-42.

3 Chan, Lois, Mai (1994), *Cataloging and Classification An Introduction*, McGraw-Hill International Editions.

4 Davis, Mills (2006), Semantic Wave 2006, Part-1: Executive Guide to Billion Dollar Markets A Project10X Special Report, *Semantic Technology Conference*, San Jose, Califorma, January.

5 Gruber, T.R. (1993). A Translation Approach to Portable Ontology Specifications, *Knowledge Acquisition*, **5**, pp.199-220.

6 Horrocks, P.F., Patel-Schneider and Harmelen, F. van (2003), From SHIQ and RDF to OWL: The making of a Web Ontology Language, *Journal of Web Semantics*, **1**,(1), pp.7-26.

7 *http://www.w3.org/TR/owl-guide/*

8 Baader, Franz and Werner, Nutt (2003), Basic Description Logics in The *Description Logic Handbook: Theory, Implementation and Applications*, Diego Calvanese, Deborah McGuinness, Daniele Nardi, Peter Patel-Schneider (Eds.), Cambridge University Press, pp.43-95.

9 McBride, B. (2002), "Jena", *IEEE Internet Computing*, July/August.

10 Kruk, Sebastian Ryszard, Decker, Stefan and Zieborak, Lech (2005), JeromeDL ¬ Reconnecting Digital Libraries and the Semantic Web, *WWW2005*, May Chiba, Japan.

11 Synak, Marcin and Kruk, Sebastian Ryszard (2005), MarcOnt Initiative ¬the Ontology for the Librarian World, *2nd European Semantic Web Conference (ESWC)*, Heraklion, Greece, June.

12 Davies, John, Duke, Alistair and Thurlow, Ian (2006), Applying Semantic Web Technology in a Digital Library. Posters of the *3rd European Semantic Web Conference (ESWC)*, Budva, Montenegro, June.

13 Project SIMILE (2005), Semantic Interoperability of Metadata and Information in unlike Environments, *MIT SIMILE Proposal*, July.

14 Harit, Gaurav, Chaudhury, Santanu and Ghosh, Hiranmay (2004), Managing Document Images in a Digital Library: An Ontology guided Approach, *Proceedings of the First International Workshop on Document Image Analysis for Libraries (DIAL'04)*.

15 Klein, Michel and Visser, Ubbo (2004), Semantic Web Challenge 2003, *IEEE Intelligent Systems*, May/June.

16 Shadbolt, Nigel, Gibbins, Nicholas, Glaser, Hugh, Harris, Stephen and Schraefel, M.C. (2004), CS AKTive Space or how we learned to stop worrying and love the Semantic Web, *IEEE Intelligent Systems*, **19**(3), pp.41-47.

Appendix

Schema for Resource Ontology Based on AACR2

Class	Sub Classes	Data Properties	Object Properties
Resource		ClassNo	hasResourceType
Resource Type		Name	
GeoRegion		Name	
	Place	Name, Address	
Language		Name	
Author		First Name, Middle Name, Last Name	
Responsibility		Author Role	has Author
Title	Title Proper	Chief Title, Alternative Title, Supplied Title, Devised Title	
	Parallel Title	Chief Title in Another, Script	hasLanguage
	Variant Title	Half Title, Caption Title, Running Title, Cover Title, Spine Title, Panel Title, Title Block Title, Title on Container, Data set Name, Binder's Title	

Contd...

Class	Sub Classes	Data Properties	Object Properties
	Key Title	Key Title, Romanized Title	
Edition Area		Number, Version, Interest	hasGeoRegion hasResponsibility
	Parallel	Script	hasLanguage
	Revision	Script	hasLanguage
Manufacturer		Name, Date	hasPlace
Publisher		Name, Abbreviated Name, Contact Person, Remarks, Status, Communication Details, Year, Date, Name of Printer, Date of Printing, Address	hasPlace
Physical Description		Volume, Pages, Leaves, Columns, Braille, Tactile system, Illustrative, Accompanying Material, Material descriptor	
	Dimension	Height, Width, Depth, Diameter	
Series		ISSN Number, Other Standard Number	hasResponsibility, hasTitle
	Sub Series		HasResponsibility, hasTitle
Note		Summary, Content, Numbers	hasLanguage, hasResponsbility,
Standard Number	Document Identifier	Standard Number, Other Number	
	Terms of Availability	Price, Qualification	
Supplementary Details		Independently, Dependently	
Mathematical Data Area		Scale, Projection, Coordinates, Equinox, Magnitude	

Chapter 4

Low-level Visual Features with Semantics-based Image Retrieval

V.P. Subramanyam Rallabandi[i]

[1]*National Brain Research Centre*
Manesar, Gurgaon, Haryana, India
rvpsubramanyam@yahoo.com

Abstract

In content-based image retrieval there is a need to reduce the gap between the high- level semantics of visual objects and the low-level features such as color, texture and shape descriptors extracted from them. In this paper, we develop an image retrieval system that bridges the gap between low-level visual features and high- level semantics and extracts a similarity measure directly from the data itself using machine learning. We proposed a fuzzy color histogram for color features and Bayesian estimation for texture features and Lie descriptors for shape features. We have used unsupervised Kohonen's Self-Organizing Maps (SOM) technique to train the images and our own indexing scheme with reference system based on R-tree SOM.

Keywords: Relevance Feedback, R-tree SOM, Fuzzy Color Histogram, Bayesian Distance, Lie Descriptors, Diffeomorphisms, Coarse Features, Semi-fine Features, Semantic Analysis.

---

[i] The present work is done at Delhi College of Engineering, Bawana Road, Delhi-42.

4.1 Introduction

Research in Content-based image retrieval (CBIR) today is a lively discipline, expanding its breadth as the access to visual information is not only performed at a conceptual level, using keywords as in the textual domain, but also at a perceptual level, using objective measurements of visual content[1]. There have been a large number of CBIR systems developed in the recent years such as IBM'S QBIC project[2], VisualSeek[3], PhotoBook[4], PicSOM[5], PicHunter[6], MIRROR[7] and lot more. There are different kinds of paradigms of retrieval systems such as Query by Picture Example (QBPE), Query by Image Content (QBIC)[8] and Relevance Feedback (RF) mechanism. Anyhow the image querying becomes an iterative process where the retrieval system is only a tool in the hands of a human expert. But most of the CBIR systems are commonly based upon non-semantic approaches employing primitive image information like color, texture, shape, spatial relations or mixtures of these features and etc. However, in many image database applications, the semantic content is more desirable because it facilitates the high-level application tasks[9]. This is manifested by difficulties in setting fair comparisons between CBIR systems and in interpreting their results. These problems have hindered the researchers from doing comprehensive evaluations of different CBIR techniques. The complete survey on content-based retrieval for multimedia images is given in[10-12]. One key issue to be faced is the identification and extraction of semantic information from the visual data. One approach to solving this approach is to associate high-level semantic information with the low-level vision data. Several systems that attempt to bridge this gap can be found in[13-14]. The retrieval of images from databases using semantic queries has been described in[15-16] and[17]. The digital library project of Stanford University has given a standard proposal for internet retrieval and search in the year 1997 in their technical report[18]. Some of the CBIR systems such as PicToSeek[19], DrawSearch[20], Image Rover[21] designed based on client-server paradigm. An image retrieval using distributed system over the internet developed by HP lab is available online[22]. Recently IBM developed a multimedia retrieval system MARVEL[23].

A major work reported in this paper is to demonstrate that semantic analysis of the image content plays a critical role in the understanding and retrieval of images. The techniques presented in this work can potentially be generalized for analyzing different types of complex images through the interaction of both low-level image analysis and semantic reasoning. The present system is developed using unsupervised SOM, and topology preserving mapping from the image descriptor space to a two-dimensional lattice or a grid of neural networks.

4.2 General Concepts of Content-Based Image Retrieval

4.2.1 Query by Picture Example

With low-level visual features, it is not possible to base a content-based image query on verbal terms like in text-based retrieval. Therefore, other query methods must be applied. With query by picture example (QBPE), the image queries are based on example images shown either from the database itself or some-external location[24]. The similar type of image retrieval by examples has been developed by R.Brunelli[25]. The user classified these example images as relevant or irrelevant to the current retrieval task and the system uses this information to select such images the user is most likely to be interested in.

4.2.2 Relevance Feedback

Generally a CBIR system is unable to retrieve the best available images in its first response. As a consequence, satisfactory retrieval results can be obtained only if the image query can be turned into an iterative and interactive process towards the desired image(s). The iterative refinement of a query is known as relevance feedback (RF). Lot of techniques has been found in literature such as Support Vector Networks[26], Boosting[27], etc. But out of them, relevance feedback is a powerful technique for interactive image retrieval[28-30]. RF can be seen as a form of supervised learning to steer the subsequent query rounds by using the information gathered from the user's feedback. We have used relevance feedback with semantic refinement to get accurate results.

4.2.3 Multi-feature Indexing

With the current state of image processing technology, image retrieval can not generally be based on abstract conceptual level. Therefore, lower-level pictorial features need to be used. This creates the basic problem of CBIR: the gap between high-level semantic concepts used by humans to understand image content and the low-level visual features used by a computer to index the images in a database. One method to tackle this issue is to use several image visual features in parallel and combine their responses in an effective manner.

4.2.4 High-level Semantics-based Image Retrieval

The survey shows that the state-of-the-art techniques in reducing the 'semantic gap' include mainly 5 categories: (1) using object ontology to define high-level concepts, (2) using machine learning tools to associate low-level features with query concepts, (3) introducing relevance feedback (RF) into retrieval loop for continuous learning of users' intention, (4) generating semantic template (ST) to support high-level image retrieval, (5) making use of both the visual content of images and the textual information obtained from the Web for WWW (the Web) image retrieval.

4.3 Proposed Image Retrieval System

The proposed semantics-based image retrieval system is a framework for research on algorithms and methods for content-based online retrieval depending on visual features of the image along with the high-level semantic analysis of the image. Earlier, we have developed an image retrieval system based on the low-level visual features such as color, texture and shape descriptors[31]. This system is developed using relevance feedback technique and proposed our own indexing scheme using R-tree. This system uses several SOMs in parallel for retrieving images from the database. These parallel SOMs have been trained with separate datasets obtained from the image data with different feature extraction techniques. The different SOMs and their underlying feature extraction schemes impose different similarity functions on the images. Every image query is unique and the users of this system have their own transient view of image similarity and relevance. Therefore, a system structure capable of holding many simultaneous similarity representations can adapt to different kinds of retrieval tasks.

4.3.1 R-Tree Structure SOM

The image indexing method used in this system is the R-tree SOM. The SOM defines an elastic topology-preserving grid of points that is fitted to the input space. Thus it can be used to visualize multi dimensional data, usually on a two-dimensional grid[32]. The map attempts to represent all the available observations with an optimal accuracy by using a restricted set of models. As the SOM algorithm organizes similar feature vectors in nearby neurons, the resulting map contains a representation of database where similar images, according to the given feature are located near each other.

The fitting of the model vectors is usually carried out by a sequential regression process, where $t=0, 1,2,...,t_{max} -1$ is the step index. For each input sample $x(t)$, first the index $c(x)$ of the best-matching unit (BMU) or "winner model" $m_{c(x)}(t)$ is identified using the condition.

$$\forall i : \left\| x(t) - m_{c(x)}(t) \right\| \leq \left\| x(t) - m_i(t) \right\| \tag{4.1}$$

Instead of the usual distance metric, Euclidean measure we used special semantic metrics, Semantic label frequency distribution similarity (SFDS). After finding the BMU, a subset of the model vectors constituting a neighborhood centered around node $c(x)$ are updated as

$$m_i(t+1) = m_i(t) + h(t;c(x),i)(x(t) - m_i(t)) \tag{4.2}$$

Where $h(t;c(x),i)$ is the neighborhood function, a decreasing function of the distance between the ith and $c(x)^{th}$ nodes on the map grid. This regression is reiterated over the available samples and the value of $h(t;c(x),i)$ is allowed to decrease in time to guarantee the convergence of prototype vectors m.

We have used a special form of the algorithm, R-tree SOM. The idea is to map objects into points in finite dimensional space, and to use multi attribute access methods (also referred as spatial access methods) to cluster them to search for them. The spatial access methods form three classes: i) R-trees and rest of R-tree family, ii) linear quad trees, iii) grid files. Several of these methods explode exponentially with the dimensionality, eventually reducing to sequential scanning. The R-tree based methods seem to be most robust for higher dimensions, provided that the fan-out of R-tree nodes remains greater than two[33]. Much detail about R-trees can be found in[34]. The R-tree SOM reduces the time complexity of the search compared to ordinary one-dimensional tree SOM. The R-tree represents a spatial object by its minimum bounding rectangle (MBR). Data rectangles are grouped to form parent nodes, which are recursively grouped to form grandparent nodes and eventually, a tree hierarchy[35].

In our experiments, we have used four-level R-trees whose layer sizes have been 4×4, 16×16, 64×64 and 256×256 units. In the training of lower SOM levels, the search for the BMU has been restricted to the 10×10 neuron area below the BMU on the above model. Every image has been used 100 times for each training each of the SOM levels. After training each SOM hierarchical level, that level is fixed and each neural unit on it is given a visual label from the database image nearest to it. We have considered color, texture and shape features. These features have been used to create a R-tree SOM of images. In similarity mapping, images in neighboring map unit are assumed to be not only semantically correlated but also of their visual similarity. We have used message digest algorithm (MD5) for dimension reduction by random mapping[36]. The images are the visual labels on the surface of the 16×16 sized SOM layer.

4.3.2 Self-organizing Relevance Feedback

Relevance feedback has been implemented in this system by using the parallel SOMs as shown in Fig. 4.1. Each image seen by the user of the system is graded by the user as either relevant or irrelevant[37]. All these images and their associated relevance grades are then projected on all the

SOM surfaces. This process forms on the maps areas where there are: 1) many relevant images mapped in same or near by SOM units; 2) relevant and irrelevant images mixed; 3) only irrelevant images; 4) no graded images at all. Out of these, the cases (1) and (3) indicate that the corresponding content descriptor agrees well with the user's conception on the relevance of the images; whereas the case (2) is an indication that the content descriptor can not distinguish between relevant and irrelevant images.

When we assume that similar images are located near each other on the SOM surfaces, we are motivated to spread the relevance information placed in the SOM units also to the neighboring units. This is implemented by low-pass filtering the map surfaces. All relevant images are first given positive weights inversely proportional to the number of relevant images. Likewise, irrelevant images receive negative weights that are inversely proportional to the number of irrelevant images such that the overall sum of these relevance values becomes zero. The values are then summed in the BMU's of the images and the resulting sparse value fields are low-pass filtered. Each image used as a visual label on the SOM surface is thus given a qualification value that depends on the local denseness of positive responses on the map and indirectly, on the feature extraction methods capability to reflect the user's view of image relevance.

4.4 Low-level Visual Descriptors

The visual content descriptors define the syntax and semantics of each feature representation. A simple feature such as color, texture and shape may have several descriptors representing different relevant aspects. Description Schemas (DS) specify the structure and semantics of relations between their components, which can be either descriptors or other DS's. Finally the description definition language XML is used to specify the existing descriptors and DS's and for defining new ones. The present system defines not only the descriptors but also special metrics to be used with the descriptors when calculating the similarity between images. There were 63 visual features extracted from the images. Of these there were 9 color moments for the three-color channels, 42 local statistics (mean, standard deviation, etc.) for texture and 12 for the shape.

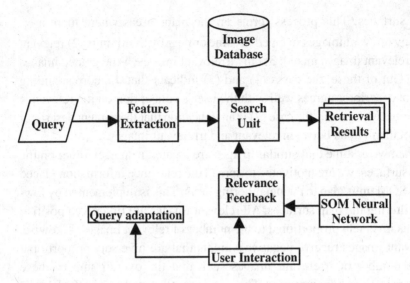

Fig. 4.1: Relevance Feedback (RF) mechanism.

4.4.1 Color Feature Descriptors

The dominant color descriptor is composed of CEILAB color coordinate system. Since RGB color has been most commonly used for representing color images, intuitively we need to perform nonlinear color space transformation from RGB to CEILAB pixel-by-pixel. We first quantize uniforming the given RGB color space to n color bins (i.e. $16^3 = 4096$ color bins). We proposed an approach using Fuzzy Color Histogram (FCH) for the retrieval of color images[38]. We employed fuzzy c-means clustering algorithm not only to classify the clusters but also to obtain the membership matrix at the same time.

4.4.2 Texture Feature Descriptors

In this approach, we train using 1x1,3x3, 5x5 image blocks (i.e. 1+9+25=35) from one image per texture class. Using this approach, we have found that the texture images in the same class differed either by perspective or contrast and changes in contrast do not pose a problem to classification since it does not change appearance of texture. When training on all images in a class the texture cluster is able to generalize the differences in perspective by increasing the spread of the cluster. However, when training by using one particular image or perspective, the clusters are tuned to the specific perspective so that they are enabling to capture feature vectors obtained at different perspectives. To classify an image block from an unknown texture class, we first obtain the texture features. Then, the image is classified as a texture by choosing the texture data corresponding to the closest cluster in the feature space. To determine the spread as well as the centroid of the class we have used simplified Bayesian distance as the metric to determine the "closeness". Under the conditions that the features are independent and Gaussian, the Bayesian distance provides maximum likelihood (ML) classification. Under these assumptions, the likelihood function for a feature vector $\vec{V}$ belonging in texture class is

$$p(\vec{v} = \vec{v} / L = 1) = \prod_{i=1}^{n_f} \frac{1}{\sqrt{2\pi}\,\sigma_{i,l}} \exp(-(v_l - \mu_{i,l})^2 / 2\sigma_{i,l}^2) \quad (4.3)$$

where v_i represent the elements of the feature vector, nf corresponds to the total number of features, $\mu_{i,l}$, $\sigma_{i,l}$ represents average and standard deviation for the ith feature over all image blocks in the texture class l. The ML classification is achieved by choosing the class l which minimizes the simplified Bayes distance function

$$d_l = \sum_{i=1}^{n_f} 2\log \sigma_{i,l} + \left(\frac{v_l - \mu_{i,l}}{\sigma_{i,l}} \right)^2 \quad (4.4)$$

It can be shown that when a priori probability for a texture classes are equal, ML classification minimizes expected classification errors[39]

4.4.3 Shape Feature Descriptors

In our space of shapes, every shape is represented by a diffeomorphism of the unit circle to itself, that is smooth function $f: R \rightarrow R$ which is differentiable, invertible and satisfies $f(x+2\pi) = f(x)+2\pi$. The Lie algebra of the group G is given by vector space of smooth vector fields on the circle: $\phi(\theta)\dfrac{\partial}{\partial \theta}$ where $\phi(\theta + 2\pi) = \phi(\theta)$. The ad joint action of $g \in G$ is the linear map from Lie(G) to itself by the conjugation map $h \to g^{-1} \circ h \circ g$ from G to itself[40]. We can expand such a ϕ in a Fourier series

$$\varphi(\theta) = \sum_{n=-\infty}^{\infty} a_n e^{in\theta} \qquad (4.5)$$

Where $\bar{a}_n = a_{-n}$

The norm on Lie(G) is defined by

$$\|\varphi\|^2 = \sum_{n=2}^{\infty} (n^3 - n)|a_n|^2 \qquad (4.6)$$

The null space of this norm is given by those vector fields whose only Fourier coefficients are a_{-1}, a_0, a_1. i.e., the vector fields which are exactly those tangent to the Mobius sub groups H, in the Lie algebra of H.

4.4.4 Iconic Image Analysis

In this section, we have described the iconic analysis of an image. We choose 64×64 subimages as the basic processing unit. For each subimage, coarse feature detectors examine the normalized color and grey level histograms of the sub images. The rotation invariant histogram features of each sub image are passed to neural network which assigns coarse feature labels to the sub images. In addition, another coarse label result can be obtained from the semi fine detectors whose fine feature detection result can be mapped into one of the coarse features.

The semi fine detector extracts texture measurements that are based on Bayesian distance. These semi-fine feature detections based on multiple size windows are also applied to the sub images. Except for the sub images corresponding to feature boundaries whose semi fine features are computed from the original 64×64 window size, the features of the other sub images are computed with different window sizes 64×64, 128×128 and so on. The labels are assigned to subimages in analyzed image and we call this labeling result a label map. This label map defines the semantic content and the spatial relationship of the various features found on the image. Sometimes it may give erroneous labels. However, the erroneous labels can be corrected subsequently through the analyses and detection procedure by the semantic analyzer with the help of the knowledge base and fine feature detectors.

4.5. Semantic Analysis of Images

4.5.1 Semantic Reasoning and Contextual Knowledge

The semantic analyzer is initially presented with three matrices (label map) produced from the coarse and semi-fine feature detectors and has to identify potentially erroneous labels to correct for them. The most obvious cue for the semantic analyzer is that the labels obtained from different visual descriptors may conflict with each other and the labels produced from the same detector may also conflict with each other. The semantic analyzer must therefore reconcile mutually conflicting classifications. Given the label maps which contain possible erroneous labels, the semantic analyzer aims to do the following:

i) Improve the accuracy of the recognition results using high-level contextual language. It may also invoke fine detectors to confirm the reasoning hypotheses.

ii) Analyze the semantic content of the whole image and recording the semantic content, which forms the basis for generating a textual annotation for the image.

The analysis or reasoning process in the semantic analyzer is closely correlated to the content in the knowledge base, which includes the prior knowledge of all semantic features at the two levels about their legitimate visual and contextual attributes. Especially the information generated from the confusion matrix is also recorded and updated in the knowledge base. Confusion matrices which recorded performance statistics are computed from the training and testing procedures as well as from previous performance of the detectors on data. This gives us information on how much any two detected features are similar to each other. Such information is then summarized into the knowledge base, either at coarse level or fine level, a set of possible confusion candidates based on the relationships of these confused features in descending order according to the similar percentage, describing how similar any two features are, or how many and how much other features are similar to the given feature. The system refines the knowledge base through the classification process as the confusion matrices are updated.

When there is more than one detector for the recognizing one type of features in our system the case for detecting the features at coarse level, the semantic analyzer forms its own primitive label matrix according to the relative accuracy of the different detectors for a given class as recorded in the confusion matrices for the detectors. The analysis starts from those images which have a high probability of being correct and gradually expands the scope of analysis based on the previous analyzed labels. When reasoning using contextual, the confusion candidates are compared and chosen for correcting the wrong labels if they are more coherent with the context. This estimate gives a list of features that are consistent with the given image. If any feature labels that is inconsistent with the query image are found on the label map, another feature which is consistent with the image is chosen from its confusion candidates. If this fails, it chooses the next most similar confusion candidate which is coherent with the context. If all these fail, i.e. cannot find the above two kinds of similar features, then change the label to the majority label among its neighbours.

There are many different operations involved in the analysis procedure such as a) neighbour analysis and region analysis, b) region searching and grouping, c) finding boundaries of the image, d) spatial relationship analysis. This is an interactive process where the images interact with, support or refute each other and finally come up with a more coherent and consistent label matrix. We call it as semantic reasoning.

4.5.2 Analysis and Detection

The process of semantic analysis in detail has been given in Fig. 4.2. To do this, the semantic analyzer generates a list of feature hypotheses, which happens in the following cases:

i)   A confusion candidate is chosen from the knowledge base and no suitable candidate is available from the knowledge base.

ii)   The semantic analyzer has very weak confidence about the confusion candidates. To judge whether a candidate is weak or not is based on the similar percentage that is calculated from the confusion matrices. In these above two cases, the semantic analyzer trigger more fine detectors according the context including the fine detector for the analyzed feature itself.

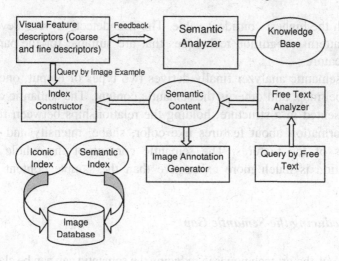

Fig. 4.2: Process of semantic analysis.

iii) The semantic analyzer expects certain features should be present but they have not been recognized within the label map. This happens when two features normally appear together while any one has been confirmed.

The fine feature detectors are a set of detectors specially designed to examine the visual properties of particular fine features that may need to be further confirmed the design principle of these detectors is based on spatial features such as shape structure, contour, neighbouring distance, etc. were used in these fine detectors. The accuracy rates of such detectors are high, but they require much more computation than the statistical coarse and semi-fine feature detections and hence, should only be invoked on demand. When invoking a specialized feature detector, the semantic analyzer passes at the same time the region of interest and particular feature to the detector which subsequently returns a confidence value to the semantic analyzer. The confidence values of different parameters such as color content, neighbour intensity, texture, the distance measure as well as its boundary have different weighting values. In the end, the semantic analyzer compared the returned confidence values from the different detectors to verify the hypotheses. This process of analysis and detection may go through several iterations before coming up with a stable better result. The semantic analyzer will select the one with the highest confident value. The fine detectors were developed using pattern recognition techniques that are suitable for the particular image features.

The semantic analyzer finally derives two types of output, one is the final label map, and other is the semantic content. The semantic content is represented in a structure, holding the relationships between features and information about features like color, shape, intensity and spatial relations of the features. The semantic content of the whole image information is much more exhaustive than the sample content of the image.

4.5.3 *Reducing the Semantic Gap*

The state-of-the-art techniques in reducing the semantic gap can be classified in different ways from different points of view. For example, by considering the application domain, they can be classified as those targeting at artwork retrieval, scenery image retrieval, web image retrieval, etc. In this paper, we focus on the techniques used to derive high-level semantics and identify five categories as follows: (i) Using object ontology to define high-level concepts[26], (ii) Using supervised or unsupervised learning methods to associate low-level features with query concepts, (iii) Introducing RF into retrieval loop for continuous learning of users' intention, (iv) Generating semantic template (ST) to support high-level image retrieval, (v) Making use of both the textual information obtained from the Web and the visual content of images for Web image retrieval. Many systems exploit one or more of the above techniques to implement high-level semantic-based image retrieval. For example, (iii) is often combined with (i), (ii) or (v) or (v) is usually combined with the other four techniques.

In some cases, semantics can be easily derived from our daily language. For example, sky can be described as 'upper, uniform, and blue region'. In systems using such simple semantics, firstly, different intervals are defined for the low-level image features, with each interval corresponding to an intermediate-level descriptor of images, for example, 'light green, medium green, dark green'. These descriptors form a simple vocabulary, the so-called 'object-ontology' which provides a qualitative definition of high-level query concepts. Database images can be classified into different categories by mapping such descriptors to high-level semantics (keywords) based on our knowledge, for example, 'sky' can be defined as region of 'light blue' (color), 'uniform' (texture), and 'upper' (spatial location). A typical example of such ontology-based system is presented in[41]. In this system, each region of an image is described by its average color in lab color space, its position in vertical and horizontal axis, its size and shape.

4.5.4 *Evaluation of Semantic Reasoning Approach*

To evaluate the advantage of using semantic reasoning to supplement visual content analysis, 63 feature units were selected at random for each image class and we have examined these images. Each class has about 100 images. By comparing the images before semantic reasoning and after semantic reasoning, we observed that on an average about 32 features successfully corrected by the semantic analyzer, means that the accuracy of whole image feature extraction is improved approximately by 50%; and 40% remained correct, about 8% removed wrong and about 2% changed from being correct to incorrect. The performance of the semantic analyzer can be improved incrementally by i) implementing more fine feature detectors; ii) improving the performance of visual feature descriptors and iii) improving the descriptive power of the knowledge base by adding more knowledge details for certain features.

4.5.5 *Image Retrieval using Semantic Content*

Three associated similarity measurements were designed to compare most frequent semantic labels, local neighbor pattern of semantic labels and semantic label frequency distribution. Semantic label (SL) is based on all the coarse regions of the image, which in fact roughly describes how the coarse features like texture, intensity, color, edge detection and shape are distributed in the image. SL is defined as follows:

```
Similarity=0
For all Windows do
Winsim=1
Sort coarse labels of retrieved images by frequency
For each coarse label of the retrieved image
If coarse label is same as most frequent coarse region of query image
Winsim =Winsim * C (where C is a constant, 0.75 taken)
End For loop
```

Similarity + = Winsim
End For loop
SL = Similarity/ Number of windows.

Neighbourhood Similarity (NS) uses a matrix to record the co-occurrence frequencies of the 63 feature labels of the eight nearest neighbours against those of the centre image. Each element n(i,j) of the matrix records how many times the center subimage being labeled i while the label of any one neighbour is j . Since we have employed 63 labels, we have considered a 63×63 matrix.

$$s_q, s_r = \frac{w_I}{w_T - w_I} \qquad (4.7)$$

where w_I is the number of subimages labeled as input query and w_T is the total number of subimages.

$$similarity = \sum_{i=0}^{n_f} \sum_{j=0}^{n_f} \left| n_q(i, j)s_q - n_r(i, j)s_r \right| \qquad (4.8)$$

where n_f is the total number of fine labels, n_q and n_r are the fine labels in the query and retrieved images, s_q and s_r are the scaling factors in the query and retrieved images respectively.

$$NS = \exp(-\frac{similarity}{w_N}) \qquad (4.9)$$

where w_N is the number of subimages which have eight connected neighbors.

Semantic label frequency distribution similarity (SFDS) directly counts the frequency of 63 fine labels occurring in the image. For each image, the system only needs to compare the 63 entries; therefore the computation time is much shorter than the 63 entries i.e. shorter than NS. SFDS is defined as follows:

$$similarity = \sum_{i=0}^{n_f} \left| F_q(i)s_q - F_r(i)s_r \right| \qquad (4.10)$$

where F_q and F_r are the frequencies of fine label i for the queried and retrieved images respectively and s_q and s_r are same as mentioned above.

$$SFDS = \exp(-\frac{similarity}{w_N}) \qquad (4.11)$$

The retrieval performance has been normalized between 0 and 1. The retrieval performance using various similarity measures for different classes are given in Table 4.1. We found that the accuracy rates using NS and SFDS are very much better and higher than SL, which actually uses less semantic information in the measurement. From our experiments, we found that SFDS is the best choice among these all similarity measures.

Table 4.1: Retrieval performance of various similarity measures for different classes

Class	SL	NS	SFDS
Flower	0.68	0.85	0.92
Car	0.73	0.82	0.89
Building	0.66	0.79	0.86
Tiger	0.75	0.81	0.9
Plane	0.71	0.78	0.89
Sunset	0.72	0.78	0.93
Bird	0.59	0.69	0.81
Elephant	0.67	0.79	0.88

4.6 Experimental Results and Discussion

4.6.1 Image Database

The image database is selected subset of the Corel image gallery[42], which is a collection of professional photos, web images, animations, videos and clips. We selected about 5,000 jpeg images from photo gallery as our natural image database. It should be noted that Corel photo gallery use semantic concepts to group the photos each with 100 images. Firstly, some images have the same or similar content but divided into different directories. Based on the above considerations, we construct an image database of 5,000 images of 50 classes with each group having 100 images.

4.6.2 Results and Discussion

We selected about 50 classes to evaluate the retrieval performance based on similarity measure. Some of the classes used in experiments are "flowers", "cars", "buildings", "tigers", "planes", "sunsets", "birds", "elephants", etc. In relevance feedback, the retrieved images are shown in the screen each time, while the remaining images are left for another round of feedback if the user actually has responses. The user clicks on similar images as positive examples while leaving the unclicked ones as negative examples. In order to get the performance evaluation we simulate the user's behavior as follows: Each time 100 images were shown to the user, the user should click all the similar images to submit positive examples. After that, the system learns the images and the results are updated iteratively in response to the user's interaction in the later stages based on semantic analysis of images. For each concept, the precision and recall are averaged over all the query images belonging to that concept, instead of just averaging over several random selected queries. The computation of the whole average should be a more objective evaluation. The query retrieval results of the images are shown in the Fig. 4.3 (a)-(j) and Fig. 4.4 (a)-(j).

4.7 Conclusion

The present image retrieval system is mainly developed based on the low-level (visual) descriptors of the image such as color, texture and shape descriptors along with the high-level semantic analysis of the image content. This system is based on R-trees SOMs in implementing RF mechanism from the user. As the system uses many parallel SOMs, each trained with separate visual content descriptors, it is straightforward to use any kind of features. This is a very desirable property, as it suggests that we can initiate queries with a large number of parallel descriptors and this system focuses on the descriptors which provide the most useful information for the particular query instance. Various similarity measures have been proposed using semantic labels and through our results we found that SFDS is the best choice among all these similarity measures. This system indeed improved the best recall-precision levels obtained earlier with pre-selection of the low-level visual features.

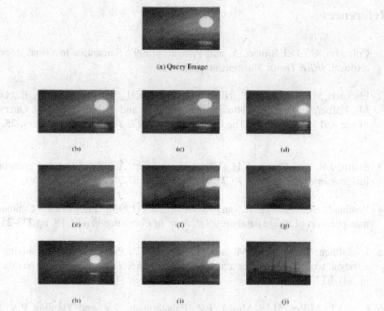

Fig. 4.3: Query results for "yellow sunsets".

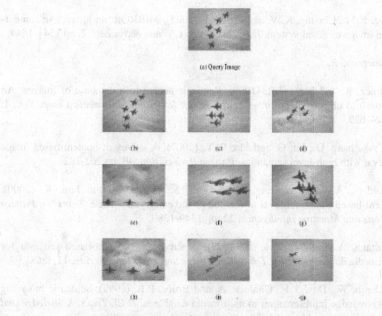

Fig. 4.4: Query results for "blue sky with planes".

References

1   Colombo, C., Del Bimbo, A. and Pala, P. (1999), Semantics in visual information retrieval, *IEEE Trans. Multimedia*, pp.38-53.

2   Flickner, M., Sawhney, H., Niblack,W., Ashley, J., Huang, Q., Dom, B., Gorkani, M., Hafner, J., Lee, D., Pettovic, D., Steele, D. and Anker, P. (1995), Querying by image and video content: The QBIC system, *IEEE Trans. on Computers*, **25**, pp.23-32.

3   Smith, J.R. and Chang, S.F. (1996), VisualSeek: A fully automated content-based image query system, *Proc. ACM Multimedia*, pp.87-98.

4   Pentland, A., Picard, R. and Sclaroff, S. (1996), Photobook: Content-based manipulation of image databases, *Int. Jour. of Computer Vision*, **18**, pp.233-254.

5   Laaksonen, J., Koskela, M. and Oja, E. (2002), PicSOM: Self-organizing image retrieval with MPEG-7 content descriptors, *IEEE Trans. on Neural Networks*, **13**, pp.841-853.

6   Cox, I.J., Miller, M.L., Minka, T.P., Papathoman, T.V. and Yianilos, P.V. (2000), The Bayesian image retrieval system: PicHunter theory, implementation and Psychological experiments, *IEEE Trans. Image Processing*, **9**, pp.20-37.

7   Wong, K.M., Cheung, K.W. and Po, L.M. (2005), MIRROR: an interactive content-based image retrieval system, *IEEE Int. Symp. Circuits & Systems*, **2**, pp.1541-1544.

8   Flickner, *op.cit.*

9   Martinez, A. and Serra, J.R. (1999), Semantic access to a database of images: An approach to object-related image retrieval, *6th Int. Conf. Multimedia Comp. Sys.*, **1**, pp.624-629.

10 Liu, Y., Zhang, D., Lu, G. and Ma, W.Y. (2007), A survey of content-based image retrieval with high-level semantics, *Pattern Recognition*, **40**, pp.262-282.

11 Smeulders, A.W.M., Worring, M., Santini, S., Gupta, A. and Jain, R. (2000), Content-based image retrieval at the end of the early years, *IEEE Trans. on Pattern Analysis and Machine Intelligence*, **22**, pp.1349-1380.

12 Yoshitaka, A. and Ichikawa, T. (1999), A survey on content-based retrieval for multimedia databases, *IEEE Trans. Knowledge and Data Engineering*, **11**, pp.81-93.

13 Al-Khatib, W., Day, Y.F., Ghafoor, A. and Bruce, P.B. (1999), Semantic modeling and knowledge representation in multimedia databases, *IEEE Trans, Knowledge and Data Engineering*, **11**, pp.64-80.

14 Cha, G.H. and Chung, C.W. (1999), Indexing and retrieval mechanism for complex similarity queries in image databases, *Jour. Visual Comm. Image Representation*, **10**, pp.268-290.

15 Colombo, *op.cit.*

16 Yang, B. and Hurson, A.R. (2005), Ad hoc image retrieval using hierarchical semantic based index, In *Proc. 19th Int. Conf. on Advance Information Networking and Application*, **1**, pp.629-634.

17 Zhang, H.J. (2003), Learning semantics in content-based image retrieval, In *Proc. 3rd Int. Symposium on Image and Signal Processing and Analysis*, **1**, pp.284-288.

18 Digital Library Project (1997), Standford University, Technical Report Available online at *http://www. diglib. stanford.edu/~testbed/doc2/WebBase.html*.

19 Gevers, T. and Smeulders, A.W.M. (2000), PicToSeek: Combing color and shape invariant features for image retrieval, *IEEE Trans. Image Processing*, **9**, pp.102-119.

20 Di Sciascio, E. and Mongiello, M. (1999), DrawSearch: A tool for interactive content- based image retrieval over the net, *Proceedings, SPIE*, **3656**, pp.561-572.

21 Sclaroff, S., Taycher, L. and Casia, M.L. (1997), Image Rover: A content-based image browser for the world wide web, In *Proc. IEEE workshop content-based access image and video libraries*, pp.2-9.

22 Gunther, N.J. and Beretta, G. (2000), Image retrieval using distributed system over the internet: BIRDS-I HP Labs, *http://hpl.hp.com/techreports/2000/HPL-2000-162.html*

23 MARVEL System, *http://research.ibm.com/marvel/news.html*

24 Chang, N.S. and Fu, K.S. (1980), Query by picture example, *IEEE Trans, Software Engineering*, **6**, pp.512-524.

25 Brunelli, R. and Mich, O. (2000), Image retrieval by examples, *IEEE Trans. Multimedia*, **2**, pp.164-171.

26 Cortes, C. and Vapnik, V. (1995), Support vector networks, *Machine Learning*, **20**, pp.273-297.

27 Tieu, K. and Viola, P. (2000), Boosting image retrieval, In *Proc. Computer Vision and Pattern Recognition*, **1**, pp.228-235.

28 Chung, K.P. and Fung, C.C. (2005), Multi-layer kernel-based approach in relevance feedback content-based image retrieval system, In *Proc. Int. Conference on Machine Learning and Cybernetics*, **1**, pp.405-409.

29 Hoi, C.H. and Lyu, M.R. (2004), A novel log-based relevance feedback technique in content-based image retrieval, *Proc. ACM Int.Conference on Multimedia*, pp.24-31.

30 Rui, Y., Huang, T.S., Ortega, M. and Mehrotra, S. (1998), Relevance Feedback: A power tool in interactive content-based image retrieval, *IEEE Trans. on Circuits and Systems for Video Technology*, **8**, pp.644-655.

31 Rallabandi, V.P.S. and Sett, S.K. (2007), Image retrieval using R-tree self-organizing map, *Data and Knowledge Engineering*, **61**, pp.524-539.

32 Kohonen, T. (2001), *Self-Organizing Maps*, Third Edition, New York: Springer-Verlag.

33 Frakes, W.B. and Baeza-Yates, R. (1992), *Information Retrieval: Data Structures and Algorithms*, Prentice-Hall, Englewood Cliffs, NJ, USA.

34 Manolopoulos, Y., Nanopoulos, A., Papadopoulos, A.N. and Theodoridis, Y. (2006), *R- trees, Theory and Applications*, Springer Verlag.

35 Beckmann, N., Kriegel, H.P., Schneider, R. and Seeger, B. (1990), The R-Tree: An efficient and robust access method for points and rectangles, *ACM SIGMOD*, pp.323-331.

36 Message Digest Algorithm (1995), *http://www.itl.nist.gov/fipspubs/index.html*

37 Benitez, A.B., Beigi, M. and Chang, S.F. (1998), Using relevance feedback in content- based image meta search, *IEEE Trans. Internet Computing*, **2**, pp.59-69.

38 Rallabandi, V.P.S. and Sett, S.K. (2005a), Color image retrieval using fuzzy color histogram, In *Proc. Int. Conf. on Systemics, Cybernetics and Informatics*, pp.477-480.

39 Fukunaga, K. (1990), *Introduction to Statistical Pattern Recognition*, Academic Press.

40 Rallabandi, V.P.S. and Sett, S.K. (2005b), Motion deformation, shape averaging and image registration using Lie Algebra, In *Proc. Beijing Int. Conference on Imaging: Technology and its Applications for the 21st Century*, pp.324-325.

41 Mezaris, V., Kompatsiaris, I. and Strintzis, M.G. (2003), An ontology approach to object-based image retrieval, *In Proc. of ICIP*, **II**, pp.511–514.

42 The Corel Corporation, *www. Corel.com*.

Chapter 5

Narrowing the Semantic Gap in Image Retrieval: A Multimodal Approach

William I. Grosky[1] and Rajeev Agrawal[1]

[1]*Department of Computer and Information Science*
University of Michigan-Dearborn, Michigan, USA
wgrosky@umich.edu
rajeev.k.agrawal@gmail.com

Abstract

Low-level color and texture image features have been used in the past for image clustering and retrieval applications. These approaches that use such image attributes as color and texture suffer from a number of problems, such as capturing semantics and formulating queries. One widely popular but highly inefficient solution to this problem is to annotate images with keywords manually, after visually examining them. The image collection can then be queried on these keywords. The quality of this method, however, is dependent on the perception of the person annotating the images. In most of the existing image retrieval research work, all features are considered to belong to one modality, but recently, multimodality has been used for more effective image retrieval. In this approach, low-level features, text annotations, image metadata etc. constitute modalities. The major challenge in this approach is how to combine different modalities, which may have different data types. Another challenge is that a multimodal approach creates a very large size vector representation of the image. We need an efficient technique to reduce it to manageable size. In this chapter, we discuss various image modalities, modality fusion techniques, the curse of dimensionality, and our approach to deal with multimodality.

Keywords: Image Retrieval, Text Annotations, Low level Features, Image Retrieval Modalities, Multimodal Approach, Modality Fusion Techniques.

5.1 Introduction

It is important to preserve and maintain an inventory of cultural heritage related images, which is, after all, the documentation of our present and past history. There is a huge amount of cultural heritage (CH) images in digital form, or in more traditional form, in museums, libraries, and other archives, either as public or private collections. It is a great endeavor to make this collection accessible to people in an efficient and effective manner. In the context of cultural images, narrowing down the so-called semantic gap is very important, as cultural images don't just represent *any* images, they have stories to tell. Simply using low-level features are not really helpful; we need the semantic information associated with them. The problem is further compounded due to the heterogeneity of the cultural heritage images. The image collection may not be available in digital form, and it may not have good text annotations available. CH images are catalogued via machine readable metadata such as Dublin Core[1] or VRA Core[2]. Categories for the Description of Works of Art (CDWA) describes the content of art databases by articulating a conceptual framework for describing and accessing information about works of art, architecture, other material culture, groups and collections of works, and related images. CDWA includes 512 categories and subcategories[3]. Cataloging Cultural Objects (CCO) is an attempt to create a data standards initiative for the cultural heritage community[4]. It provides descriptive standards for art, architecture, cultural objects, and their images. CCO maps to the CDWA core and VRA Core 4.0 metadata element sets to query databases using search by similarity methods. MPEG-7, formally named *Multimedia Content Description Interface*, has been designed keeping in mind a variety of applications that can be stored (on-line or off-line) or streamed (e.g. broadcast, push models on the Internet), and can operate in both real-time and non real-time environments[5]. MPEG-7 Visual Description Tools consist of basic structures and descriptors that cover the following basic visual features: color, texture, shape, motion, localization, and face recognition.

In the earlier years of content-based image retrieval (CBIR), low-level features, such as color and texture, were used either in narrow domains to identify two sets of images in one of two categories, or in a broad domain, where images were classified into different categories using clustering techniques. Low-level features have been successful for specific applications such as face, fingerprint, and object recognition. The gap between low-level visual features and semantic concepts mediated by an image is still a big problem. To improve retrieval results, many researchers have tried to use region-based features by representing images at the object-level, or used relevance feedback (RF) techniques[6], which incorporate users' perceptions of the images. Many techniques have also been developed to apply information retrieval techniques in the context of image retrieval. These techniques have been applied solely on the textual annotations and also in conjunction with low-level features of the image objects. The biggest problem in this approach is to have a good quality of annotations, which is time consuming and highly subjective. To extend the annotation list, WordNet[7] has been used in several systems, which further improves the results. Annotations have also been used to group images into a given number of concept bins, but the mapping from image space to concept space is not one-to-one, since it is possible to describe an image using a large number of concepts. No generic, direct transformation exists to map low-level representation into high-level concepts. The gap between low-level features and text annotations has been identified as the *semantic gap*. While addressing the area of cultural image retrieval, it has been widely recognized that the family of image retrieval techniques should become an integration of both low-level visual features addressing the more detailed perceptual aspects, and high-level semantic features represented in metadata standards. Although efforts have been devoted to combining these two aspects of visual data, the gap between them is still a huge barrier in front of researchers. Intuitive and heuristic approaches do not provide us with satisfactory performance. Therefore, there is an urgent need for finding and managing the latent correlation between low-level features and high-level concepts. How to bridge this gap between visual features and semantic features has been a major challenge in this research field.

Another challenge, which researchers still are struggling with, is the curse of dimensionality: multimedia data is inherently of high-dimensionality, making it difficult to carry out efficient querying. Thus, it is extremely interesting that various techniques for dimensional reduction have also been found to improve semantic retrieval, forming so-called concepts from low-level features. This chapter discusses these techniques and shows that using them in the same fashion as they have been used in traditional textual information retrieval produces quite interesting results.

5.2 Multimodal Image Representation and Retrieval

5.2.1 *Representing Image Data*

The information retrieval problem has been posed as 'matching of queries with words to documents with words'. From a user's perspective, however, retrieval is based more on a concept than on a set of words. LSA was first proposed in Deerwester, *et al.*[8] to overcome the deficiencies of term-matching retrieval by treating the unreliability of observed term-document association data as a statistical problem. To organize and search a large text collection, clustering traditionally has been used to discover the inherent concepts embodied there[9]. The basic idea is to extract unique keywords from the set of documents and consider these words as features and then represent each document as a vector of weighted word frequencies in this feature space. A term-document matrix is created, in which rows represent the textual keywords and columns represent the documents. Then, LSA is applied on this term-document matrix to discover the latent relationships between correlated words and documents.

After successful applications of LSA in text retrieval, researchers tried to apply this technique in the image application domain. The problem here is to describe what a term is in an image. The earliest applications used manual text annotations to describe an image, similar to the terms in a document in text retrieval. It is not an easy task to build a system entirely on manual text annotations. Another approach is to use the low-level features (descriptors) of an image. These features can be extracted automatically, unlike manual annotations. This approach has 3 steps:

- Extracting image features
- Reduction of feature vector dimensions
- Query image collection using some similarity metric

In one of the earliest papers, Swain and Ballard[10] use color for high-speed image location and identification. Color histograms of multicolored objects are used, providing a robust and efficient representation for indexing the images. In Jain, *et al.*[11], an image is represented by three 1-D color histograms in the red, green and blue channels, while a histogram of the directions of edge points is used to represent general shape information. A, so-called, blobworld representation[12] is used to retrieve images. This approach recognizes the images as a combination of objects, making both query and learning in the blobworld more meaningful to the user. In all these works, color is the fundamental unit used to represent an image, which is very similar to the keywords in a text document. However, the representation of the color features may vary in the different systems, ranging from histograms to indexing. The QBIC system[13] stores color, texture, shape, sketch and object information of each image and uses techniques similar to information retrieval techniques. In this system, it is possible to integrate all of these in one single query. The user can specify the color proportion, select regions of relevant texture and draw a sketch of the query image. In this system, dimensional reduction was used to reduce the time taken to calculate image similarities, which was an operation of quadratic time-complexity. In Photobook[14], PCA is used to create eigenimages, which are small sets of perceptually-significant coefficients. This technique is referred to as *semantics-preserving image compression*. These low-level features have been used as terms, over which to apply standard information retrieval techniques.

In other approaches, images have been divided into blocks of pixels and then each block is described using low-level features. Various text retrieval techniques, such as inverted files, term weighting and relevance feedback are then applied on the blocks of an image[15]. In Westerveld[16], image contents are combined with textual contents. The low-level image features used are HSV color space and Gabor texture filters. The retrieval results for the text and image features are better than image-only and text-only results. Similar results are achieved in Grosky, *et al.*[17]

5.2.2 *Taking the Advantage of Modalities*

Previously, we discussed that an image contains multiple modalities such as color, texture, text. A single modality may not be enough to classify an image to the correct category. For example, if we select the color as a discriminative feature, several images may have same color, but when combined with another modality, such as texture, they can be classified to their respective categories with higher confidence.

An important question to answer in a multimodal approach is what constitutes the modalities. In any multimedia element, it is possible to have the features of that element be extracted from different sources, e.g. a video shot may have visual features such as color and texture, audio features, and textual features, each source being one modality. In most of the existing image retrieval research work, all features are considered to belong to one modality, but recently, multimodality has been used for more effective image retrieval. We present here our idea of using visual keywords, which, first appeared in Picard[18]. This works with images, not words, and helps in recognizing visually similar events, so-called *visual synonyms*, using both spatial and motion similarity. Visual keywords can be based on color, texture, pattern, and objects in the image or any other user-defined features, depending on the domain. Visual keywords are created by cropping domain-relevant regions from sample images. These regions are then assigned labels and sub-labels to form a thesaurus and a vocabulary, respectively[19]. Additionally, the low-level features are extracted from these cropped regions to form feature vectors to represent visual keywords. A keyblock-based approach[20] encodes each image as a set of one-dimensional index codes linked to the keyblocks in the codebook, analogous to considering a text document as a linear list of keywords. For each semantic class, a corresponding codebook is generated. However this approach does not have any invariant properties and requires domain knowledge while encoding the images. More recently, the visual keyword approach has been used for visual categorization using support vector machines (SVM) and naïve Bayes classifiers[21]. Objects and their image locations are discovered by using a visual analogue of a word, formed by vector quantizing low-level features[22], and extracting a large number of overlapping, square sub-windows of random sizes, at random positions from the training images[23]. In a biomedical domain, ViVos (Visual Vocabulary) is developed to summarize an image automatically, to identify patterns that distinguish image classes and to highlight interesting regions in an image[24]. In all the above approaches, only the low-level features have been used to construct the visual keywords. We augment the visual keyword approach by utilizing the textual keywords to form a multimodal vector representation of an image[25].

5.2.3 Modality Fusion Techniques

A single modality may not be enough to classify an image to the correct category. For example, if we select color as a discriminative feature, several images may have the same color, but when combined with another modality, such as texture, they can be classified to their respective categories with higher confidence. Each modality extracts certain aspects of an image and they are inter-dependent with each other. In the presence of many modalities, it is important to identify the best way to fuse them. The fusion schemes can be based on whether we fuse the image data from different modalities first and then conduct experiments or do it the other way round[26].

● Definition 1 (Early Fusion). A fusion scheme that integrates unimodal features before learning concepts.

● Definition 2 (Late Fusion). A fusion scheme that first reduces unimodal features to separately learned concept scores; then these scores are integrated to learn concepts.

In early fusion, we need a one-step learning phase only, whereas late fusion requires an additional learning step. According to the architecture, fusion schemes can be grouped into three main categories; parallel, serial combination, and hierarchical. The parallel architecture has a very simple layout: all the individual classifiers are invoked independently, and the results of each of them are combined. The results may be selected based on equal weight or they may be assigned different weights, based on certain user selected criteria. In a serial combination, individual classifiers are applied in a linear fashion. In this scheme, the sequence of applying the classifiers is important. The classifiers having low computation costs are applied first, followed by the ones which have a higher computation cost. In the hierarchical approach, the individual classifiers are placed into a decision-tree like structure. There are various fusion methods, which can be distinguished from each other in their trainability, adaptivity, and requirements on the output of individual classifiers. A comparison of various fusion schemes can be found in Jain, *et al.*[27], based on these three criteria. Some of the popular ones are product combination, majority voting, min-max aggregation, weighted sum, adaptive weighting, borda count, class set reduction, bagging, boosting, neural tree.

In Kittler, *et al.*[28], there is a common theoretical framework for a class of fusion schemes, where individual classifiers use distinct features to estimate the posterior probabilities given the input pattern. A sensitivity analysis of the various schemes to estimation errors is carried out to show why the sum or average rule outperforms the other rules for the same class. In the product combination, it is assumed that all modalities are independent of each other. We can estimate the posterior probability of an image to belong to a certain class by multiplying the aposteriori probabilities generated by the individual classifiers for each modality. The problem in this approach is that it is difficult to have independent modalities and therefore posterior probabilities cannot be estimated correctly. In the weighted-sum approach, the weighted average of the scores from multiple modalities are taken. In estimating posterior probabilities, the sum rule is less sensitive to noise then the product rule. Therefore, the product rule is appropriate where the posterior probability for each modality can be estimated accurately and the sum rule is most appropriate for combining different estimates of the same posterior. In the majority-voting rule, a pattern is presented to each classifier, which provides a score that is either as a whole assigned to one class label or divided into several labels. The label which receives more than a certain threshold of the total scores is considered as the final classification result[29]. More discussion on modality independence, the curse of dimensionality and fusion-modal complexity can be found in Wu, *et al.*[30]. An iterative similarity propagation approach is proposed to explore the relationship between web images and their textual annotations for image retrieval[31].

5.2.4 Closing the Gap Using Various Image Features

The semantic gap is the principal focus of multimedia retrieval research[32]. In simple terms, the semantic gap in content-based retrieval is that multimedia data is captured by devices like scanners, digital cameras, camcorders, etc. in a format which is optimized for storage and retrieval. Therefore, this data cannot be used to understand what the object *means*. In addition to that, user queries are based on semantic similarity, but the computer can process similarity only by data processing. In early systems, the semantic gap was not recognized and more reliance was given on low-level representation. The results were not very good. Later, to bridge this gap, text annotations of images/video by humans were used, in spite of the interpretation of these objects by annotators. One of the immediate advantages was to use text information retrieval techniques in multimedia retrieval. These techniques were applied solely on the text annotations and also in conjunction with low-level features of the objects. The results were encouraging. The annotation lists were also used to group the images into a certain number of concepts, but the mapping from image space to concept space is not one-to-one, since it is possible to describe an image using a large number of words. While assigning keywords to images, humans can see a broad view of the image or can break apart the image into small pieces, where these small pieces may be labeled individually. There is no direct transformation to map low-level representations into high-level concepts; e.g. a car may be red, but a red color does not mean a red car. Also, merely assigning keywords is not enough to capture the semantics existing in the image. It is a relatively easy task to manage the semantic gap in a narrow domain, such as family pictures, but computationally highly complex in broad domains, such as all the images on the Internet. For example, in a face detection system, it is possible to identify a person using only low-level features, provided that the system has a content to concept mapping.

In general, the semantic gap starts at the low-level features and goes to the semantics[33]. Sometimes, we may identify some of the objects in an image, but the context of these objects in that particular image may be missing. Another popular technique to bridge this gap is to use relevance feedback (RF) from the users[34]. This feedback may contain both positive and negative values. In this approach, a user is presented with an initial set of images, and then the user provides feedback. This user feedback is used to modify the query results. This process may be repeated until the user is satisfied with the results, and this feedback may then be used for future retrieval results from other users. In general, the semantic gap is quite critical to the design of good content-based multimedia retrieval techniques.

5.2.5 *Approaches to Efficient Image Retrieval*

The most important issues in the context of general information retrieval, identified in Croft[35] are relevance feedback, information extraction, multimedia retrieval, effective retrieval, routing and filtering, interfaces and browsing, efficient and flexible indexing and retrieval, distributed information retrieval, integrated solutions. This list has not changed significantly in the last 13 years. Multimedia retrieval is now the focus of information retrieval techniques. We are facing much the same issues even today. We will discuss in this section broad approaches to efficient multimedia retrieval techniques.

We discuss the many retrieval techniques, starting from simple text-based to the more complex multimodal-based ones:

- *Text-based retrieval:* In general, the information about images is stored in databases as keywords or descriptive text. This is also called keyword-based indexing. The query is formulated based on the form of keywords, and is matched with the stored keywords and/or descriptive text. The images can be organized by topics for search and retrieval using database queries. This approach returns the results very fast but has its own limitations, because text-based descriptions are not considered accurate and precise and are often incomplete. Also, it is not feasible to generate descriptive text for a wide variety of data. It is very cumbersome and expensive to annotate multimedia data manually. For example, the largest directory system on the Internet, http://dmoz.org, needs 74,719 human editors to classify 4 million links into 600,000 categories. Another problem with text annotation is that it may not conform to any defined vocabulary in a particular domain and may not describe the relations of the objects. This approach has been used in indexing news/sports video, images, and songs using the associated text available. Sato, Kanada, Hughes, and Smith[36] proposed a system for news video caption recognition which consists of spatial filters to segment the words from image and video OCR. Recently Shih, *et al.*[37], proposed a semantics understanding system to interpret the superimposed captions on sports videos.

- *Feature-based similarity:* Feature-based similarity search and retrieval have been used since the time when multimedia content-based retrieval systems came into existence. These techniques are primarily based on computer vision algorithms. There are three important aspects of content-based retrieval systems: feature extraction, representation, and retrieval. We have discussed different types of features above which can be extracted from an image. The features can be extracted at a global level to represent the entire image or the image is partitioned into parts and then features are computed from each part. The criteria to partition an image is dependent on the type of application. If the idea is to search for an object, then object segmentation would be advantageous. Object segmentation works best for a narrow domain application. Another type of segmentation is *weak segmentation*, which can be achieved by dividing an image into salient regions. In video retrieval, a shot can be represented by one or more key frames. After feature extraction, images can be represented as a set of vectors. While searching and retrieving similar images for a query image from a given image set, a similarity measure between a query image and data set images is used to determine the closest n images from the image set. There are different distance measures in the literature, such as Euclidean, city block, Chebyshev, Minkowski, quadratic, Canberra, Pearsons correlation coefficient etc.[38]. This similarity can also be computed based on salient features, object silhouettes, and structural features. QBIC[39], Virage[40], PhotoBook[41], VisualSEEk[42] are some examples of feature-based image retrieval systems.

- *Human-centered:* Since multimedia systems are closely related to human perception of the multimedia objects, there has been attempt to develop systems which incorporate human behavior and their needs. These types of systems extend the scope from a data-centric approach to a more human-centric approach. Human-centered multimedia systems take the advantage of the research from multiple disciplines like computer vision, multimedia, psychology, pattern recognition, AI, etc. In a human-centered approach, the main issues are[43]:
  - How humans understand and interpret multimedia signals (feature, cognitive, and affective levels).
  - How humans interact naturally (emotion, mood, attitude, and attention levels).
  - How can we personalize video delivery services and how can we meet affective retrieval requests?
  - Multimodal emotion recognition: how can we achieve a more natural and effective human computer interface (esp. in virtual environments) using speech and facial expression recognition?
  - Interactive frameworks: systems that learn visual concepts from user input for automatic detection and recognition (train my computer to automatically detect scenes, objects, or events of interest).
  - Conceptual structures for multimedia indexing: what do we index, how do we index it, and how do we organize it?

In Broek *et al.*[44], an object-based image retrieval (OBIR) scheme is introduced, which is based on how humans perceive color. It uses an 11 color quantization scheme and the color correlogram. It is known that humans use 11 color categories, namely, red, green, blue, yellow, orange, brown, pink, purple, black, white, and gray in processing color. These 11 color categories are considered as being universal and as being optimal[45]. The color correlogram[46] is constructed from an image by estimating the pairwise statistics of pixel color. A large number of textural features can be derived from the color correlogram to characterize the content of the image, such as: energy, entropy, correlation, inverse difference moment, inertia, Haralick's correlation, cluster shade, and cluster prominence. An understanding of the usage of multimedia objects by the users can help in returning more relevant results. Most of the video search engines employ algorithms to analyze the results of the user's preferences and accordingly return the results. Mongy, Bouali, and Djeraba[47] have presented a framework to analyze video usage mining using Markov models. In an experiential multimedia environment, users apply their natural human senses directly to observe data and information of interest related to a particular event[48]. Therefore, the same set of multimedia information can be retrieved in different ways, depending on the context in which the user needs it. In experiential environments, the focus is on the user's perspective and intuitive interfaces are provided for the user to creatively manipulate multimedia data from these multiple perspectives.

- *Machine learning-based:* After feature-based retrieval methods, machine learning or pattern recognition is the most explored area in multimedia information retrieval. Learning-based methods have generated significant interest among researchers in bridging the semantic gap. Learning-based methods determine associations between low-level features of the multimedia objects and their semantic descriptions. Machine learning-based methods can be classified into supervised and unsupervised learning or classification. In supervised learning, there is a set of predefined classes already known and a new multimedia object is classified into one of these already existing classes. There are three important steps in supervised learning:
  - Decide the set of training examples, like a set of images or videos.
  - Input feature representation
  - Decision making

The above steps may vary, depending on the problem domain. The four commonly used approaches are template matching, statistical classification, syntactic or structural matching, and neural networks[49]. The PCA and Karhunen-Loeve (KL) transform have been used for the linear description of multimedia data. It is recognized that human-in-the-loop is the best approach for efficient multimedia retrieval. To close the gap between high-level concepts and low-level features, relevance feedback techniques are used to learn from the users. The user is posed certain questions after the results of a query are returned to the user. These responses can be used to refine the results in the short term, or can be accumulated for long-term improvement of retrieval performance[50]. It is not possible to gather the labeled data with its true categories clearly identified. In unsupervised learning, we need to construct the decision boundaries using a model, which can fit to the input data set. Unsupervised learning is a very difficult problem, because data can form clusters with different sizes, which may not be according to the existing true labels. To learn object categories automatically from unlabeled images, each image is represented by an unordered set of local features. Then, all images are embedded into a space where they cluster according to their partial-match feature correspondences. A spectral clustering technique is used to recover the primary groupings among images, which is based on the pair-wise affinities between input images[51].

- *CH image retrieval techniques:* Cultural image digital libraries employ similar techniques as described above. The CH image retrieval schemes work mostly in a narrow domain, e.g. an art collector might be interested in certain types of objects or patterns. A CH image retrieval system, which uses color and texture histograms for statistical description and texture and shape descriptors to describe shape content is described in Boujemaa, *et al.*[52]. In Birkbeck, *et al.*[53], a set of CH objects, which are previously captured as geometric and appearance models, are presented for users' queries. The CH objects are rich in content, describing events, monuments, places, people, etc., and distributed across different locations. To integrate CH sources on the Web, CIDOC CRM and CRM core ontologies are described in Sinclair, *et al.*[54]. This metadata which exists in different CH object collections, are mapped to a common ontology, which allows unified access. MultiMatch is a multilingual search engine designed specifically for the access, organization and personalized presentation of CH information[55]. The users can formulate queries using different modalities such as free text, similarity matching, or metadata. It also provides browsing capability to navigate the collection, using a web directory-like structure based on the MultiMatch ontology.

5.3 Dimensionality Reduction Techniques

5.3.1 The Curse of Dimensionality

The curse of dimensionality was identified and defined by Bellman[56], in connection with the difficulty of optimization by exhaustive enumeration on product spaces and referring to "the exponential growth of hyper volume as a function of dimensionality". In statistics, the convergence of any estimator to the true value of a smooth function defined on a space of high dimension is very slow. Essentially, the concept holds that high dimensional data is hard to work with because of large space and time complexity. Another important question to answer here is how many dimensions are good enough to work with. If we add more features, it can increase the noise and so the rate of error. The idea of dimensionality itself usually refers to problems adhering in fitting models, estimating parameters, or optimizing a function in many dimensions. The curse of dimensionality problem should be viewed from qualitative, rather than quantitative point of view. The dimensionality reduction techniques are used in many application areas such as human and computer vision, signal processing, text analysis, neuroscience, genetics, biomedical, financial, satellite imagery etc.

5.3.1.1 The Problems Caused by High Dimensionality

It has been observed that it becomes exponentially more difficult to find global optima for the parameter space, as the dimensionality of the input data space increases, therefore to find appropriate model for the input data space. In the area of neural network, the complexity of network can become unmanageable when the number of inputs into the network exceeds few hundreds. Therefore, it is practical to pre-select variables among a large set of input variables that are likely to predict the dependent variables of interest[57]. As the dimensionality of the input data space (i.e., the number of predictors) increases, it becomes exponentially more difficult to find global optima for the parameter space, i.e., to fit models. In practice, the complexity of neural networks becomes unmanageable when the number of inputs into the neural network exceeds a few hundreds or even less, depending on the complexity of the respective neural network architecture. Hence, it is simply a practical necessity to pre-screen and pre-select from among a large set of input (predictor) variables those that are of likely utility for predicting the outputs (dependent variables) of interest[58].

In multimedia retrieval applications, the feature vectors are used to store information to represent high dimensional data. Such vectors may represent anything from RGB data of individual pixels to texture and shape data for an image, and multimedia data similarity queries are based upon nearest neighbor searches of this data. In processes where the dimension of the feature vectors continues to increase, problems arise as the data tends toward the boundary of the data region and the result is that the time for a 'nearest neighbor searches' increases rapidly as the dimensionality increases. An interactive computer application called jCurse that can illustrate the "curse of dimensionality" by allowing the user to view a number of data distributions and perform distance measurements using a variety of metrics is in Eccles, *et al.*[59]. They also argue that the expected distance increases as the dimension increases in the case of maximum, Manhattan, and Euclidean distance, with distribution models of uniform, Gaussian, Chi-Square, exponential and a mix of these for all components of the feature vector. Tesic[60] discusses the issue in terms of capturing and organization of large volumes of images, such as scientific and medical data and notes that such projects require new information processing techniques in the context of pattern recognition and data mining. In multimedia databases, the volume of the data is very large, and so are the feature vectors. It is impractical to store all the extracted feature vectors from millions of images in main memory. The amount of time needed to access the feature vectors on storage devices overwhelmingly dominates the time needed for the search. This problem is further complicated when the search is to be performed multiple times and in an interactive environment. The high dimensionality of data can cause increased time and space complexity, degradation in the algorithm/system performance and decreased performance in nearest neighbour search, clustering and indexing.

5.3.1.2 Overcoming the Curse

There are 2 ways to overcome the curse of dimensionality in multimedia search and retrieval. First is related to search the approximate results of a multimedia query, and the second is to reduce the high dimensional input data to low dimensional representation. In most cases, the users are interested in retrieving the results, which are closed to their query, therefore exact search and retrieval can be wasteful and not required. A standard method, which has been very popular, is to map the data items into a high dimensional feature space as points. The feature space can be indexed using multidimensional indexing scheme[61]. The similarity search is then equivalent to hyper-spherical range search. This search will return all multimedia objects, which are similar to query object, but within a certain threshold. The problem in this method is highlighted in Beyer, *et al.*[62], if the data dimension is large, then the maximum and minimum distances to a given query point in high–dimensional space are almost the same under a wide range of distance metrics and data distributions. All points converge to the same distance from the query point in high dimensions, and the concept of nearest neighbours becomes meaningless.

The nearest neighbour search in high dimensions is useful when the underlying dimensionality of the data is much smaller than the actual dimensionality and when the search space is limited to only a cluster to which the query point belongs. A novel data structure termed Spatial Event Cube (SEC) for conceptual representation for complex spatial arrangements of visual thesaurus entries in large multimedia datasets is suggested by Tesic[63]. This space can be used to discover simple spatial relationships in scientific dataset using the perceptual association rule algorithm, to distill the frequent visual patterns in image and video datasets in order to discover interesting patterns.

Another possible approach is described by Chavez *et al.*[64] with the use of a probabilistic technique for fixed radius searching on general metric spaces. or approximate algorithm. They state that these algorithms are acceptable in most cases "because in generation the modelization as a metric space already carries some kind of relaxation, so finding some close elements is usually as good as finding all of them".

5.3.2 *Dimensionality Reduction Techniques*

Dimensionality reduction, reducing the number of random variables involved in an operation, has been one of the most active research areas of machine learning in the recent years.

There are several different approaches, such as *feature selection*, which involves finding a subset of features by means of a filter, and *feature extraction*, which involves using a mapping of the multidimensional space to fewer dimensions. In some applications, it is possible to use new representations in which there has been some loss. There is a trade-off between preserving important aspects of original data and the dimensions desired. It is also possible to measure the degree of loss with a loss function, which provides a quantitative means for measuring errors in the representation of data; different loss functions may mean different low-dimensional representations. The dimensionality reduction techniques have applications mainly in the following two categories: visualizing/plotting high dimensional data for analysis in 2 or 3 dimensions, and improving the performance for search and retrieval applications, which uses the data for analysis.

In feature selection, an appropriate subset of the original features is found to represent the data. The criteria to select appropriate features are dependent on the application domain. This method is useful when a limited amount of data is present, but represented with a large number of features. For example, in diagnostic use of gene expression data, a classifier is used to determine the disease of a patient based on the expression of thousands of genes. For this, the classifier is to be trained from data of only several tens of patients[65]. It is crucial to determine a small set of relevant variables to estimate reliable parameter. The advantage of selecting a small set of features is that you need to use few values in the calculations.

In feature extraction, new features are computed using the original features, without losing any important information. Feature extraction methods can be divided into linear and non-linear techniques. Linear techniques are based on to get the resultant feature set Y, which are derived using a linear combination of the original feature set X. The linear feature extraction process generally uses a weight vector w to optimize a criterion, which is also considered as a quality parameter.

In the next section, we introduce our framework for multimodal-based image retrieval, using the non-linear dimensional reduction technique of *diffusion maps*. This technique provides a framework based on diffusion processes that allow one to obtain a multiscale description of the geometric structures of the data, as well as of spaces of functions defined on the data.

This approach uses the ideas from spectral graph theory, harmonic analysis and potential theory[66]. In this framework any arbitrary data set can be parameterized to build embeddings, called diffusion maps. It is then possible to define a meaningful metric on the data using the, so-called, *diffusion distance*.

5.4 A Framework for Multimodal-Based Image Retrieval

5.4.1 Visual Keyword Construction

Let I be a set of n images. Each image is divided into non-overlapping tiles, after which we extract various features from each tile, resulting in T, k-element feature vectors, where T is the total number of tiles in all the I images. Let V be the desired number of visual keywords. We then cluster the set of feature vectors into V clusters, each cluster corresponding to one of the V visual keywords. Our approach treats each tile like a word in a text document, counting the number of times tiles from each bin appear in an image. Tile (feature) vectors are formed using simple low-level features, such as color histograms, textures, etc., as well as the more sophisticated Scale Invariant Feature Transforms (SIFT) descriptors[67] or MPEG-7 descriptors. SIFT is a transformation that transform images into scale-invariant coordinates relative to local features. SIFT generates a large number of features that densely cover the image over the full range of scales and locations. In SIFT, keypoints are detected by checking the scale-space extrema. The descriptor of each keypoint is based on the gradient magnitude and orientation in a region around the keypoint in a sample tile of certain scale. MPEG-7 descriptors support some degree of interpretation of semantics determination, and can be passed onto, or accessed by, a device or computer code[68]. The procedure to create visual keywords is completely unsupervised and does not involve any image segmentation. The granularity of the number of visual keywords is a parameter selected by the user, and may vary depending on the domain. In a narrow domain, a small number of visual keywords are appropriate due to a high degree of tile similarity. But in a broad domain, a larger number of visual keywords may be desired.

Another important parameter to consider is the selection of template size to create tiles, since this size has a direct effect on the computation costs. A small template size will result in large number of tiles and hence higher computation costs. This is a trade-off between quality and speed. A template size of 32×32 pixels is appropriate while using MPEG-7 descriptors. We use the scalable color descriptor (SCD) with 64 coefficients, which are good enough to provide reasonably good performance, the color layout descriptor (CLD) with 12 coefficients, found to be best trade-off between the storage cost and retrieval efficiency, and the color structure descriptor (CSD) with 64 coefficients, sufficient enough to capture the important features of a tile. Hence, a tile vector has 140 coefficients. We note that each of the three MPEG-7 descriptors are of different sizes. Therefore, each descriptor is normalized individually. After obtaining the normalized MPEG-7 descriptors, we use the high-dimensional clustering algorithm, *vcluster*[69], to cluster all the tiles into the desired number of clusters. Each cluster will represent a visual keyword. After the classification, an image is then described by a vector, whose size is equal to the number of clusters. The *j*-th element of this vector is equal to the number of tiles from the given image that belongs to the *j*-th cluster. The visual keyword-image matrix is then formed, using the image vectors as columns. Finally, we normalize each column vector to unit length and generate the normalized visual keyword-image matrix T_{vis}.

5.4.2 *Multimodal Image Representation Using Fusion of Visual and Textual Keywords*

There is a variety of information associated with the images in addition to low-level features. This may be in the form of content-independent metadata, such as time stamps, locations, image formats or content-bearing metadata. Content-bearing metadata describes the higher-level concepts of the image. The text associated with images has been found to be very useful in practice for image retrieval; for example, newspaper archivists index largely on captions[70]. Smeaton and Quigley[71] use Hierarchical Concept Graphs (HCG) derived from Wordnet[72] to estimate the semantic distance between caption words. In this paper, we use textual keywords and fuse them with visual keywords to create a multimodal image representation. We first create a term-document matrix (T_{tex}). To control the morphological variations of words, we use Porter's stemming algorithm[73]. The minimum and maximum term (word) length thresholds are set to 2 and 30, respectively.

We obtain a large number of modalities (features) in the form of visual and textual keywords. These modalities are not completely independent of each other; we need to find an effective strategy to fuse them. Though LSA and ICA can be used for this purpose, they need a good estimate of the number of independent components and only perform best under some error-minimization criteria. In our approach, we adopt a diffusion maps approach, discussed earlier, for the fused multi-modality matrix $T_{vis-tex}$, which is obtained after concatenating the visual keywords-image matrix T_{vis} and the textual keyword-image matrix T_{tex}. Below, is a brief description of the nonlinear diffusion kernel[74] used in our technique.

Let Ω represent the set of columns in $T_{vis\text{-}tex}$ and x, y be any two vectors in Ω. Then we can define a finite graph $G = (\Omega, W_\sigma)$ with n nodes, where the weight matrix W_σ (x, y) is defined as:

$$W_\sigma(x,y) = \exp\left(-\left(\frac{|x-y|}{\sigma}\right)^2\right) \tag{5.1}$$

where lx - yl is the L2 distance between vector x and y. Let

$$q_\sigma(x) = \sum_{y \in \Omega} W_\sigma(x,y).$$

Then we can have a new kernel:

$$W_\sigma^\alpha(x,y) = \frac{W_\sigma(x,y)}{q_\sigma^\alpha(x) q_\sigma^\alpha(y)} \tag{5.2}$$

The parameter α is used to specify the amount of influence of the density in the infinitesimal transitions of the diffusion. We can obtain the anisotropic transition kernel $p_\sigma(x,y)$ after applying the normalized graph Laplacian construction to $W_\sigma^\alpha(x,y)$:

$$d_\sigma(x) = \sum_{y \in \Omega} W_\sigma^\alpha(x,y) \tag{5.3}$$

and

$$p_\sigma(x,y) = \frac{W_\sigma^\alpha(x,y)}{d_\sigma(x)}. \tag{5.4}$$

Matrix $p_\sigma(x,y)$ can be viewed as the transitional kernel of a Markov chain on Ω. The diffusion distance D_t between x and y at time t of a random walk is defined as

$$D_t^2(x, y) = \left\| p_t(x, .) - p_t(y, .) \right\|_{1/\phi_0}^2 \tag{5.5}$$

$$= \sum_{z \in \Omega} \frac{(p_t(x, z) - p_t(y, z))^2}{\phi_0(z)} \tag{5.6}$$

where ϕ_0 is the stationary distribution of the Markov chain.

The diffusion distance can be represented by the right eigenvectors and eigenvalues of matrix $p_\sigma(x, y)$:

$$D_t^2(x, y) \cong \sum_{j \geq 1} \lambda_j^{2t} \left(\psi_j(x) - \psi_j(y) \right)^2 \tag{5.7}$$

ψ_0 does not show up because it is a constant. Since the eigenvalues tend to 0 and have a modulus strictly less than 1, the above sum can be computed to a preset accuracy $\delta > 0$ with a finite number of terms. If we define

$$s(\delta, t) = \max\{j \in N \text{ such that } |\lambda_j|^t > \delta |\lambda_1|^t\}, \tag{5.8}$$

up to relative precision δ, then we have

$$D_t^2(x, y) \cong \sum_{j=1}^{s(\delta, t)} \lambda_j^{2t} \left(\psi_j(x) - \psi_j(y) \right)^2 \tag{5.9}$$

Therefore, we can have a family of diffusion maps ψ_τ, $\tau \in N$, given by

$$\Psi_t : x \to \left(\lambda_1^t \psi_1(x), \lambda_2^t \psi_2(x), ..., \lambda_{s(\delta, t)}^t \psi_{s(\delta, t)}(x) \right)^T \tag{5.10}$$

The mapping $\psi_t : \Omega \to R^{s(\delta, t)}$ provides a parameterization (fusion) of the data set Ω; in other words, a parameterization of the graph G in a lower-dimensional space $R^{s(\delta, t)}$, where the rescaled eigenvectors are the coordinates. The dimensionality reduction and the weight of the relevant eigenvectors are dictated by both the time t of the random walk and the spectral fall-off of the eigenvalues. This diffusion mapping represents an effective fusion of visual and text keywords and is a low-dimensional representation of the image set. The values of σ and α in the diffusion kernel are set to 10 and 1 respectively for all of our experiments.

5.4.3 Image Retrieval Using Multimodal Image Presentation

LSA has been used for document retrieval, where documents are represented as vectors, in which each dimension corresponds to a term.

The main idea of LSA is to lower the dimension of documents and reconstruct the matrix using a lower dimensionality. In searching relevant documents, the rank k approximation, A_k, with the smallest acceptable error with respect to the original matrix, A, is used. This approximation translates the term and document vectors into a concept space. We write this approximation as $A_k = U_k S_k V_k^T$. In this equation, U_k and V_k are the matrices of the left and right singular vectors and S_k is the diagonal matrix of singular values. Given a query vector q, we have to transform the query to the concept space by $q_{new} = S_k^{-1} U_k q$. Then, we compare q_{new} with the concept-space representation of other documents, via the cosine similarity. In our approach, the low dimensional representation obtained from the diffusion kernel is similar to the term-document matrix in reduced dimension space in information retrieval.

It has been argued in Bast, *et al.*[75] that the ability to identify pairs of related terms is the core concept of spectral retrieval. In almost all versions of LSA, while creating the reduced rank term-document matrix, a fixed low sub-dimensional subspace is selected. Therefore, the qualities of these schemes depend on this selection. When varying the dimensions and looking at the curve of relatedness score for each term-pair, it is found that the shape of this curve indicates the term-pair relatedness. Therefore, any fixed choice of dimension will not be appropriate for all the term pairs. In the algorithm proposed by the authors, for each term pair, the number of dimensions varies depending on when the relatedness score is at or below zero. We have adopted this approach in our multi-modal keyword based retrieval.

In this section, we will discuss various experiments conducted to investigate the effectiveness of our multimodal keyword framework, using the well-known Corel image dataset and the *LabelMe* collection available through the MIT AI Lab[76]. We selected 999 images belonging to 10 categories from the *Corel* dataset and 658 images belonging to 15 categories from *LabelMe* (Fig. 5.1). The details of the datasets are given in Table 5.1. The MILOS software[77], based on the MPEG-7 XM model, is used to extract the color descriptors SCD, CSD, and CLD.

Table 5.1: Details of the datasets

Dataset	#Images	#Tiles	#Visual Keywords	#Text Keywords
LabelMe	658	165750	1500	506
Corel	999	95904	900	924

For both the datasets, we measure the precision at 10% and 30% recall and the average precision at 10%, 20%, ... and 100% recall. The values vary between 0 and 1. We considered the entire collection of images in our database as the query data set to avoid favoring certain query results. We are interested in answering the following two questions:

1. Is there any improvement in the image retrieval results using our multimodal keyword representation, over the low-level feature representation?

2. Is the diffusion kernel approach an effective approach to fuse different modalities?

To answer the first question, we conduct experiments using the entire image as one visual keyword and compare it with the multimodal keywords. To answer second question, we use the diffusion kernel to get a lower-dimension representation of each image before retrieval. Additionally, to examine the effectiveness of diffusion kernel, we also use Latent Semantic Analysis (LSA) to fuse the keywords in low-level feature space and in multimodal feature space. Here is the list of all experiments:

- Full size images using LSA *(fslsa)/* Tiles of each image using LSA *(tslsa)*.
- Full size images *(fsdk)/* Tiles of each image *(tsdk)* using the diffusion kernel.
- Full size images + text keywords *(fstklsa)/* Tiles of each image + text keywords using LSA *(tstklsa)*.
- Full size images + text keywords *(fstkdk)* / Multimodal (Tiles of each image + text) keywords obtained using diffusion kernel *(tstkdk)*.
- Only text keywords *(txt)* obtained using the diffusion kernel.

Fig. 5.1: Sample images from LabelMe.

The results are shown in Table 5.2 and Table 5.3. In each table, the first column shows the results for *LabelMe* and the second column shows the results for *Corel* datasets. The results show that multimodal keywords give the best results at an average precision level. In most cases, they also show improved performance at 10% recall level. As we increase the recall level, multimodal keywords consistently show better performance. The next best result is obtained when full-size images and text keywords are combined. Using the text keywords alone falls behind this.

Table 5.2: Precision results (full size images)

Experiment type	10% recall		30% recall		Av. Prec.	
fslsa	.67	.74	.51	.59	.41	.45
fsdk	.68	.75	.51	.60	.42	.46
fstklsa	**.81**	**.83**	**.64**	**.69**	**.49**	**.53**
fstkdk	**.84**	**.85**	**.67**	**.70**	**.55**	**.54**
Txt	.77	.81	.68	.69	.52	.51

Table 5.3: Precision results (tiles)

Experiment type	10% recall		30% recall		Av. Prec.	
tslsa	.69	.72	.54	.57	.44	.45
tsdk	.69	.75	.57	.61	.45	.50
tstklsa	**.80**	**.87**	**.68**	**.76**	**.56**	**.62**
tstkdk	**.81**	**.86**	**.69**	**.77**	**.59**	**.63**

Using only low-level image features provides worse results as compared to multimodal keywords. We also observe that there is no significant difference in the case of using only low-level features as to whether we use the entire image or tiles. We also see that using text keywords alone is better than using low-level features of the full-size image, which indicates that at a higher recall value, the utility of using low-level features diminishes. These results are consistent for both the datasets used in our experiments. Another important observation is that visual keywords alone are better than using low-level features for entire images. Based on the experimental results, we can now answer the questions listed in the beginning of this section:

- There is a significant improvement in the retrieval results when we use multimodal keywords, as is evident from Table 5.2 and Table 5.3. This indicates that the multimodal representation is better than low-level features or text representation.
- The diffusion kernel performs better than LSA while at the same time saving computation cost, avoiding high dimensionality and finding the modalities which are the most representative of a large feature set.

5.5 Conclusion

In this chapter, we have described multimodal image retrieval in some detail, including our approach to this important problem. Our techniques in this area pay particular attention to the problem of the *semantic gap*, how to retrieve particular images that the user has in mind. We have seen that dimensional reduction over multiple modalities, especially the non-linear technique of diffusion maps, helps us in the solution to this problem. Such techniques can certainly be applied to video and other event-based environments.

References

1 Dublin Core Metadata Element Set, Version 1.1. 2008, retrieved Nov 14, 2008, *http://dublincore.org/documents/dces/*.

2 VRA Core, 4.0, (2007), retrieved Nov. 14, 2008, *http://www.vraweb.org/projects/vracore4/ index.html.*

3 Categories for the Description of Works of Art (CDWA), retrieved Nov 14, 2008 *http://www.getty.edu/research/conducting_research/standards/cdwa/index.html*

4 Baca, M., Harpring, P., Lanzi, E., McRae, L., Whiteside A. (Eds.) (2006), *Cataloging Cultural Objects: Guide to Describing Cultural Works And Their Images*, Chicago: American Library Association.

5 MPEG-7 Standard. International Organization for standardization ISO/IECJTC1/SC29/ WG11 *http://www.chiariglione.org/mpeg/standards/mpeg-7/mpeg-7.htm.*

6 Belongie, S., Carson, C., Greenspan, H. and Malik, J. (2002), Recognition of Images in Large Databases Using Color and Texture, *IEEE Trans. PAMI*, **24**(8), pp.1026-1038.

7   Fellbaum, C. (Ed.) (1998), *WorldNet: An Electronic Lexical Database*, MIT Press, Massachusetts, USA.

8   Deerwester, A., Dumais, S.T., Landauer, T.K., Furnas, G.W. and Harshman, R.A. (1990), Indexing by latent semantic analysis, *Journal of the American Society of Information Science*, **41**(6), pp.391-407.

9   Dhillon, I.S. and Modha, D.S. (2001), Concept Decompositions for Large Sparse Text Data Using Clustering, *Machine Learning*, **42**(1), pp.143-175.

10 Swain, M. and Ballard, D. (1991), Color Indexing", *Int. Journal of Computer Vision*, **7**(1), pp.11-32.

11 Jain, A. K., and Vailaya, A. (1996). Image Retrieval Using Color and Shape, *Pattern Recognition*, **29**(8), pp.1233-1244.

12 Carson, C., Belonge, S., Greenspan, H. and Malik J. (2002),Blobworld: Image Segmentation using Expectation-Maximization and its application to image querying, *PAMI*, **24**(8), pp.1026-38.

13 Faloutsos, C., Barber, R., Flickner, M., Hafner, J., Niblack, W., Petkovic, D. and Equitz, W. (1994), Efficient and Effective Querying by Image Content, *Journal of Intelligent Information Systems*, **3**(3/4), pp.231-262.

14 Pentland, A., Picard, R. and Sclaroff, S. (1994), Photobook: Content-Based Manipulation of Image Databases, *SPIE: Storage and Retrieval for Image and Video Databases*, pp.34-47.

15 Squire, D.M., Muller, W., Muller, H. and Pun, T. (2000), Content-Based Query of Image Databases: Inspirations from Text Retrieval, *Pattern Recognition Letters*, **21**, pp.13-14.

16 Westerveld, T. (2000), Image Retrieval: Content Versus Context, *Proc. of the RIAO Conf.*, Paris, France, pp.276-284.

17 Grosky, W. I. and Zhao, R. (2002), Negotiating the Semantic Gap: From Feature Maps to Semantic Landscapes, *Pattern Recognition*, **35**(3), pp.693-600.

18 Picard, R.W. (1995), Toward a Visual Thesaurus, *MIRO*, Glasgow.

19 Lim, J. H. (2001), Building Visual Vocabulary for Image Indexation and query Formulation, *Pattern Analysis and Applications*, **4**, pp.125-139.

20 Zhu, L., Rao, A. and Zhang, A. (2002), Theory of keyblock-based image retrieval", *ACM Trans. Inf. Syst*, **20**(2), pp.224-257.

21 Csurka, G., Dance, C., Fan, L., Willamowski, J., and Bray, C. (2004), Visual

categorization with bags of keypoints, *ECCV Workshop on Statistical Learning in Computer Vision*.

22 Sivic, J., Bussell, B., Efros, A. A., Zisserman, A. and Freeman, B. (2005), Discovering Objects and Their Location in Images, *ICCV*.

23 Maree, R., Geurts, P., Piater, J. and Wehenkel L. (2005), Random Subwindows for Robust Image Classification, *CVPR*, **1**, pp.34-40.

24 Bhattacharya, A., Ljosa, V., Pan, J., Verardo, M. R., Yang, H., Faloutsos, H. C. and Singh, A.K. (2005), ViVo: Visual Vocabulary Construction for Mining Biomedical Images, *ICDM*.

25 Agrawal, A., Grosky, W. I., and Fotouhi F. (2006), Image Clustering Using Multimodal Keywords, *SAMT*, pp.113-123.

26 Snoek, C., Worring, M. and Smeulders, A.W.M. (2005), Early versus late fusion in semantic video analysis, *ACM Multimedia*, pp.399-402.

27 Jain, A.K., Duin, R.P.W. and Mao, J. (2000), Statistical pattern recognition: A review, *Tran. on Pattern Analysis and Machine Intelligence*, **22**(1), pp.4-37.

28 Kittler, J., Hatef, M. and Duin, R.P.W. (1996), Combining classifiers, *Intl. Pattern Recognition*, pp.897-901.

29 Xu, L., Krzyzak, A. and Suen, C.Y. (1992), Methods for Combining Multiple Classifiers and Their Applications in Handwritten Character Recognition, *IEEE Trans. Systems, Man, and Cybernetics*, **22**, pp.418-435.

30 Wu, Y.E., Chang, Y.K., Chang, C. and Smith, J.R. (2004), "Optimal multimodal fusion for multimedia data analysis", *ACM MM*, pp.572-579.

31 Wang, X., Ma, W., Xue, G. and Li, X. (2004), Multi-model similarity propagation and its application for web image retrieval, *ACM MM*, pp.944-951.

32 Smeulders, W.M.A., Worring M., Santini, S., Gupta A. and Jain, R. (2000), Content based image retrieval at the end of the early years, *IEEE Transactions on Pattern Analysis and Machine Intelligence*, **22**(12), pp.1349-1380.

33 Hare, J.S., Lewis, P.H., Enser, P.G.B. and Sandom, C.J. (2006), Mind the Gap: Another Look at the Problem of the Semantic Gap in Image Retrieval, *SPIE, Multimedia Content Analysis, Management, and Retrieval*, **6073**(1).

34 Hoi, S.C.H., Lyu, M.R. and Jin, R. (2006), A Unified Log-Based Relevance Feedback Scheme for Image Retrieval, *Transactions on Knowledge and Data Engineering*, **18**(4), pp.509-524.

35 Croft, W. B. (1995), What Do People Want from Information Retrieval? (The Top 10 Research Issues for Companies that Use and Sell IR Systems), Center for Intelligent Information Retrieval Computer Science Department, University of Massachusetts, Amherst.

36 Sato, T., Kanada, T., Hughes, E. and Smith, M. (1998), Video OCR for Digital News Archives, *IEEE Workshop on CAIVD*, pp.52-60.

37 Shih, H.C, and Huang, C.L. (2006), A Robust Superimposed Caption Box Content Understand-ing for Sports Video, *IEEE Workshop on Multimedia Information Processing and Retrieval*, pp. 867-872.

38 Webb, A.R. (2002), *Statistical Pattern Recognition*, John Wiley, 2nd edition.

39 Niblack, W., Barber, R. Equitz, W., Flickner, M. D., Glasman, E. H., Petkovic, D., Yanker, P., Faloutsos, C. and Taubin, G. (1993), The QBIC Project: Querying Images by Content Us-ing Color, Texture, and Shape, *Storage and Retrieval for Image and Video Databases*, San Jose, CA, pp.173-187.

40 Bach, J.R., Fuller, C., Gupta, A., Hampapur, A., Horowitz, B., Humphrey, R., Jain, R., and Shu, C.F. (1996), Virage image search engine: An open framework for image management, *Storage and Retrieval for Still Image and Video Databases*, **2670**, pp.76-87.

41 Pentland, *op.cit.*

42 Smith, J.R. and Chang, S.F. (1997), Visually searching the Web for content, *IEEE Multimedia*, **4**(3), pp.12-20.

43 Jaimes, A., Sebe, N. and Perez, D.G. (2006), Human-Centered Computing: A Multimedia Perspective, *ACM Multimedia*, California, USA.

44 Broek, E.L. van den, Rikxoort, E. M. van, and Schouten, Th. E. (2005), Human-Centered Object-Based Image Retrieval, *Lecture Notes in Computer Science (Advances in Pattern Recognition)*, **3687**, pp.492-501.

45 Berlin, B., and Kay, P. (1969), *Basic color terms: Their universals and evolution*, University of California Press, Berkeley.

46 Huang, J., Kumar, S.R., Mitra, M., Zhu, W. and Zabih, R. (1997), Image Indexing Using Color Correlograms, *CVPR*, pp.762-768.

47 Mongy, S., Bouali, F., and Djeraba, C. (2005), Analyzing User's Behavior on a Video Data-base, *ACM MDM/KDD Workshop on Multimedia Data Mining*, Chicago, IL, USA.

48 Jain, R. (2003), Experiential computing, *Communications of the ACM*, **46**(7), pp.48-54.

49 Jain, R. (2000), *op. cit.*

50 He, X., Ma, W., King, O., Li, M. and Zhang, H. (2003), Learning a semantic space from user's relevance feedback for image retrieval : Conceptual and dynamical aspects of multimedia content description, *IEEE Trans. Circuits Syst. Video Technol.*, **13**(1), pp.39-48.

51 Grauman, K. and Darrell, T. (2006), Unsupervised Learning of Categories from Sets of Partially Matching Image Features, *IEEE Conference on Computer Vision and Pattern Recognition (CVPR)*, New York City, NY.

52 Boujemaa, N., Ferecatu M. and Gouet, V. (2002), Approximate search vs. precise search by visual content in cultural heritage image databases, *MIR*.

53 Birkbeck, N., Cobzas, D., Espiritu, C., Jagersand, M. and Yerex, K. (2005), Image-based capture, modeling and rendering for cultural heritage, *Proc. of the Canadian Annual Conf. on Graphic Interface*, Vancouver.

54 Sinclair, P., Lewis, P., Martinez, K., Addis, M. and Prideaux, D. (2006), Semantic web integration of cultural heritage sources, *WWW. ACM*, New York, NY, pp.1047-1048.

55 Amato, G., Debole, F., Peters, C., and Savino, P. (2008), The MultiMatch Prototype: Multilingual/Multimedia Search for Cultural Heritage Objects, *ECDL*, Aarhus, Denmark.

56 Bellman, R., (1961), *Adaptive Control Processes: A Guided Tour*, Princeton, Princeton University Press.

57 StatSoft (2005), Electronic Textbook, *http://www.statsoft.com/textbook/glosc.hmtl.*

58 *ibid.*

59 Eccles, I., and Su, M. (2004), Illustrating the curse of dimensionality numerically through different data distribution models, *International Symposium on information and Communication Technologies*, **90**, pp.232-237.

60 Tesic, J. (2004), Managing large-scale multimedia repositories, Ph.D. Thesis, Vision Research Lab, University of California, Santa Barbara.

61 Guttman, A. (1984), R-trees: A dynamic index structure for spatial searching, *ACM SIGMOD*, pp.4757.

62 Beyer, K. S., Goldstein, J., Ramakrishnan, R., and Shaft, U. (1999), When Is "Nearest Neighbor" Meaningful? *International Conference on Database Theory*, Springer-Verlag, **1540**, pp.217-235.

63 Tesic, *op. cit.*

64 Chavez, E., and Navarro, G. (2003), Probabilistic proximity search: Fighting the curse of dimensionality in metric spaces, *Inf. Process. Lett.*, **85**(1), pp.39-46.

65 Tibshirani, R., Hastie, T., Narasimhan, B. and Chu, G. (2002), Diagnosis of multiple cancer types by shrunken centroids of gene expression, *Proc. National Academy of Sciences of the USA*, **99**(10), pp 6567-6572.

66 Coifman, R.R., and Lafon, S. (2006), Diffusion maps, *Applied and Computational Harmonic Analysis*, **21**(1), pp.5-30.

67 Lowe, D.G. (1999), Object Recognition from local scale invariant features, *ICCV*.

68 Manjunath, B.S., Salembier, P. and Sikor, T. (Eds) (2002), *"Introduction to MPEG-7 Multimedia Content Description Interface*, John Wiley & Sons.

69 Karypis, G. (2003), Cluto: A clustering toolkit, release 2.1.1, *Technical Report 02-017*, University of Minnesota, Department of Computer Science.

70 Markkula, M. and Sormunen, E. (1988), Searching for photos — journalists' practices in pictorial IR, In the *Challenge of Image Retrieval. Electronic Workshops in computing.*

71 Smeaton, A.F. and Quigley, I. (1996), Experiments on Using Semantic Distances Between Words in Image Caption Retrieval, *SIGIR*, pp.174-180.

72 Fellbaum, *op.cit.*

73 Rijsbergen, C.J., Robertson, S.E. and Porter, M.F. (1980), New models in probabilistic information retrieval, *British Library Research and Development Report*, **5587**.

74 Coifman, *op.cit.*

75 Bast, H. and Majumdar, D. (2005), Why Spectral Retrieval Works, *SIGIR*, Salvador, Brazil, pp.11-18.

76 Russell, B., Torralba, A., Murphy, K. and Freeman W.T. (2007), LabelMe: A database and web-based tool for image annotation, *Int. Jour of Computer Vision*.

77 Amato, G., Gennaro, C., Savino, P. and Rabitti, F. (2004), Milos: a Multimedia Content Management System for Digital Library Applications, *ECDL*, **3232**, pp.14-25.

Chapter 6

Challenges in the Recognition and Searching of Printed Books in Indian Languages and Scripts

R. Manmatha[1] and C.V. Jawahar[2]

[1]*Department of Computer Science,*
University of Massachusetts, Amherst, MA, USA
manmatha@cs.umass.edu
[2]*Center for Visual Information Technology*
International Institute of Information Technology, Hyderabad, India
jawahar@iiit.ac.in

Abstract

Optical character recognizers have been combined with text search engines to successfully build digital book libraries in a number of European languages. The recognition of printed books in Indian languages and scripts is, however, still a challenging problem. This paper describes some of the challenges in building recognizers for Indian languages. Challenges include the complexity of some cursive scripts, the large number of classes, the paucity of annotated data sets and the document quality. However, content-level browsing and accessing document images is immediately required for accessing image collections in digital libraries. We describe some possible approaches to this problem including techniques to directly search the text using word spotting.

Keywords: Indian Languages, Indian Scripts, Content level Browsing, Image Retrieval, Digital Libraries, OCR, Recognizers, Search System, Word Spotting.

119

6.1 Introduction

Books, newspapers and magazines form an important part of a society's cultural heritage. To enhance cultural communication within a society, it is important to provide easy access to such material. This is being currently achieved for many European languages such as English, French and Russian by projects such as the Million Book project, Google Books or the Internet Archive. Books, newspapers and magazines are scanned, converted to text using commercial optical character recognition (OCR) software and then indexed for search. Making handwritten material searchable in a similar manner is still difficult (even for English) and we will not discuss that further. There is significant interest in making printed material in Indian languages searchable in the same manner – for example the Digital Library of India (DLI)[1, 2] is such an attempt. However, there are no good commercial recognizers available for Indian languages. Major challenges in developing such recognizers include the variety of languages and scripts in India. Additional challenges include the large number of character classes in many of these scripts and the lack of good annotated data sets.

Why is it difficult to build OCR systems for Indian languages? There are probably good financial reasons why companies have not tried to build OCR systems for Indian languages unlike say Chinese. Much of the formal internal and external communication in companies, large organizations and even much of the government in India still takes place in English. The language of high-end business in India is primarily English. This has proven financially advantageous to India for example in the software industry. However, it also means that there is less of a financial incentive to build Indian language OCRs. Here we will focus on the technical difficulties in recognizing Indic documents. While that the language of business may be English, Indian languages are widely used in communications between people and form an important intermediary in preserving the culture. A significant number of newspapers, magazines and books get printed in these languages and it would be useful to search such material. While considerable historical material in Indian languages exists on palm leaf manuscripts and as inscriptions on structures, these are much beyond what current technology can recognize and we will, therefore, not discuss such material further.

OCR systems first have to find the layout of a document image to find possible text regions. The text blocks are segmented into words and characters. This is followed by a recognition phase using a classifier. The accuracy of the pattern classifier is improved by post-processing with the help of a dictionary or for research systems an appropriate language model. In a number of scripts (for example Latin scripts) it is straightforward to divide words into characters using white space as long as good quality printed documents are used. This makes it possible to use character recognizers built for each character thus simplifying the problem. Note that this assumes that the layout analysis as well as word/character segmentation work well. In a number of Indian languages a line *Shirorekha* connects characters making character segmentation trickier. In addition, with natural degradations in the document, characters (or symbols) in the image may get cut into multiple parts. Multiple characters can also get merged into one unit. Such degradations make recognition challenging. Finally, Indian languages have a potentially large numbers of character classes. We touch upon these points later.

There are some techniques which can potentially simplify this problem; one can recognize words rather than characters thus avoiding the character segmentation problem[3]. This technique is not favored for good quality printed Latin scripts since the characters can usually be cleanly segmented. However, it is used in handwriting and is also likely to be good for noisy text. Directly recognizing each word leads to a large expansion of character classes but has been successfully used for example in historical handwritten recognition[4]. A modification of this approach adapted from speech recognition involves segmentation and recognition, at the same time, using an HMM – again a technique used for print in some cases[5] and widely used for handwriting[6]. Manmatha[7] gives a brief overview of document image recognition while Nagy[8] reviews the recent literature in the area. Pal and Chaudhuri[9] survey the state of the art in Indian scripts.

For many digital libraries, recognition is considered as a prerequisite to developing a search engine. Often, however, the output of the recognition is not directly viewed by the user in many situations. In such cases search can avoid OCR completely. Search has the advantage that it is usually not reliant on accurately finding every word. Rather, context is implicitly used in search (as with multiple word queries). Search systems produce a ranking from which the user selects the most appropriate or relevant result. This means that while the result must be in the top n, it does not have to be the top result.

At least two different approaches exist for searching scanned images of text directly. The first one based on word spotting[10-11] involves clustering similar word images together in the dataset using image matching (notice that we are talking about clustering the test dataset and not the training set). The clusters that are formed can either be annotated by a user (one annotation per cluster rather than one per image) or alternatively searched directly using an image query. Since people prefer text queries, a reverse annotation step can be performed where the text query produced by a person is converted to an image query by creating a glyph. For printed words creating a reverse annotation is possible[12]. A number of image matching steps have been tried although dynamic time warping has been the most successful for both handwriting and print[13-15] including printed Indian scripts. Dynamic time warping is, however, slow and problems arise when trying to scale this approach to large corpora. Alternative techniques have been suggested in this case. One proposed for handwriting involves converting the handwritten features to discrete segments using clustering[16]. Another, tried for printed books in Hindi and Telugu involves using locality sensitive hashing to index printed books[17]. This latter approach is sensitive to font variations but given that much of a book is in a single font, it can be searched well using this approach.

A second approach involves image annotation techniques[18]. Here, a set of word images from a training set is annotated with the correct word. The words are automatically segmented and continuous features computed which are in turn transformed to discrete features. A statistical mapping is then learned between the discrete features of a word and its English rendering using the training set. The word segmentation and feature extraction are repeated for the test set and the word images are automatically annotated with their textual versions using the statistical model. A single word image may be annotated with large numbers of words and associated probabilities. Given a query, a language modeling based retrieval approach is then used to rank the documents. Note that for multi-word queries it is possible that the top annotation for any single word may not be the best match for the query if a number of the other words in the query bias it towards a different answer. This relevance model based approach has been successfully used for historical handwriting but has not been tested for printed Indian languages.

In this chapter we focus on methods which enable us to search printed digital libraries without doing explicit character recognition. We first present some of the challenges in designing robust recognizers for Indic scripts. We then look at word spotting and the proposed uses for searching Indian scripts. Given that traditional word spotting approaches can be slow, we consider the use of indexes using locality based hashing to search word images rapidly. Finally, we conclude the chapter.

6.2 Challenges for Indic OCRs

The languages of India belong to either the Indo-European or Dravidian language families with a small number (in terms of speakers) belonging to the Austro-Asiatic and Tibeto-Burman language families. Roughly speaking most speakers of Dravidian languages are concentrated in the south of India while the rest of India has speakers of languages derived from Sanskrit (an Indo-European language). The Austro-Asiatic and Tibeto-Burman languages are found in small pockets. There are possibly more than 200 languages in India. However the twenty two official languages in India are Assamese, Bengali, Dogri, Gujarati, Hindi, Kashmiri, Konkani, Maithili, Manipuri, Marathi, Nepali, Oriya, Punjabi, Sanskrit, Sindhi, Urdu (all Indo- European), Kannada, Malayalam, Tamil, Telugu (all Dravidian), Bodo (Tibeto- Burman) and Santhali (Austro-Asiatic). The situation is further complicated since all the Dravidian languages have loan words from Sanskrit – in particular Telugu has a substantial fraction of its vocabulary derived from Sanskrit. For most speakers, Hindi and Urdu are essentially the same language. The two main distinctions between them are a) that Hindi's vocabulary is more Sanskritized while Urdu's vocabulary borrows more heavily from Persian and Arabic and b) Hindi is written in Devanagari while Urdu is written in an Arabic derived script. However, the latter difference means that Hindi and Urdu require separate OCR systems.

Many of these languages have their own distinct scripts. For example, each of the four main Dravidian languages has its own script which are very different from each other and from those of other Indian languages. This is unlike Europe where a large number of languages share a Latin alphabet with small variations. A number of these languages are spoken, written and read by significant populations. Hindi (including Urdu) has about

600 million native speakers, Telugu about 75 million and Malayalam about 37 million speakers. All these languages have significant printed books and resources and OCRs are immediately required to make them accessible. The largest newspaper in India by circulation Dainik Jagran is a Hindi newspaper.

A good OCR algorithm has two important components – a layout recognition step and a step which recognizes the segmented characters. While a lot of work has been done on recognizing isolated characters/words in Indian scripts and languages, it is not often recognized that an essential element in building a good OCR is a good layout recognition algorithm which describes how the page is formatted. For example, a good layout analysis algorithm extracts out the image and text parts and segments the text into groups such as columns, paragraphs, sentences, words and characters. Layout analysis as well as segmentation is difficult for many reasons. For Indian scripts, the complex shapes and their scattered distribution on a 2D plane makes many text blocks similar to line drawings and pictures. The situation gets further complicated when the printed text is generated using word processors which are designed for scripts and fonts in European languages. This has a direct bearing on the arrangements of glyphs and their spacing. A quick look at the distance-angle plot of components in English and Telugu (in Fig. 6.1), reveals that the symbol distribution in Telugu is highly general (distributed) while that in English is highly structured (clear peaks seen in Fig. 6.1(a)). An empirical comparison of segmentation algorithms[19] argues that many popular algorithms are not directly applicable to many of the Indian scripts. Popular algorithms available in the literature use local geometric information in the form of distance between connected components to develop segmentation algorithms. In many situations (as in Fig. 6.2), the inter-line spacing may be smaller than the intra-word spacing. In summary, not enough work has been done on layout analysis for Indian languages and current layout analysis algorithms produce segmented characters which are noisy and the results applied to isolated characters and words do not directly translate to real documents. Hence, more work is needed on Indian languages to recognize real output from document images.

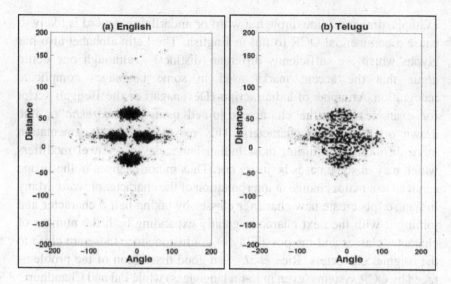

Fig. 6.1: Segmentation of Indian language documents is often challenging due to the complexity of glyph distribution (a) Distance-Angle plot for English (b) Distance-Angle plot for Telugu.

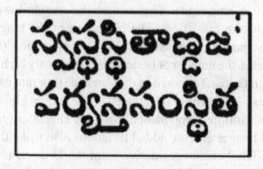

Fig. 6.2: At places inter-line spacing may be even smaller than intra-character spacing within a word.

In virtually all scripts (such as Latin, Cyrillic, Chinese, Japanese and Korean) for which commercial OCR has been successful, characters or the corresponding units are separated by a space. Thus for good quality documents it is possible without a great deal of effort to segment individual characters in these scripts. In these languages, problems arise when the documents are noisy or complex since the layout recognition and character segmentation is then more likely to fail. For example, drawing a line through a word or underlining a word is likely to cause a commercial OCR to fail in English. The Latin alphabet also has glyphs which are sufficiently different (distinct) – although one could argue that the accent marks used in some languages complicate recognition. A number of Indian scripts (Devanagari or the Bengali script for example) have the characters joined using a *Shirorekha* or line drawn on top of the characters. This makes character segmentation more difficult. In addition most Indian languages use vowel modifiers which may in some cases be just a dot. Thus minor changes in the image can lead to a major change in interpretation of the character or word. Many Indian scripts create new character classes by taking half a character and joining it with the next character greatly expanding both the number of character classes and the possibility of confusion since these are close to the original characters. Ricé *et al.*[20] is a good discussion of the problems faced by OCR systems (even in Latin languages) while Pal and Chaudhuri[21] survey character recognition in Indian scripts. We now expand on these difficulties.

A large number of characters are present in Indian scripts compared to that of European languages. This makes the recognition difficult for conventional pattern classifiers. The basic unit of the language *akshara* may be a consonant(C), a consonant-vowel combination (CV), CCV or CCCV. This makes the number of basic units enormously high, though many of these valid units are rarely used in the language (but rare use complicates training). These aksharas may consist of a single glyph (connected component) or multiple components. Complex character graphemes with curved shaped images and the added inflations also make the recognition difficult. Additional challenges derive from the large number of similar/ confusing characters. Fig. 6.3 shows some of the pairs of similar characters in Malayalam. The variation between these characters is extremely small. Even humans find it difficult to recognize them in isolation. However, we usually read them correctly from the context. Such issues in the recognition process also increases the need for computational resources. Increased computational complexity and memory requirements due to the large number of classes, has been a bottleneck in developing robust OCR systems.

The lack of standard databases, statistical information and benchmarks for testing, are another set of challenges in developing robust OCR systems for Indian languages. This has prevented the scaling of available results to

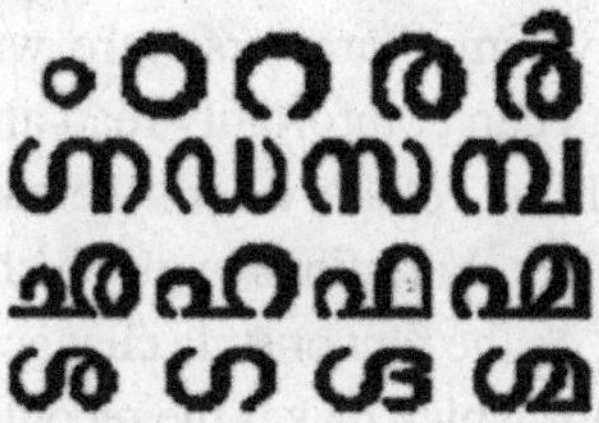

ം ഠ റ ഭ ർ
ഗ ഡ സ ബ
ഇ ഹ ഫ മ
ശ ഗ ങ ഡ

Fig. 6.3: Examples of similar characters in Malayalam.

large document collections. The absence of large standard datasets also makes it difficult to develop OCR systems robust to natural variations. The lack of well developed language models makes conventional post-processors practically impossible. Many languages like Malayalam and Telugu have very complex language structures, which does not make them attractive candidates for using linguistic post-processing (e.g. using dictionaries, bigrams).

Unicode/display/font related issues in building, testing and deploying working systems, have slowed down research in the development of character recognition systems for Indian languages. Many standard representations such as Unicode fail to encode all the valid characters in many of the Indian scripts. Such representational issues seriously affect the development of software and systems. In some scripts the same character can be written in multiple ways and all the multiple methods may co-exist in the same document. This has possibly happened because of script revisions which have happened officially or un-officially at various times. Fig. 6.4

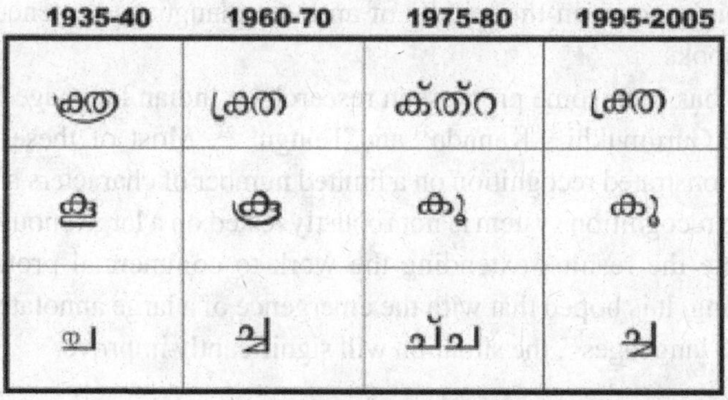

1935-40	1960-70	1975-80	1995-2005
ക്ത	ക്രത	ക്ത്റ	ക്രത
ക്ള	ക്ള	കൂ	കൂ
ഄ	ച്ള	ച്ച	ച്ള

Fig. 6.4: Examples of changes in script with time.

shows how three Malayalam characters were written during periods of time. Present day readers can comfortably read all these variants. Fig. 6.5 shows a similar example in Telugu where the same character (shown in Hindi) get written in Telugu. Variations in glyph/shape of a character could happen due to font/style. As the font or style changes the glyph of a character also changes considerably, which makes the recognition difficult.

Fig. 6.5: The same Telugu characters are written in different ways. The first column shows a Hindi character and the other columns show the corresponding – with the same sound – Telugu characters written in different ways.

A significant population of Indian educated people can read, write or comprehend multiple languages. Many Indian language documents contain foreign language words (printed in the same or a foreign script). In practice, script separation at word or character level is difficult. Fig. 6.6 demonstrates that highly similar shapes exist across characters. The appearance of foreign or unknown symbols in the document makes the recognition difficult, and sometimes unpredictable. For example, English words might occur in the middle of an Indian language sentence even in printed books.

There has been some progress in research on Indian language OCRs in Bangla,[22] Gurumukhi,[23] Kannda[24] and Telugu[25-26]. Most of these attempts have demonstrated recognition on a limited number of characters and pages. Since the recognition system is not robustly tested on a large enough corpus to validate the results, extending the work to commercial prototypes is challenging. It is hoped that with the emergence of a large annotated corpus for Indian languages[27], the situation will significantly improve.

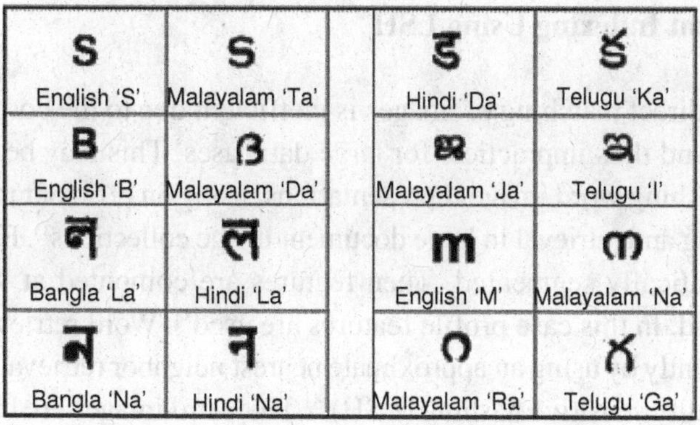

S English 'S'	**S** Malayalam 'Ta'	**ड** Hindi 'Da'	**୪** Telugu 'Ka'
B English 'B'	**ß** Malayalam 'Da'	**ൠ** Malayalam 'Ja'	** a** Telugu 'I'
ল Bangla 'La'	**ल** Hindi 'La'	**m** English 'M'	**ന** Malayalam 'Na'
न Bangla 'Na'	**न** Hindi 'Na'	**O** Malayalam 'Ra'	** X** Telugu 'Ga'

Fig. 6.6: Similarity of characters across scripts.

6.3 Word Spotting and Recognition Free Matching

Word spotting has been tried for many different kinds of documents both hand-written and print. Rath and Manmatha[28] used dynamic time warping (DTW) to compute image similarities for handwriting. The word similarities are then used for clustering using K-means or agglomerative clustering techniques. This approach was adopted in Jawahar *et al.*[29] for printed Indian language document images. To simplify the process of querying, a word image is generated for each query and the cluster corresponding to this word is identified. In such methods, efficiency is achieved by significant offline computation. Gatos *et al.*[30] used word spotting for old Greek typewritten manuscripts for which OCRs did not work. One advantage of word spotting over traditional OCR methods is that they take advantage of the fact that within corpora such as books the word images are likely to be much more similar, which traditional OCRs do not do.

Many of these techniques (for example DTW) are computationally expensive and do not scale very well. Inspite of this, Sankar *et al.*[31] successfully indexed 500 books in Indian languages using this approach by doing virtually all the computation offline. This made the retrieval instantaneous. Avoiding DTW, Rath *et al.*[32] demonstrated the use of direct clustering of word image features on historical handwritten manuscripts. However, clustering is itself an expensive operation. An alternative to doing this efficiently using locality sensitive hashing (LSH) will be discussed in the next section.

6.4 Efficient Indexing Using LSH

However, direct matching of images is inefficient due to the complexity of matching and thus impractical for large databases. This may be solved by directly hashing word image representations, using an efficient mechanism for indexing and retrieval in large document image collections[33]. First, words are automatically segmented. Then features are computed at word level and indexed. In this case profile features are used[34]. Word retrieval is done very efficiently by using an approximate nearest neighbor retrieval technique called locality sensitive hashing (LSH)[35]. The word images are hashed into hash tables using features computed at word level. Content-sensitive hash functions are used to hash words such that the probability of grouping similar words in the same index of the hash table is high. The sub-linear time content-sensitive hashing scheme makes the search very fast without degrading accuracy. Experiments on a collection of Kalidasa's – the classical Indian poet of antiquity – books in Telugu demonstrate that 20,000 word images may be searched in a few milliseconds. The approach thus makes searching large document image collections practical.

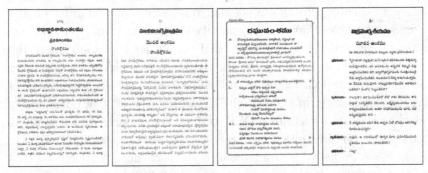

Fig. 6.7: Sample document images from Kalidasa's books in Telugu.

The query image and example search results are shown in Fig. 6.8. The first two rows show correct results. The last column in the last two rows shows examples where erroneous words may be retrieved although they appear somewhat visually similar.

The results of queries containing words of different sizes and style types are shown in Fig. 6.9. Such results are obtained by querying the same word

Query Image	Some of the Retrieved Images			
భగవతి!	భగవతి.	భగవతి!	భగవతి	భగవతి!
నిపుణికా	నిపుణికా	నిపుణికా	నిపుణికా	నిపుణికా
ద్వితీయాంకము	ద్వితీయాంకము	ద్వితీయాంకము	ద్వితీయాంకము	తృతీయాంకము
శరత్	శరత్	శరత్	శరత్	శరది

Fig. 6.8: Results: Example (Telugu) words searched for input queries.

Query Image	Some of the Retrieved Images			
ఋతుసంహారమ్	ఋతుసంహారం	ఋతుసంహారము	ఋతుసంహారమ్	ఋతుసంహారము
విదూషకుడు	విదూషకుడు	విదూషకుడు	విదూషకుడు	విదూషకుడు
అంకము	అంకము	అంకము	అంకము	అంకము

Fig. 6.9: Results: Words with small variations in style and size are retrieved.

in multiple books of the collection. Using the same query on two different books of the collection retrieves words which are content-wise similar.

Indian language words have small form variations. For example, the same word may have different case endings. Such words are also searched correctly using the proposed solution. Example results of such queries are shown in Fig. 6.10 (row 2). The retrieved words have the same stem, which is due to the similarity in image content. There are limits to the font variations that can be handled by the proposed retrieval technique. Experiments show

Query Image	Some of the Retrieved Images			
ప్రియురాలా!	ప్రియురాలా!	ప్రియురాలా!	ప్రియురాలికి	ప్రియురాలిని
చంద్రుని	చంద్రుని	(చంద్రుని)	చంద్రుడే	చంద్రుల
శ్లోకములు	శ్లోకములు	శ్లోకములు	శ్లోకము	శోకమును

Fig. 6.10: Results: Words with small form variations are retrieved as relevant.

that we cannot use combinations of different font words but such combinations are very unlikely to occur in books.

The proposed hash based search is sub-linear and much faster than exhaustive nearest neighbour search. The experiments were conducted on data sets of increasing size (by 5,000 words) in each iteration. The maximum number of words used were around 45,000. With the use of the maximum size data set, the maximum time to search relevant words was of the order of milliseconds. The experiments were conducted on an AMD Athlon 64 bit processor using 512 MB memory.

6.5 Discussions, Conclusion and Future Directions

Clearly, word spotting using locality sensitive hashing can successfully retrieve documents in response to query if the font variations are small. The method is also extremely fast. The approach used at word level avoids character segmentation and complexities which may arise therein. Finally, like all word spotting techniques it leverages the actual data set (rather than just a training set). The method has also been tried on some other Indian languages besides Telugu.

However, if font variations are large the method does not work as well. This may be due to feature limitations and also technique limitations. Gradient features may possibly improve results. One can also envision other approaches which involve a combination of recognition and locality sensitive hashing approaches. Other approaches which may be successful include image annotation based approaches.

The difficulties inherent in Indian scripts implies that we need to think out of the box and build robust systems which have better layout analysis systems and recognizers. Even OCR systems for English are not that robust to noise. Underlining a word can make the OCR system fail. The widely reported recognition rate of 99% for English OCR systems is misleading since its only true for good quality printed documents in standard fonts. It hides robustness problems when layouts are complex or there is noise. We believe building recognition and search systems for Indian languages/scripts may give us the opportunity to build better systems for all languages/scripts.

6.6 Acknowledgments

R. Manmatha was supported in part by the Center for Intelligent Information Retrieval. Any opinions, findings and conclusions or recommendations expressed in this material are the author(s) and do not necessarily reflect those of the sponsor. We wish to thank the editors of this book and in particular Dr. Usha Munshi for inviting us to participate in a workshop on cultural heritage artifacts and being patient with us during the writing of this book.

References

1 Ambati, V., Hari, L., Balakrishnan, N., Reddy, Raj and Jawahar, C.V. (2006), Process and Architecture for Digital Library of India, In *Proc. of ICDL*.

2 Sankar, K.P., Ambati, V., Pratha, L. and Jawahar, C.V. (2006), Digitizing a million books: Challenges for document analysis, In *Proc. DAS*, pp.425-236.

3 Madhvanath, S. and Govindaraju, V. (2001), The role of holistic paradigms in handwritten word recognition, *IEEE Trans. on Pattern Analysis and Machine Intelligence*, 23(2), pp.149-164.

4 Lavrenko, V.T. Rath, M. and Manmatha, R. (2004), Holistic word recognition for handwritten historical documents, In *Proc. of the Int'l Workshop on Document Image Analysis for Libraries*, pp.278–287, Palo Alto, CA (January 23-24).

5 Lu, Z., Schwartz, R., Natarajan, P., Bazzi, I. and Makhoul, J. (1999), Advances in the bbn byblos ocr system, In *ICDAR*, pp.337-340.

6 Vinciarelli, A., Bengio, S. and Bunke, H. (2004) Offline recognition of unconstrained hand• written texts using hmms and statistical language models, *IEEE Trans. Pattern Anal. Mach. Intelligence*, 26(6), pp.709-720.

7 Manmatha, R. (2009), Document image analysis and recognition, In ed. B. Wah, Wiley *Encyclopedia of Computer Science and Engineering*, 2, pp.1022-1031.

8 Nagy, G. (2000), Twenty years of document image analysis in PAMI, *IEEE Transactions on PAMI*, 22(1), pp.38-62.

9 Pal, U. and Chaudhuri, B.B. (2004), Indian script character recognition: A survey, *Pattern Recognition*, 37(9).

10 Rath, T.M. and Manmatha, R. (2003), Word image matching using dynamic time warping, In *CVPR*, 2, pp.521-527.

11 Balasubramanian, A., Meshesha, M. and Jawahar, C.V. (2006), Retrieval from document image collections, In *DAS*, pp.1-12.

12 Sankar, K.P. and Jawahar, C.V. (2007), Probabilistic reverse annotation for large scale image retrieval, In *CVPR*.

13 Rath (2003), *op. cit.*

14 Balasubramanian, *op.cit.*

15 Konidaris, T., Gatos, B., Ntzios, K., Pratikakis, I., Theodoridis, S. and Perantonis, S.J. (2007), Keyword-guided word spotting in historical printed documents using synthetic data and user feedback, *IJDAR*, **9**(2), pp.167-177.

16 Rath, T.M. and Manmatha, R. (2007), Word spotting for historical documents, *IJDAR*, **9**(2), pp.139-152.

17 Kumar, Anand, Jawahar, C.V. and Manmatha, R. (2007), Efficient search in document image collections, In *Proc. of ACCV*, pp.586-595.

18 Rath, T.M., Manmatha, R. and Lavrenko, V. (2004), A search engine for historical manuscript images, In *SIGIR*, pp.369-376, ISBN 1-58113-881-4.

19 Kumar Sesh, K., Kumar Sukesh, K. and Jawahar, C.V. (2007), On Segmentation of Documents in Complex Scripts, In *Proc. of International Conference on Document Analysis and Recognition (ICDAR)*, **2**, pp.1243-1247.

20 Rice, S., Nagy, G. and Nartkey, T. (1999), Optical Character Recognition: An Illustrated Guide to the Frontier, (Kluwer Academic Publishers).

21 Pal, *op.cit.*

22 Chaudhuri, B. and Pal, U. (1998), A complete printed Bangla OCR system, *Pattern Recognition*, **31**(5), pp.531-549, (May).

23 Lehal, G.S. and Singh, C. (2002), A complete OCR system for Gurmukhi script, In *Proceedings of the Joint IAPR International Workshop on Structural, Syntactic, and Statistical Pattern Recognition*, pp.358-367, London, UK, Springer-Verlag.

24 Ashwin, T. and Sastry, P. (2002), A font and size-independent OCR system for Kannanda documents using svm, In *Sadhana*, **27**.

25 Negi, A., Bhagvati, C. and Krishna, B. (2001), An OCR system for Telugu, In *ICDAR '01: Proceedings of the Sixth International Conference on Document Analysis and Recognition* Washington, DC, USA, IEEE Computer Society.

26 Jawahar, C.V., Kumar, Pavan M. and Kiran Ravi, S.S. (2003), A bilingual OCR for Hindi-Telugu documents and its applications, In *Proc. ICDAR*, pp.408-412.

27 Jawahar, C.V. and Kumar, A. (2007), Content-level annotation of large collection of printed document images, In *ICDAR*, pp.799-803.

28 Rath (2003), *op.cit.*

29 Balasubramanian, *op.cit.*

30 Konidaris, *op.cit.*

31 Sankar (2007), *op.cit.*

32 Rath (2007), *op.cit.*

33 Kumar, Anand, *op.cit.*

34 *ibid.*

35 Datar, M., Immorlica, N., Indyk, P. and Mirrokni, V.S. (2004), Locality-sensitive hashing scheme based on p-stable distributions, In *SOCG*, pp.253-262, ISBN 1-58113-885-7. doi: http://doi.acm.org/10.1145/997817.997857.

Construction and Statistical Analysis of an Indic Language Corpus for Applied Language Research

Prasenjit Majumder[1], Mandar Mitra[1] and B.B. Chaudhuri[1]

[1]*Computer Vision and Pattern Recognition Unit*
Indian Statistical Institute, Kolkata

prasenjit.majumdar@gmail.com
{mandar,bbc}@isical.ac.in

Abstract

In recent times, the languages of South Asia have become an important research area for the language engineering community. Unfortunately, this research is seriously hampered by the dearth of suitable corpora. The only easily available text corpus in Indian languages is the multilingual DoE corpus, which contains texts excerpted from different genres, like fiction, text book articles, translation, and mass media. We found this corpus unsuitable for applied research in the areas of Information Retrieval (IR), and Information Extraction (IE). For these purposes, a news corpus is far more suitable. Since there was no Bangla (Bengali) news corpus available, we decided to construct one. To the best of our knowledge, this is the first corpus of its kind; it is also significantly (about 5 times) larger than the DoE corpus. This paper describes the construction of the new corpus. We provide some justification for our choice of source, and describe the technical details of how the text was collected from on-line sources on the Internet. Some statistics about the new corpus are also presented. Some of this statistical information is shown to be useful for building IR systems.

Keywords: News Corpus, Indic Language, Information Retrieval, Web Crawling, Text Encoding.

7.1 Introduction

With the increasingly widespread penetration of computers and the Internet in South Asia in general, and in the Indian sub-continent in particular, a rapidly growing amount of textual information in South Asian languages is becoming available in electronic formats. There is an increasing demand for efficient and effective tools to organize and search through this available information. These languages are, therefore, becoming important research areas for the language engineering community[1-2]. Unfortunately, this research is seriously hampered by the lack of suitable corpora. According to Baker and McEnery[3], "There is a dearth of work on Indic languages. The need to focus on Indic languages was further strengthened by our major review (with over 80 research centers world wide responding) of the needs of the community. Indic languages are the ones that most researchers want to work with but cannot because of the lack of corpus resources."

The only commonly available Indian language corpus is a multilingual corpus developed under a program titled *Technology Development for Indian Languages (TDIL),* sponsored by the Department of Electronics, Govt. of India. This corpus, commonly referred to as the *DoE corpus,* contains texts in 12 officially recognized Indian languages. However, the corpus has certain drawbacks which render it unsuitable for applied research in the areas of Information Retrieval (IR), Information Extraction (IE) and Natural Language Processing (NLP). The IR/IE/NLP research community typically uses news corpora for experimentation. Since there was no Bangla (Bengali) news corpus available, we decided to construct one. This paper describes the construction of the new corpus.

We begin by discussing the DoE corpus and its limitations (Section 7.2). Next, we briefly review some standard corpora commonly used in IR and IE research (Section 7.3). In Section 7.4, we describe the actual acquisition of the corpus. Some basic statistical properties of the corpus are presented in Section 7.5. We conclude with a discussion of future work in Section 7.6.

7.2 Limitations of the DoE Corpus

The DoE corpus consists of a total of about 10,000 documents, and contains texts in 12 Indian languages, including Assamese, Bangla (Bengali), Hindi,

Tamil, Telugu, and Urdu. Dash and Chaudhuri[4] have described the construction of this corpus, with special emphasis on the Bangla section of the corpus. The motivation behind the construction of the DoE corpus was to capture a representative sample of the language for computational study and analysis. Accordingly, the corpus draws on sources from various genres, e.g. fiction, scholarly articles on various subjects (fine arts, social science, natural science, etc.), mass media, translations, etc. As a result, even though the corpus has become a useful resource for the study of Indian languages *per se,* preliminary IR experiments with this corpus show that it is unsuitable for IR, IE and applied NLP research. In this section, we first review the resources commonly used for empirical research in the areas of IR and IE, and then briefly describe our experience with using the DoE corpus for IR experiments.

7.2.1 *Information Retrieval and Information Extraction*

Broadly speaking, the goal of an IR system is to find useful information corresponding to a user's query, from a given collection of documents. Web search engines such as Google, Altavista and Yahoo are possibly the most familiar examples of IR systems. The search facility provided with CD-ROM encyclopedias are also often based on IR techniques.

Perhaps the most important problem faced by an IR system is that the information contained in the documents is unstructured, i.e. it is couched in free-flowing, natural language; likewise the users' queries may be phrased in natural language, or in terms of keywords. Various models have been proposed to tackle this problem. These models attempt to represent the semantic information contained in a document in a structured form that can be stored and handled by a computer. Since the representation is approximate, experimental validation is an important part of most IR research. In other words, any proposed technique has to be tested on realistic sample data to evaluate its usefulness. The sample data, or test corpus, consists of three components: (i) a document corpus, (ii) a set of sample queries, and (iii) relevance judgements, i.e. information about which documents in the corpus are relevant to a given user query. The effectiveness of a proposed technique can then be estimated by evaluating its ability to retrieve relevant documents for a given query.

Information Extraction is a more specific task that aims to extract key pieces of information from a given document, in accordance with a pre-specified set of requirements. This information can be represented in a structured form (e.g. as a filled-in template) and stored in a database. For example, an IE system may analyze newswires and transcripts of radio and television broadcasts to find and summarize descriptions of terrorist activities. In recent years, a considerable amount of research activity has focused on achieving an even more specific goal: given a user question, a system should provide a specific answer, instead of requiring the user to search for the answer in a set of retrieved documents. This problem is usually referred to as *Question Answering (QA)*.

The IR, IE, and QA research communities make extensive use of test corpora to evaluate, improve and fine-tune models and techniques. Section 7.3 contains some references to the use of corpora in IR/IE/QA research.

7.2.2 *IR Experiments with the DoE Corpus*

One of our main research interests was in IR from Bangla documents. Bangla is used by about 250 million people of Eastern India and Bangladesh (where it is the national language). It is the fifth-most popular language in the world. For research on Bangla IR, one of our first requirements was a suitable Bangla document corpus. We started with the Bangla section of the DoE corpus, collected 50 sample queries from various potential users, and gathered relevance judgments for these queries and the document corpus. Our preliminary studies revealed the following limitations of this setup:

- The number of documents in this corpus is only 1270. Given that actual IR systems have to deal with enormous amounts of data (several orders of magnitude larger than the DoE corpus), we concluded that this corpus was unrealistically small.
- Since the documents are from diverse genres, the number of relevant documents for any given query is small (less than 5). Voorhees[5] has shown that when queries have very few relevant documents in a test corpus, the results of IR experiments are unreliable, in the sense that commonly used evaluation measures are unstable. This makes the DoE corpus unsuitable for conducting IR experiments.

We therefore decided to construct a Bangla corpus suitable for performing Information Retrieval and Extraction experiments. In the next section, we review similar corpora used by the community for research on other languages. These serve as a model based on which we constructed our corpus.

7.3 Use of News Corpora for IR/IE Research

Empirical research in IR and IE has a long history. At present, the Text REtrieval Conference (TREC)[6] series is probably the best-known forum for IR experimentation. Organized by NIST every year since 1992, TREC provides a uniform platform for the evaluation of IR techniques. TREC participants are provided with a list of queries and a text corpus. They are asked to run their systems on those queries and submit the search results, which are then evaluated using standard quantitative measures. Both English and non-English corpora are used in TREC, and these are drawn predominantly from news sources, e.g. Wall Street Journal, Associated Press, Financial Times, Los Angeles Times, etc.

A similar, standardized platform for empirical research and evaluation in the area of Information Extraction is provided by the Message Understanding Conferences (MUC). The first MUC was organized by DARPA in 1987; MUC-7, the last in the series, was held in 1997[7]. The text data used in these conferences is also taken from newswire articles.

The Cross Language Evaluation Forum (CLEF)[8], organized every year since 2000, targets the evaluation of mono- and multi-lingual information retrieval systems for European languages. A wide range of European languages like French, Dutch, Portuguese, Bulgarian, and Hungarian etc. have been addressed so far in CLEF. The corpora used for these languages are drawn entirely from leading news sources of the respective languages.

For Asian languages, the NTCIR workshops[9] constitute the best-known platform for IR system evaluation. The languages considered so far at NTCIR are Chinese, Japanese and Korean. Here too, news articles constitute the main source of test data. Text collections are constructed by using articles from the leading newspapers in these languages e.g. People's Daily and Xinhua newswire for Chinese, Mainichi for Japanese, and Korean Economic Newspaper for Korean.

To the best of our knowledge, no such large-scale test collections exist for Indian languages. Becker and Riaz[10] have described the construction of an Urdu corpus, but the corpus is small (less than 50,000 words). This corpus, once again, consists of news articles and columns which are taken from the Urdu site of the British Broadcasting Corporation.

In keeping with the prevalent practice of using news corpora for IR/IE research, we decided to construct a reasonably large collection of news articles in Bangla. The next section describes the process of corpus acquisition.

7.4 Corpus Acquisition

7.4.1 Source Selection

One traditional, manpower-intensive method of corpus acquisition is to manually input the text from documents that are available as hard copies. This method is expensive; further, the possibility of typographic errors is high. In comparison, document acquisition from the Internet is a low-cost and effective alternative. The lack of manpower resources constrained us to consider only sources that are already available on the Internet.

Fortunately, several leading Bangla dailies are available on the Internet. On the other hand, the content representation formats chosen by these newspapers creates a problem that is peculiar to Internet content in Indian languages. The Unicode standard for Indian languages is still being formulated and has not yet been finalized. In the absence of a universally (or even widely) accepted standard, content in these languages is frequently represented in terms of font codes rather than character codes. In other words, a character is represented by the numerical code(s) for the glyph(s) that make(s) up the visual representation of that character. The set of glyphs and their numerical codes could be different for different fonts for the same language. The same character can, therefore, be represented by two different numerical codes in two different Web pages. This is in contrast to English, other European languages, and some of the major Asian languages, for which character encoding schemes have long been standardized. Thus, while any given English character is always represented by the same numerical code in any HTML file independent of its source, this is not true of Bangla.

We found about 20 online Bangla dailies published from India, Bangladesh, and Canada (see *http://directory.google.com/Top/World/*

Bangla/Sambad for some examples). We considered the websites of five prominent dailies, *Aajkaal, Anandabazar Patrika, Bartaman,* and *Pratidin,* published from India, and *Jaijaidin* published from Bangladesh. *Jaijaidin* provides its news articles as pdf files. Extracting the textual content from a pdf file is difficult. *Pratidin* puts up its articles in the form of GIF images of text documents; an accurate Optical Character Recognition (OCR) system would be required to extract the textual content of these articles. Each of the other newspapers uses its own custom font and encoding scheme to display the text of the news articles. Of these, only *Anandabazar* provided access to a sizeable archive of previous issues; the archives of the other two papers contained only about 30 issues (i.e. 1 month's back issues) at a time. These considerations led us to select *Anandabazar Patrika* as our source. This selection can also be justified from another point of view: *Anandabazar* is the largest circulating printed Bangla daily in India, with a daily circulation of about 1,000,000 copies.

7.4.2 Data Collection

Like any other daily, each issue of Anandabazar covers regional, national and international news. The articles cover diverse subjects including politics, sports, culture, science, commerce, arts and entertainment, etc. Most importantly, at the time of corpus construction, the Anandabazar website provided access to an archive of all daily issues from 2001 and 2002.

We used the open-source program *wget* (*http://www.gnu.org/software/wget/wget.html*) to automatically traverse and download the archived articles from the years 2001 and 2002. Each individual article is an HTML file; all articles from a single day (usually numbering about 100) are stored in a separate folder with the date as the folder name. The date format used by Anandabazar is 1yymmdd where yy, mm, dd stands for the year, month, and day respectively.

The visual layout of the articles follows a structure that is commonly found in many online newspapers. Each page is divided into three vertical columns, with the news text being displayed in the central column. The other columns (and sometimes a footer at the bottom of the page) serve as margins, or contain links that can be used to navigate the website, as well as advertisements. We preprocessed the files by first deleting those portions that appear on all pages (e.g. margins, navigational panels, advertisements). We also identified and removed all images, banners, animation, and sound files. All color and style related markup was also deleted. This preprocessing yields a simple HTML file that contains only <FONT> and <P> (paragraph) tags. The textual content of interest lies between the <FONT> tags.

This text is displayed using a set of three custom fonts with the help of the Portable Font Resource (PFR) technology (also known as dynamic fonts) developed by Bitstream, Inc. (*http://www.bitstream.com/*). Since the text is represented in terms of non-standard font codes, we first had to convert the encoding to ISCII[11] (Indian Script Code for Information Interchange, described in Bureau of Indian Standards Document No. IS:13194-1991), a standard character code widely used within India. ISCII forms the basis of Unicode assignments for Indian scripts; the present corpus can thus be converted easily into Unicode 4.0.

The complexity of this conversion process was compounded by two factors:

1. Firstly, three different fonts were used to display the content. The fonts have overlapping glyph sets, and each font uses its own idiosyncratic encoding schemes.
2. The font files were not available for downloading. Thus, a table of glyphs and corresponding numeric codes had to be manually constructed for each font by painstakingly comparing the original HTML source and displayed forms of a large number of pages.

After the glyph-vs-numeric-code tables were constructed, a program for converting glyph codes to ISCII character codes was written. This program takes the preprocessed HTML files, and converts them to text files with a small amount of markup: each article is assigned an identifier, marked up using <DOCNO>, </DOCNO> tags; the actual content of the article is enclosed within <TEXT> and </TEXT> tags; paragraphs are separated by blank lines. An example of a marked-up file is shown in Fig. 7.1. These files were then passed through a post-processing stage, where certain articles such as fictional features were deleted from the corpus.

The following table compares the size of the final Anandabazar corpus with the older DoE corpus. As can be seen, the new corpus is about five times larger than the DoE corpus in terms of number of words contained. The next section presents more statistics about the corpus.

```
<DOC>
<DOCNO>1010709_9kol6.pc</DOCNO>
<TEXT>
২৪ আষাঢ় ১৪০৮ সোমবার ৯ জুলাই ২০০১

অফিসপাড়ায় আগুন

স্টাফ রিপোর্টার

রবিবার ভোরে মহাকরণের পিছনে একটি বহুতলের ১০ তলায় আগুন লাগে। আগুনে পাঁচ-
ছ'টি অফিসের জিনিসপত্র পুড়ে যায়। দমকলের ১০টি ইঞ্জিন গিয়ে ছ' ঘণ্টার চেষ্টায় আগুন
আয়ত্তে আনে। প্রাথমিক তদন্তে দমকল অফিসারদের ধারণা, শীততাপনিয়ন্ত্রণ যন্ত্র থেকে
আগুন লাগে। সেই আগুন ছড়িয়ে পড়ে। আগুনে হতাহতের কোনও খবর পাওয়া যায়নি।
পুলিশ ও দমকল সূত্রে জানা গিয়েছে, এই দিন ভোর সোয়া ৫ টার সময় কোল ইণ্ডিয়া
ভবনের উল্টো দিকে ২৩ এ নেতাজি সুভাষ রোডের একটি ১২ তলা ভবনের ১০ তলায়
আগুন দেখা যায়। এই বহুতলে সরকারি-বেসরকারি মিলিয়ে প্রায় ৩০০ অফিস ভাড়া
রয়েছে।
</TEXT>
</DOC>
```

Fig. 7.1: A typical document of the Anandabazar corpus.

7.4.3 *Toolkit*

In order to be really useful to language researchers, a corpus has to be shareable or distributable. Researchers can then conduct various studies using the same body of text, and compare their findings. Unfortunately, since the Anandabazar corpus consists of copyrighted material, we do not have the distribution rights for this corpus[i]. However, the content is publicly available on the Web. We have therefore constructed a freely available toolkit (written in Microsoft Visual C++ version 5, and tested on Windows9x, 2000, XP) that can be used by interested researchers to create a copy of

---

[i] The publisher is currently considering a proposal to make the corpus publicly available for research purposes.

Table 7.1: A comparison of the DoE and Anandabazar corpora

	No. of words	Unique words	No. of documents
DoE	3,500,000	183,000	1,274
Anandabazar	17,238,792	305,568	53,049

the corpus locally from the content available on the Web. The toolkit consists of the following components:

1. Font code to ISCII converter: The converter takes care of converting the font encoded content in the original HTML pages to the ISCII character coding scheme. It also strips off the unnecessary portions of the HTML page and replaces it by the simple markup scheme mentioned above.
2. Corpus cleaner/postprocessor: This module eliminates those files that should not be included in the corpus, e.g. the horoscope, weather, and fiction pages. It is also possible to set a threshold with respect to file size, so that only those documents which are longer than the threshold are retained.
3. Statistical tool: This component contains code to calculate the various statistics reported in this paper.
4. Browser: This provides an interface where a Bangla document can be viewed and edited.

7.5 Statistical Analysis

Some basic statistical information about the corpus is presented in Table 7.2

7.5.1 Document Statistics

Table 7.2 shows that the variation in document lengths is noticeable. Documents vary between 175 bytes and nearly 28 Kbytes in length, with a mean length of about 2 Kbytes and a *standard deviation of over 1 Kbyte*.

To give an idea of the diversity of subjects covered by the articles in the corpus, Table 7.3 shows the most frequently occurring broad categories of documents in the corpus, along with the number of documents in these categories.

Table 7.2: Basic statistics about the Anandabazar corpus

Corpus Size		Document Length Statistics	
Size in Mbytes	112	Minimum	175 bytes
No. of documents	53,048	Maximum	27,988 bytes
Word-level Statistics		Mean	2,217 bytes
Total no. of words	17,176,286	Median	1,810 bytes
No. of distinct words	308,554	Mode	2,219 / 511 bytes
Avg. word length	4.34 bytes	Standard deviation	1,724
Avg. sentence length	12		

Table 7.3: Most frequently occurring categories in the corpus

10424 Rajya (state news)	7037 Khela (sports news)	2503 Editorial
9723 Kolkata (city news)	2913 Business	550 Rabimela (Sunday spls.)
7687 Desh (national news)	2702 Bidesh(foreign news)	265 Music

7.5.2 *Sentence and Word-level Statistics*

The distribution of sentence lengths (in number of words) and word lengths (in bytes) is shown in the Fig. 7.2. Most words are between 4 and 5 bytes long. This observation is in agreement with the statistics reported earlier by Dash and Chaudhuri[12].

A marked difference between the DoE corpus and this corpus is that the average sentence length is more than 1.5 times that in the DoE corpus. On average, a sentence in this corpus contains 12.40 words, whereas for the DoE corpus, the number was 8. We conclude that the style of writing used in news stories uses longer sentences than usual. Fig. 7.3 shows two example sentences from the Anandabazar corpus, with sentences consisting of 31 and 56 words respectively.

Table 7.4 shows a list of the 20 most frequent words occurring in this corpus. The most frequently used words in this corpus are [o] followed by [na]. Interestingly, both words are polysemous and have varied usages. Note that all the words listed are function words or *stopwords*, i.e. they are

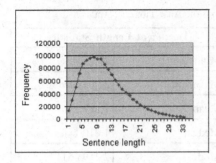 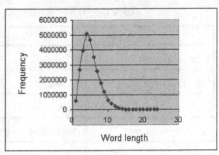

Fig. 7.2: Distribution of sentence and word lengths.

সূর্যোদয় দেড় টাকা, বৃষ্টিপাত ২০ পয়সা, তাপমাত্রা ৫০ পয়সা, বাশ্পীভবনের পরিমাণ এক টাকা-আবহাওয়া সংক্রান্ত এই তথ্যগুলি বিভিন্ন বেসরকারি সংস্থা ও ব্যক্তির কাছে এই দরেই বিক্রি শুরু করেছে রাজ্যের কৃষি দফতর।

অর্থ দফতরের অনুমতি ছাড়া গঙ্গা ভাঙ্গন রোধের দফতর (দুনম্বর ডিভিশন) একটি গাড়ির জন্য দু'লক্ষ, বহরমপুর সেচ দফতর একটি গাড়ির জন্য ১.২০ লক্ষ হাজার টাকা, দামোদর সেচ বিভাগ দু'টি গাড়ির জন্য ২.৭৮ লক্ষ টাকা, কাঁথিতে একটি গাড়ির জন্য ২.১২ লক্ষ এবং তিস্তা খাল প্রকল্পের সদর বিভাগে তিনটি গাড়ির জন্য ৩ লক্ষ ২০ হাজার টাকা খরচ করা হয়েছে।

Fig. 7.3: Example of long sentences in the corpus.

not related to the subject matter of the documents in which they occur. In other words, they cannot be used as keywords to index any document. This also suggests a straightforward method for constructing a stopword list that can be used in a Bangla IR system: (i) a list of the *n* (usually 300 - 400) most frequently occurring words is constructed; (ii) the list is manually checked and potential keywords are eliminated from the list of stopwords.

In contrast to the most frequently occurring words (which are stopwords), the most frequently occurring word bi-grams and tri-grams are often useful as key-phrases that may be used to index documents. Table 7.5 lists some of the word bi-grams and tri-grams that occur most frequently in the corpus.

Table 7.4: List of 20 most frequent words

Freq.	% Corpus	Term		Freq.	% Corpus	Term	
196397	1.14	ও	ভ্গল্ক্ষ	69043	0.40	নিয়ে	ভ্ললন্দ্ক্ষ
144100	0.84	না	ভ্দ্ক্ষ	65552	0.38	এবং	ভ্জ্লন্দ্ক্ষ
144033	0.84	এই	ভ্ন্দ্নন্ক্ষ	64639	0.37	হয়	ভ্ড়ল্প্ঠৈক্ষ
114264	0.66	করে	ভ্লপ্জন্দ্ব্ক্ষ	64378	0.37	কোনও	ভ্লক্গুচ্ঠক্ষ
109030	0.63	থেকে	ভ্0্দ্লন্দ্ব্ক্ষ	61646	0.36	তার	ভ্ব্জ্ক্ষ
95839	0.56	এ	ভ্ন্দ্ক্ষ	61539	0.36	তা	ভ্ব্ক্ষ
78925	0.46	এক	ভ্জল্ক্ষ	60182	0.35	সেই	ভ্ব্ন্দ্নক্ষ
72750	0.42	যে	ভ্ব্ত্ব্লন্দ্ক্ষ	60043	0.35	কিন্তু	ভ্ললন্দ্ব্ড়ক্ষ
72437	0.42	আর	ভ্জ্জক্ষ	57280	0.33	জন্য	ভ্ব্ত্ব্গুল্লক্ষ
70528	0.41	সঙ্গে	ভ্ব্ক্গুল্দ্ধক্ষ	54045	0.31	হয়েছে	ভ্ড়ল্ন্দ্ব্ত্ত্রভ্ড়ক্ষ

It is clear that all these "phrases" can be used as key-phrases to index the documents in which they occur. In fact, for English, this technique of identifying useful multi-word indexing units (usually termed *phrases*), based on simply counting the frequency of word bi-grams or tri-grams and selecting all bi-/tri-grams that occur often enough as potential key-phrases, has been shown to be as effective as more sophisticated techniques based on syntactic processing[13].

7.6 Conclusion and Future Work

This paper describes the construction of a large corpus of Bangla news articles, the first of its kind. Such a corpus is expected to fulfill a long- standing need of the language research community interested in working on Indic languages. The construction process consists essentially of acquiring textual material from the web, and storing the text in a "standard" character-encoding scheme. Some basic statistical information about the corpus has also been presented; information about the frequency of single words and word bi-grams and tri-grams can be useful for building components of an IR system, e.g. stopword lists, and list of candidate key-phrases.

Table 7.5: Some frequently occurring word bi- and tri-grams

Bengali Phrase	Translation	Remarks
স্টাফ রিপোর্টার	staff reporter	
নিজস্ব সংবাদদাতা	our correspondent	
রাজ্য সরকার	state government	
বুদ্ধদেব ভট্টাচার্য্য	Buddhadeb Bhattacharya	name of the Chief Minister
লক্ষ টাকা	lakh Rupees	monetary amount
হাসপাতালে ভর্তি	hospital admission	
কেন্দ্রীয় সরকার	Central Government	
মুখ্যমন্ত্রী বুদ্ধদেব ভট্টাচার্য্য	Chief Minister Buddhadeb Bhattacharya	
দক্ষিন ২৪ পরগনা	South 24 Parganas	name of a district
১৪ জৈষ্ঠ ১৪০৯	14th Jaishtha 1409	date string
পাকিস্থানের প্রেসিডেন্ট মুসারফ	Pakistan's President Musharraf	
রাজ্য সম্পাদক অনিল	State Secretary Anil	
নীলরতন সরকার মেডিকেল	Nilratan Sarkar Medical	name of a college
প্রধানমন্ত্রী অটলবিহারী বাজপাই	Prime Minister Atal Behari Vajpayee	
বিশ্ব হিন্দু পরিষদ	Vishwa Hindu Parishad	name of an organization

In order to use this corpus for IR/IE research, some amount of supplementary information/annotation is needed. A set of about 30 sample queries has been constructed. We are currently in the process of collecting relevance judgments for these queries. For this purpose, we have adopted the *pooling* methodology used at TREC. A number of diverse retrieval strategies are used to retrieve 100 (say) documents for a given query. A *document pool* is constructed for each query by taking the union of all the documents retrieved for that query by the various strategies. This pool is then manually inspected and relevance assessments are made.

Besides the basic IR task of retrieving relevant documents in response to a query, there are a number of other information-processing problems for which a corpus is a useful resource. Research efforts on these problems typically use a news corpus for experimentation (see the TREC proceedings for more details). For example, *Topic Detection and Tracking (TDT)* is a challenging task where a system has to first identify, or *detect,* those news stories that discuss an event or topic that has not already been reported in earlier stories. Topic tracking consists of starting with a few sample stories and finding all subsequent reports that discuss the same topic. Since the Anandabazar corpus contains news articles from 2001 and 2002, it has stories covering the major national and international events of that time, e.g. the 11th September bombing of the World Trade Center, and may be used as a test-corpus for TDT experiments. Similarly, the corpus, suitably annotated, can serve as an experimental test-bed for document categorization and filtering. News articles are also a rich source of proper nouns and can thus be used for training and testing Named Entity Identification (NEI) techniques.

If the corpus is further supplemented by a comparable corpus in another language (say English), the pair of corpora will prove to be a vital resource for research on Cross-Lingual Information Access and Retrieval (CLIA/ CLIR) and related problems. For example, a pair of comparable Bengali and English corpora may be used to construct a basic named-entity identifier (NEI) for Bengali. Using one of the publicly available NEIs for English, a set of NEs could be identified in the English corpus. These could then be transliterated into phonetically similar Bengali strings. We could then tag as NEs words in the Bengali corpus that approximately match the strings obtained by transliteration. Experimental results show that more than 60% of the English names can be correctly identified in Bengali text using this approach (details of this study have been reported by Majumder *et al.*[14].

Such enhancements, along with extensive annotation of the corpus (with relevance judgments, parts of speech information, named entities, subject categories, etc.) are expected to be completed under an initiative launched by the Government of India in 2006 (*http://tdil.mit.gov.in/*). The final annotated corpus is expected to even more useful as a resource for applied language research in Bangla.

References

1   Wong, K.F. and Tsujii, J. (eds.) (2003), *ACM Transactions on Asian Language Information Processing (TALIP)*, **2**(2), **2**(3), ACM Press.

2   Gey, F., Kando, N. and Peters, C. (2002), Workshop reports: cross language information retrieval: a research roadmap, *ACM SIGIR Forum*, **36**(2).

3   Baker, P. and McEnery, A. (1998), Needs of language-engineering communities: corpus building and translation resources, *MILLE working paper 7*, Lancaster University.

4   Dash, N. and Chaudhuri, B.B. (2000), The process of designing a multidisciplinary monolingual sample corpus, *International Journal of Corpus Linguistics*, **5**(2), pp.179-197, John Benjamins.

5   Voorhees, E.M. (1998), Variations in relevance judgments and the measurement of retrieval effectiveness, *Proceedings of the 21st annual international ACM SIGIR conference on research and development in information retrieval*, pp.315-323.

6   Text REtrieval Conference, *http://trec.nist.gov/*.

7   Chinchor, N. (1997), Overview of MUC-7, *Proceedings of the 7th Message Understanding Conference*, *http://www.itl.nist.gov/iad/894.02/related_projects/muc/index.html*.

8   Peters, C. (2005), *What happened in CLEF 2005?* Introduction to the Working Notes, *Working Notes for the CLEF 2005 Workshop*.

9   Kando, N. (2002), Overview of the Third NTCIR Workshop, *Proceedings of the 3rd NTCIR Workshop*, *http://research.nii.ac.jp/ntcir/workshop/OnlineProceedings3/*.

10 Becker, D. and Riaz, K. (2002), A study in Urdu corpus construction, *Proceedings of the 3rd Workshop on Asian Language Resources and International Standardization*, COLING-02

11 ISCII Standard, *http://tdil.mit.gov.in/standards.htm*.

12 Dash, *op.cit.*

13 Mitra, M., Buckley, C., Singhal, A. and Cardie, C. (1997), An Analysis of Statistical and Syntactic Phrases. *Proc. 5th RIAO Conference on Computer-Assisted Research of Information*, pp.200-214.

14 Majumder, P., Mitra, M., Sarkar, N., Mitra, P. and Datta, K. (2006), Bengali Name Identification Using A Noisy Comparable Corpus, *Proc. Intl. Conf. on Emerging Applications of IT (EAIT)*, pp.41-44. Elsevier Press.

Chapter 8

Heritage Preservation in Digital Way — A Contemporary Research Issue

A. Chatterjee[1] and S.G. Dhande[1]

[1]Cad Laboratory
Indian Institute of Technology
Kanpur, India
{achat, sgd}@iitk.ac.in

Abstract

The present paper discusses the work of digitization of cultural heritage of India. Non-contact digitizing system is the only practical choice for high resolution scanning of sculptures and artifacts. They collect from 20 to more than 25,000 points per second and provide resolution of better than 0.001-inch to 0.020-inch, depending on technology. T1his work is carried out at Indian Institute of Technology, Kanpur and in Allahabad University and focuses mainly on Buddhist deities Hariti and Gajlaxmi. We will discuss about the digitization of these artifacts, concept of Rapid Prototyping, Reverse Engineering. In the paper we will also discuss the detail of the development of the Rapid Prototype of Buddha statue in FDM (Fused Deposition Modeling). Certain research issues pertaining to reconstruction and databases are also discussed.

Keywords: Digitization, Non contact, Triangulation, Rapid Prototyping, Reverse Engineering, Fused Deposition Modeling (FDM), Digital Watermarking.

8.1 Introduction

Heritage as it is defined in Webster's dictionary "a tradition etc. handed down from one's ancestors or the past", is any nation's reckoning about its people, culture, behavior etc. Right from Harrapa- Mohendojoro civilization in Indus Valley in Indian sub continent to Maya Culture in Mexico, it bears the signs and symbols of a nation's glorious past. It also indicates how a nation did in past in areas of science, education, culture etc. Heritage is an insight in the valid facets of any country's history, religious and cultural contrasts and its indigenous lifestyles still untouched by the trappings of modernity. Indian civilization is over 6000 years old and its culture is a medley of amazing diversities and starling contradictions, but above all, it represents the multifaceted aspects of India as a whole.

Around the fourth century A.D.[1], Chinese traveler Fa-Hien visited Mathura, a place 180 KM east of New Delhi. He has mentioned in his notes that about twenty monasteries existing at that time on both sides of the river Yamuna where about three thousand monks used to meditate. The second Chinese traveler, Hien-Tsang, came to India in about seventh century A.D. and also noted about these monasteries and about two thousands monks living there. So there are lot of Buddha and other Hindu sculptures excavated and some of them are in the process of decay now.

Our cultural heritage is slowly eroding, "explains Learning Sites president, Donald H. Sanders". Ancient archaeological sites have been vandalized and damaged, and most of them naturally erode over time. Visual representations of those sites, like slides or photographs, suffer from image degradation after many years. Thus, what we are witnessing is not only the deterioration of the actual antiquities themselves, but also of the only surviving original visual records of those monuments. Sites once accessible to scholars and the visiting public are rapidly disappearing and, as photographic emulsion peels off old glass plates at an alarming rate, documentation of these places is disappearing as well. So a new need has been felt for documentation and obtaining geometrical model in the field of cultural heritage[2-3].

Many of the most exciting area of research lie between and across the boundaries of traditional discipline and the greatest challenges for our society need to be met by a marriage of the arts and humanities with science.

8.1.1 Kausambi School of Art

Kausambi[4] was the capital of *Chedi-vatsa areas*, one of the prominent areas into which the Indo-Aryan people were divided, and the scene of several important events in the Buddha's life. It has one of Asoka's pillar and a little further on the ruins of the Ghositarama, first built during the Buddha's lifetime. The huge ancient ramparts of the city though now all in ruins are also interesting. The earlier specimens of art have their close parallel in *Bharhut* and *Sanchi* and deal with events and scenes in Buddha's life. They are in low relief and the treatment, on the whole, in archaic. The nativity scene on a plaque is one of the earliest depictions of Buddha's Birth in Indian art.

8.2 Objectives

The present work is related to the development of a tool using all the modern and high-end technologies namely CAD, Reverse Engineering, Rapid Prototyping. The objective of the work is divided into the following tasks[5]:

- Scan the Sculpture/model using high quality digital scanner and test the design, using computer aided engineering analysis.
- To record and archive morphological features of heritage artifacts
- To do the research work and explore the potential of 3D vision for applications in heritage or as an input to virtual reality environments,
- Visualize product with Rapid Prototyping.
- Make changes in the design as per original model requirements and finalize it.

Technology under study will allow artists, sculptors, archaeologists, and researchers to view, analyze, and even reproduce artifacts digitally. As an initial demonstration sculptures made out of clay were digitized using an optical scanner and digital models created. The models thus created can form archives, which could be manipulated at any time to view, edit or fabricate.

8.3 Methodology

8.3.1 Data Collection

Scanning is a procedure of capturing the points, which collectively depicts the outer geometry of an object. There are various scanners available for 3D scanning e.g. 3D optical scanner, Laser scanner, Touch probe mechanical scanner etc. In the present study ATOS 3D optical scanner of GOM is used. (Fig. 8.1: ATOS Scanner)

Measuring procedure of ATOS scanner is as follows[6]: The ATOS head is mounted on a tripod or stand and is positioned freehanded in front of the measuring object. There is no need for additional hardware like for example table feed motion setups or robots. The measurement consists of projecting different fringe patterns onto the object's surface using a white light projection unit and capturing these patterns by two integrated cameras at either side of the sensor head. In some seconds the ATOS software calculates precise 3D coordinates of up to several million-object points. The result of each measurement is directly displayed. The system monitors both its calibration and the influence of environmental conditions by itself, so that reliable, precise and fast measurements can be made, even under rough conditions. All measurements are automatically transformed into a common object coordinate system. The complete 3D data set can then be exported using standard file formats for an easy post processing.

8.3.2 Point Cloud Processing

8.3.2.1 Alignment

The point cloud of the objects overlaps in various places when displayed in the 3D windows. Due to the system dependent measuring errors, we may get gaps between the clouds. Alignment operation is used to align point cloud in such a way that the gaps between them are minimized.

8.3.2.2 Merging

After the alignment of the various scanned views of the object, merging is done to get a consensus surface of the object. Once this consensus

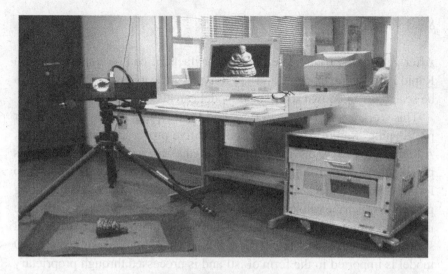

Fig. 8.1: ATOS standard digital optical scanner.

data is available we can get do the polygonization to get the triangulated data file.

8.3.2.3 *Polygonization*

A point cloud can be converted into triangle mesh without overlapping areas. Depending upon the surface finish the triangles are of various sizes. An even surface is described with large triangles, uneven areas with small triangles.

8.3.2.4 Hole Filling

If there are holes in the surface, they are filled. Hole filling basically uses the method of triangulation or surface fitting to calculate the extra points to fill the hole area. The triangulation method computes the points taking the boundary of the hole and generates almost a planer surface to fill the hole while surface-fitting method takes the neighboring surface nature of the hole into consideration to compute the points to fill the hole.

8.3.3 Prototyping

After getting the triangulated data of artifacts, it can be imported into a Rapid Prototyping machine and a prototype can be made. Artifacts can also be scaled up and down so a scaled model can also be obtained.

This work uses Stratasys FDM Rapid Prototyping System (Fig. 8.2) for prototyping. Rapid Prototyping uses additive process for model making. Additive process is the exact reverse of the subtractive process .In this process material is manipulated so that successive portion of it combines to form the desired object[7]. Rapid Prototyping is a Layer by layer manufacturing process in which the whole model is divided into horizontal layers and machine makes the prototype building these layers on one upon another. The Fig. 8.2 shows the Stratasys FDM1650 RP Machine[8]. In Stratasys system, the CAD model is imported in the form of .stl and is processed through proprietary software Insight. This software sliced the 3D model into horizontal layers after the part is oriented for optimum build position and any support structure is automatically detected and generated by software. The slice thickness can be set anywhere between 0.051 to 0.762 mm. Tool path of the build process is generated, which is downloaded to the FDM machine[8].

Fig. 8.2: Stratasys FDM1650 rapid prototyping system.

Creation of prototype from 3D digitized model is schematically represented below.

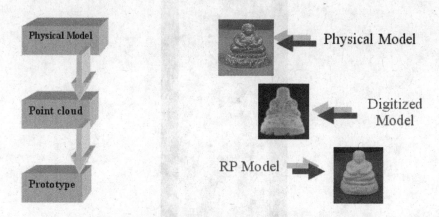

Fig. 8.3: Pictorial representation of reverse engineering process.

8.4 Some Research Findings

8.4.1 Sculptures and their Quantitative Information

Squeezing Lady (Fig. 8.4) is also a good depiction of a 2nd Century lady. Buddha's Lamp is one of the great findings of Allahabad University archaeologists. This lamp was in the form of Lotus. It was donated by Bhikshu Dharmpradipa to be used in Gandh-Kuti; a room where the Buddha had resided inside the monastery. There is an inscription at the bottom of the lamp. *"Venerable Dharmpradip, the Sakya-Bhiksu"*. To the best of my

Table 8.1: Related information of squeezing lady

Sculpture Material	Red Sand
Height	61 cm
Period	2nd Century
Total points obtained (After processing)	3,00,000
Processing Time	2 Hrs
Time taken to scan	4.5 Hrs

Fig. 8.4: Point cloud data of squeezing lady.

knowledge, this lamp is the only lamp available today in the whole world. This is a meritorious gift in honour of lord Buddha for the Gandh-Kuti at Ghositarama. Fig. 8.5 shows the point cloud data of Lamp and information related to point cloud is given in Table 8.2.

Table 8.2: Related information of lamp

Sculpture Material	Clay (Terracotta)
Height	18 cm
Total points (after processing)	5,98,710
Processing Time	1.5 Hrs
Time taken to scan	2 Hrs

8.4.2 Standing Buddha

This is an important and valuable artifact depicting the standing figure of Lord Buddha. It is made of Red stone. Fig. 8.6 shows the point cloud data of standing Buddha and information related to point cloud is given in Table 8.3.

Fig. 8.5: Point cloud data of the lamp of Lord Buddha.

Table 8.3: Related information of Buddha

Sculpture Material	Red Stone
Height	49 cm
Total points obtained	18,06,131
Processing Time	2 Hrs
Time taken to scan	2.5 Hrs

Fig. 8.6: Point cloud data of standing Lord Buddha.

8.4.3 Deity Gajalaxmi

Kausambi is deservedly famous for its terracotta art. Gajagamini constitute a classic in Indian Terracotta art. It anticipates the superb modeling of sculptures of the succeeding period. Fig. 8.7 shows the point cloud data of Deity Gajlaxmi and information related to point cloud is given in Table 8.4.

Table 8.4: Related information of Deity Gajlaxmi

Sculpture Material	Clay (Terracotta)
Height	73 cm
Total points obtained (before processing)	2,21,23,660
Processing Time	6 Hrs
Time taken to scan	4 Hrs

Fig. 8.7: Point cloud data of Deity Gajlaxmi.

8.5 Research Issues

8.5.1 Cataloguing of 3D Digital Data

An important research issue is to find out the way to catalogue the 3D digital data. If the 3D data is centrally archived or to some extent even if they are not, techniques are required for indexing the work with in each client library. There is a great need to create graphical catalogue for the digitized art. In case of 2-D images local indexing may be done by catalogue containing thumbnail images. In case of 3D data thumbnail should be interactive allowing the library user to examine the work from all the angles. They should be light weighted for browsing on a low cost PC or even in a laptop. Unfortunately computer capable of rotating 3D model in real time are expensive and even a low detail. 3D models of complex object require huge funding both in hardware and software.

8.5.2 Storage Problem for Enormous 3D Data

There are several research problems associated with 3-D scanning. It provides large data sets. During our scanning in Mathura and Allahabad University museum we acquired a data of 20 GB by scanning 32 sculptures. Creating .stl model out of it will produce another 10 GB. In this way if we create archive of all artifacts in museum it may produce more than terabytes of data. The enormous size of 3D archive makes it unlikely that a library will be maintaining the local copies of them. Certainly on-line storage is out of the question. At the current price of Rs. 100 per GB disc, it will take Rs. 50,000 to keep the 500 GB of database. No library can be able to spend so much money for a single work. It has proposed that 3D data must be stored centrally and distributed on demand to libraries.

8.5.3 3D Digital Watermarking

Recently, much interest is being taken in methods to protect the copyright of digital data and preventing illegal duplication of it[10]. However, in the area of CAD/CAM and Computer Graphics, there are no effective ways to protect the copyright of 3D geometric models. The 3D geometric model, such as surface model, solid model or polygonal model can be recognized as valuable products of intellectual activities in CAD, CAM and Computer Graphics systems. The current situation of the distributed engineering environment increases opportunities to exchange digital data of geometric models between various organizations through Internet. It also increases the possibility of theft of the geometric model by duplication. Therefore the copyrights of the geometric model must be strongly protected from theft. However, so far, almost all current digital watermarking techniques are only focused on the copyright protection of digital text, image, video and sound data. And very little research on digital watermarking for 3D geometric models has been done. Watermarking is one of the copyright protection methods where an invisible watermark is secretly embedded into the original data[11].

8.5.4 Life of Digital Data

Another research issue is the method of storing 3-D models. In the 2D works the images can be printed on the paper at high resolution and saved. In the event of a digital achieve becomes unreadable or un-decodable, it can be re-constructed. 3D model have no natural printed representation. Rapid prototyping technology could be used to make physical replicas but the cost of making such replicas is also high. The replicas do not capture color or surface finish and we cannot make of large objects also. Thus it is important to preserve digital model themselves. Due to size and complexity of the 3D models techniques that are being developed for achieving digital information will have to be extended.

8.6 Conclusion

In India, from 600 century B.C. to 4th century B.C. there was well-established kingdom and golden era in every walk of life in general and arts in particular. The art reached its peak during 325 A.D to 600 A.D during Gupta period[12]. Expression of celestial happiness, love and kindness were chiseled out and a concrete form was given to stone. A straight nose, elongated horizontal eyes, sharp curved eyebrows and other super human features can easily be experienced in these sculptures. Therefore, it is indeed a calling of this century how to preserve these art forms, which are thousands years old and so rich in its depiction and beauty. The methodology and process to preserve the artifacts and sculptures have been established, using the technology available today.

But this process needs more refinements and some algorithm needs to be developed to reconstruct or regenerate the sculptures. It has been seen in many times during excavation process the statues or sculpture gets damaged or a statue or sculptures of some very ancient ages like 320 B.C. excavated in deformed state, so one needs to develop some methodology to regenerate these artifacts in original form. It calls for an algorithm to be developed in general to heal the geometrical model found damaged or disfigured. Research is undergoing now to develop the algorithm that will take care of the problem and preservation of heritage in a virtual way will be cent percent successful once the research is complete and produce desired outcome.

8.7 Acknowledgement

This work was funded by the Info-Sculpture project of Media Lab Asia program of Ministry of Communication and Information Technology, Government of India. We also acknowledge to Allahabad University for extending their support to carry out the scanning in their museum. Our special thanks go to Prof. Rai, Senior Professor and Head of the Ancient History Department of Allahabad University for providing all the help for this research.

References

1 Prasad, J. (1952), *Master Pieces from Mathura Museum*, New Age Publishing, Darya Ganj, New Delhi, p.182

2 Miyazaki, Daisuke, Ooishi, Takeshi, Nishikawa, Taku, Sagawa, Ryusuke, Nishino, Ko, Tomomatsu, Takashi, Takase, Yutaka and Ikeuchi, Katsushi, The Great Buddha Project: Modeling Cultural Heritage through Observation, CAD Center, Tokyo, Japan, *http:// www.cvl.iis.u-tokyo.ac.jp/papers/all/0031.pdf*

3 Digital Michel Angelo Project: Stanford University, *http://graphics.standard.edu/ projects/mich/*

4 Sharma, G.R. (1980), *History to Prehistory: Archaeology of the Ganga Valley and the Vindhyas*, (General Editor: Sharma, G.R., Editorial Board: Clark, J.D. and Thapar, B.K., Managing Editor: Mandal, D.) Allahabad, Department of Ancient History, Culture, and Archaeology.

5 *http://www.iitk.ac.in/MLAsia/infosculpt.htm*

6 *ATOS Users Manual*

7 Kai, Chua Chee, Fai, Leong Kah, *Rapid Prototyping*, John Wiley & Sons, p.17, 94.

8 *www.stratasys.com*

9 *ibid.*

10 Kanai, Satoshi, Date, Hiroaki and Kishinami, Takeshi, Digital Watermarking for 3D Polygons using Multiresolution Wavelet decomposition, *Proc. Sixth IFIP WG 5.2 GEO-6, 1998,* Hokkaido University, Japan, *http://minf.coin.eng.hokudai.ac.jp/members/kanai/wm1-geo6.pdf*

11 *ibid.*

12 Prasad, *op.cit.*

Chapter 9

Digitising European Renaissance Prints — A 3-year Experiment on Image and Text Retrieval

Marie-Luce Demonet[1]

[1]*François-Rabelais University*
Tours, Centre National de la Recherche Scientifique, France
marie-luce.demonet@univ-tours.fr

Abstract

This paper presents an overview of an on-going study on digitization of old European renaissance documents at CESR, the research centre with which the author is attached. Three collections of digital resources are being developed at the CESR: Musicology (dealing with a corpus of Renaissance Songs), Architecture for Art History and the BVH program (Virtual Humanistic Libraries). The BVH contains a selection of Renaissance books located in different departmental libraries. The significant items that are so far not digitized by other libraries are selected. About 2,000 books (comprising of about 800,000 pages) out of about 50,000 books have been scanned by the CESR in collaboration with others. However, preservation of these documents is not the only requirement of this project. It also attempts to provide some kind of access inside the images of the texts. Document's images are classified into different groups mainly based on to the format (for printed material) like folios, quartos, octavos, etc. Books are further classified according to their graphic contents (e.g. medical books with large anatomy engravings, technical books with schemas, folk books with used woodcuts, maps and atlas, cosmographies, and so on). An application called AGORA (Analyseur Graphique pour OuvRages Anciens = Graphic analyzer for rare books) is used for primary structure analysis and segmentation of imaged documents. Indexing of documents makes use of the key-words coming from the Iconclass thesaurus, a set of semantically and hierarchically organized trees of keywords describing the works of art and ornaments, down to the smallest details, actions, foregrounds and backgrounds. Manuscripts zones are described mainly with metadata and annotations, and eventually with the same topics. In future, the names of personalities are also to be indexed as for mythological entities, with an alphanumeric number, to allow multiple queries inside collections of artifacts, book illustrations, archives, paintings, etc. Therefore, in the website of BVH, the images will comprise not only text in image form, but all the graphic elements extracted from the digitized documents, properly indexed and accessible by means of a double standard search engine, connected to the Iconclass thesaurus. Simultaneous visualisation of images and texts, will be rendered possible by the organization of metadata and XML/TEI encoding. However, in doing so, the first challenge is to build and connect a network of databases linked to the Iconclass thesaurus, so that one can find any item in any base from a range of hierarchized keywords and provide immediate access to the images the user is looking for. The second challenge is the treatment of multinlingualism offered by Iconclass. And final challenge is to test automatic procedures of encoding: until now, encoding is done by hand; but with automatic image retrieval and similarity analysis (processed in Tours), one can expect to save time-consuming encoding.

Keywords: Page Layout, Renaissance OCR, Thesaurus, Image Identification, Text Encoding.

9.1 Introduction and the Tours Centre for Renaissance Studies

The Tours Centre for Renaissance Studies (Centre d'Études Supérieures de la Renaissance, CESR, Tours) is a research institute for humanities, a department belonging to the University François-Rabelais and to the French National Centre for Scientific Research (Centre National de la Recherche Scientifique, CNRS UMR 6576). It was created in 1956, based on the previous model of the Centre for Studies in Medieval Civilisation in Poitiers. It is specialised in interdisciplinary studies (philosophy, European languages and literatures, musicology, history, art history, history of the book, history of sciences) and is devoted to the period stretching from the late Middle Ages to Early Modern times (1400-1650), from Petrarch to Descartes. At present, a total of some 44 researchers work at the Centre, along with more than 20 adjunct researchers belonging to other laboratories or universities.

This institute for higher education is also a teaching facility for about 150 postgraduate students, 50 of whom are doctoral candidates. The two-year Master's programme is specialised in Renaissance studies, including required coursework in history of the book. For the second year, students can choose a traditional programme that is based on coursework and research, or they may choose a professional programme, which provides an initiation to library science and to digitisation of rare or fragile documents.

The Centre supports several interdisciplinary projects, three of which deal particularly with digitisation: 1) in musicology ('Images of music'), an EU-funded project in 2001-2003 for a Corpus of Renaissance Songs, and from there other projects of digitising manuscripts and books of music have also developed (directed by P. Vendrix); 2) in architecture ('Architectura', http://www.cesr.univ-tours.fr/architectura/index.asp), with a digitisation project of 300 books, treatises on architecture of the sixteenth and seventeenth centuries, started in 2003 (directed by Y. Pauwels and F. Lemerle) in collaboration with the National Institute for Art History and the National Art School in Paris; 3) in literature, the 'BVH' program, or 'Bibliothèques Virtuelles Humanistes' (Virtual Humanistic Libraries, *http://www.bvh.univ-tours.fr*), directed by Marie-Luce Demonet, also started in 2003 in collaboration with several public and research libraries[1-4]. Other databases joined the BVH website during the year 2008:

- 'De *Minute en Minute*', transcribed archives of notaries, coming from public repositories (*http://193.52.215.193/Minutes/presentation.htm*), directed by Pierre Aquilon (who is also director of the national Incunabula Catalogue);
- *Dionis* (digitised database of Renaissance medical books of the University Library in Tours, *http://193.52.215.193/Dionis/index.asp*), directed by Jacqueline Vons, in collaboration with the Medical Library in Paris (BIUM)[i];
- The French database for sixteenth century texts, '*Epistemon*', with original transcriptions (http://www.cesr.univ-tours.fr/Epistemon/index.htm), started by M.-L. Demonet in Poitiers in 1998.
- The Rabelais database, previously on a server at the University of Nice (*http://lolita.unice.fr*)

Currently, the Centre has its own research library, with more than 55,000 titles, 4000 of them being rare books, from the sixteenth century and later. The first two digitised books (in 2000) came from this collection: *De humani corporis fabrica* by Vesalius (1543) and *De laudibus sanctae crucis* by Raban Maur (1503), a post-incunabulum famous for its illustrations. This initial experiment has shown both the promise and the limits of raw digitisation: further research is needed to enhance the possibilities made available by such a tool, owing to proper encoding and indexing, query software, and tools for analysis.

---

[i] Bibliothèque InterUniversitaire d'odontologie et de Médecine de Paris (Odontologic and Medical Library), belonging to the University of Paris-V.

9.2 The BVH Project

The BVH project is part of a larger plan that envisages preservation of written heritage in general, not only printed texts but also archives and some manuscripts.

The BVH is a virtual library of high-quality digitised documents, containing a selection of Renaissance books located in the departmental libraries of the Région Centre (Orléans, Blois, Tours, Bourges and eight smaller community libraries) and other partners (Poitiers, Lyons, Troyes, The Medical Library in Paris (BIUM), and Bibliothèque Mazarine)[ii]. Between 2003 and 2008, the team selected a first set of interesting titles that are not already digitised by other libraries such as the Bibliothèque nationale de France (BnF, the 'Gallica' website, its digital library, *http://gallica2.bnf.fr/*). In August 2006, the BVH was accepted as a member of the BnF network, and, since December 2006, Gallica has included it in its catalogue[5]. Conversely, and owing to the OAI protocol, the BVH allows researchers to browse the catalogues of the BIUM and Troyes. The new version of Gallica 2 (launched in Autumn 2008), gives access to Gallica's catalogue from the BVH. Through collaboration with the BnF, the BVH program will participate in the European Digital Library project, and will bring its expertise within the field of rare book database processing and harvesting. Moreover, the Centre is also qualified to train students (professional Master's degree candidates) in the procedure of rare document digitisation; several have subsequently been hired in this field.

9.3 Selection of the Corpus

The books digitised within the BVH project were originally printed in many countries of Europe (mainly France, England, Germany, Italy, Switzerland, Spain, and Holland), and they offer a large spectrum of formats, fonts, page layouts, images and illustrations. The selection of 2,000 books — i.e. 800,000 pages — out of about 50,000 owned by regional libraries has been done by

---

[ii] The Bibliothèque Mazarine is an academic library which owns a very rich collection of Renaissance books ; its catalogue is in progress. This library, the BnF and the Bibliothèque de l'Arsenal are the main resources in Paris for the period.

the CESR (Toshinori Uetani) with the collaboration, for classical texts and manuscripts, of another research institute of the CNRS, the IRHT (Institut de Recherche et d'Histoire des Textes, Institute for Research and History of Texts)[iii] located in Paris and Orléans. This collaboration has carried out the digitisation, in Tours, of a first set of 280 volumes (from October 2003 to Decembre 2008), already available online, plus 370 others (200,000 pages) digitised from May 2007 to December 2008 (Tours and Orleans) that must be classified and indexed before being published online. A second call for 200 more books will be launched in June 2008 for another project (Châteauroux and Blois libraries) that started in January 2009. It will probably be necessary to revise our initial ambitions of reaching a total amount of 2,000 volumes before 2010: this target would require immediately hiring four more specialists and technicians. Digitisation itself can be a rather quick process, but verifying the copy, writing the description, and processing the database itself is time-consuming, and an interval of nearly one year is needed between digital acquisition and online publication. This scale has nothing in common with the one million (or more) book projects.

9.4 Digitisation

The laboratory utilises a specific scanner that is mainly intended for rare book collections. It is specialised in high definition results while preserving the old and fragile documents: the books are not flattened under a pane of glass, they can be processed half-opened, so that they do not destroy the binding; pages are turned manually (demonstrations of automatic page flippers do not inspire entrusting fragile documents to them). The CESR organises its own database owing to the pre-processing system: different sets are selected, mainly according to the format (for printed material), folios, quartos, octavos, etc. A second classification separates the books according to their graphical content (except for ornamental letters, which can be found in any book): medical books with large anatomy engravings, technical books with schemas, folk books with woodcuts, maps and atlases, cosmographies, and so on. The scenarios that will be used for image retrieving and indexing

---

[iii] Section of Humanism (Marie-Elisabeth Boutroue).

require this organisation in order to rationalise the process.

The companies that digitise the books within this programme, in parallel with our own digitisations, are asked to use the same kind of scanner with the same requirements. In the laboratory, images of the books are processed by special software (BookRestorer), in order to eliminate line curving and spots if necessary, and quality is assured by a specialised operator, who must show technical skills and have a good knowledge of particularities of early printing. These images, corrected or not, are transmitted to computing partners[iv] for tests and research on image treatment and OCR development (see Fig. 9.1). The computing teams have agreed on a 300 dpi colour standard and light compression (JPEG 2000 at 5 %); between 10 and 20 % of images are randomly and systematically reviewed by the team (not by the company). Delays can occur when the operator misses pages (that is easy to see, but takes a long time to rectify), or when blurred images must be scanned again. The digitisation using a 120° mode avoids any possibility of error on a missing page.

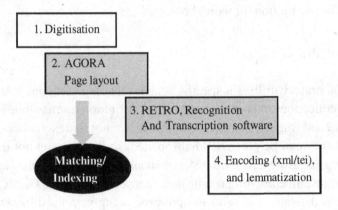

Fig. 9.1: Project levels.

[iv] LI-RFAI (Tours University, Jean-Yves Ramel): AGORA and RETRO software; L3I (University of La Rochelle, Jean-Marc Ogier): matching images, image structure analysis, page layout ; Paris V (Nicole Vincent), Rouen (Pierre Heroux, Thierry Paquet), Rennes (Bertrand Couasnon), Nancy (Antoine Tabbone): manuscript recognition, word spotting, metadata organization ; INRIA (National Institute for Applied Computing, Paris), Jean-Daniel Fekete: document structure, visualisation.

Two levels of quality are achieved: a book can be published online, first with a minimal description and treatment, and a basic pdf format; secondly, with enhanced specificities: pdf with mrc compression, zooming, and image extraction and retrieval, one of the options suggested in the menu. Storage (now on Gold CDs) is already a problem, and will soon be a bigger one: tiff format is not saved any more, as the computing teams do not need it to process the documents; no storage solutions have been decided yet either in France or in Europe, and the cost of keeping, copying and retrieving old files is getting higher and higher. The CDs should be controlled and duplicated every 3 to 5 years, with a copy on a hard drive Raid 5 (10 to 20 to at the present time, on a second server, in use from October 2008).

9.5 Target Documents

The CESR is aware of the standard practices of digital libraries within the communities of research in the humanities: searching, retrieving, modifying, annotating, and creating a personal sub-database, sharing information and knowledge. The present situation requires considerable adaptability: it is important to create routines for efficiency, and also to be very flexible because of the technological evolution expected in the following years. Moreover, taxonomy of historical documents and the corresponding needs of the users (archivists, historians, art historians, literature experts, book historians) being not exactly the same, harmonisation is necessary to obtain a general agreement on basic classification and keywords.

Topics that guide the selection of books are:

- Main European authors (with a special interest in the Rabelais corpus, sources and European adaptations of the time)
- Sources for the history of sciences, technology and medicine
- Law and political literature
- Religious documents (especially from the Reformation and Counter- Reformation)
- Projects based on certain library collections or research projects with a specific aim, such as linguistic books, dictionaries and the first polyglot vocabularies.

This list is by no means definite. Any request from readers, be they scholars or not, is taken into consideration. There is no charge to the reader, but the digitised book is published online. Precise reference is required from users desiring to publish the document, and, if the original belongs to a partner library, the library itself collects the potential fees. All terms concerning copyright and intellectual property were discussed in 2003-2005 with the librarians, collection-holders, and institutions (Universities, CNRS, communities), and a contract has been signed with each of them.

9.6 Layout Analysis and Document Categorization

After using the appropriate software (e.g. BookRestorer) to remove blemishes frequently found in old documents and applying digitisation quality and compression levels, every book is treated by software that is developed by the computing team in Tours (LI-RFAI): AGORA (Analyseur Graphique pour OuvRages Anciens = Graphic analyser for rare books) which gives primary structure analysis and segmentation. It has been used since 2005 by the CESR-BVH and its enhancement speeds up the automatic selection of image and text zones for further treatment[6-10].

AGORA is able to separate the different image zones and to provide specific image databases (Fig. 9.2). The manuscript zones (margin annotations, *ex libris* or possession marks, signatures on the front page, and sometimes interlinear translations or commentaries) can be analysed separately. They are worthy of interest for the identification of printers and authors. Such famous writers as Montaigne are known for having widely practiced this kind of personal annotation: scholars (and also booksellers) are eager to find new attributions of valuable handwriting. The IRHT humanist database (BUDE) offers information about owners and a manuscript sampling (*http://web_bude.irht.cnrs.fr/php/login.php*). The automatic indexing of these zones, and of the zones within the zones, will help specific queries inside the image database of manuscripts. Thus, the scenarios will be adapted to other sets of documents, with identification of semantic zones – using the proper denominations from the history of printing – and the relations between the zones. The structure of the page and the document will be closely related to that of the XML/TEI pattern, in order to automatically help AGORA develop new scenarios.

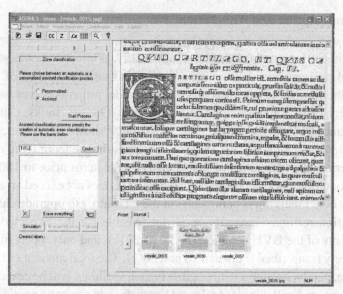

Fig. 9.2: AGORA: zone detection.

Scholars take part in testing interactive and easy-to-use generic scenarios for AGORA processing. Some tests have already been done, and we have been able to detect the difficulties of adapting the scenarios to the specificities of each category of book. The training can be supplied by users belonging to the humanities community, who are able to provide the appropriate names for printing specificities, which are the main labels (margins, difference between annotation and commentary, legends, printers' 'signatures,' etc.), the same labels being used within the <div> tags of the TEI descriptions. It is still necessary to test the various thresholds of image analysis, choosing what the priority is for the reader. For example, the headline that is repeated on the top of every page can be placed in a special database to clear the other text zones, because it is not a priority to process them with OCR. A second version of AGORA is now in experimentation, using more intuitive guidelines, and training can also be drawn out of examples: the user chooses among several scenarios, launches one of them with the search engine, and corrects or adapts afterwards. Modeling and interaction are alternately used, in order to improve the quality of results as well as the quality of the following requests and answers.

9.7 Transcription and Annotation

The digitisation process alone is not satisfactory. While it complies with the minimal preservation requirements, it does not offer any kind of access inside the images of the texts. All large-scale projects advertise their capability of searching inside the hidden text (Google Books, Gallica 2, Europeana), but when the text mode is visible, it shows a poor percentage of efficiency. The OCRs that are now available show encouraging results, considering the difficulties of image analysis for items prior to 1800. But raw recognition, for example with Fine Reader 9, does not exceed an average of 60%: benchmarking is being done in the laboratory to upgrade character recognition results. Transcription is not feasible for the expected 2,000 documents of the BVH database (by 2010-2011), and only a part of it will be entirely transcribed (between 10 and 20%). The total amount of the text database, nearly 200 items with original French spellings, will be nevertheless significant, and will allow for relevant linguistic and semantic queries.

Enrichment has a twofold purpose: for the metadata that describe the images and the texts (bibliographical information, description of the copy), and the data extracted from image recognition and text transcription (after the proper annotation). As the first one should be solved by OAI protocols and Open Archive exchange systems, we are dealing mostly with the second objective, so that we can offer much added value to the image and the transcript.

9.8 Image-and-Text Capacities

The international context of virtual libraries shows a large demand on new technical possibilities to process large amounts of text and image data. The CESR has contacts with other European libraries (Budapest, Wolfenbüttel, Glasgow…) and North American universities (in Toronto, Chicago, Virginia) that have digitisation projects and websites. To increase the availability of the databases and the efficiency of queries, especially on images, computing teams are requested for building and testing new tools for automatic recognition, mapping, matching images and indexing. These operations are very important to improve the usability of digitised books, now available in virtual libraries all over the world when they contain images, ornaments, portraits, capital letters or other illustrations. Mostly, the communities of users require a free and easy access to the text and to the image of the text, the possibility of clicking from one to another, and extracting knowledge at different levels. Digital libraries often show excellent digitised texts, scrolling and leafing options, and no more. Downloading is not always possible. Thus, dealing with image treatment and text searching, as well as enrichment between the two, is a challenge we are aware of.

In the BVH website, the images will comprise not only text in image form, but all the graphic elements extracted from the digitised documents, properly indexed and accessible by means of an image search engine, connected to the Iconclass thesaurus. Simultaneous visualisation of images and texts will be rendered possible by the organisation of metadata and XML/TEI encoding, and appropriate automatic linking. (Fig. 9.3)

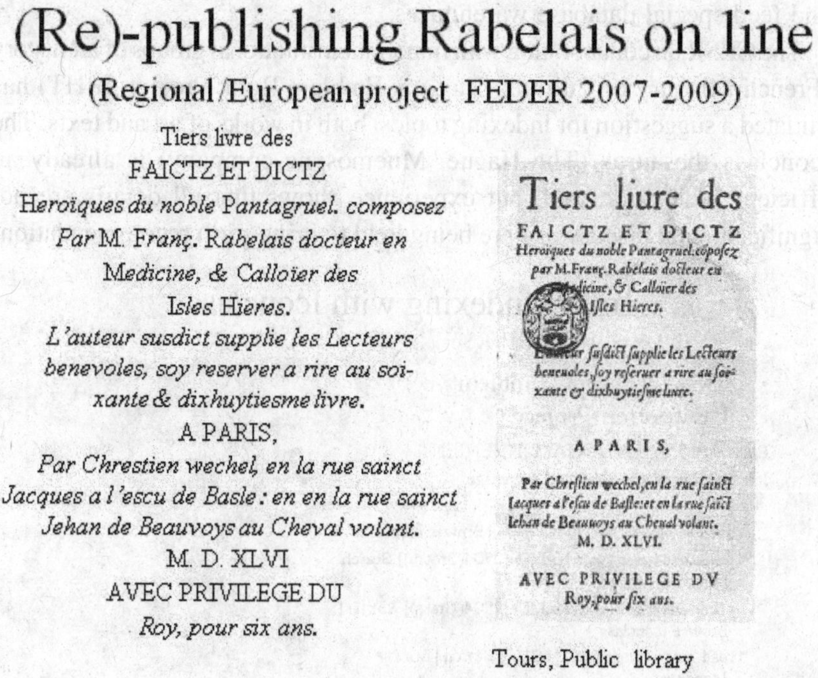
(Re)-publishing Rabelais on line
(Regional /European project FEDER 2007-2009)
Tiers livre des
FAICTZ ET DICTZ
Heroïques du noble Pantagruel. composez
Par M. Franç. Rabelais docteur en
Medicine, & Calloïer des
Isles Hieres.
L'auteur susdict supplie les Lecteurs
benevoles, soy reserver a rire au soi-
xante & dixhuytiesme livre.
A PARIS,
Par Chrestien wechel, en la rue sainct
Jacques a l'escu de Basle : en en la rue sainct
Jehan de Beauvoys au Cheval volant.
M. D. XLVI
AVEC PRIVILEGE DU
Roy, pour six ans.
Tiers liure des
FAICTZ ET DICTZ
A PARIS,
M. D. XLVI.
AVEC PRIVILEGE DV
Roy, pour six ans.
Tours, Public library

Fig. 9.3: Text and image of the text.

9.9 Automatic Thesaurus for Early Modern Images

For the scholar, and also for the amateur and the non-academic user, a common indexation for images coming from different sources would be a considerable improvement. The CESR already has experience in offering image indexing with a prior homemade indexation thesaurus, and we could see the limit of individual choices, even when a specialist of art history does them. First of all, in order to improve the automation of the process, we will recognize similar images and index them simultaneously, which will save time and money. Most of the time, online virtual libraries offer large image databases with a basic browsing and screen display, without proper indexing, and with no way of searching inside the images. The content access is, at best, facilitated by hyperlinks from a table of contents, typed by operators. Academics in the humanities would appreciate new tools that could recognize and select text and image zones, analyze and compare the zones to classify and feed special database warehouses.

The CESR, in collaboration with important institutional groups of art history (French Ministry of Culture, Glasgow Emblem Book Project, IRHT) has initiated a suggestion for indexing topics, both in works of art and texts. The Iconclass thesaurus (The Hague, Mnemosyne company) is already an efficient indexation tool, but experience shows that all details are not significant, and discussions are being held to bring forth recommendations

Image indexing with Iconclass

* Model: Glasgow Emblem' Digitization Project

Paradin 1551: FATA VIAM INVENIENT.
Iconclass Keywords Relating to the image:

 * boulder, stone [25H1124] Search | Browse Iconclass
 * plants and herbs (with NAME) [25G4(Broom)] Search | Browse Iconclass
 * plants and herbs (with NAME) [25G4(Grass)] Search | Browse Iconclass
 * road-cross, 'mont-joie' [46C117] Search | Browse Iconclass

Fig. 9.4: Description of images.

about indexation levels (Fig. 9.4). Domain ontology (in the linguistic sense) and particularities must be maintained in a way that does not generate a gigantic number of results. The names of individuals should also be indexed, as well as mythological entities, with an alphanumeric number, to enable multiple queries inside collections of artefacts, book illustrations, archives, paintings, etc. To our knowledge, this endeavour does not seem to have been foreseen by European-funded projects. As a real innovation in this field, the Iconclass thesaurus will also be used for manuscripts and transcriptions, and the tagging of the xml text data files will include its keywords. Thanks to this common search tool, the user will be able to ask for a specific topic in heterogeneous databases.

The first challenge is to build and connect a network of databases linked to the Iconclass thesaurus, so that one can find any item in any base from a range of hierarchized keywords and provide immediate access to the images one is looking for. In a sub-database in development, keywords belonging to the Iconclass thesaurus are associated, a set of semantically- and hierarchically-organized trees of keywords describing the works of art and ornaments, down to the smallest details, actions, foregrounds and backgrounds. The relevance of small detail naming is verified. The results of high-level and low-level information are compared and tested from the point of view of the end-user. The second challenge is the treatment of multilingualism offered by Iconclass: the keywords are codes, and the online request can be written in any of the four languages in which the thesaurus is translated: English, French, German and Italian. Dutch, Spanish, Finnish, Hungarian, Japanese and twenty other languages are also partially available. The third challenge is to test automatic procedures of encoding: until now, encoding has been done by hand, but with automatic image retrieval and similarity analysis (processed in Tours), one can expect to save time-consuming encoding.

9.10 Character Recognition

The pre-processing by AGORA is crucial to improve the efficiency of the off-the-shelf OCR that is being developed by the CESR and computing teams. The RETRO program (REconnaissance et TRanscription par Ordinateur, Computer transcription and recognition), offers semi-automatic text transcription and multiple full-text queries (94% to 98% recognition). AGORA helps by dividing graphic elements and text blocks, whereas RETRO applies a new method of sorting fonts and auto-training (no character recognition, no compression) before the association with the ASCII character. Manual interventions are limited to verification and encoding.

AGORA + RETRO enable the reconstruction of 80% of the original text in an electronic format in only a few hours. A full transcription can be achieved either by labeling all models of patterns of characters or by using a syntactic processing which allow the automatic recovering of missing characters by using lexicons. For example, a book of 150 pages having more than a million characters provide 20.000 different patterns models of characters or symbols. The manual labeling of the first 182 patterns models which occur the more frequently in the book enable the reconstruction of 85% of the original transcription in ASCII format (Fig. 9.5).

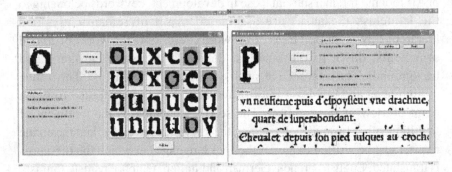

Fig. 9.5: Transcription software.

This rate is sufficient for a query with a search text engine that accepts missing characters. The number of different character patterns to edit manually depends on the regularity of the printing and the quality of the document preservation. Usually, the number of different character patterns represents 2% of all the characters of the book. Assisted transcription increases the transcription speed by 98%, which is the average redundancy rate of character patterns measured on Renaissance books.

9.11 Document Structure and Encoding

The acquisition is based on transcripts of original texts, copyright-free and available, though copy-protected. The main language is the French of that period (that of the beginning of modern French), as well as transcripts from Latin and from other vernacular languages (e.g. Italian). The transcripts do not reproduce modern critical editions, but singular copies presented under a common form, that is 'neutral' and 'patrimonial', neither diplomatic nor modernised. The diplomatic level is processed by an application (Dissimilog)[v] that automatically displays brevigraphs such as characters with tildes, and converts the i-j and u-v to the modern typing system. The first level of annotation (the tagging in XML/TEI language) allows adding information to the transcript corpus by means of specific coding, though not restrained to a confined community of researchers. In 2007 and 2008, in collaboration with other research teams dealing with old and middle French texts and the National Computing Institute (INRIA), the CESR has been working on an encoding manual[vi], approved by this community and compatible with the different existing OAI protocols, and with the standards of the Europeana portal. It is important that these image-and-text resources constitute a true corpus with its own distinctiveness: it will also be a good sample for a wider repository about Early Modern Europe, which will be an efficient means of diffusing the results of the research. Every tag has been discussed and included within a platform (Millefeuille, under Eclipse) that displays the tagged elements. A second edition of this manual will be published in 2009, with a supplement dealing with pointers, graphics, SVG and image marking.

This tagging, voluntarily, is not very thorough: we do not want to make choices that are too specific. Corrections are limited to obvious printing mistakes, and tagged as such. Only the divisions of the text, the typographic elements, the main structure, the selection of basic divisions such as prefaces, chapters, tables of contents, line breaks and page breaks, are considered as indispensable, especially to link these parts to the digitised volumes. Also for linguistic reasons, the encoding goes as far as <name>, <persName> and <geogName> in order to prepare an historical annotation, but the granularity of the tags will be added by other users. All other tags (quotations, speakers)

---

[v] Developed by Thierry Vincent (Ecrit.com company, Poitiers).

[vi] Centre d'Études Supérieures de la Renaissance (Dufournaud, N., Demonet, M.-L., *et al.*), with the help of Jean-Daniel Feket (INRIA), Manuel d'encodage TEI-Renaissance (Renaissance TEI encoding Manual), online on the BVH website, http://www.bvh.univ-tours.fr/XML-TEI/index.asp, July 2008.

are optional. Linebreaks </lb> ou pagebreaks </pb> cutting the words are a tough topic to deal with: after having thought about several solutions with the TEI consortium (a new, tag, a new element, a new attribute...), the team admitted that the most efficient way of processing the words at the end of the lines would be to transcribe without any special tagging, and to use, for the query system, an other "linear" text under the visible one[vii].

Manuscripts and archives are treated the same way: if metadata catalogue descriptions are different (EAD instead of Dublin Core), this will affect only the headers that could contain both kinds of document definitions. From our point of view, the content can be encoded through the same tagging system as for the printed material: keywords for the topics, TEI encoding for texts.

9.12 Linguistic Multi-annotation: Detecting Ambiguities

The availability of Renaissance texts in their digital format and the emergence of lexicometrical tools and browsers modify the practice of source-exploring[11-14]. Annotation is a procedure that inserts information about text units within the text, besides TEI tagging: for instance, we can identify, for a unique graphical form, diverse information such as its lemma or its grammatical category. It enables the enhancement of lexicometric practice (lexical statistics on text forms) on the textual and linguistic planes. We wish to combine a wide coverage of linguistic resources (as much information as possible) with an efficient 'disambiguation' (i.e. choosing among information and selecting what is relevant). A tool such as AnaLog, developed by the University of Poitiers[viii], enables the study and the visualisation of ambiguities such as they potentially exist in linguistic resources and are instantiated in the texts. The purpose is to pass from several resources to texts, from texts to resources, to compare and contrast the information.

[vii] The software will be Philologic, with the help of the University of Chicago (Mark Olsen).
[viii] Marie-Hélène Lay, FORELL laboratory, University of Poitiers.

9.13 Conclusion

The BVH digital library is not only an image-and-text library, but also an experimental resource website, offering the results of a double-layered examination of digital heritage. Text processing and image processing is the twofold – and ambitious – goal, in order to satisfy all kinds of readers.

References

1 Busson, S, and Uetani, T. (2003-2008), 212 books online, *http://www.bvh.univ-tours.fr.*

2 Demonet, M.L., Uetani, T. and Geonget, S. (2000-2007), Seventeen transcripts in Cornucopie, Renaissance French texts online, (33 others forthcoming), *http:// www.cesr.univ-tours.fr/Epistemon.*

3 Demonet, M.L. (2004), La Renaissance numérique : les 'bibliothèques virtuelles humanistes', in Digital technology and philological disciplines, Lebrave J.-L., Bozzi, A. (eds), Castelvecchio Pascoli, *Linguistica computazionale*, **20-21**, pp.175-185.

4 Geonget, S. (2002), Les bases textuelles en ligne : une analyse des politiques éditoriales, Frantext et Gallica in L'*édition* électronique en littérature et dictionnairique: évaluation et bilan, Rouen, *http://www.canalc2.tv/ video.asp? idvideo=1384*

5 Demonet, M.L. (2007), Les Bibliothèques Virtuelles Humanistes au Centre de la Renaissance de Tours, Chroniques de la BnF, *http://www.bnf.fr/pages/infopro/ journeespro/pdf/poles_pdf/poles2006_pdf/Demonet.pdf*, pp.1-23.

6 Journet, N, Eglin, V, Ramel, J.Y. and Mullot, R. (2006), Dedicated texture based tools for characterisation of old books, *2nd IEEE International Conference on Document Image Analysis for Libraries*. Lyons (France), pp.60-70.

7 Ramel, J.Y., Leriche, S., Demonet, M.L. and Busson, S. (2007), User-driven Page Layout Analysis of historical printed Books, in *International Journal on Document Analysis and Recognition*, **9**(2-4), pp.43-267.

8 Ramel, J.Y., Busson, S. and Demonet, M.L. (2006), AGORA: The Interactive Document Image Analysis Tool of the BVH Project, *2nd IEEE International Conference on Document Image Analysis for Libraries*, Lyons (France), pp.145-155.

9 Ramel, J.Y. and Leriche, S. (2005), Segmentation et analyse interactives de documents anciens imprimés, Traitement du Signal, *Presses universitaires de Grenoble*, **22**(3), pp.209-222.

10 Wandmacher, T. and Antoine, J.Y. (2007), Methods to integrate a language model with semantic information for a word prediction component, in *EMNLP-CoNNL'2007*, Prague, submitted.

11 Demonet, M.L. and Lay-Antoni, M.H. (2000), L'adaptation d'un analyseur au corpus rabelaisien, in JADT 2000 (Journées d'Analyse de Données Textuelles), Lausanne, École Polytechnique, *http://www.cavi.univ-paris3.fr/lexicometrica/jadt/jadt2000/pdf/89/89.pdf*, pp.1-8.

12 Demonet, M.L. and Lay-Antoni, M.H. (2000), Informatisation et lemmatisation du corpus rabelaisien, *Le Médiéviste et l'ordinateur*, **38**(Feb.), pp.28-40.

13 Demonet, M.L. (2000), Du papier au texte électronique et inversement : dernières évolutions du corpus rabelaisien, in Foire des études françaises, Wooldridge R. (ed.), Toronto, *http://www.etudes-francaises.net/*, pp.1-12.

14 Demonet, M.L. (1994), *Electrochronicques de Rabelais, CD-Rom*, (ed.), 2000 pages of transcripts of main Rabelais original editions, in collaboration with Brunet E. (Nice University), online between 1995 and 2006 (soon to be integrated in BVH).

Chapter 10

Measuring Document Similarity with Information Retrieval Techniques

Sudip Sanyal[1]

[1]*Indian Institute of Information Technology Allahabad, India*
ssanyal@iiita.ac.in

Abstract

This article presents a review of some techniques that have been found to be useful for measuring the similarity between documents. After defining measures of similarity, the article describes some of the standard preprocessing steps that are useful. The binary search models and vector space models are then examined. The sources of shortcomings in these models are identified and the manner in which latent semantic analysis overcomes some of them is described. Further improvement, using the probabilistic semantic analysis, is then described. Avenues for further improvements, using language models are also suggested.

Keywords: Information Retrieval Techniques, Binary Search Models, Vector Space Model, Latent Semantic Analysis, Probabilistic Semantic Analysis, Language Models.

10.1 Introduction

With the advent of large scale storage of data, as in digital library systems or data ware-houses, we have the associated problem of retrieving the relevant data/information. One can, of course, argue that if the data is properly indexed then we can retrieve it efficiently using standard data base technologies. However, in practice, the data may be unstructured or semi-structured. Indexing this form of data manually is a time consuming and error prone process. A typical scenario will help clarify this point:

Assume that we have a large collection of heritage documents and we decide to preserve it digitally. In order to achieve this goal we decide to convert the documents in a suitable digital format and save them on some suitable media. The indexing of the documents would be done using some metadata in a specified format like Dublin Core[1]. If a user wants to retrieve a particular document, then she/he would have to know the metadata. Also, the accuracy of the retrieval system would depend on the accuracy of the metadata i.e. if the metadata is not accurate then the correct document will not be found. However, preparation of correct metadata would require the services of a human expert who is knowledgeable about the particular document and the domain that the document belongs to. This is not always feasible, particularly when the number of documents is large and they cover a wide variety of domains.

It is quite feasible that the requirements of the user are not satisfied even if we assume that proper indexing of all the documents have been done. This is because quite often the user may be looking for a set of documents on a particular topic. A possible scenario for this situation would be as follows:

A user wants to learn about the historical importance of Allahabad. The user may not have any idea of the metadata for such documents. For example, the user may not know the names of the authors or the titles of the relevant documents. Indeed, it is entirely feasible that there is no single document that is devoted to exactly this topic. Instead, there may be several documents that contain sections devoted to this topic but the title of the document (or other metadata associated with the document) may not reflect this fact. A suitable retrieval system should be able to locate these documents and present them to the user.

An examination of the above common scenarios lead us to a different type of retrieval system that does not depend on the metadata. Instead, we want an information retrieval system. The user should be able to represent her/his needs in terms of some key words, or a fragment of a document or a natural language query. The system would then have to find all relevant documents that meet the needs of the user and present them in a suitable manner. The key observation is that we are trying to build a system that searches the entire corpus for all relevant documents. This is not an easy task. To begin with, we have to define as to what we mean by the term "relevant". We also have to build suitable measures for relevance. More importantly, we will have to build suitable algorithms that can be used for locating the relevant documents. As we will see later, the scalability of these algorithms is a critical factor that needs to be considered. The primary task of these algorithms will be to measure the similarity between a pair documents. One member of this pair is the query of the user and the other will be from the corpus of documents. Another design goal of these systems would be to make the system as independent as possible of the language (natural) being used.

In this work we shall examine the above issues. We will review various algorithms available for measuring document similarity and examine their suitability from the point of view of accuracy, scalability and language independence. To begin with, we will define the measures of accuracy. Then we will examine the vector space model for information retrieval. The more sophisticated latent semantic indexing will be analyzed in some detail. We will then proceed with the probabilistic latent semantic indexing method. We will also examine how the performance of these systems can be improved with some natural language processing. In the concluding section we shall examine future enhancements for these systems.

10.2 Measures of Accuracy

Information retrieval systems are not perfect. There can be two different reasons for the imperfection. The first is that the user did not formulate the query properly. This is unfortunately true even though, at first sight, this may appear as an excuse for imperfection. To elucidate this point let us continue with the example given above i.e. a user wants all documents that discuss the historical importance of Allahabad.

Let us assume that the information retrieval system accepts the query from the user as a set of key words. What are the key words that the user may supply? Most probably the set of key words would be "historical", "importance" and "Allahabad". Is the set adequate? Does it really capture the needs of the user? The system would not find a document that referred to Allahabad by its historical name "Prayag". On the other hand it may locate a document that has the words "important" and "Allahabad" but which does not discuss history in any way. It may discuss the strategic importance of the air base in Allahabad.

The second reason for the imperfection of information retrieval systems is the fact that the algorithms used for measuring similarity may have some short coming. The short coming may be due to some simplifying assumption made about natural languages (recall that the query would be formulated in some natural language) or the algorithm may be making some assumption about the language model. We shall examine these issues in detail when we examine various algorithms in subsequent sections. For the time being we would like to build some measures of accuracy so that we have an objective process for comparing the performance of the algorithms.

If we examine the example given above, we find that the system may make two types of errors. In the first case the system may fail to locate a relevant document. In the second case the system may locate a document that is not relevant.

Corresponding to the two types of errors we define two types of measures for accuracy: Precision and Recall.

- *Precision* is the ratio of the number of documents that were actually relevant to the total number of documents that were retrieved.
- *Recall* is the number of relevant documents retrieved to the total number of relevant documents in the corpus.

Thus, the first type of failure is addressed by precision while the second type of error is addressed by recall. As we will see later, quite often we can improve precision by lowering recall and *vice versa*. Thus, it is difficult to use these measures to judge the accuracy of a given method for information retrieval. Usually a single measure can be obtained by using the F-score which is the median of the precision and recall values. It is relevant to point out at this stage that the pattern recognition community uses a related, but slightly different, set of measures of accuracy. The preferred measures of error in that domain are false positives and false negatives. However, in this article we will be using precision and recall for measuring accuracy. Having looked at the methods for measuring accuracy, we will now proceed to examine the usual preprocessing steps that are required before implementing the actual information retrieval algorithms.

10.3 Preprocessing and Representation of Documents

Each document in the collection is usually preprocessed and represented in a specific fashion for information retrieval. We will examine the preprocessing steps and the method of representation. The main preprocessing steps are tokenization, stop word removal and stemming. One may use additional preprocessing steps like named entity recognition, anaphora resolution etc. We will briefly examine the importance of the first three steps in this section. The effect of including the last two steps will be taken up in a later section.

- *Tokenization* is the process of identifying the individual units that will form the basis of document clustering or information retrieval. Tokenization is important because the user query will also be formulated in terms of words that will be mapped to these tokens. For a language like English, or for Indian languages, this may appear to be a simple process of removing the punctuation marks and identifying the words. However, complications can (and do) occur due to the usage of abbreviations etc. Thus, knowledge of the usage patterns of a language is required for proper tokenization. This preprocessing step becomes considerably more complicated for languages like Chinese. This is because these languages quite often do not have gaps between words. Thus, identification of individual words is a difficult task for these languages. Often, this complication is handled by using a dictionary lookup. Once the tokenization is complete, the next step is stop word removal

- *Stop word removal* is the process of identifying and removing stop words. Stop words are commonly occurring words like "is", "a", "the" etc. The reason for removing them is that they do not carry information that is useful for the document retrieval task i.e. these words do not help us to differentiate documents. For example, we can not guess the domain that a document belongs to if we are only given the frequency of occurrence of the word "is". The presence of these words actually lowers the precision of the retrieval algorithms. Extensive lists of these words are available for most modern languages and their removal is quite straightforward. After the removal of the stop words, the next step is stemming.

- *Stemming* is the process of reducing all the remaining words to their respective stems. It is worth stressing that stemming finds the stem, and not the root, of the words. The effect of stemming can be best understood with the example below:

- *Original text:* Faced with a string of resignations and bitter feuding in his Labour party, embattled British Prime Minister Tony Blair on Thursday said he will step down within a year but refused to set a definite departure date
- *Stemmed text:* face with a string of resign and bitter feud in hi labour parti, embattl british prime minist toni blair on thursdai said he will step down within a year but refus to set a definit departur date

The above result was obtained using the well known Porter stemmer[2]. One may well wonder why we stem at all. While it is true that we often lose the original word, the advantage of stemming lies in the fact that the same distortion is introduced whenever the same word occurs. Thus, words like "boy" and "boys" will be stemmed to "boi" while "boyish" will remain "boyish". From the point of view of information retrieval, both "boy" and "boys" carry similar information while "boyish" has a different sense (and different part of speech too). Thus, the process of stemming reduces the total number of tokens (or terms) and also reduces similar words to a common term. This not only enhances the efficiency of the subsequent algorithms in terms of speed but also improves their accuracy.

The above steps reduce a given document to a set of terms. We now need a sensible way of representing the documents. Conceptually, we can represent the documents as a table or matrix. This matrix is called the term-document matrix. Assume that we have a set of N documents $D = \{D_1, D_2, D_3, \dots, D_N\}$. The total set of distinct terms in the corpus of N documents is $T = \{T_1, T_2, T_3, \dots, T_M\}$. The term-document matrix is an (N x M) matrix whose $(i, j)^{th}$ element represents the importance of the jth term in the ith document. Different information retrieval techniques use different measures for this importance. We shall see different methods for calculating the value of the matrix elements when we examine the individual techniques for measuring document similarity. It is pertinent to point out at this stage that while we can look at the term-document matrix as a matrix, in practice we prefer to use a slightly different data structure for holding the values. The reason is that the term-document matrix is highly sparse where most of the matrix elements are zero. Thus, a more convenient structure, called the inverted file is used in practice. This structure creates a list of records. One record corresponds to one term in the corpus. Each record contains the matrix elements corresponding to each document which uses that term. Only entries corresponding to the non-zero matrix elements are kept. This alternative structure leads to more efficient implementations of the algorithms.

We should realize that there are some implicit assumptions in the above forms of representation. These are that we are assuming that the order of the terms does not affect the retrieval process. Also, the ordering of the documents does not affect the algorithms either. We now proceed to examine various methods for measuring document similarity.

10.4 Binary Similarity Models

In the binary model, if a term appears in a document, the corresponding element of the term-document matrix is equal to one, else it is equal to zero. Various similarity measures can be defined using this form of the term-document matrix. The commonly used measures are the Common Features Model[3], the Contrast Model and the Ratio Model[4] and the Distinctive Features special case of the Contrast Model[5]. However, these models were not found to be very effective in an empirical evaluation of models of text document similarity[6]. The primary cause for the poor performance of these models is two features of natural language texts. These are synonymy and polysemy.

- *Synonymy* is the case when several words have the same sense. For example, in a given document, the word 'car' and 'automobile' may be used interchangeably. However, the document similarity measure would treat them as distinct terms. Thus, if the user provides 'car' as a key word in the query then the document containing 'automobile' would not be retrieved even though they were relevant to the query. Thus, synonymy reduces recall.

- *Polysemy* is the situation when a single word can have more than one meaning. For example, the word 'bank' can be a river bank or a financial institution. Thus, if the user gives 'bank' as a query key word then the system would retrieve documents containing both types 'banks' while the user obviously had only one type in mind. Thus, polysemy reduces precision.

The above analysis leads us to the conclusion that the limitations of this representation (and these models) can be overcome if we could, somehow, look at the meaning of the words. This leads us to various semantic models. However, before examining the models that try to capture semantics, we will first look at the vector space model in the next section.

10.5 Vector Space Model

A closer look at the binary models reveal that we give equal importance to the terms that occurred a single time in the document and those that occurred several times. This appears to be counter-intuitive. If a document is about Allahabad, then it stands to reason that the term 'Allahabad' would occur several times. Thus, the importance of the term 'Allahabad' should be higher for that document and it helps us to distinguish this document from others that do not contain this term. In order to capture this aspect we should use the frequency of the terms in the term-document matrix.

On the other hand, if a particular term occurs very frequently in almost all documents, then it does not help us in distinguishing various documents in the corpus. The stop words, mentioned in section 2 above, represent an extreme case of such words. Thus, if a term appears in most documents, then its importance should be reduced in the corresponding elements of the term-document matrix. This aspect is captured by a factor called inverse document frequency. Thus, a popular method for calculating the elements of the term-document matrix is the (term-frequency x inverse-document-frequency) which is often abbreviated as *tf-idf*. In this scheme the matrix elements are calculated as:

$$W_{a,b} = tf_{a,b} * idf_b = tf_{a,b} * \log\left(N / df_b\right) \qquad (10.1)$$

where,
N = number of documents in the document-collection
idf_b = inverse document frequency
$tf_{a,b}$ = term frequency i.e. the frequency of occurrence of term 'b' in document 'a'
df_b = the number of documents in which the term 'b' occurred in the corpus.
Entropy based measures are also well known.

Given the term-document matrix, the vector space model[7] looks upon each document as a vector in the M dimensional space created by the M terms. The similarity between a pair of documents, D_p and D_q, is then calculated using a cosine similarity measure

$$\cos \theta_{pq} = D_p \cdot D_q / \left| D_p \right| * \left| D_q \right| \tag{10.2}$$

If two documents, 'p' and 'q', are similar then they will point in similar direction in the M dimensional term space. Thus, the corresponding value of θ_{pq} will be small and the value of Cos θ_{pq} will be close to one. On the other hand, if two documents are dissimilar then the corresponding value of Cos θ_{pq} will be close to zero. Figure 10.1 below shows a hypothetical term space of two dimensions for a corpus of the three documents. Documents '1' and '2' are similar to each other while '3' is dissimilar to them. Figure 10.1 also helps us understand why we often find that a rise in precision leads to a fall in recall and *vice versa*. In general, document 'p' will be considered similar to document 'q' if the value of Cos θ_{pq} is greater than a threshold value. Now, raising the threshold would allow less number of documents to be considered similar to the target document i.e. recall would drop and precision would rise. On the other hand, lowering the value of the threshold would have the opposite effect. It would allow a greater number of documents to come within the limit, thus raising recall but lowering precision.

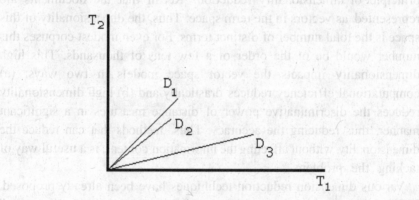

Fig. 10.1: A hypothetical term space for a corpus of three documents and two terms.

Instead of using the cosine similarity measure we could have used other measures like

$$\text{Inner Product} = \sum D_{pj} * D_{qj}$$

Dice Coefficient $\quad = 2 \sum D_{pj} * D_{qj} \Big/ \Big\{ \sum D_{pj}^2 + \sum D_{qj}^2 \Big\}$

Jaccard Coefficient $\quad = \sum D_{pj} * D_{qj} \Big/ \Big\{ \sum D_{pj}^2 + \sum D_{qj}^2 - \sum D_{pj} * D_{qj} \Big\}$

In the above expressions the summations run over all the terms.

An analysis of the vector space models shows that while it produces higher accuracy compared to the binary models, they do not address the problems of synonymy and polysemy outlined above. As mentioned earlier, these issues can be addressed if we take the semantics into account. In other words, we have to go beyond the surface structure and delve deeper.

10.6 Latent Semantic Analysis

Latent semantic analysis (LSA) is a statistical/mathematical technique to elicit and infer relationship among usage of words in a given context. It does not use any artificial intelligence methods or natural language processing techniques. It tries to explore something about meaning of the words and about the topics in text-documents[8-9]. LSA is based on the principle of dimensionality reduction. Recall that the documents are represented as vectors in the term space. Thus, the dimensionality of this space is the total number of distinct terms. For even modest corpuses this number would be of the order of a few tens of thousands. This high dimensionality impacts the vector space models in two ways: (a) computational efficiency reduces drastically and (b) high dimensionality reduces the discriminative power of distance measures in a significant manner, thus reducing the accuracy. Thus, methods that can reduce the dimensionality, without affecting the information content, is a useful way of tacking the problem.

Various dimension reduction techniques have been already proposed. These techniques can be treated as a promising way to extract the "concepts" from unstructured data. These document reduction techniques can be classified in two categories: (a) Feature Selection and (b) Feature Transformation

- *Feature Selection* methods sort all the terms using a suitable mathematical measure that are computed from the documents.

Examples of such methods are: Document Frequency, Mean Tf-IDf and Term Frequency Variance.

- *Feature Transformation* methods assign vector space representation of the collection of documents into lower dimension subspace. The new dimensions are linear combinations of the original ones. Well known methods in this category are Latent Semantic Analysis, Random Projection, Independent Component Analysis, Principal Component Analysis. Out of these, LSA has proved to be very efficient in the area of text analysis and will be the topic of the present section.

The initial steps in LSA are the same as that of vector space models i.e. after the preprocessing of text in the documents the entire corpus is represented as a term-document matrix. LSA takes this term-document matrix as input and applies Singular Value Decomposition (SVD) on it. In SVD, a matrix is decomposed into the product of three other matrices. If $W = \{W_{a,b}\}$ represents the term-document matrix then SVD yields.

$$W = R_0 S_0 C_0 \tag{10.3}$$

One component matrix, R_0, explains the original row entities as vectors of derived orthogonal factor values while another component matrix, C_0, describes the original column entities in the same way. The third component is a diagonal matrix, S_0, containing scaling values. When the three components are matrix-multiplied, the original matrix, W, is reconstructed.

SVD is a very useful technique because it provides a simple procedure for an ideal approximate fit using smaller matrices. If the singular values in S_0 are arranged by size, the initial 'k' largest may be kept and remaining smaller fixed to zero. The multiplication of the resulting matrices is a matrix (which is nearly equal to the original matrix) and is of rank 'k'. It can be shown that the new matrix is almost equal to the original matrix in the least square sense. This observation implies that the information contained in the original term-document matrix is nearly conserved, but the dimensionality of the space is reduced to 'k'. If the resulting matrices are W_{new}, R_{new}, S_{new} and C_{new} respectively then the similarity between all pairs of documents in the corpus can be measured by computing ($W^T_{new} \times W_{new}$) while the similarity between all pairs of terms can be found by computing ($W_{new} \times W^T_{new}$).

The value of 'k' is a parameter whose choice is of critical importance. This is because it decides the amount of dimension reduction. Ideally it should be small enough so that all the sampling errors can be ignored but large enough to capture all the real structure in the data. Each value in the new representation is calculated as a linear combination of the original cell values. As a result of this, any change in the cell value of original matrix is reflected in the values of newly reconstructed matrix with reduced dimensions. The dimension reduction step has cut down matrices in a manner that terms that occurred in some contexts will appear with larger or smaller predictable frequency. Also, some words that did not appear actually now do appear, fractionally.

Once the dimensionality reduction has been completed, we can measure the similarity between documents using the cosine or some other suitable measure. These measurements are now performed in the 'k' dimensional space.

If we calculate the similarity between pairs of terms then we find that synonymous words appear close to each other. This is revealed from the values obtained after calculating (W_{new} x W^T_{new}). Thus, in practice, while it is observed the LSA gives a better measure of similarity between documents, the problems of polysemy remains. We thus turn to a very sophisticated method next which reduces the problem of polysemy.

10.7 Probabilistic Latent Semantic Analysis

The basis of PLSA is the Aspect Model[10]. It is a latent variable model for co-occurrence data which combines a hidden aspect or class variable A_l € A = {A_1, A_2, A_3, ... A_k} for each observation i.e. with each occurrence of terms T_j € T = {T_1, T_2, T_3, ... , T_M} in a document D_i € D = {D_1, D_2, D_3, ... , D_N}. An observed pair (D_i, T_j) can be obtained, while the hidden class variable 'A_l' is eliminated. Converting the whole process into a joint probability model yields

$$P(d,t) = P(d) * P(t|d) \qquad (10.4)$$

where

$$P(t|d) = \sum P(t|a) * P(a|d) \qquad (10.5)$$

and the sum is over all aspects.

The crucial issue is the introduction of the aspects. The first observation is that these aspects are hidden (hence the term 'latent' in the title of the section). One can get an intuitive feel of these new entities by looking at them as something that is smaller than documents and larger than individual terms. Roughly speaking, we can say that a document is made of aspects and the aspects are built out of individual terms. One should not look at aspects as sentences. Instead, one should look upon them as a collection of terms that tend to occur together in different contexts. Since these aspects are hidden, so one has to 'discover' them. This essentially entails determining the probabilities *P(t|a)* and *P(a|d)* given the term-document probabilities *P(t|d)*. *P(t|a)* represents the probability of observing a term given an aspect (or topic) and *P(a|d)* is the probability of observing an aspect given a document.

The conditional probabilities can be determined using a well known method of statistics, namely the Expectation-Maximization algorithm. This method maximizes the log-likelihood to evaluate the probabilities. In summary, the method reduces to an iteration of an expectation step and a maximization step. The steps can be summarized as follows:

- Inputs: term-document matrix T(t , d), t=1:M, d=1:N and the number A of aspects/topics sought
- Initialize arrays P_1 and P_2 randomly with numbers between [0,1] and normalize them row-wise to 1
- Iterate until convergence

  For d=1 to n, For t =1 to m, For a=1: A

$$P_1(t,a) \leftarrow P_1(t,a) \sum_{d=1}^{N} \left\{ T(t,d) * P_2(a,d) / \left\{ \sum_{a=1}^{A} P_1(t,a) * P_2(a,d) \right\} \right\} \tag{10.6}$$

$$P_2(a,d) \leftarrow P_2(a,d) \sum_{t=1}^{M} \left\{ T(t,d) * P_1(t,a) / \left\{ \sum_{a=1}^{A} P_1(t,a) * P_2(a,d) \right\} \right\} \tag{10.7}$$

$$P_1(t,a) \leftarrow P_1(t,a) / \sum_{t=1}^{M} P_1(t,a) \tag{10.8}$$

$$P_2(a,d) \leftarrow P_2(a,d) / \sum_{a=1}^{A} P_2(a,d) \tag{10.9}$$

- Output: arrays P_1 and P_2 , which hold the estimated parameters P (t |a) and P (a| d) respectively.

As can be seen, the adjustable parameters are the convergence condition and the number of aspects/topics, A. The latter plays a role similar to that of the parameter 'k' in LSA and its choice is critical.

One can easily find the terms that are important for a given aspect as well as the aspects that are important for a document. Moreover, polysemous words will appear in more than aspect. For example, a simple meta-search-engine was built[11] using PLSA. This search engine accepted the user query (in the form of a set of key words) and fired the query to three basic search engines namely Google, Yahoo and MSN. PLSA was run on the top ten results returned by the three search engines. The number of aspects was usually 5 or 6. The results displayed by the meta-search-engine showed the words relevant to each of the aspects. During experiments the system was deliberately given query key words that are known to be polysemous. One example is shown below and the query was "thread". This term is used in the context of "textiles", "clothes", "sewing" etc. The same word is also used in the context of programming as in "multi-threading" etc. Table 10.1 gives a sample output of the query.

Table 10.1: Results using the query = "thread" with PLSA

Topic 1	Topic 2	Topic 3	Topic 4	Topic 5
Thread	Fangohr	Auckland	Gigalink	Showcase
System	Firms	Zealand	BridesMaid	Prices
Java	Hungry	NZ	ThreadDesign	Boutiques
Class	Stock	Necklace	www	Dj
lang	Flavor	Crochet	dress	Thousands
process	sure	Paris	collection	Cocktails

As we can see, the algorithm was quite successful in discriminating between different uses of the same word. Similar results were obtained for other polysemous queries.

Experiments were also performed for measuring the similarity between pairs of documents for a collection of fifty documents. The same documents were also scored for similarity by human beings. A comparison of the results delivered by the algorithm with the scores given by humans shows a high correlation. The results given by PLSA are, in general, superior to those obtained using LSA. In the next section we shall discuss possible improvements to PLSA by using suitable language inputs.

10.8 Role of Language Inputs

In this section we shall examine how the results can be improved if some language inputs are used as a part of the preprocessing. The first is, unfortunately, language dependent but the second is language independent.

If we examine the process being followed by each of the methods described above, we find that a common input is the term-document matrix. The matrix elements are calculated using the *tf-idf* method which depends on frequency of occurrence of the terms in a document. Now, let us consider the following hypothetical "document":

Ram was the son of King Dasharath. He ascended to the throne of Ayodhya after defeating Ravana and returning from exile.

The frequency of "Ram" in the above document is one because the word occurs only once. However, a closer look reveals that the frequency should have been two instead of one. The reason is that the pronoun "he" in the second sentence also refers to "Ram". The above observation implies that we should resolve the pronouns before constructing the term-document matrix. This would allow a more accurate representation of the document using the term-document matrix. One can extend the above idea further by trying to resolve all anaphors. For example, a document on the "Taj Mahal" may refer to the monument as "Taj Mahal", "The Taj" etc. By recognizing that all such terms refer to the same entity we again improve our term-document matrix. As we can see, the resolution of pronouns and other anaphors is language dependent. Fairly standardized tools exist for this purpose for the English language and similar tools are needed for other languages. Actual experiments on measuring document similarity shows that these preprocessing steps lead to some improvement in the accuracy.

A second language input is in building good language models. As is well known, every document has a large number of function words and some content bearing words. The stop words mentioned earlier are examples of function words. Since these words do not help us in discriminating between documents, so they can be dropped from the term-document matrix. This has two advantages. The first is that such a step improves the accuracy of the system. The second is that algorithms like LSA or PLSA require extensive computations. The amount of computation depends critically on the number of terms. Thus, a reduction in the number of terms improves the efficiency of these algorithms. Thus, we need a language model that is able to identify function words. Fortunately, the function words are found to obey a Poisson distribution in a corpus. This observation has been found to be true for several languages. Thus, one can create distributions of all distinct terms in a corpus, identify the ones that follow the Poisson distribution and mark these as function words. Once these are discarded from the term-document matrix then we will be able to build a more accurate and efficient system.

10.9 Conclusion

This article presents several alternative ways of measuring the similarity between documents. An examination of the results obtained by the more traditional methods lead us to the PLSA. The results obtained by PLSA are certainly very promising. Further avenues for improvements, using different types of language inputs, are also discussed. Of course, the system is still far from perfect. One can improve the efficiency of the system by using various types of clustering or classification algorithms. Similarly, we can improve the accuracy by building better language models and using these models to improve the algorithms. These are the topics for future research and their success would lead to efficient and accurate methods for locating relevant information from vast repositories like the modern digital libraries or the internet.

References

1 *http://dublincore.org/documents/*

2 Jones, K.S. and Willet, P. (1997), *Readings in Information Retrieval*, San Francisco: Morgan Kaufmann, ISBN 1-55860-454-4.

3 Shepard, R.N. and Arabie, P. (1979), Additive clustering representations of similarities as combinations of discrete overlapping properties, *Psychological Review*, **86**(2), pp.87-123.

4 Tversky, A. (1977), Features of similarity, *Psychological Review*, **84**(4), pp.327-352.

5 Rohde, D.L.T. (2002), Methods for binary multidimensional scaling, *Neural Computation*, **14**(5), pp.1195-1232.

6 Pincombe, B. (2005), Comparison of Human and Latent Semantic Analysis (LSA) Judgements of Pairwise Document Similarities for a News Corpus, *DSTO-RR-0278, Technical Report*, Australian Government, Department of Defence.

7 Salton, G. (1970), Automatic text analysis, *Science*, **168**, pp.335-343.

8 Deerwester, S. *et al.* (1990), Indexing by latent semantic analysis, *Journal of the American Society for Information Science*, **41**(6), pp.391-407.

9 Landauer T.K., Foltz, P.W. and Laham, D. (1998), An Introduction to Latent Semantic Analysis, *Discourse Processes*, **25**, pp.259-284.

10 Hofmann, T. (1999), Probabilistic Latent Semantic Indexing, *Proceedings of the 22nd Annual International ACM SIGIR Conference on Research and Development in Information Retrieval*, pp.50-57.

11 Aatre, A.A. (2007), Meta-Search Engine based on Query-Expansion using Latent Semantic Analysis and Probabilistic Latent Semantic Analysis, *M.Tech. Thesis*.

Chapter 11

Intinno: A Web Integrated Digital Library and Learning Content Management System

Udit Sajjanhar[1], Mayank Jain[1], Arpit Jain[1] and Pabitra Mitra[1]

[1]Computer Science and Engineering
Indian Institute of Technology, Kharagpur, India
{udits,mjain,pabitra}@iitkgp.ac.in

Abstract

The article describes the design of Intinno, an intelligent web based learning content management system. The system aims to circumvent certain drawbacks of existing learning management systems in terms of sparsity of content, lack of intelligent search and context sensitive personalization. The sparsity problem is solved by using web mining to crawl learning content from the web. Automatic annotation is used to archive the crawled content into a digital library. Multiparameter indexing and clustering is done to provide intelligent content based search. Finally, context sensitive and personalized recommendation on content is supported. The system is available online at http://www.intinno.com

Keywords: Learning Content Management System, Web Mining, Digital Library, Intelligent Content based Search.

11.1 Introduction

A Learning Management System (or LMS) is a software tool designed to manage user learning processes[1]. LMSs go far beyond conventional training records management and reporting. The value-add for LMSs is the extensive range of complementary functionality they offer. Learner self-service (e.g. self-registration on instructor-led training), learning workflow (e.g. user notification, teacher approval, waitlist management), the provision of online learning, on-line assessment, management of continuous professional education, collaborative learning (e.g. application sharing, discussion threads), and training resource management (e.g. instructors, facilities, equipment), are some of the additional dimensions to leading learning management systems[2].

In addition to managing the administrative functions of online learning, some systems also provide tools to deliver and manage instructor-led synchronous and asynchronous online teaching based on learning object methodology. These systems are called Learning content management systems or LCMSs. An LCMS provides tools for authoring and re-using or re-purposing content as well as virtual spaces for learner interaction (such as discussion forums and live chat rooms). The focus of an LCMS is on learning content. It gives authors, instructional designers, and subject matter experts the means to create and re-use e-learning content more efficiently[3].

The current course management systems have a number of drawbacks which hinder their wide acceptance among teachers and students. One of them being the problem of cold start. Instructors who begin to make up a course don't have the material to start up. Seamless content reuse is often not possible. Materials presented may lack coverage of the subject area and thus fail to cater information needs of all students in a class. On the other hand, students while studying or reading a lecture have to waste a lot of their time in searching for relevant resources from the web.

We aim to build a system which solves the above problems to a large extent. The web interfaced educational digital library will solve the cold start problem faced by instructors. While putting up new course, assignment or a lecture, similar resources would be available from the digital library either by search or by recommendations. Also, while reading a lecture/tutorial a student would be recommended relevant material from the web and thus would save him time spent in looking for relevant resources[4]. The system will have the additional benefit of acting as a collaboration platform among students by building up of networking of courses.

The main focus of our system (called Intinno) is to mine the free and open source material available on the web[5] to build up a quality collection of learning material. Such material is automatically annotated and archived in a digital library and later intelligently searched or recommended.

11.2 Architecture of Intinno

The functionalities provided by the system include, web mining, learning content management, search and recommendation. Accordingly, Intinno has the following major components:

1. Web Miner for Learning Content
2. Information Extraction and Automatic Annotation Module
3. Digital Library and Content Search Module
4. Personalization and Content Recommender System

A block diagram of Intinno system is shown in Fig. 11.1 The system tasks may be mainly classified into the following major steps: (i) Building up of digital library from the content crawled from the web. The subtasks of this step are (a) Collection of resources from the web, (b) Automatic Tagging of collected data for indexing. Step (ii) Search for similar material, namely,

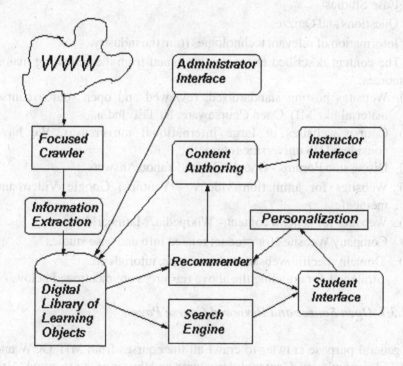

Fig. 11.1: Intinno architecture: Block diagram.

similar courses and similar content (lectures/ tutorials/ assignments). Step (iii) Personalized recommendation by using the context information of current user and the current course. Each of the above contents are described in details in the subsequent sections.

11.3 Mining Learning Resources from Web

Web being a rich repository of learning content, we attempt to collect high volume of learning material from web using a web miner[6]. The type of content required for the digital library would include.

1. Courses
2. Assignments
3. Lectures and Tutorials
4. Animation and Videos
5. Case Studies
6. Questions and Quizzes
7. Information of relevant technologies from the industry.

The content described above can be mined from the following major resources:

(a) Websites hosting standardized, reviewed and open source course material like MIT Open Courseware, NPTEL India.

(b) Course websites of large international universities. We have considered US universities currently.

(c) Discussion Forums - Google Groups, Yahoo Answers

(d) Websites for animations/videos – Youtube, Google Video and metacafe

(e) Websites for general content – Wikipedia, Mathworld

(f) Company Websites for product related info and case studies

(g) Domain specific websites for questions, tutorials etc.
   Strategies for crawling the above resources are mentioned below.

11.3.1 Open Source and Reviewed Course Pages

A general purpose crawler to crawl all the courses from MIT OCW and NPTEL is employed. Content is structured and thus is easier to crawl. Also it provides us a list of basic courses to include in the digital library. Courses from MIT OCW can be downloaded directly and the download data is arranged into folders. The content from NPTEL is ad hoc and cannot be downloaded directly. Hence, data downloaded from NPTEL will have to be catalogued.

11.3.2 Content from University Course Pages

Full crawl is not possible in this case and we opt for focused crawling[7]. Focused crawling is possible due to the following observations in most universities page structures.

- Every University page has a page listing all its schools and departments
- Every Department will have a page listing all its faculty members
- Every faculty member will have links of the courses on his home page.

The above structure is utilized to tune the focused crawler.

We also attempted direct search on Google for university course material. Using Google search keywords of the form: <name of course> course page syllabus etc.. often returns course page. However this approach has the problem of manually listing the names of all the courses in order to reach them. The problem lies in the fact that we don't have a exhaustive list of courses.

Another issue involved for such course pages is that of extraction of learning content from courses on the web. The data downloaded from an course on the web, may be arranged in various ways and needs to be processed to extract the relevant information. Here we propose a simplistic algorithm for doing it in each of the following two cases:

- *Case 1:* All the data of a particular course lies on one page. In this case different kinds of data will be under corresponding headings. For example all the assignments of a particular course will be under the assignments headings and all the questions will be under the questions heading. To extract data from such a course, we detect the headings on a particular page and we hypothesize that all the data under a heading is of that type. The algorithm has about 65% accuracy.

- *Case 2:* The course page has separate links for separate kind of data i.e. the assignments are on one page and the questions on another. We assume that these separate pages have such an anchor text that indicates the type of content on the page. For example the main course has links to Assignments/Lectures and Quizzes. To extract data from such a course we assume that type of content on each page to be given by the anchor text on the hyperlink.

11.3.3 Unstructured Data: Discussion Forums and Animation Videos

Full Crawl is irrelevant and is also not possible. Focused crawling is the approach adopted. From the courses already stored in the digital library now extract a set of keywords, including, (i) Terms from the name of the course, (ii) Terms from the syllabus of the course, and (iii) Terms from assignment heading/name, Lecture heading/name.

Next we search for discussions/Animations/Videos from the web which match the above list of keywords and index the results obtained above with the keywords with which they were found and the content of the entity obtained.

11.3.4 General Purpose Collections like Wikipedia

Full Crawl of Wikipedia is possible and can be obtained as a single XML document. However, full crawl/download may not be necessary and may in fact weaken precision of the search on digital library. We use a keyword based focused approach described above to limit the pages being indexed in wikipedia. Each wikipedia article can be characterized as lectures or tutorials. While indexing the articles of Wiki more importance should be given to the headings and the sub headings on the page.

11.3.5 Websites of Industrial Corporations

Websites in this categories will have to be handpicked and will be few in number. Examples of company websites includes whitepapers, manuals, tutorials obtained from research lab of companies like IBM, Google, Microsoft, GE. Handpicked websites of popular corporate training resources like those offering questions/quizzes on C and those offering tutorials like How Stuff Works.

11.4 Information Extraction for Automatic Content Tagging

Content crawled from all the sources mentioned in the previous section is annotated using the following tags before it is archived in the digital library.

(a) Name of the Course
(b) Name of the institute
(c) Name of instructor
(d) Type of content – Assignment/Lecture/Tutorial
(e) Type of file – pdf/html
(f) Expected standard of students
(g) Timeline of when the course was taught
(h) Original source link
(i) Indexing/Meta Tags

In addition to the above tags we also store some entity specific metatags that are important from the point of view of indexing and parameterized search. They are also used for information fusion and integration from multiple sources. For both the above category of tags hand crafted wrappers are used for information extraction[8].

11.4.1 Annotating Course Objects

When a course is downloaded, then in addition of the first 8 tags it has the following labels as its meta tags:

1. Name of the Course
2. Terms from the description of the course
3. Terms from the syllabus of the course
4. Terms from the headings of individual assignments/Lectures from that course. (This will ensure that the meta tags describing the course have elements from the course content itself.)

These terms will represent the indexable units from a course as a whole. A course will be searched by giving a query using these terms.

11.4.2 Annotating Course Sub-elements

The elements from a course are:
• Assignments

- Lectures/Tutorials
- Questions/Quiz
- Discussions
- Animations/Video/Pictures

All these elements will be stored by filling the 8 tags described above. The Indexing/Meta tags of the material obtained from a course will be:

1. Name of the course
2. Type of entity (i.e. Assignments/Lectures/Tutorials etc)
3. Name of entity i.e. name of the assignment/lecture
4. Content from the entity itself i.e. the assignment itself.

11.4.3 Annotating Wikipedia Content

The content from Wikipedia will be stored by filling the 8 tags of the form above. The type of content from wikipedia will have a default type of Lecture/tutorials. The meta tags in case of Wikipedia will be the terms from the articles itself. While indexing more importance will be given to the terms appearing in the headings and the sub headings of a wiki page.

11.4.4 Annotating Discussions/Animations/Video

The content will be downloaded by giving keywords as search queries at the respective sources. The indexing meta terms in this case will be:

- the terms used for query
- terms from the content itself.

Adding the search keywords in the meta tags ensures that information about related course/course material is added in the tags of the entity. This will ensure that if the search is made in the name of the course then related material also turns up in the results.

11.5 Searching the Digital Library

We provide two additional capabilities in addition to keyword based search, namely (i) Content based search for similar courses, and (ii) Intelligent search for course materials (i.e. if a search is given for material on biochemistry course then materials from molecular biology course should also turn up in the results.)

To find similar courses we will perform hierarchical clustering on the courses since courses by nature are a hierarchical. To perform clustering on courses we need a similarity measure between different courses and these similarity measures are defined in terms of:

1. Document similarity measure between the course syllabus. Jaccard co-efficient could be used as a measure here.
2. Similarity between the Meta Tags of a course. The meta tags of a course have elements from the content of a course and thus similarity between meta tags will ensure a similarity measure between courses based on content of courses.
3. There are some ontologies which are available for different domains. We will collect these ontologies and similarity measure between courses may be defined as the distance between courses in these ontologies.

A combination of above 3 measures will be used to perform clustering of courses. The clustering of courses is performed offline.

11.5.1 Tag Augmentation

The clustering of courses are used to perform tag augmentation in the following manner.

1. For all the courses in one cluster, the tags of a particular course belonging to the cluster will be augmented by the tags of all the courses in that cluster.
2. Also for the content of a particular course, its meta tags will be augmented with names of other courses in the same cluster.

Step 1, above will ensure that given a query for a course like biochemistry, similar courses like molecular biology will also appear in the search results. Step 2 above will ensure that if search for material with some keywords then material from related courses would also come in the search results.

11.5.2 Ranking of Search Results

The above clustering of courses and the augmentation of tags will facilitate intelligent search of courses/material. But the search results need to be ranked too. The following criteria may be used in ranking the courses/course materials:

1. Measure indicating the authority of the source of the material (For example university from where the material is picked)
2. Cosine similarity measure on the tags by the keywords
3. Courses with more content may be ranked higher
4. For content being searched, content from similar courses may be given more preference.
5. Also content from courses or even courses with same difficulty level as the user may be given more preference.

The criterion 4 and 5 above use personalized information. The information used are: i) difficulty level of the user and ii) the courses that have been taken by the user. Thus we can say that our ranking algorithm is personalized for every user.

11.6 Personalized Recommendation

Students studying a particular page (content) will be recommended similar contents. This recommendation will be:

1. Content Based i.e. Content from the digital library similar to the one being read will be recommended.
2. Content Diversified: i.e., if the person is currently studying Lectures then he/she will be recommended questions/quizzes/assignments. However on the other hand if the person is busy doing assignments or solving questions then he/she will be recommended lectures/tutorials on that particular subject from the digital library.
3. Recommendation will be based on a learning approach where for some content the actual goodness of the link would be learned by the number of clicks on the recommended links.
4. Recommendation will be personalized i.e. it will be based on the courses that the user has done and also on his/her level of understanding which can be judged from his courses list.

11.7 Implementation and Deployments

The Intinno system[9] may be used online at http://www.intinno.com. Currently there are about ten courses archived in the digital library are being added soon. The system currently crawls about 1000 university sites in *.edu* domain in addition to well known educational material resources. It also mines a number of hand picked websites.

Intinno is under use for the undergraduate courses for all departments at Indian Institute of Technology Kharagpur. User feedbacks are being collected for further improvement of the system.

11.8 Conclusion and Future Work

The philosophy behind Intinno was to use web mining techniques to develop an intelligent education portal. Key features include, web crawling, avoidance of cold start, automatic annotation, sophisticated indexing, intelligent search and personalized recommendation of content.

The system is under development and machine learning and data mining techniques are explored to improve the quality of user experience. Quantitative evaluation of search and recommendation performance is also being carried out.

References

1 Wikipedia : *http://www.wikipedia*

2 Cole, J. and Foster, H. (2007), *Using Moodle: Teaching with the Popular Open Source Course Management System* (O'Reilly Media Inc.).

3 Devedzic, V.B. (2003), Key Issues in Next Generation Web Based Education, *IEEE Trans. System Man Cybernetic: Part C*, **33**, p.339.

4 Dolog, P., Henze, N., Nejdl, W. and Sintek, M. (2004), Personalization in distributed e-learning environment, in WWW04: *Proc. Intl. Conf. World Wide Web*.

5 Bergmark, D. (2002) Collection synthesis, in JCDL'02: Proceedings of the *2nd ACM/IEEE-CS joint conference on Digital libraries*, (ACM, New York, NY, USA).

6 Chakrabarti, S. (2002), *Mining the Web: Discovering Knowledge from Hypertext Data* (Morgan-Kauffman).

7 *ibid.*

8 Kushmerick, N. (1999), Gleaning the Web, *IEEE Intelligent Systems*, 14, p.20.

9 *http://www.intinno.com.*

Chapter 12

A Radiologist's Digital Workbench: Balancing Representation and Access Challenges for Medical Images

Mayank Agarwal[1] and Javed Mostafa[2]

[1]*School of Information and Library Science*
University of North Carolina at Chapel Hill
Chapel Hill, NC, USA

magarwal@email.unc.edu

[2]*Information Science and*

Biomedical Research & Imaging Centre
University of North Carolina at Chapel Hill
Chapel Hill, NC, USA
jm@unc.edu

Abstract

Although significant advances have been made in the field of information retrieval, the field has not seriously engaged in challenges associated with effective and efficient access to image data. Similarly, the area of medical image computing and computer assisted intervention failed to realize the gains that could be achieved by leveraging the advances in information retrieval, particularly in query languages and interaction models. In this paper we attempt to bridge this gap by surveying and analyzing literature from both domains. We specifically focus on the following areas: medical image formats, data modeling, textual semantic access and image surrogates, and image query models. We conclude the paper with a discussion on interaction and interface evaluation. The survey is presented based on a framework of achieving a balance between image representation and image access challenges.

Keywords: PACS, Image Representation, Content based Image Retrieval, Access Challenges, Radiology Information System, Relevance Feedback.

12.1 Introduction

Over the past three decades, since Magnetic Resonance Imaging was introduced there has been substantial increase in the use of MRI as a preferred radiological imaging tool. These days radiologists and clinicians are demanding instantaneous access to images. This brings forth the biggest challenge in terms of storage, retrieval, and presentation of these images. The complexity of the task can be gauged by the fact that Fujitsu Services recorded the 100 millionth patient image in its data center in December 2006[1].

The state-of-the-art in medical imaging owes its existence to DICOM (Digital Imaging and Communication in Medicine) which as a *defacto* standard describes how to store, format and exchange biomedical images and image-related information[2]. Development of standards lead to the development of RIS (Radiology Information System).

While RIS handles the more administrative and textual functions like reporting, scheduling, billing etc, PACS on the other hand deals with more subtle issues related to imaging like collection, storage, accessibility and distribution. RIS serves the purpose of providing the right information to the right people at the right time in the right format and providing necessary support to PACS.

12.2 Medical Image Management

PACS initially came to light with the First International Conference and Workshop on Picture Archiving and Communication Systems held in Newport Beach, California in January 1982. But it did not came to the fancy of clinicians until 1989 mainly because of the restrictions in terms of limited know how of the computer assisted technology, limited storage, etc.

PACS essentially is a medical image facility to assist radiologists in interpreting the images more accurately. PACS has been developed keeping in mind the aim to provide the right image at the right time in the right place. The PACS architecture has 3 major components viz. image acquisition, PACS core system, and displays[3].

Image acquisition is where the patient scans are fed in to the system. One strategy is to allow the image to be transferred directly from the imaging instrument at the full resolution. While the other strategy of frame grabbing, digitize the analog voltage being sent to the display device. The digitization process limits the resolution to a fixed number of bits[4]. Examples of digital image acquisition involves computer radiography and digital radiography, film digitizers which are used to digitize the X-Rays or scans already on films.

PACS core system handles the function of search and retrieval, and how these images need to be organized. PACS core is composed of

- Image Archival System
- Image Management System
- RIS Communicator

DICOM defines the standards for Image Archival System. The archival system subsumes most often a relational database to map the path of the storage to the actual image and the other metadata to facilitate almost instantaneous retrieval and search process. DICOM also defines the type of queries that need to be supported by the archival system given the patient information and the test information. Redundant Array of Inexpensive Disks (RAID) is used for backup and disaster management.

Image Management System allows for communication between PACS and other components/databases of the system. It facilitates the storage and retrieval by deciding which node in the system should receive the images. The node can either be the database or the display workbench. The system also allows the data administrator to ensure data integrity and rectify any errors that might have creeped in during the acquisition process.

RIS communicator is important for the system as it prepares and passes the scheduling and test information to PACS. Furthermore, it verifies the demographic details of the subject before the scans are sent to PACS for storage. The RIS-PACS interface provides PACS with the metadata associated with the scans.

To enable radiologists and clinicians interact with the data stored in PACS and RIS, displays are required. The decision for the type of display required is guided by what requirements it needs to cater to. It can be a review workstation or diagnostic workstation. The diagnostic workstation are typically high resolution displays while on the contrary the review workstation has just the enough resolution to allow for reporting and analysis of the scans and related information[5]. However, with the advancements in web based technologies, the line between diagnostic and review displays is blurring and they are moving towards a web-based architecture. This in turn is leading to a wider acceptance of PACS as a desired system for medical image management.

12.2.1 Medical Image Formats and Storage Challenges

12.2.1.1 Digital Imaging and Communication in Medicine

In 1982 the American College of Radiology and the National Electrical Manufacturers Association came together to a consensus on a standard format called ACR-NEMA 2.0 to store medical images. ACR-NEMA defined a header to specify the image related metadata such as image dimensions, the depth per pixel etc, along with the imaging device information which was followed by the actual image pixel data.

In 1994 at the annual meeting of the Radiological Society of North America various imaging equipment participated and lead to the development of the ACR-NEMA 2.0 successor called DICOM. DICOM information objects are definitions of the information to be exchanged. NEMA has defined unique identifiers to correctly classify various image types. For example, RT is used for identifying modality of type Radiation Therapy, and MR is used for identifying modality of type Magnetic Resonance. DICOM has both normalized and composite information objects[6].

DICOM also has various service class which associate each information object with a command to be executed on that object instance. For example, Storage Service Class is used to store images or reports, Query/Retrieve Service Class causes a storage device to be queried and information retrieved, etc[7]. Since, there are both normalized and composite information objects there are corresponding service class for each of them. DICOM can support multi-dimensional image data to be encapsulated in a single DICOM data object. DICOM allows for pixel data to be compressed using variety of compression algorithms like JPEG, or run length encoding. DICOM also integrates the patient information in the DICOM object only so that they are never separated.

Development of DICOM standards has lead to considerable improvement in image quality. The DICOM Grayscale Standard Display Function based on Barten curve specifies the luminance or intensity that need to be produced based on the input value which renders the image to give a consistent quality across various display options.

12.2.1.2 *Analyze*

ANALYZE is a format being developed and supported by Mayo Clinic. An ANALYZE image consists of at least two files

- an image file
- a header file

The header file provides information about the dimensionality, history of the pixel data including the patient information such as patient id, scan number, etc. The image file contains uncompressed pixel data for the images. The control information for the image data is described in header file. One respect in which ANALYZE differs from DICOM is, DICOM encapsulates the header and the pixel data into a single entity[8].

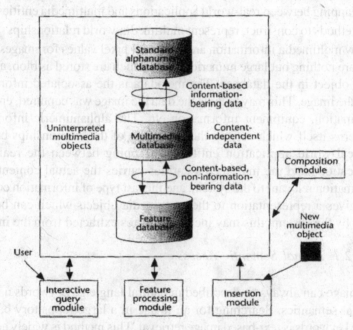

Fig. 12.1: A generic architecture for a multimedia information system.

The images in question will be used by people primarily that can be classified into two categories. One that require high resolution and quality and involves computer scientists, statisticians and the other that wants the data to be accessible in real time including medical students, commercial business[9]. To address the needs of both the group a compromise in terms of both speed of access and resolution quality has to be reached.

12.2.2 Data Modeling

As soon as we start talking about retrieval of image and multimedia information, how the content is organized becomes important. The generic data model from a multimedia perspective should capture 5 types of information[10]

- Raw multimedia information
- Metadata
- Alphanumeric information
- Mapping between real-world applications and multimedia entities
- Methods to construct, represent multimedia-world relationships

Raw multimedia information are the actual pixel values for images. Often they are nothing but large numeric strings which are stored as blob, a binary large object in the database. The metadata is the associated information with the image. This may include the data the image was captured, encoding information, equipment information etc. The alphanumeric information concerns itself which defines the properties of the relationships between the real-world application entities[11]. Mapping between the real-world applications and the multimedia entities carries the actual content based information relevant to the system, and the last type of information connects and gives a representation to the multimedia objects which can be acted upon by the system, this may include features extracted from the images.

12.2.2.1 Textual Semantic Access

An image can always be described in natural language keywords using the textual semantics. Searching for an image in a large repository based on those keywords is text-based image retrieval. This method is widely accepted as the information retrieval techniques for text, and have been there for quite a long time. It is also more intuitive for the end users to use.

However, searching based on the textual information has its problems as well. It assumes that such information is always available which is not always the case[12]. In such cases manual annotation of the images are required which is not a objective method to generate the associated information. Additionally, it is context-sensitive and tiresome job. The perspective in which end user describes an image can be entirely different from that of the person who documented the image. The same image can be interpreted in various ways by the same person in different space and time. There will be inconsistencies between different users of the system[13]. It is not uncommon for users to lack the domain centric knowledge to come up with keywords required for a good match[14].

To overcome the problem of limited domain knowledge one solution can be to show the description images similar to the user query[15]. To alleviate other problems user can be asked to provide relevance feedback on the search results to assist system learn over time.

12.2.2.2 *Image Surrogates*

A visual way to facilitate searching is called image surrogate search. The visual surrogate search approach attempts to mimic the keyword or textual search approach. The idea is to identify exemplar images that represent the actual image content (hence the use of the term surrogate) and allow the user to employ the surrogates in a query to retrieve similar images. A key challenge is to establish a systematic and effective way to determine surrogates. For example, if the collection happens to be a set of MRI images from Alzheimer patients, a good method would be grouping the images into various stages of disease progression and for each key stage selecting an image which depicts the condition most clearly and accurately. Hence, assuming the full spectrum of disease progression has n stages, then there would be n surrogates that would be pre-selected, just as key-words are pre-selected for indexing and searching purposes.

Upon selection of surrogates, the next challenges involve adopting one or more query models to allow the user to employ them in search. Several query models will be discussed in a later section, however, it is important to note here that surrogates are most closely associated with the Query-by-Example (QBE) modality of searching. The QBE approach was originally developed by IBM as a way to overcome some of the complexities associated with more formal querying approaches such as SQL. In the most simplest implementation of the QBE modality the user is presented with table structures as templates (with the columns labeled with field names) and the user is supposed to type in a literal value under one or more columns to formulate a query, which from a system's perspective is to be interpreted as a demand for records whereby the corresponding fields have the exact same values. For surrogate-based QBE search modality, the expectation is that the user will be able to specify one or more surrogates and formulate a query whereby the system will attempt to find images from a collection that match the surrogate/s. The difference with traditional QBE searching is that the actual examples (i.e., the surrogates in this case) must be displayed in some manner so that the user may select one or more from them. The presentation and browsing of surrogates is not a trivial matter as the means for doing so may directly impact how users may formulate queries and ultimately how effective these queries are. An innovative and empirically proven approach is known as the "fish-eye" design. It is thus called because in this approach the surrogate of interest is placed or moved to the center and system then retrieves associated surrogates and arrays them around the central surrogate. With the focus thus established on the main surrogate the user then can review related surrogates and refine the query accordingly. Upon selection of a satisfactory set of surrogates the user then can request the system to retrieve the corresponding image and associated data.

The image surrogate approach is deemed to be an essential way to facilitate searching as it is not always feasible or practical to express the actual image attributes in textual form. In certain instances "pointing to a representative image" which contains the target attribute/s would be a fast and accurate way to initiate a search. The related challenges in implementing a surrogate-based search involves selection of appropriate surrogates, which may turn out to be a manual and intellectually demanding task. Upon selection of surrogates, associating them to the actual images in the collection leads to another set of challenges. The association process, which is actually the indexing stage, can be conducted in a pre-coordinated fashion, whereby the appropriate images are directly linked to one or more surrogates in the index. The association between surrogates and images can also be established after the query is specified (i.e., after the user selects a surrogate). The association conducted after the query specification is referred to as post-coordination and this of course needs to be conducted automatically based on a matching process between attributes of the selected surrogate and image attributes. If a fish-eye type interaction modality is supported then association among surrogates would also need to be established in a pre-coordinated way. It should be clear to the reader by now that linchpin of surrogate-based search is a process for establishing association among surrogates and images (and potentially among surrogates themselves). A significant amount of accuracy can be gained by engaging manual indexers to establish direct links among items as a pre-coordinated indexing procedure. Such an indexing scheme however is expensive and may be unsustainable as the collection size grows. Hence, a means is necessary to detect critical attributes of images automatically and use these attributes for "on the fly" association (i.e., post-coordinated) adapting to the demands of user's query. The process for detection of attributes is highly dependent on feature extraction techniques, which will be discussed in the section that follows.

12.2.3 Image Content and Indexing

Handling image content and effective indexing for fast access is another important issue when talking about content-based retrieval. Faster searching is achieved through a process of feature extraction and dimensionality reduction which are described in the following sections.

12.2.3.1 Feature Extraction

Feature extraction is defined as a process of creating a representation for, or a transformation from the original data. This is accomplished using filters similar to the ones used by humans[16]. As an example set of Gabor filters can be used to characterize the texture. Various features such as color, shape, texture, spatial layout have been used for the purpose of content-based retrieval.

Color histogram is a vector where each entry stores the number of pixels of a given color in the image[17]. Color histograms have been used in IBM's QBIC[18], Virage[19]. Retrieval using color has proved effective for databases ranging in size from 66[20] to 1440[21]. However, with the increasing database size they lose their effectiveness because since they record only the color information, two images with same color histograms can have entirely different appearance.

An improvement over color histograms called color correlogram[22] was proposed to take into consideration the spatial correlation of colors along with the color distribution. It represents the histogram as a three-dimensional object where the first and the second dimension corresponds to the color for any pixel pair and the last dimension represents their spatial orientation. When compared to color histogram it provides better retrieval results however, its use is restricted by the computational costs involved.

Texture has also been widely used as a feature for indexing in content-based retrieval. Various statistical methods such as Tamura feature, Fourier spectra, Markov random field, filters such as Gabor and wavelet transforms are used to represent the image texture. Tamura, *et al.* looked at the texture as humans perceive texture. They defined six texture features including coarseness, contrast, directionality, line-likeness, regularity and roughness. The first three have found successfully used for retrieval purposes in QBIC[23]. Coarseness according to Tamura, *et al.*[24] is a measure of the granularity of the image. Contrast captures the dynamic range of gray levels in an image, together with the polarization of the distribution of black and white. Directionality measures the total degree of directionality. This is accomplished by first detecting all the edges in an image and then taking the angle and the magnitude at each pixel.

A bank of orientation and scale sensitive Gabor filters can also be used to extract the texture information by computing the mean and standard deviation of the output of the application of the filters in frequency domain[25, 26].

In the field of medical imaging often the features are computed from local region of interest. Mattie, *et al.*[27] describes the application of color, morphology, texture, and spatial relationship to digital image cytometry and cell image retrieval. ASSERT[28] uses feature extraction to identify diseases such as emphysema in high-resolution computer tomography. It uses gray-scale, texture, shape, etc. as features. It relies on a physician-in-the-loop approach, where a physician first marks the pathology bearing regions and then features are computed from those PBRs.

12.2.3.2 Dimension Reduction

When dealing with high spectral images, 3D volumetric medical images, the image feature vectors usually are of high dimensionality, but due to the problems associated with such multi-dimensional data[29], reducing the dimensions in the data seems to be a reasonable alternative. The problem of dimension reduction can be stated as given a random variable $X=(x_1,...,x_p)^T$, find a random variable $Y=(y_1,...,y_k)^T$ such that $k \leq p$ and

Y effectively captures the information conveyed in X[30].

The most commonly used dimension reduction technique today is principal-component analysis (PCA)[31]. Principal component analysis tries to find the variables such that they are most separated i.e. they have the maximum variances. Application of PCA drops the directions with small variances. The problem with PCA is that it is an unsupervised technique and hence it does not take into account the contextual information associated with the feature[32].

Singular Value Decomposition (SVD) is similar to PCA. Application of SVD is equivalent to rotating the axis and projecting the features on the new axis such that the new feature vectors[33]. SVD decomposes the feature vectors into uncorrelated orthogonal vectors[34]. The disadvantage with SVD being the computational cost involved and with an image where the feature space is very large, the cost can be a prohibitory factor. In SVD the data is broken down as

$$X = AY + M + V \qquad (12.1)$$

where M represents the mean and V represents the variance[35]. An extension to SVD, Generalized Singular Value Decomposition (GSVD) can give improved results[36].

Linear Discriminant Analysis is a well known supervised dimension reduction technique which is capable of using the class label and other contextual information into consideration[37, 38]. LDA aims to maximize the separation between the means of projection and minimize the variance between each projected class. LDA fails when the contextual information is captured by the variance but not the mean. LDA also tends to over fit the training data.

Given a $n \times n$ similarity measure matrix, Multi-dimensional scaling (MDS) produces a k-dimensional representation of a p-dimensional matrix to reflect the information contained in the similarity matrix[39]. A rule of thumb to determine the maximum number of k, is to ensure that there are at least twice as many pairs of items then the number of parameters to be estimated, resulting in $p \geq 4k + 1$[40-41]. In MDS a low-dimensional representation is obtained by minimizing certain cost functions such as the distance between the feature points in the original space to the reduced dimensional space. Wu, *et al.*[42] proposed a modified version of MDS called Weighted Multi-dimensional scaling (WMDS) to ensure that the M nearest neighbours to an image are preserved and the ordinal relationship is maintained in the reduced space.

FastMap[43] uses a pivot based approach to dimensionality reduction. The idea behind FastMap is that given only the $N \times N$ distance matrix for objects that belong to some unknown n-dimensional space, the algorithm tries to project these object-points onto a k-dimensional space. FastMap recursively projects the pivot objects on one less dimensional hyperplane.

Experiments by Moravec and Snásel[44] conclude that SVD was slow for the retrieval purposes but produces the closest match followed by FastMap.

12.2.4 Image Query Models

A query model defines the interaction modality and the type of content the user is permitted to use in formulating search requests. Due to the wide variety of data the user may use (a combination of textual and image attributes) and the various ways these data may potentially be expressed, the range of different query models possible is quite large. Traditionally, only text-based approaches dominated in retrieval systems. In recent times, some visual attribute-based approaches have become available but in medical image retrieval systems such approaches are still quite rare. In the following sections we discuss the query models under three broad categories, namely textual, visual, and integrated cues.

12.2.4.1 Text-based Queries

Queries that treat image as an entity and search for images based on the verbal description are the text based queries. An example of a text based query can be "find all the images of a rose". The obvious problem with such an technique is that it is context sensitive. Since, in the domain of radiological imaging the similarity between images is defined according to the stage of the disease, severity, and treatment, the problem is more prominent. Pu[45] points out that of the 2.4 million queries almost 19% are failed searches. Smeaton and Quigley[46] describes a system that uses textual queries on the image captions to search for the images.

12.2.4.2 Visual cue Queries

With more technological innovations taking place than ever, more and more visual data is being produced. It has become imperative to efficiently find relevant information from this pool. While an image can be described in words, it is already rich in itself. An image can be accurately described in terms of colors[47-49], shapes[50-55], texture, spatial layout[56-60], and other visual features. Finding images based on content in the image, as opposed to the textual annotation is broadly known as Content Based Image Retrieval (CBIR). The content based image retrieval leads to high degree of effectiveness in terms of finding the closest match. In a typical content- based image retrieval system, an image is represented as a multi-dimensional feature vector. For finding an image, the user provides the system with an example image or a sketch, which allows the system to represent them as a feature vector. The system then calculates the similarity metrics between the feature vectors in the database and the input feature vector which helps in the retrieval process. To make the search effective, efficient indexing scheme needs to be in place. Users can be asked to provide relevance feedback which can be used to refine the query to retrieve more logical and meaningful results.

Some popular content-based image retrieval systems are, QBIC[61], ViewFinder[62], IBM Multimedia Analysis and Retrieval System[63].

12.2.4.3 Integrated Queries

It has often been noted that the performance of either stand-alone text-based queries or visual-cue queries are far from accurate. To overcome the limited searching capabilities of monomodal techniques, often integrated queries are used for searching and retrieval. Since the images are returned by searching on both semantic meaning and the pixel information for integrated queries, the results are much more relevant to the query[64]. For example a search on the term Alzheimer will return the MR scans of all the Alzheimer's disease patients. And given a query image of a MRI scan for which there is no information about the disease the patient has, the visual cue search process will return as result all the similar MR scans. However, a search on a query which is a combination of both the above queries i.e. a search on term Alzheimer with features similar to the given query image is likely to return the MR scans of all the Alzheimer's disease patient which have similar visual characteristics to the input image. Favela and Meza[65] combine content-based image retrieval using wavelet transforms with textual access method on the captions to get a combined index.

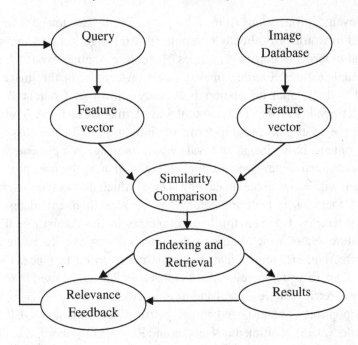

Fig. 12.2: Overview of content-based image retrieval.

One key issue in supporting searches based on both textual and visual cues is the potential of confusing the user due to the increase in number of different cues and the large number of combinations that are possible. In Viewfinder, one approach we have applied to support integrated queries is to permit the user to specify for a query different weights for individual attributes and thus indicate their preference for certain attributes over others. For example, in one version of ViewFinder, developed to search NASA mission images, it is possible for the user to review all the textual metadata and three major types of visual cues (color, shape, and texture) and assign different weights to specific attributes. These weights are subsequently used by during ranking of the hit set to determine the order of presentation. These weights are changeable at any time, on a per query basis. Often the size and scope of the image collection may influence what queries produce the best results.

Over time, the size and nature of the collection are likely to change. The user's experience with the system, as he or she interacts with the system and determine the relationship between their queries and corresponding responses produced by the system, also influences the effectiveness of the queries. These factors indicate a need for an iterative approach to query formulation, involving a cycle of trial and feedback. We discuss a class of technique known as relevance feedback which take into account these factors and also attempt to increase the user's power to express the semantics associated with their query demands.

12.2.4.4 Query Refinement

Despite the developments in the field of content based image retrieval, the existing systems are still not able to match upto the performance of the text based systems available. The techniques in use lack the ability to capture the semantic meaning of the image in the feature vector itself. Moreover, often the semantics are human-sensitive[66]. To address this issue, interactive relevance feedback is used. Relevance feedback tries to capture the context of the image by allowing users to tell the system what they expect from it by marking each result as positive or negative. Based on the feedback by the users the system refines the query to come up with improved results.

Initial relevance feedback learning algorithms were adopted from the domain of text retrieval. These algorithms tried either to refine the query or perform re-weighting. In the query point model the user query is pushed towards the positive examples and away from the negative counterparts. In MARS system, Rocchio's formula[67] is used to iteratively move the query point. According to Rocchio's formula, if Q represents the query, and F be the set of all image features of which F_R being relevant and F_N being irrelevant, and N_R and N_N being the number of images in F_R and F_N respectively. The modified optimal query can be expressed as:

$$Q' = \alpha Q + \beta \left(\left(\frac{1}{N_R} \sum (F_i) \in F_R \right) \right) - \gamma \left(\left(\frac{1}{N_N} \sum (F_i) \in F_R \right) \right) \quad (12.2)$$

Experiments have shown that the retrieval performance is improved using Rocchio's formula even in the case of images similar to textual access methods.

While on the other hand in re-weighting scheme the system re-assess the importance of each dimension of the feature vector. This can be achieved by promoting or demoting the weights associated with the distance metric for each dimension. Consider a situation where a one query result is marked as a positive response to it. In this scenario, the feature vectors that help with the significant matching are considered more important while on the other hand those with smaller contribution are less important for that query[68]. For a feature f of the image, the new weight, w_i can be computed as:

$$w_i = w_i \cdot \left(1 + \overline{\delta} - \delta_i\right)$$ 12.3)

$$\delta = \left| f(Q) - f\left(A_j^+\right) \right|$$ (12.4)

where $\overline{\delta}$ represents the mean value of δ, $f(A_j^+)$ represents the feature f for the promoted image A_j^+. On the grounds of same reasoning we can say for a negative example, the weights can be updated as:

$$w_i = w_i \cdot \left(1 - \overline{\delta} + \delta_i\right)$$ (12.5)

A model for updating the weights can be based on Bayesian framework[69]. Bayesian framework tried to model the problem of relevance feedback as an answer to the question, "given a history of display/action pairs, what is the probability that a given datum, $I_i \in I$, is equal to the target I_t, where I represents the large image database, I_t is the target image being searched for, and I_i is the set of images being shown to the user after i_{th} iteration".

After simplifications the model can be depicted by the following equations.

$$P\{I_i | a_i \ldots a_k, D_1 \ldots D_k, U\} \propto P\{I_i\} \prod_k P\{a_k | I_i, D_k, U\}$$ (12.6)

Decision trees have also been used for relevance feedback[70-71]. Ishikawa, *et al.*[72] presents an approach to relevance feedback that takes into consideration diagonal queries. They define diagonal queries as the queries that have non-zero covariance.

12.2.5 Interaction and Interface Evaluation

According to Shaw[73], for Information Retrieval systems the difficulties for the end-users increases if they are asked to interact with an unfamiliar computer system. User-interaction is central to the image retrieval process. The process starts with the user specifying a visual representation of the image, the representation which can either be an example image, or a sketch and fine-tuning the parameters of importance.

The effectiveness of the retrieval system should be evaluated in terms of the retrieval performance and the usability of the interface. The retrieval performance is often times measured in terms of precision and recall. Recall is defined as the proportion of the relevant images retrieved from a collection for a topic:

$$Recall = \frac{number\ of\ relevant\ images\ retrieved}{total\ number\ of\ relevant\ images\ in\ the\ collection} \quad (12.7)$$

Precision is the proportion of returned images that are relevant to the query:

$$Precision = \frac{number\ of\ relevant\ images\ retrieved}{total\ number\ of\ images\ retrieved} \quad (12.8)$$

Often times a compromise between recall and precision must be made, since improving one sacrifices the other. As the number of images retrieved increases, recall increases which leads to a decrease in precision. To compensate for this variety of aggregate measures such as F-score, recall- precision table, MAP (Mean Average Precision), ANMRR (Average Normalized Modified Retrieval Rank)[74] are used. However, MAP is most frequently used for evaluation of the retrieval performance. MAP is calculated by taking mean of average precision (AP) across all queries.

Valdivia, *et al.*[75] in their experiment finds out that adding more textual information to the system increases the effectiveness significantly.

Desealers, *et al.*[76] presents a comprehensive study for the medical image retrieval task. For their experiment they combined the textual information retrieval with the low level features. They used FIRE (Flexible Image Retrieval Engine) as the image retrieval engine. Their results were similar to Valdivia, *et al.*

Martínez-Fernández, *et al.*[77] using the GNU Image Finding Tool (GIFT) reported results for 3 tasks for the medical image retrieval task. They found that with relevance feedback in place the quality of results stayed same. However, with textual information added to the search process the results were significantly improved with relevance feedback.

The other important criterion for an IR system is evaluating the system from the perspective of human computer interaction. It concerns itself with the usability of the design where usability is defined as a measure of the ease with which a system can be learned or used, its safety, effectiveness and efficiency, and the attitude of its users towards it[78].

Run	Average Precision	%
mirabase.qtop	0.0942	100.0%
mirarf5.1.qtop	0.0942	100.0%
mirarf5.qtop	0.0941	99.8%
mirarf5.2.qtop	0.0934	99.1%

One of the earliest studies for the usability of the interface that supported multiple image query models was conducted by Mostafa and Dillon. Eight solvable search questions were given to 18 (7 male/11 female) library and information science students. The results of the experiment showed that the success rate were above 80% for both the interfaces, 83% and 84% respectively for visual-verbal and verbal interfaces. Users preferred to use visual surrogates for known item searches.

Venters, *et al.*[79] conducted a thorough user interviews to identify the user requirements. It was found that a single interface cannot satisfy the needs of all the end-users and they needed multiple interfaces which support the findings of McDonald, *et al.*[80]

They conducted 28 evaluation sessions and the participants were selected from across the 14 UK PIN offices. All the participants found the interfaces to be simple and easy to learn. They preferred browsing over other methods of access. However, with query by sketch, several participants made Type II error.

McDonald, *et al.*[81] in their study on 24 students at University of Sunderland using their system CHROMA found that the performance of the users is better with navigation tool than with sketch tool. Their study involved two types of tasks, scenarios and timed searches. The purpose of scenarios was to encourage participants to explore the system at their own pace. To capture the performance data they used the timed search task.

12.3 Conclusion and Research Opportunities

The area of medical image retrieval when compared to the broad field of IR is still at a relatively early stage of development. Significant advances have been made in automated approaches for feature extraction and image analysis. From a retrieval perspective however these advances have been under-utilized in devising new and innovative ways of retrieving images from large collections and manipulating the retrieved images dynamically to answer user's questions. Opportunities exist to create new image query models and integrating image mining, particularly in specific disease domains.

Another potential direction of development is in introducing multi-modality in medical image searching. It may be possible to allow the user to sketch out a rough shape or trace a shape on image surrogates as a way to formulate queries; this capability would help the user define a more accurate search when the search cannot be defined easily using textual and numerical data. Finally, to make faster progress in research, it would help if more attention is placed upon the creation of "gold standard" data sets – images that have been pre-labeled according to individual attributes present in them. These pre-labeled images would be useful in assessing the accuracy of automated classification and post-coordination algorithms. Additionally, making available modular test-bed systems that support critical functions such as indexing, query models, ranking, and display would be helpful as they would reduce the burden associated with development, by allowing the researcher to keep all the major functions constant while varying and evaluating the specific function under development.

References

1   Services, F., 100 million patient images stored, *http://www.fujitsu.com/uk/ news/pr/ fs_20061213.html.*

2   Rosslyn, N.E.M.A., *Digital imaging and communications in medicine* (di• com).

3   Dreyer, K.J., Hirschorn, D.S., Thrall, J.H. and Mehta, A. (2005), *PACS: A Guide to the Digital Revolution*, (Springer-Verlag New York, Inc., Secaucus, NJ, USA), ISBN 0387260102.

4   *ibid.*

5   *ibid.*

6   Rosslyn, *op.cit.*

7   Horri, S.C., A nontechnical introduction to dicom, *http://www.rsna.org/Technology/ DICOM/intro/services.cfm.*

8   Foundation, M., Analyze7.5 file format.

9   Berman, L., Long, R. and Thoma, G. (1994), Challenges in providing access to digitized x-rays over the internet, In *Proceedings of the 23rd AIPR Workshop.*

10 Grosky, W.I. (1994), Multimedia information systems, *IEEE MultiMedia*, 1(1), pp.12-24, ISSN 1070-986X, doi: http://dx.doi.org/10.1109/93.295262.

11 *ibid.*

12 Rowe, L.A. and Jain, R. (2005), ACM sigmm retreat report on future directions in multimedia research, *ACM Trans. Multimedia Comput. Commun. Appl.*, 1 (1), pp.3-13, ISSN 1551-6857, doi: http://doi.acm.org/10.1145/1047936. 1047938.

13 Keister, L. (1994), User types and queries: impact on image access systems, In eds. Fidel, R., Smith, P.J., Hahn, T.B. and Rasmussen, E.M., *Challenges in Indexing Electronic Text and Images*, Medford, NJ, USA, Information Today, Inc.

14 Zheng, W., Ouyang, Y., Ford, J. and Makedon F.S. (2003), Ontology-based image retrieval, In *WSEAS MMACTEE-WAMUS-NOLASC.*

15 Zhang, C., Chai, J. Y. and Jin, R. (2005), User term feedback in interactive text- based image retrieval. In SIGIR'05: *Proceedings of the 28th Annual International ACM SIGIR Conference on Research and Development in Information Retrieval*, pp.51-58, New York, NY, USA, ACM. ISBN 1-59593-034-5. doi: http://doi.acm.org/10.1145/1076034.1076046.

16 Jin, J.S., Indexing and Retrieving High Dimension Visual Features, *Multimedia Information Retrieval and Management*, eds. Feng, D., Siu, W.C., Jhang, H.J., pp.178-203, Springer ISBN 3-540-00244-8.

17 Pass, G. and Zabih, R. (1999), Comparing images using joint histograms, *Multimedia Syst.*, **7**(3), pp.234-240, ISSN 0942-4962. doi: http://dx.doi.org/10.1007/s005300050125.

18 Flickner, M., Sawhney, H., Niblack, W., Ashley, J., Huang, Q., Dom, B., Gorkani, M., Hafner, J., Lee, D., Petkovic, D., Steele, D. and Yanker, P. (1997), *Query by image and video content: The qbic system*, pp.7-22.

19 Bach, J.R., Fuller, C., Gupta, A., Hampapur, A., Horowitz, B., Humphrey, R., Jain, R. and Shu, C.F. (1996), Virage image search engine: An open framework for image management, In *Storage and Retrieval for Image and Video Databases (SPIE)*, pp.76-87.

20 Swain, M.J. and Ballard, D.H. (1991), Color indexing, *Int. J. Comput. Vision*, **7**(1), pp.11-32, ISSN 0920-5691. doi: http://dx.doi.org/10.1007/BF00130487.

21 Flickner (1997), *op.cit.*

22 Huang, J., Kumar, S.R., Mitra, M., Zhu, W.J. and Zabih, R. (1997), Image indexing using color correlograms, In CVPR'97: *Proceedings of the 1997 Conference on Computer Vision and Pattern Recognition (CVPR'97)*, p.762, Washing• ton, DC, USA, IEEE Computer Society. ISBN 0-8186-7822-4.

23 Flickner (1997), *op.cit.*

24 Tamura, H., Mori, T. and Yamawaki, T. (1978), Textural features corresponding to visual perception, *IEEE Transactions on System, Man and Cybernetics*, **8**, pp.460-473 (June).

25 Manjunath, B.S. and Ma, W.Y. (1996), Texture features for browsing and retrieval of image data, *IEEE Trans. Pattern Anal. Mach. Intell.*, **18**(8), pp.837-842, ISSN 0162-8828. doi: http://dx.doi.org/10.1109/34.531803.

26 Wu, P., Manjunanth, B., Newsam, S. and Shin, H. (1999), A texture descriptor for image retrieval and browsing, Content-Based Access of Image and Video Libraries, (CBAIVL'99) *Proceedings, IEEE Workshop* on. pp.3-7, (1999). doi: 10.1109/IVL.1999.781114.

27 Mattie, M.E., Staib, L., Stratmann, E., Tagare, H.D., Duncan, J. and Miller, P.L. (2000), Pathmaster: Content-based cell image retrieval using automated feature extraction, *Journal of American Medical Informatic Association*, **7**(4), pp.404-415 (July), URL http://www.jamia.org/cgi/content/abstract/ 7/4/404.

28 Shyu, C.R., Brodley, C.E., Kak, A.C., Kosaka, A., Aisen, A.M. and Broderick, L.S. (1999), Assert: A physician-in-the-loop content-based retrieval system for hrct image databases, *Comput. Vis. Image Underst.*, **75**(1-2), pp.111-132, ISSN 1077-3142. doi: http://dx.doi.org/10.1006/cviu.1999.0768.

29 Jain, A.K., Duin, R.P.W. and Mao, J. (2000), Statistical pattern recognition: A review, *IEEE Trans. Pattern Anal. Mach. Intell.*, **22**(1), pp.4-37, ISSN 0162-8828. doi: http://dx.doi.org/10.1109/34.824819.

30 Fodor, I.K. (2000), A survey of dimension reduction techniques, *Technical report*.

31 Jollifie, I.T. (1986), *Principal Component Analysis*, (Springer-Verlag, Berlin; New York).

32 Fodor, *op.cit.*

33 Wu, P., Manjunath, B.S. and Shin, H.D. (2000), Dimensionality reduction for image retrieval, In *IEEE International Conference on Image Processing (ICIP 2000)*, **3**, pp.726-729 (Sep), URL http://vision.ece.ucsb.edu/ publications/00ICIPeng.pdf.

34 Hull, D. (1994), Improving text retrieval for the routing problem using latent semantic indexing, In SIGIR'94: *Proceedings of the 17th Annual International ACM SIGIR Conference on Research and Development in Information Retrieval*, pp.282–291, New York, NY, USA, Springer-Verlag New York, Inc. ISBN 0-387-19889-X.

35 Vinay, V., Cox, I.J., Wood, K. and Milic-Frayling, N. (2005), A comparison of dimensionality reduction techniques for text retrieval, In *ICMLA'05: Proceedings of the Fourth International Conference on Machine Learning and Applications*, pp.293-298, Washington, DC, USA, IEEE Computer Society, ISBN 0-7695-2495-8. doi: http:// dx.doi.org/10.1109/ICMLA.2005.2.

36 Howland, P., Jeon, M. and Park, H. (2003), Structure preserving dimension reduction for clustered text data based on the generalized singular value decomposition, *SIAM J. Matrix Anal. Appl.*, **5**(1), pp. 165-179, ISSN 0895-4798. doi: http:// dx.doi.org.libproxy.lib.unc.edu/10.1137/S0895479801393666.

37 Jain, *op.cit.*

38 Hastie, T., Tibshirani, R. and Friedman, J. (2001), The *Elements of Statistical Learning*, Springer Series in Statistics, (Springer New York Inc., New York, NY, USA).

39 Cox, T.F. and Cox, M.A.A. (2000), Multidimensional Scaling, Second Edition, (Chapman & Hall/CRC, September), ISBN 1584880945, URL *http://www.amazon.ca/ exec/obidos/redirect?tag=citeulike09-20\&path=ASIN/1584880945.*

40 Fodor, *op.cit*

41 Cox, *op.cit.*

42 Wu, P., Manjunath, B. and Shin, H. (2000), Dimensionality reduction for image retrieval, *Proceedings of International Conference on Image Processing*, **3**, pp.726-729, doi:10.1109/ICIP.2000.899557.

43 Faloutsos, C. and Lin, K.I. (1995), Fastmap: A fast algorithm for indexing, data-mining and visualization of traditional and multimedia datasets, In *SIGMOD'95: Proceedings of the 1995 ACM SIGMOD International Conference on Management of Data*, pp.163-174, New York, NY, USA, ACM, ISBN 0-89791-731-6. doi: http://doi.acm.org.libproxy.lib.unc.edu/10.1145/223784. 223812.

44 Moravec, P. and Snasel, V. (2006), Dimension reduction methods for image retrieval, Intelligent Systems Design and Applications, *ISDA'06, Sixth International Conference*, **2**, pp.1055-1060 (Oct.). doi: 10.1109/ISDA.2006. 253757.

45 Pu, H.T. (2004), A query analytic model for image retrieval, In eds. Chen, Z., Chen, H., Miao, Q., Fu, Y., Fox, E.A. and Lim, E.P., ICADL, **3334**, *Lecture Notes in Computer Science*, pp.378-387, Springer, ISBN 3-540-24030-6.

46 Smeaton, A.F. and Quigley, I. (1996), Experiments on using semantic distances between words in image caption retrieval, In SIGIR'96: *Proceedings of the 19th Annual International ACM SIGIR Conference on Research and Development in Information Retrieval*, pp.174-180, New York, NY, USA, ACM. ISBN 0-89791-792-8, doi: http://doi.acm.org.libproxy.lib.unc.edu/10.1145/ 243199.243261.

47 Gray, R.S. (1995), Content-based image retrieval: color and edges, Technical Report PCS-TR95-252, Dartmouth College, Computer Science, Hanover, NH (March), URL *http://www.cs.dartmouth.edu/reports/TR95-252. ps.Z.*

48 Pass, *op.cit.*

49 Mathias, E. and Conci, A. (1998), Comparing the infiuence of color spaces and metrics in content-based image retrieval, In SIBGRAPHI'98: *Proceedings of the International Symposium on Computer Graphics, Image Processing, and Vision*, p.371, Washington, DC, USA, IEEE Computer Society. ISBN 0-8186-9215-4. doi: http://dx.doi.org/10.1109/ SIBGRA.1998.722775.

50 Wong, W.T., Shih, F.Y. and Liu, J. (2007), Shape-based image retrieval using support vector machines, fourier descriptors and self-organizing maps, *Inf. Sci.*, **177**(8), pp.1878-1891, ISSN 0020-0255. doi: http://dx.doi.org/10.1016/ j.ins.2006.10.008.

51 Sebastian, T.B. and Kimia, B.B. (2002), Metric-based shape retrieval in large databases, In ICPR'02: *Proceedings of the 16th International Conference on Pattern Recognition (ICPR'02)* 3, p.30291, Washington, DC, USA, IEEE Computer Society, ISBN 0-7695-1695-X.

52 Mehrotra, R. and Gary, J.E. (1998), Shape-similarity-based retrieval in image databases, In *Image description and retrieval*, pp.55-86, New York, NY, USA, Plenum Press, ISBN 0-306-45925-6.

53 Grosky, W.I. and Mehrotra, R. (1990), Index-based object recognition in pictorial data management, *Comput. Vision Graph, Image Process*, **52**(3), pp.416-436, ISSN 0734-189X. doi: http://dx.doi.org/10.1016/0734-189X(90) 90085-A.

54 Super, B.J. (2002), Fast retrieval of isolated visual shapes, *Comput. Vis. Image Underst.*, **85**(1), pp.1-21, ISSN 1077-3142. doi: http://dx.doi.org/10. 1006/cviu.2002.0959.

55 Mehtre, B.M., Kankanhalli, M.S. and Lee, W.F. (1997), Shape measures for content based image retrieval: A comparison, *Inf. Process. Manage.*, **33**(3), pp.319-337, ISSN 0306-4573. doi: http://dx.doi.org/10.1016/S0306-4573(96) 00069-6.

56 Chang, S.K., Shi, Q.Y. and Yan, C.W. (1987), Iconic indexing by 2-d strings, *IEEE Trans. Pattern Anal. Mach. Intell.*, **9**(3), pp.413-428, ISSN 0162-8828.

57 El-Kwae, E.A. and Kabuka, M.R. (1999), A robust framework for content-based retrieval by spatial similarity in image databases, *ACM Transactions on Information Systems*, **17**(2), pp.174-198, ISSN 1046-8188. doi: http: // doi.acm.org/10.1145/306686.306689.

58 Sung, S.Y. and Hu, T. (2006), Iconic pictorial retrieval using multiple attributes and spatial relationships, *Knowledge-Based Systems*, **19**(8), pp.687-695, ISSN 0950-7051. doi: http://dx.doi.org/10.1016/j.knosys.2006.05.013.

59 Chang, J.W., Kim, Y.J. and Chang, K.J. (1997), A spatial match representation scheme for indexing and querying in iconic image databases, In *CIKM'97: Proceedings of the Sixth International Conference on Information and Knowledge Management*, pp.169-176, New York, NY, USA, ACM, ISBN 0-89791-970-X. doi: http://doi.acm.org/10.1145/266714.266890.

60 Gudivada, V.N. (1994), Tessa – An image testbed for evaluating 2-d spatial similarity algorithms, *SIGIR Forum.*, **28**(2), pp.17-36, ISSN 0163-5840. doi: http://doi.acm.org/10.1145/195498.195502.

61 Flickner, M., Sawhney, H., Niblack, W., Ashley, J., Huang, Q., Dom, B., Gorkani, M., Hafner, J., Lee, D., Petkovic, D., Steele, D. and Yanker, P. (1995), Query by image and video content: The qbic system, *Computer.*, **28**(9), pp.23-32, ISSN 0018-9162. doi: http://dx.doi.org/10.1109/2.410146.

62 Albertson, D.E. Mostafa, J. and Fieber, J. (2002), Video searching and browsing using viewfinder, In *TREC*, URL *http://dblp.uni-trier.de/db/ conf/trec/trec2002.html #AlbertsonMF02.*

63 Natsev, A., Smith, J.R., Tesié, J., Xie, L. and Yan, R. (2008), Ibm multimedia analysis and retrieval system, In CIVR'08: *Proceedings of the 2008 international conference on Content-based image and video retrieval*, pp.553-554, New York, NY, USA, ACM, ISBN 978-1-60558-070-8. doi: *http://doi. acm.org/10.1145/1386352.1386427.*

64 Lu, G. and Williams, B. (1999), An integrated www image retrieval system, In The *Fifth Australian World Wide Web Conference.*

65 Favela, J. and Meza, V. (1999), Image retrieval agent: Integrating image content and text, *IEEE Intelligent System*, **14** (5), pp. 36-39, ISSN 1094-7167. doi: h t t p://doi.ieeecomputersociety.org/10.1109/5254.796086.

66 Rui, Y., Huang, T., Ortega, M. and Mehrotra, S. (1998), Relevance feedback: A power tool for interactive content-based image retrieval, *IEEE Transactions on Circuits and Systems for Video Technology*, **8**(5), pp.644-655 (Sep).

67 Rocchio, J.J. (1971), Relevance feedback in information retrieval, In ed. Salton, G, The SMART Retrieval System – *Experiments in Automatic Document Processing*, Prentice-Hall, Inc.

68 Huang, J., Kumar, S.R. and Mitra, M. (1997), Combining supervised learning with color correlograms for content-based image retrieval, In *MULTIMEDIA'97: Proceedings of the fifth ACM international conference on Multimedia*, pp.325-334, New York, NY, USA, ACM. ISBN 0-89791-991-2.

69 Cox, I., Miller, M., Omohundro, S. and Yianilos, P. (1996), Pichunter: Bayesian relevance feedback for image retrieval, *Proceedings of the 13th International Conference on Pattern Recognition*, **3**, pp.361-369, (Aug).

70 MacArthur, S.D., Brodley, C.E., Kak, A.C. and Broderick, L.S. (2002), Interactive content-based image retrieval using relevance feedback, *Comput. Vis. Image Underst.*, (2), pp.55-75, ISSN 1077-3142. doi: http://dx.doi.org/10. 1006/cviu.2002.0977.

71 MacArthur, S., Brodley, C. and Shyu, C.(2000) Relevance feedback decision trees in content-based image retrieval, In CBAIVL'00: *Proceedings of the IEEE Workshop on Content-based Access of Image and Video Libraries (CBAIVL'00)*, p.68, Washington, DC, USA, IEEE Computer Society. ISBN 0-7695-0695-X.

72 Ishikawa, Y., Subramanya, R. and Faloutsos, C. (1998), Mindreader: Querying databases through multiple examples, In VLDB'98: Proceedings of the 24rd International Conference on Very Large Data Bases, pp.218-227, San Francisco, CA, USA, Morgan Kaufmann Publishers Inc. ISBN 1-55860-566-5.

73 Shaw, D. (1991), The human-computer interface for information retrieval, *Annual Review of Information Science and Technology*, **26**, pp.155-195.

74 Group, M.V. (1999), Description of core experiments for mpeg-7 color/texture descriptors, *ISO/MPEGJTC1/SC29/WG11 MPEG98/M2819* (July).

75 Valdivia, M.T. Martín, Cumbreras, M.A.G, Díaz-Galiano, M.C., López L.A.U. and Ráez, A.M. (2005), The university of jaén at imageclef 2005: Adhoc and medical tasks. In *Ref. DBLP:conf/clef/2005*, pp.612–621. ISBN 3-540-45697-X.

76 Deselaers, T., Weyand, T., Keysers, D., Macherey, W. and Ney, H. (2005), Fire in imageclef 2005: Combining content-based image retrieval with textual information retrieval, In *Ref. DBLP:conf/clef/2005*, pp.652-661, ISBN 3-540-45697-X.

77 Martínez-Fernández, J.L., Villena-Román, J. García-Serrano, A. and Cristóbal, J.C.G (2005), Combining textual and visual features for image retrieval, In *Ref. DBLP:conf/clef/2005*, pp.680-691, ISBN 3-540-45697-X.

78 Nielsen, J., (1993), *Usability Engineering*, (Morgan Kaufmann Publishers Inc., San Francisco, CA, USA), ISBN 0125184050.

79 Venters, C.C., Hartley, R.J., Cooper, M.D. and Hewitt, W.T. (2001), Query by visual example: Assessing the usability of content-based image retrieval system user interfaces, In PCM'01: *Proceedings of the Second IEEE Pacific Rim Conference on Multimedia*, pp.514-521, London, UK, Springer-Verlag. ISBN 3-540-42680-9.

80 McDonald, S., Lai, T.S. and Tait, J. (2001), Evaluating a content based image retrieval system, In SIGIR'01: *Proceedings of the 24th annual international ACM SIGIR conference on Research and development in information retrieval*, pp.232-240, New York, NY, USA, ACM. ISBN 1-58113-331-6. doi: http://doi.acm.org/10.1145/383952.383993.

81 *ibid.*

Chapter 13

A Conceptual Model Metadata of Thai Palm Leaf Manuscripts

Nisachol Chamnongsri[1], Lampang Manmart[1], Vilas Wuwongse[2]
and Elin K. Jacob[3]

[1]*Information Studies Program*
Faculty of Humanities and Information Science
Khon Kaen University, Thailand
nisachol@sut.ac.th, lamman@kku.ac.th
[2]*School of Engineering and Technology*
Asian Institute of Technology, Thailand
vilasw@ait.ac.th
[3]*School of Library and Information Science,*
Indiana University, USA
jacob@indiana.edu

Abstract

This paper presents a semantic approach in the development of a metadata conceptual model for the development of a metadata scheme to represent palm leaf manuscripts (PLMs). The approach is based on the requirements of users, of collection management, and of PLMs characteristics to facilitate their retrieval in digital collections. Then, the IFLA's Functional Requirements for Bibliographic Records (FRBR) was adapted to extract the appropriate metadata elements and its relationship. The FRBR model uses a structured, four-level hierarchy to represent an intellectual work with multiple titles, editions or formats. Because FRBR focuses on representation of the conceptual work rather than the physical entity, it must be modified for representation of PLMs. In this modified model, the level of work applies to the physical PLM rather than its conceptual content; expression applies to the scripts, languages, and literary styles in which the PLM occurs; manifestation applies to the formats in which each expression is

243

available; and item applies to individual copies of a single format of reproduction. The modified model has been used to devise a metadata schema where each level has its own set of elements.

Keywords: Metadata Model, FRBR Model, Metadata Schema Development, Palm Leaf Manuscript, Cultural Heritage.

13.1 Introduction

In the new, knowledge-based world economic system, 'the production, dissemination and use of knowledge are crucial factors for enhancing economic growth, job creation, competitiveness and welfare'[1]. In Thailand, the 9th National Economic and Social Development Plan, 2002-2006, continued in the 10th Plan, 2007-2011, proposes that 'Thailand will become more competitive through the development of innovations by integrating modern science and technology and local wisdom. This approach will lay the foundation of Thailand's intellectual capital that can be used to develop competency and strengthen economic and social foundations for long-term, sustainable growth'[2].

For example, the One Tambol One Product (OTOP) project encourage villagers in each district to create original products by applying local wisdom or resources and modern technology, thereby giving the old products added value and new marketplace appeal[3].

Local wisdom, which is being promoted as one of the country's strengths, 'is a holistic, knowledge-based approach rooted in local circumstances such as the experiences and problem-solving skills of our Thai ancestors'[4] that are recorded in ancient documents. Palm Leaf Manuscripts (PLMs) is a form of ancient document that comprises a significant documentary heritage of the Isan people of Northeastern Thailand. These manuscripts contain a vast amount of knowledge that can be classified into eight categories: Buddhism (or Religion), Tradition and Beliefs, Customary Law, Economics, Traditional Medicine, Science, Liberal Arts, and History. 70% of the content recorded in PLMs consists of Buddhist stories and doctrine and 30% records local wisdom in the form of folktales, diaries, poetries, ethics, customary law, rites and rituals.

However, the local wisdom recorded in these manuscripts is often difficult to access and use. There are several obstacles: 'PLMs are scattered in many places, such as temples and households in rural areas, making them difficult to collect'[5]; 'they are regarded as holy objects and their owners may not allow access to them; some of the original manuscripts have disappeared or been destroyed'[6]; 'manuscripts that have survived are very fragile and easily damaged'[7]; and, perhaps most importantly, the languages in which they are written are either archaic or undergoing shift. Additionally, 'access to the content of the original manuscripts is problematic because they are written in archaic orthographies'[8], requiring expert translation. Recent (2000s) researches and preservation projects have been trying to collect and register palm leaf manuscripts that are scattered in many places, such as temples and households, and to transcribe these manuscripts, microfilm them for preservation, digitize these manuscripts to make them easy to access and use, and to preserve the original manuscripts. However, access to knowledge in digitized palm leaf manuscript is still a problem for users.

13.2 The Characteristics of Northeastern Thai Palm Leaf Manuscripts, Their Management, and Their Users

Northeastern Thai PLMs vary in size. A standard palm leaf manuscript is generally 5-6 cm. in width and 50-60 cm. in length with 48 pages (24 leaves written on both sides). PLMs can be as short as 15 cm. or as long as 80 cm. and can vary as to the number of pages (i.e., leaves). 'The people of Isan use different sizes in different ways: the longer PLMs are used as textbooks to record Buddhist stories and doctrine'[9], while 'the shorter ones are used as notebooks to record local wisdom related to daily life'[10]. The languages in which PLMs are written are either local or undergoing shift (Pali, ThaiIsan, Pali-ThaiIsan, Old Thai, and Khmer); and the manuscripts are written in four archaic orthographies (ThamIsan, ThaiNoi, Khmer, and Old Thai), requiring expert translation. Because the length of a PLM is determined by its physical dimensions rather than their content, a single manuscript may record many stories or a single story may require more than one manuscript. Furthermore, one PLM could be inscribed in various scripts and languages;

in addition one story/PLM could be inscribed in many literary styles – the manner in which the inscribers express the story (e.g. outstanding, fine, ordinary, etc.).

To preserve the knowledge recorded in palm leaf manuscripts and to make it accessible to modern users, preservation projects transcribe a PLM into the modern Thai alphabet and language and then reproduce the transcription in a variety of formats. The translation process involves several transformations: from the ancient alphabet to the modern Thai alphabet, from the ancient language to the Isan language, and finally from the Isan language to modern Thai. The original PLM, its transcriptions and its translations are reproduced in the form of microfilms, photocopies, digital images, PDF files, and text files. This ensures, on the one hand, that the user who is not familiar with ancient alphabets or archaic languages can access the knowledge in these manuscripts; on the other hand, a user or researcher familiar with ancient alphabets and languages can access the original manuscripts or their reproductions. To enhance ease of access to each story or subject in a PLM, some projects will separate reproduction or image files by story rather than by putting all images in one file in an attempt to maintain the appearance of the original bound manuscript.

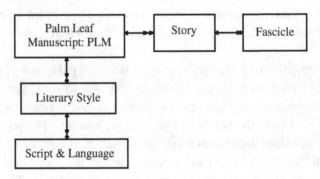

Fig. 13.1: The characteristics of a Northern Thai palm leaf manuscript.

Nevertheless, access to the knowledge in the PLMs is still a problem for users. Currently, the only access point to the manuscript is its title; but this presents a problem for the user who is not already familiar with both the content of a specific PLM and the archaic language in which it is written. Furthermore, access to individual stories is difficult when many stories are recorded in one fascicle or when a particular story has different titles in different PLMs, or the title has various spelling. Besides, each story or each manuscript written in different place will be unique even if it shares the same content with other PLMs. However, because users generally access manuscripts using the title or the subject, the title (or story) is obviously the most important access point to the knowledge contained in PLMs.

13.3 The Requirements

13.3.1 Requirements Analysis

To understand the context of the PLMs community and domain clearly the three requirement analyses were constructed (1) the unstructured interviews with three user groups – researchers, local philosophers, and graduate students, (2) the observation and unstructured interviews with the staff of four palm leaf manuscript preservation projects at four different institutes, and (3) the content analysis of the physical structure and types of content in the palm leaf manuscripts.

Because the PLMs are now being used by particular groups, therefore the subject of a user study must be real users – those who have experience in using the PLMs. A total of 20 subjects participated in the user study. They were selected from users' registration books of 4 PLM preservation projects and their publications related to the PLMs. Afterward, the snowball technique was used. There were seven graduate students from three fields; five Master students in Archeology, one in Thai language, and one PhD. student in Communication Arts. Another eight subjects were researchers from six academic institutes in five research areas: Isan history and Laos history, Eastern inscriptions and Buddhism, Isan Literature, Anthropology, Thai literature and Folklore. The last five subjects are local scholars who are paying attention in exploring knowledge in palm leaf manuscripts. All participants had experience in using palm leaf manuscripts for at least one year. The interviews were focused on how the participants carry out their searches when searching for the PLMs and its content, what is useful information in searching for the PLMs, and what they expect from the PLMs Metadata.

The collection management requirements analyzed form the observations and unstructured interviews with the project managers and staff of four palm leaf manuscript preservation projects at four different institutes. The questions focused on the current state of palm leaf manuscript management, the needs and expectations relating to metadata, and where the metadata is going to be used in the PLM management system.

Content analysis was used to analyze the physical structure and types of content in the palm leaf manuscripts. The populations were the Northeastern Thai palm leaf manuscripts stored in the National Library, Nakhon Ratchasima branch. Samples of palm leaf manuscripts were randomly selected from the PLMs registration books in the library. The total number of subjects was 30 PLMs. The samples were categorized into two groups, long PLMs and short PLMs. Under each group, the PLMs were separated according to their scripts and content.

13.3.2 Identification of Requirements

1. To access the desired content by using the reasonable access points (Title, Keywords, Subject, Place of found, Script, Language, etc.) and the user's stated search criteria. (e.g. users could search by title, if known; or they could search by title keywords or search for similar titles which would retrieve all related titles, or search for all similar content by the giving subject or the users' keywords; or they could search or limit the search using the place of found, or script; or they could search for a translation in the desired format).
2. To identify the desired manuscripts by important information such as if the same title were retrieved then users could distinguish between these PLMs, even by content recorded or physical characteristics; or they could identify the retrieved metadata by categorized in groups.
3. To select and obtain the desired PLMs (e.g. they could select PLM according to Title, Script, Language, Literary style, Place of found, Date of inscription, Physical condition, Version, and Format. Then obtain the PLMs by information about Storage place, URI, Access method and Right of use or Access restriction).

4. To display the digitized PLMs in a suitable way for individual users. Because digitized PLMs are composed of various digital files (e.g. one PLM which has 24 leaves could be composed of 24 JPEG images, and 24 text files – translation files of each leaf of this PLM could be displayed as one image one text file start from leaf number one until end; or could be displayed all images first then all text files; or the PLM could be displayed in the traditional manner, with two pages at one time – same screen, in this case page 2 and page 3 come from different leaves).

5. To preserve the PLMs in a digital form for a long time use. There is technical information dealing with attributes of digital images and the production technique associated with them (e.g. could make the preservation decisions and actions, or to know which preservation action was taken, could display and use digital PLMs when technology is changed, could ensure the authenticity of digital PLMs and the rights control).

6. Interoperability between different computer systems. Metadata elements and values should have a formal definition, defined obviously in the way that is both computer and human understandable. Therefore, PLMs metadata and its content could be shared and used in the most effective way (e.g. could search and reuse PLMs metadata from different projects, could search for PLMs holding by different projects from their own project interface).

13.4 Conceptual Model of Metadata Elements for the PLMs

A conceptual model of metadata provides a framework which allows one to examine the metadata elements and its relationships, and 'provide guidelines for the extraction and use of appropriate metadata elements'[11] which will bring the productive result. 'It is a crucial component in understanding the metadata context'[12] and conceptual structure of metadata elements in a systematic way. Thus, extracting the key elements and structure of the domain in 'designing metadata schema should be based on the establishment of a data model through an analysis of the requirements of the community and the domain'[13].

The most wildly accepted conceptual model in defining metadata elements is a conceptual model that has been developed by the IFLA (International

Federation of Library Associations and Institutions) Study group on the Functional Requirement for Bibliographic Records.

13.4.1 The FRBR Model

The Functional Requirements for Bibliographic Records (FRBR) model was proposed by the International Federation of Library Associations and Institutions (IFLA)[14] in 1998. FRBR is a conceptual model that defines a structured framework and the relationships between metadata records by focusing on the kinds of resources that a data record describes. In order to solve the problem of searching for intellectual work in a digital library, where one work may have a variety of titles, versions and/or formats, FRBR uses a hierarchical structure that establishes relationships between four levels of representation: a work, its *expression(s)*, an expression's *manifestation(s)*, and the individual *item(s)*. This approach ensures that the user will be able to select the most appropriate version or format of the desired work.

'The hierarchical model of FRBR for group 1 entities was inspired by the entity relationship model for relational databases and by the concept of inheritance'[15], which ensures that the properties (or data elements) described at superordinate levels of representation are inherited by all the subordinate levels nested under them. FRBR lays the foundation for hierarchical catalogue records by recognizing the difference between a particular works, several expressions of the work, various formats in which an expression exists, and the particular item:

- *Work* represents an intellectual concept of works, identified by titles and realized through its relationship with expression;
- *Expression* represents the various versions or revisions of a work established in its relationship with one or more manifestations;
- *Manifestation* represents the physical embodiment of an expression;
- *Item* represents the individual unit of a manifestation.

A *Work* is realized through its *Expression*, which is embodied in a *Manifestation*, which is exemplified by an *Item*.

Group 2 entities (Person, Corporate body) deal with the responsibility for intellectual content and the reproductions of manifestation. Group 3 entities (Concept, Object, Event, Place) are a content topic. The FRBR model assists

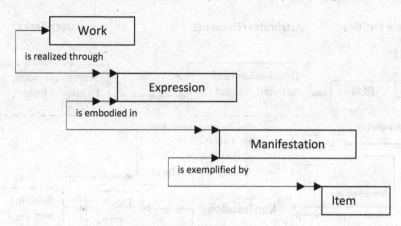

Fig. 13.2: FRBR Model: Primary entities and relationships (IFLA 1998).

in identifying and defining relationships between key entities at each level and the horizontal relationships between entities at the same level. Therefore, FRBR provides guidelines for the extraction and use of appropriate metadata elements; especially for complicated documents such as film, music or museum material, which may have a range of expressions and formats. It is widely accepted and frequently used in digital library projects as a model for an analysis of the metadata requirements and the development of metadata schemas[16, 17]. In addition, analysis of FRBR and user tasks when searching for bibliographic records we can know the key function of each entity which assists us in extracting appropriate metadata elements for each entity at each level to support each function. For example, when searching for documents in "Traditional medicine", a user would start their search with the content topic, or search by title if known. In the FRBR model '*Work*' represents the intellectual concept which would be defined by attribute '*Title*', '*Uniform title*', '*Subject*', and '*Keyword*' which directly responds to the 'find' task. We will consider the key functions for each entity and its elements in the metadata system which provided useful guidelines in designing metadata schema for a particular community.

13.4.2 Adapting FRBR Model to PLMs Metadata Model

According to the analysis of Nagamori and Sugimoto 'the four levels model of FRBR is an excellent framework to explicitly separate the intellectual

Main Entities   Attributes/Elements   User Tasks

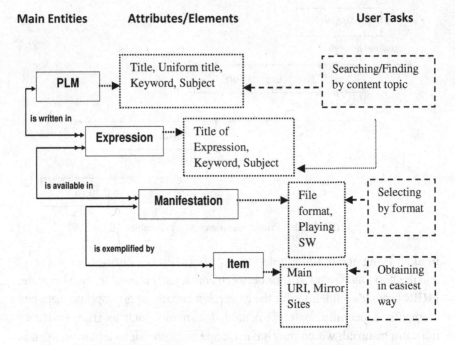

Fig. 13.3: Analysis of metadata elements by matching entities of
the FRBR model with user tasks.

content and physical characteristics of a resource'[18]. This hierarchical relationship offer an opportunity for the development of metadata scheme that will enable the user to discover, select, locate, and access PLMs in the most appropriate versions and formats. Moreover, this model can be used to develop metadata that will support manuscript preservation and rights control management. However, the concept of work as the top level in the FRBR model is not suitable for the representation of PLMs since FRBR focuses on work as a conceptual entity. Because a PLM exists as a physical rather than a conceptual entity, an effective metadata schema must consider orthographies and languages, the physical and digital formats in which those expressions are available, and the individual copies of a given manifestation.

Accordingly, the revised FRBR model applies the concept of work to the physical manuscript – the PLM, which may contain one or more stories or only a part of a story. The expression applies to two entities (1) Expression

(Original) includes scripts, languages and literary styles in which the original PLMs occur: languages (Khmer language, Pali language, Isan language, and Old Thai language), scripts (Khmer, ThamIsan, ThaiNoi, or Thai), literary styles (outstanding, fine, ordinary) (2) Expression (Translation) for the transcription versions (Modern Thai and English). The manifestation addresses the various formats in which each expression is available: the original fascicle, microfilm, photocopy, digital image (formatted for archiving and distribution), and text files in both modern Thai and archaic alphabets. Manifestation can be separated into two entities the Manifestation (Original) and Manifestation (Reproduction). The item applies to individual copies of a single format of reproduction only, because the original PLM itself – the manuscript, is recognized as one item.

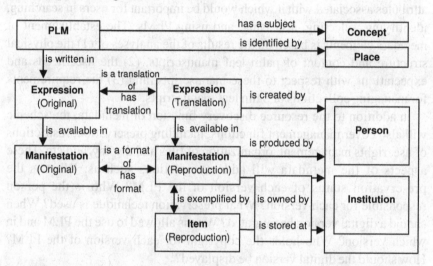

Fig. 13.4: A Model of the relationships between the key entities in PLM metadata.

There are 14 relationships in the model showing the relationships between three groups of entities separated into two groups: both by vertical and by horizontal. The vertical relationships are the hieratical relationships between group 1 entities which separate content and its carriers; these are *written in, is available in*, and *is exemplified by*. The horizontal relationships are the relationship between group 1 entities, which link the original PLM to its reproduction formats and versions. Other groups of horizontal relationships are (1) the relationship between group 1 entities and group 3 entities, *has a subject* links the original PLM to the concept of content, *is identified by* links PLM to Place. Although the intellectual concept – that is, the stories recorded in a PLM – may show little variation across PLMs, the treatment of the story which reflect local wisdom: because the style of the PLM's author will reflect the traditions and beliefs of their communities, each story and therefore each manuscript will be unique even if it shares the same content with other PLMs. Thus, place can shape intellectual content (2) relationships between the lower levels of group 1 and group 2 entities, which shows the responsibility of the production and reproduction of versions and formats. These are *is created by, is produced by*; and which also shows the rights of ownership of each version and format.

Each entity in the model was then identified by those characteristics or attributes associated with it which would be important for users in searching, identifying, selecting, accessing, and using PLMs. The establishment of metadata elements is based on the results of the analyses of (1) the physical structure and content of palm leaf manuscripts, (2) the user needs and expectations with respect to these manuscripts, and (3) the requirements for managing collections of palm leaf manuscripts.

In addition to the resource discovery function of metadata, the scheme will also cover management functions, including preservation, restrictions of use, rights management, organization of files and display, and etc. These aspects of the metadata will address questions such as: What is the preservation status of each version of the PLM? Who is the person responsible for each version? What preservation technique is used? When should a digital version be migrated? Who is allowed to use the PLM and in which version? Who holds the copyright for each version of the PLM? How should the digital version be displayed?

The process of designing administrative and structural metadata will require the identification of the various functions involved in collection management and use. The FRBR model can help in analyzing at which level each function applies and the relationship between functions since some functions will not apply at all levels. For example, at the level of expression, the original manuscript will not require structural metadata intended to support digital functions. Thus, the model indicates that structural metadata at each level can be linked across different functions by using the identification number assigned to a unique record.

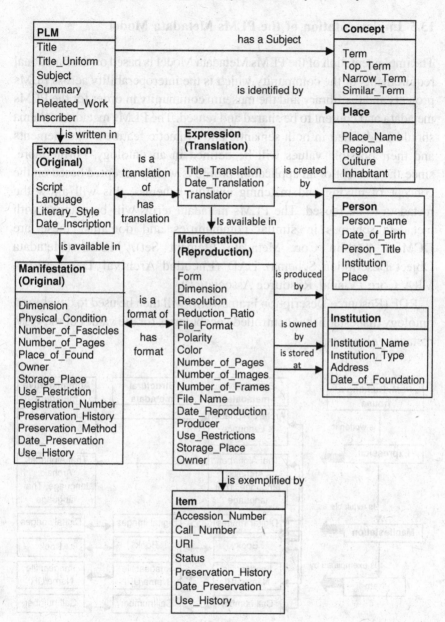

Fig. 13.5: Attributes of the entity: Example.

13.5 Implementation of the PLMs Metadata Model

The implementation of the PLMs Metadata Model is based on the functional requirements of the community which is the interoperability across PLMs projects and the library and the museum community in order for the PLMs metadata and content to be shared and reused. The PLMs metadata schema should be defined in both semantic and syntactic features. The elements and their possible values will be defined in an ontology. Furthermore, since the concept of an application profile is widely accepted based on the concept of mixing and matching existing schemas, this will allow the metadata to be reused. The PLMs metadata terms will be mapped with metadata schemas in similar communities and domains: these are DCMES (Dublin Core Metadata Element Set), MODS (Metadata Object Description Schema), EAD (Encoded Archival Description), VRA Core (Visual Resource Association).

RDF (Resource Description Framework) will then be used to develop an ontology that establishes controlled vocabularies for the values of the PLM metadata elements.

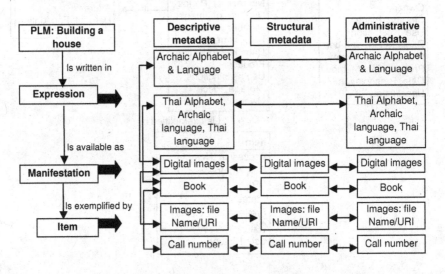

Fig. 13.6: An example of functional structure for PLM metadata.

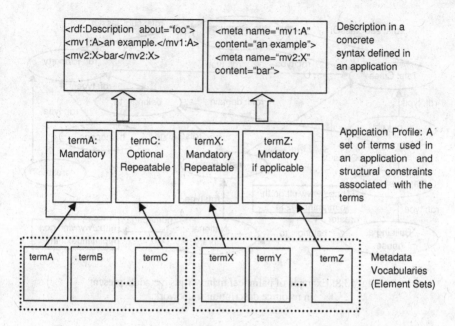

Fig. 13.7: Concept of application profile[19].

13.6 Conclusion and Future Works

Developing a metadata schema, the design of a metadata conceptual model in a systematic way based on the requirements of users, of collection management, and of document characteristics will bring a useful result. The FRBR model offers a conceptual framework for the development of a metadata scheme that will support the main functions of PLM management: resource discovery, access and use; record maintenance; digital preservation; and rights management. FRBR's four-level hierarchical model allows the metadata record at each level to represent the data applicable to the various expressions and different formats as well as individual items. Moreover, the FRBR model will be of assistance in defining those metadata elements which are required for each function of the digital collection. Reconceptualizing *work* as a representation of the original palm leaf manuscript rather the intellectual concept, FRBR's hierarchical structure provides an effective framework for the design of a metadata scheme that

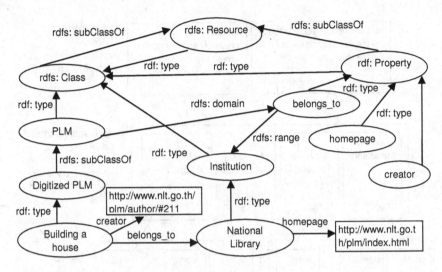

Fig. 13.8: Example of palm leaf manuscripts metadata present
in resource description framework.

can support the various functions required for access to and management of resources in PLM collections.

The next step in this research; will be to map the PLM metadata elements with metadata schemas in similar communities and domains. A set of attributes will be established to specify terms based on the functional requirements of palm leaf manuscript collection management. Then a Resource Description Framework (RDF/XML and RDFS) will be used to define the metadata scheme and ontology in order to allow reuse of the elements defined in the palm leaf manuscript metadata schema and ontology. The last step, will be the evaluation of the developed metadata for the management of PLMs by community's users.

Acknowledgments

We would like to acknowledge the grant from the Center for Research on Plurality in the Mekong Region, Khon Kaen University and a Southeast Asia Digital Library Grant from the US Department of Education administered through Northern Illinois University Library.

References

1 [UNECE] United Nations Economic Commission for Europe (2004), Knowledge-Based Economy, *http://www.unece.org/ie/wp8/kbe.htm* (accessed on 14 December 2004).

2 Office of National Economic & Social Development Board (2002), One Tambon One Product *http://ie.nesdb.go.th/gd/html/forms/Projects/TumBonProject/TumBonExPlain/ TumBonProjectExPlain.htm* (accessed on 5 February 2006), (In Thai).

3 Office of National Economic & Social Development Board (2003), The main point of the Ninth National Economic and Social Development Plan, *http://www.nesd.go.th/ interesting_menu/progress_plan/plan9_data* (accessed on 12 January 2006), (In Thai)

4 Office of the National Education Commission (1999), The policy to promote Thailand's Knowledge on education In the *Conference on management of local information*, Mahasarakham: Central Library, Mahasarakham University (accessed on 11 December 2004), (In Thai).

5 Samutkhup, Suriya and Kittiarsa, Pattana (2003), Why was a female lower garment used as a wrapper of palm-leaf manuscripts in Northeast Thailand? An anthropology approach to Isan palm leaf manuscripts, *Art & Culture Magazine*, **24**(6), pp.82-95, (In Thai).

6 (2004), Northeastern Thai Palm Leaf Manuscript Preservation Project, *http://www.msu.ac.th/BL/bailan/PAG2.ASP* (accessed on 9 December 2004), (In Thai).

7 Somboon-a-nake, Sineenart (1998), Palm leaf manuscripts: The cultural heritage of the Lanna people *Library Association Bulletin*, **42**(2), pp.25-36, (In Thai).

8 Na Thalang, Ekawit (2001), *Isan's Knowledge*, Bangkok: Ammarin 115 pp. (In Thai) Northeastern Thai Palm Leaf Manuscript Preservation Project Mahasarakham University.

9 Chantharasakha, Surajit (2001), Isan palm leaf manuscripts In *Conference on the Study of Knowledge Recorded in Palm Leaf Manuscript in Northeastern Thailand*, Mahasarakham, Thailand, 22-23 September 2001, Faculty of Humanities and Social Science Mahasarakham University, UNESCO, Chiang Mai University.

10 Na Thalang, *op.cit.*

11 Han, Sung-Kook, Lee, Hyun-Sil and Jeong, Young-Sik (2006), Conceptual model of metadata schema for records management, pp.21-31. In The 2nd International Symposium on Knowledge processing and Service for China, Japan and Korea: Metadata and Ontology, Beijing, China, *http://grid.wonkwang.ac.kr/* (accessed on 4 February 2008).

12 Nagamori, Mitsuharu and Sugimoto, Shigeo (2007), Using metadata schema registry as a core function to enhance usability and reusability of metadata schemas, pp.85-95, In Proceedings of the International Conference on Dublin Core and Metadata Applications 2007, *http://www.dcmipubs.org/ojs/index.php/pubs/article/view/35/17* (accessed on 10 February 2008).

13 Han, Sung-Kook, *et al.*, *op.cit.*

14 [IFLA] (1998), IFLA Study Group on the Functional Requirements for Bibliographic Records, *Functional Requirements for Bibliographic Records: Final Report UBCIM Publications-New Series*, **19**, Munchen: Saur, K.G., *http://www.ifla.org/VII/s13/frbr/frbr.htm* (accessed on 20 November 2004).

15 Coyle, Karen (2004), Future considerations: the functional library system record, *Library Hi Tech*, **22**(2), pp.166-174.

16 Lin, Simon C., *et al.* (2001), A metadata case study for the FRBR model based on Chinese painting and calligraphy at the National Palace Museum in Taipei, pp.51-59 In *DC-2001 Proceedings of the international conference on Dublin Core and metadata applications*, Kyoto, Japan, NII.

17 Caplan, Priscilla (2003), *Metadata fundamentals for all librarians Chicago*, American Library Association.

18 Nagamori, *et al.*, (2007), *op.cit.*

19 Nagamori, Mitsuharu (2006), Hybrid and Network-Assisted Vocabulary Interface, *http://raus.slis.tsukuba.ac.jp/* (accessed on 14 March 2008).

Chapter 14

Techniques for Extraction of Metadata from Heritage Documents

Ratna Sanyal[1]

[1]Indian Institute of Information Technology Allahabad, India

rsanyal@iiita.ac.in

Abstract

This work discusses the importance of maintaining a consistent metadata for digital archives. Various techniques for automatic extraction of metadata from textual documents are described. The Dublin Core is used as a reference model for the metadata. Techniques for automatic extraction of each element of Dublin Core are given. A common theme is the use of language independent techniques, as far as possible. Special emphasis is laid on the identification of specific features that will give us clues for automatically extracting the metadata.

Keywords: Metadata Extraction, Heritage Documents, Dublin Core, Language Independent Techniques.

14.1 Introduction

Information of our heritage is stored in different types of digital media like text, images, video, audio etc. Preserving and disseminating this information in a digital format presents unique challenges and opportunities. This work reviews some of the techniques that have been used for retrieving information from these diverse media. A common theme is the extraction of metadata from the available digitized items. This is an essential step for proper indexing of the items and plays a crucial role in the subsequent retrieval. Subsequent to the review of the existing techniques we shall focus our attention on the extraction of metadata from textual items. The techniques used for natural language processing and information retrieval will form the basis of this step. We shall discuss methods that are largely language independent. This will allow the developed techniques to work for textual heritage information of every language, with minimal linguistic dependencies. The role of structural information will also be discussed in this context.

An important aspect of dissemination is the capability of the system to offer various views, depending on the interests of the user. For example, one user may want to study images of a particular genre irrespective of the location or time. On the other hand, another user may want to examine images and text of a particular location/period. Other scenarios of user requirements are also possible. The system, therefore, has to extract the relevant metadata to satisfy these diverse requirements. Also, the indexing and retrieval techniques have to take advantage of the extracted metadata so that the most relevant results can be presented to the user.

The initial problem is to collect the heritage documents and properly place these valuable textual documents in a digital repository. This broad array of information carries with it not only the problem of immensity of scale but also the lack of any uniform structure or arrangement of text. Thus, an associated area of interest is the issue of organizing and archiving this information. We can simplify the detail and complexity of the data and the resulting information overload by grouping similar documents together, i.e. performing document classification. It is generally used to represent two kinds of analysis: Document Categorization and Document Clustering. To perform these analyses one has to extract the metadata about the documents. If we could collect almost all the heritage textual documents and classify them correctly, then we can say that our heritage documents are really kept in a repository which is in all aspects 'rich'.

In the next section, we give a brief overview of metadata. While not essential for this paper, we use the Dublin Core[1] as a suitable reference model for representation of metadata. The techniques for extraction of different elements of metadata are presented in the third section. The concluding remarks are presented in the last section.

14.2 Brief Overview of Metadata

Metadata is data about the data. While the data itself would be the actual document, image, video etc., the metadata would consist of items like title, author, publisher etc. Digital libraries are large repositories of valuable information which are accessible to the global public. Metadata is important for these libraries since it allows us to organize this information in a systematic way. Unfortunately, if the metadata is not created consistently, then the data of the organization is adversely affected. Also, it is possible that some information may be wrong or misleading and may lack authentication. This shows the importance of well organized metadata for any rich repository.

Several standards are available for metadata. Dublin Core (DC) serves as a useful reference model[2] and we assume the Dublin Core model to standardize metadata in this work. This model provides an element set for describing a wide range of resources. Simple Dublin Core (SDC) represents fifteen elements: Title, Subject and Keyword, Description, Resource Type, Source, Relation, Coverage, Creator, Publisher, Contributor, Rights Management, Date, Format, Resource Identifier and Language. The Qualified Dublin Core (QDC) represents eighteen elements. The latter includes fifteen elements of SDC and three additional elements like Audience, Provenance and Rights Holder. There are a group of element refinements (called qualifiers) for refining the semantics of elements.

Some tools are available for extracting a few DC elements. The National Library of New Zealand has released a metadata extraction tool[3]. This is capable to extract DC elements like Title (name of the file), Type, Date and time, Format, Identifier and Language (only English). Another metadata extraction tool is DC.dot[4], a Dublin Core generator for NewsAgent. This tool can retrieve a Web page and automatically generate Dublin Core HTML <META> tags. After typing a URL, this tool can extract Title, Subject, Description, Type, Format and identifier. These tools, quite often, extract the information available in the properties of digital files. They often do not examine the contents of the file itself. However, as we all know, the real information lies within the document itself.

However, we would like to emphasize that several other metadata standards are available. For example, the Open Language Archives Community (OLAC) describes another three sets of metadata[5]. The 'Work

Language' defines the information entities and their intellectual attributes as names of works and the creators, 'Document Language' and 'Subject Language'. The choice of a particular standard depends on the ultimate use of the metadata. OLAC, for example, is very useful for linguistic purposes while DC is good for information retrieval.

In the next section we shall see how various elements of the metadata can be extracted. The focus will be on identifying the specific features that carry information about a given element.

14.3 Techniques for Extraction of Metadata

Heritage textual documents can be in plain text, text with images, only image and image with caption. These may be in a variety of formats like .txt, .html, .doc, .pdf, .tif, .gif, .bmp etc. We assume that the documents have some structure including (hopefully) title (as a heading), name of author(s), sections, copyright information. We also assume that the text in documents is in Unicode / ASCII or they can be converted into these encoding formats. Automated metadata generation can be done as an experimental research, where information retrieval techniques are used on digital resources. An alternative approach is provided by applications research where content creation software and metadata generation tools are used in operational setting. For example some commercial software supports metadata generation of a number of elements that map to DC standards. However, most of these do not look at the content. In the following we discuss approaches for extracting metadata from the contents of text documents.

Before we begin to examine the techniques that can be used for extracting the metadata automatically, it is fair to say that these methods are not fool proof. In particular, automatic extraction of some elements is still an open problem. Moreover, the structural information present in most text documents, offers valuable clues for extracting certain types of metadata.

14.3.1 Extraction of Title

The first DC element is "Title" which, we can say, is the Name given to the resource. For example, the name of the book that describes the days of lord

Rama was given as "Ramayana". In this case, the name is referred as the title of the document. The techniques for automatic extraction of the title would use structural information. The specific features that are useful for extracting the title are:

- *Position of text*: the title would appear towards the beginning of the document
- *Font type, style and size*: the font type, style or size of the title is likely to be different from that of the rest of the document
- *Repetition:* the title may be repeated at specific location (e.g. bottom or top of the alternate pages) on subsequent pages.

The title may also have been created at the time of creation of document. We can extract the font information of each character of the document. A frequency analysis of the fonts would show that a large majority of the characters have been written in a particular font, with a particular style and size. These are not likely candidates for the title. We focus our attention on the characters that use infrequently used fonts in the document. We next check which of these infrequent fonts has been used in the first 5% characters of the document. In case there is more than one font appearing in the top 5% then we choose the biggest font as that of the title. Thus, by using a combination of these distinct features it is possible to extract the exact title of the document.

14.3.2 Extraction of Subject and Keyword

The next DC element is "Subject and Keyword". The description of this element is the topic of the content of the resource. For example, the subject of the book "Ramayana" is Rama. The extraction of this element is not as straightforward as that of the title because the structural information is scanty. Instead, we can use statistical information retrieval techniques to identify the most important terms/words of the document. Structural information (i.e. whether the extracted terms/words also occur in the title) can be used to enhance the accuracy. We can use the following steps for automatic keyword extraction:

- Remove all stop words and other functional words using suitable language models
- Perform Named Entity (NE) recognition

- Perform anaphora resolution
- Rank words using an algorithm like Probabilistic Latent Semantic Analysis (PLSA)[6].
- Pick the most important words of the document

A standard list is available for English stop words[7]. For other languages we can use purely statistical techniques to build language models that will identify functional and content bearing words. The functional words are (usually) not keywords and hence can be removed from further consideration as far as keyword spotting is concerned.

Named Entity Recognition is a subtask of machine translation and information retrieval. Finding similar topics will be easier if we recognize the named entities from different textual documents either in same language or even in different languages. Named entities are words which belong to certain categories like persons, places, organizations, numerical quantities, expressions of times etc. A large number of techniques have been developed to recognize named entities for different languages. Some of them are Rule based and others are Statistical techniques. The rule based approach uses the morphological and contextual evidence[8] of a natural language and consequently determine the named entities. This eventually leads to formation of some language specific rules for identifying named entities. The statistical based techniques use a substantial amount of annotated data to train a model, like Hidden Markov Model[9], Conditional Random Fields[10] and Maximum Entropy Model[11], and subsequently test it with the test data. All of these above methods require the effort of a language expert. Moreover, the annotated data required for statistical techniques is yet to be made available for Indian Languages. A new technique has been developed to recognize named entities of different languages[12]. This approach does not use the above techniques. Instead, this new approach not only reduces the burden of collecting and annotating data, but is language independent also. This method is used to build a multilingual named entity list that can be used by the named entity recognizer. This method finds the actual transliteration from an untagged corpus. For example, the transliteration for "बंगाल" is "Bangal" while the English representation is "Bengal". The basic idea is to match the two representations of the same NE, in two different languages, using a phonetic matching algorithm. This comes from the property of the NE that they are similar sounding when written in native script or any other script. However this cross-lingual matching is not a trivial task. First of all, the two strings to be matched have to be represented in the same script. We can use the tool[13] to recognize NE in English language. For Indian languages, we can adopt the different NE recognizer developed by different groups in Technology Development in Indian Languages[14].

Now the next task is to find out the anaphora from those textual documents. Anaphors are the most frequent constructs in any language, which indicate some relationship among different sentences. An anaphor is usually the pronoun used in place of some noun present in any of the preceding sentences. Presence of an anaphor depicts a semantic relation between the sentence having it and the one having its corresponding referent. The aim is to resolve the reference of the anaphor to one of the many nouns present in the preceding sentences. To understand the problem, we can analyze the following example:

Hindi Sentence: अनिता मेधावी है। वह परिश्रमी भी है।[i]

In the above two sentences, the word "वह" (she) in second sentence refers to "अनिता" (Anita).

Specifically if we can detect the corresponding nouns of those pronouns which are present in that text, that will help us to resolve the main character/ important characters of that document. For performing anaphora resolution, we can use the standard tool if the language is English. The same task can be done in Indian languages if the tool is ready. Semantic Analysis of Text-Documents has been an active area of research for the past few years[15-17]. It involves extensive use of Natural Language Processing techniques for analyzing the semantic structures of the text. Semantic analysis of a document means to analyze the meaning or transitions in meaning of the sentences or of different clauses and the relation among them. There are a number of approaches to semantic analysis. We have developed anaphora resolution as a technique of semantic analysis of text documents written in Hindi language[18]. The focus is on texts that mainly employ simple sentences, such as children's stories, short essays, etc. The technique works by locating sentences in the text that are semantically related through anaphors, analyzing their semantics and exploiting the latter for resolving

---

[i] "I" is the sentence terminator in Hindi just as "." is in English.

referents of the respective anaphors. We can also use coreference resolution from same documents or from other documents. Coreference resolution is a necessary step for effective information retrieval in a collection of large number of textual documents. Coreference is said to occur when one expression has the same referent as another expression. Coreference resolution is the process of finding coreferences in a document. For example "Mohandas Karamchand Gandhi" can be referred to as "Mr. Gandhi", "Mahatma Gandhi", "he" or even "Bapu". All these phrases corefer and the purpose of the resolution system is to find out this relationship between them[19]. This will help us to recover the information about whether similar documents are available in the same language. If we want to retrieve the same information in different languages, we should have the proper machine translation system.

PLSA[20] is a very effective language independent technique for finding the latent concepts in a given document or a set of documents. The concepts are described on the basis of the words / terms that are relevant to the concept. It can be used for measuring the similarity between a pair of documents as well as for finding the words / terms that are important for a given document. The numeric value generated by this technique is very useful for ranking words in terms of their importance. Moreover, since this method is language independent, so it can be used for any language. As we will see in subsequent sections, the ranking of the words is also useful for building a description or summary of the document.

14.3.3 Extraction of Description

The third DC element is "Description" which means an account of the content of the resource. We need the description of the document because this description can be used to preview the main text, classification or categorization of the documents, question answering, access from mobile devices (PDAs/cell phones) etc.

Now the description of the textual document may be an abstract of the document or an extraction of the important sentences. These descriptions are based on single or multiple documents, domain specific (religion, cultural heritage, healthcare, tourism …) or specific to a type of text (scientific articles, news items, short stories …). Multiple documents can be multilingual. The approaches to multilingual description are:

- Evolve techniques that are language independent (almost) - most of the extraction techniques based on scoring methods fall under this category.
- Use multilingual corpora – with machine learning algorithms, particularly clusterization.

For example, the description of any document is given at the preface part, abstract or summary section. We can use the structural and semantic information by finding the most important sentence (s) in the document.

We can adopt the same steps those we have followed for keyword extraction. The difference is that after ranking the words we can rank the sentences of the document and pick the most important sentences of the document. The sentences can then be presented in the same order as they appear in the original document. Thus, these sentences form a very concise summary of the document which is formed by extracting the most important sentences. One can improve the quality of this summary by analyzing the individual sentences for clauses[21]. It is possible to identify the important (nucleus) clauses and the less important (satellite) clauses using cue phrases[22]. The satellites are then removed and the truncated sentence is then reconstructed to make it grammatically correct.

There is a research work on multi-document summarization by sentence extraction[23]. This approach uses statistical method of generating extraction from multi-document. This approach works on any domain. However, there may be problems, as this approach is not based on any natural language techniques, so co-reference resolution factor would be missing and also passages would be disjoint among the multi-documents. An alternative system is used by the Columbia Newsblaster System which provides descriptions of topically clustered news daily since late 2001[24]. This system follows a Corpus based approach.

Intellexer Summarizer[25] is a desktop application which is based on the technique of semantic analysis of the document. This technique analyzes the document that is to be summarized and extracts the main ideas to ultimately reproduce a short summary. Intellexer Summarizer's unique feature is to produce high quality of theme and structure-oriented summarization by providing a selection of summary types. There is no restriction on the size of the document. "IBM many aspects document summarization tool"[26] highlights various angles of the content of a document. The user decides about the size of a summary and this tool produces a summary based on the user's decision. The user selects the number of sentences based on two criteria, i) Coverage and ii) orthogonality. The basic algorithm is based on the combination of document summarization problem and a greedy search strategy. Users can load a textual document and also decide the size of the summary. The system automatically generates the summary or the description of the document.

14.3.4 Extraction of Resource Type

The nature or genre of the content of the resource is also an important DC element, which is termed as "Resource Type". Though we are considering only the textual documents, but the document may be of other types. For example it may be an "Image", "Sound", "Source code" etc. or combinations of two or three can be present in a text document. The type can be extracted easily from the file extension of the document. For example: .jpg will have type "Image". The restriction is that new file extensions will have to be added in the database.

Further, the Resource Type may be refined. If a fixed vocabulary is used then classification techniques can be used for refinements. However, it should be kept in mind that fixed vocabularies are available for specific domains only. For example, one may use the AGROVOC[27] and AGRIS[28] categories for this purpose for the agriculture domain. Further refinement (like "scenery", "landscape" etc.) will require appropriate content based image retrieval algorithms.

14.3.5 Extraction of Source

Automatic extraction of the next DC element, "Source", is an open problem. Source is referred as a reference to a resource from which the present resource is derived. For example one particular image may be taken from "Page number 76 of ISBN 81-203-1470-0". Then we can say that the second one is the source of that particular image. The extraction of source is very difficult as one has to retrieve the information from a vast repository. Further complications can arise if the original source is not available in the repository in an electronic format. In that case only manual searching is possible or the information can come only from the experts in that particular domain.

The following example will clarify the point: Suppose a digital photograph of Mona Lisa is taken and added to the archive. What will be the source corresponding to this resource? Would it be the name of the original painter, the art gallery where the original picture is available or the name of the photographer? Sufficient information is not available in the photograph itself and only a domain expert would be able to give the required information. If there is seal of the organization/institutions from where the document was taken for digitization, then one can fill-up the information of the source. As the name of the source will be embedded in the image of the seal or monogram, one can use the technique cited in Jean, *et al.*[29], where the authors have discussed about the document analysis system which would extract the area of interest in grey-scale document images.

14.3.6 Extraction of Relation

The next element is "Relation". This element is described as a reference to a related resource. There are nine different types of relations as described in Dublin core. These are IsPartOf, IsVersionOf, IsFormatOf, HasFormat, IsReferencedBy, References, IsBasisFor, IsBasedOn and Requires. Automatic extraction of each type of relation is also an important and open problem. Some can be extracted automatically. For example: IsReferencedBy and References can be extracted from the structural information of the References section of a text and cross checked from the main body of the text or can be extracted from the rich repository of different documents. We need a string matching algorithm to find the similarity of the sentences from different documents. In case of image, we have to apply the text area segmentation process and isolate the image from the text. Image processing technique, like content based information retrieval should be applied to extract the whole or part of the image from the existing repository. The repository can be enriched if we store photographs of sculptures, historical places, statues etc.

Relation is an important element even for automatic indexing of documents. Though we can use coreference resolution technique[30] along with title, keywords and subject for automatic indexing, but extraction of relation would give more accurate result. Extraction of relation could help to find the links between different documents based on above mentioned nine types of relationship.

14.3.7 *Extraction of Coverage*

The next DC element, "Coverage", is referred to as the extent or scope of the content of the resource. Scope of the content can be spatial or temporal. For example, the news on "Workshop on Self-Archiving and Digital Repository" was "The Library, Documentation and Information Science Division of the Institute is organizing a four days Workshop on Self-Archiving and Digital Repository during October 31 to November 3, 2007. The program of this event includes invited lectures, discussions, hands-on training by eminent scholars, and resource persons in this field". Now if we want to know about the coverage on subject, then it should be 'Self-Archiving and Digital Repository' and if our target is to find the coverage on time then it is 'October 31 to November 3, 2007'.

The extraction of the coverage may not be possible or meaningful in every case – for example in story books etc. Coverage can be extracted from the title/abstract/sentences close to the title (if available) using cue phrases[31]. The cue phrase "during" was used in earlier example to extract the coverage in the context of time. There are approximately two hundred fifty cue phrases in English. One can build the corresponding cue phrases for other Indian languages and use them to extract this important DC element. These cue phrases are useful to detect semantic instead of structural information. Even one can classify the cue phrases in two areas as discourse and sentential using lexicon based or machine learning techniques[32].

14.3.8 *Extraction of Creator*

One important DC element is the "Creator". The description of creator is an entity primarily responsible for making the content of the resource. In other words we can say that creator is the author or writer or poet depending on the type of the document. The name of the creator can be easily extracted by using the same features that were used for extraction of the "Title" i.e. structural information, position of text, font type and style. Problems may arise in some situations. For example if the original heritage document was written by one creator and later on it was modified or translated by another creator then we have an ambiguity. In these cases we should take extra precaution and use sub-fields. We should put the fields like modifier, translator, editor etc. also as additional fields and we should keep the name of original creator at the proper field "Creator". In general, the information about translated by or modified by or edited by, is available in the beginning of the document. Therefore this information can be extracted using the same features and suitable cue phrases. In a recent research work[33], even the information about the author along with type and text has been extracted from handwritten annotation in digital documents.

14.3.9 Extraction of Publisher

The next DC element, "Publisher" is the entity responsible for making the resource available. Extraction of this element becomes easy as this information is given as 'publisher' or 'published by' words in the beginning of the document. We can use the structural information, cue phrases and other sources of information to extract the name of the publisher. Difficulty would arise if the document is handwritten and it has not been published anywhere. In these cases it is best to leave this field blank.

14.3.10 Extraction of Contributor

"Contributor" is another DC element which is defined as an entity responsible for making contributions to the content of the resource. For example the contributor may be a person or an organization or a service. For our purposes, we will assume that the contributor is the organization that created the digital content and made it available for the digital library. Information about contributor is not (usually) embedded in the document itself. The name of the contributor can be extracted from the properties of the digitized files of that document. For example, some popular formats will store information about the author, company, date of creation, date of modification etc. as properties of the file. We can extract the information about the company from this information. We should note that this actually gives us information about the organization/company that performed the digitization which may be quite distinct from the name of the organization that holds the original document.

14.3.11 Extraction of Rights Management

Automatic extraction is an open problem in the case of the next DC element "Rights Management". This element is described as the information about rights held in and over the resource. IPR, Copyright or other property rights may come under this element. For example, sometimes we face the problem when we see that Rights= "Access limited to XYZ" or Rights= "Access unlimited". However, it should also be noted in most countries the copyright laws stipulate that no person or organization holds the copyright to a document after a certain period. For example, in India, the mandatory period is till sixty years after the demise of the author. By this definition, most textual heritage documents are free of copyright. Similarly, if an author gives his own unpublished document or the organization provides the unpublished documents where the work had been done for preservation in digital media, then such documents are also free of copyright.

14.3.12 Extraction of Date

"Date" is the next DC element which is given as a date associated with an event in the life cycle of the resource. For example Date = "1998-02-16". One has to take precaution during the extraction of the date. For example, if the date is interpreted as the date of creation of the digitized content, then it can be extracted from the properties of the file containing the digitized content. However, this date is different from the date of creation of the original un-digitized matter. On the other hand, if we interpret "Date" as the date of the publication/creation of the original un-digitized document, then we have to extract this information from the first few pages of that document by locating the publisher name, edition etc. This information is given at the beginning of that document. If the document has not been published or is a handwritten that does not mention the date, then the tentative date may come out after the discussion with some domain experts. Obviously, automatic extraction is not possible in such cases since the information does not exist in the document itself.

14.3.13 Extraction of Format

The next DC element "Format" is defined as the physical or digital manifestation of the resource. For example: the Format is doc, pdf, text format or the document is beyond text documents e.g. "image/gif" format. The information can be extracted from file extension. A database of possible file extensions has to be updated regularly.

14.3.14 Extraction of Resource Identifier

Extraction of the DC element "Resource Identifier" is possible for large number of textual documents. The description of this element is an unambiguous reference to the resource within a given context. For example keywords like ISBN can be used as resource identifier if available. Identifier="ISBN 81-203-1470-0". Alternatively, we can use URL for web pages, where that web page contains information of the heritage documents and after digitization the document is kept as an electronic format. If such information is not available then file names of digital resource can be used.

14.3.15 Extraction of Language

The DC element, "Language" is described as the language of the intellectual content of the resource. For examples: Language = "Hindi" or Language = "Bengali". Information about the script can be extracted if Unicode representation of the characters is used in the document. However, in several cases, the same script is used for different languages. Thus, the specific language can be identified using multilingual dictionary lookup in such cases. The latter type of extraction technique can be used for distinguishing between Hindi and Nepali as same script, Devanagari, is used in case of both the languages.

14.3.16 Extraction of Audience

A class of entity for whom the resource is intended or useful is termed as "Audience". It is a new element introduced in QDC. This class may be determined by the creator or the publisher or by a third party. For example Audience = "Researchers and students of History". Domain experts can develop local lists of values/vocabulary for describing the classes. The specific class for a particular document can then be determined using pattern classification techniques. One can use standard supervised training algorithms for classification of the documents where the features to be used are, once again, the key words that have been extracted previously.

14.3.17 Extraction of Provenance

The second new element in QDC is "Provenance". This element is described as a statement of any changes in ownership and custody of the resource since its creation that is significant for its authenticity, integrity and interpretation. For example: Provenance is given as "This book once owned by XYZ" or "recovered by the Allahabad Museum in 2007." Automatic extraction of this element is difficult since this information is not embedded in either the document or its associated properties file. It is, in fact, buried in some other related documents. Thus, automatic extraction of this element is an open problem.

14.3.18 Extraction of Rights Holder

The third new element in QDC is 'Rights Holder' and is described as a person or organization owning or managing rights over the resource. For example: if Rights Holder = "ABC" for some document, then the keyword "copyright" or the symbol © will be available and can be used for extraction. Moreover, this information will be close to the location of the title, edition, year or publisher of the document and this structural information will allow us to extract the data.

14.4 Conclusions

Metadata helps the users to extract the resources more efficiently from the heterogeneous repository of digital libraries. This article presented the possible techniques and challenges for automatic extraction of different metadata elements of Dublin core. Existing tools are unable to extract all the elements. Certain elements of metadata can be extracted from the properties of the files containing the digitized documents. Information retrieval techniques, together with suitable heuristics based on structural information shows promise of assisting humans in the creation of consistent metadata for the remaining elements. In particular, extraction of topic, key words and summary are possible using these techniques. However, there is a paucity of tools and techniques for Indian languages and much work needs to be done in this area. Moreover, metadata will be more useful and consistent if a feedback is obtained from the users since it will help authenticate the documents.

References

1 *http://dublincore.org/documents/usageguide/*,   *http://www.dublincore.org/documents/ dces/* (latest version dated:2008-01-14).

2 *ibid.*

3 National Library of New Zealand – Metadata Extraction Tool, *http://meta-extractor.sourceforge.net/*

4 Dot-A Dublin Core generator for NewsAgent, DC., *http://www.ukoln.ac.uk/metadata/ newsagent/dc*

5 The Open Language Archives Community: OLAC, *www.language-archives.org/events/ talks/olac*

6 Hofmann, T. (1999), Probabilistic Latent Semantic Indexing, Annual ACM Conference on Research and Development in Information Retrieval, *Proceedings of the 22nd annual international ACM SIGIR conference on Research and development in information*, pp.50-57.

7 *www.ai.mit.edu/projects/jmlr/papers/volume5/lewis04a/lyr12004_rcv1v2_EADME.htm*

8 Kim, J. and Woodland, P.C. (2000), Rule Based Named Entity Recognition, *Technical Report CUED/F-INFENG/TR.385*, Cambridge University Engineering Department.

9 Robert, M. (2002), Markov models for language-independent named entity recognition, In *Proceedings of CoNLL-2002 Taipei*, Taiwan, pp.591-599.

10 McCallum, A. and Li, W. (2003), Early results for named entity recognition with conditional random fields, feature induction and web-enhanced lexicons, *Proceedings of the Conference on Natural Language Learning*, pp.188-191.

11 Uchimoto, K., Ma, Q., Murata, M., Ozako, H. and Isahara, H. (2000), Named entity extraction based on a maximum entropy model and transformation rules, *Proceedings of the 38th Annual Meeting on Association for Computational Linguistics*, pp.326-335.

12 Nayan, A., Rao, B.R.K., Singh, P., Sanyal, S. and Sanyal, R. (2008), Named Entity recognition for Indian Languages, *Proceedings of International Workshop on NER for South and South East Asian Languages*.

13 *http://nlp.stanford.edu/software/CRF-NER.shtml*

14 IJCNLP-08 Workshop on NER for South and South East Asian Languages (NSSEAL), *ltrc.iiit.ac.in/ner-ssea-08*

15 Mitkov, R. (1999), Anaphora Resolution, The State of the Art: *Technical Report*, School of Languages and European Studies, University of Wolverhampton, Stanford Street, Wolverhampton WV1 1SB, United Kingdom.

16 Wunsch, H. (2006), Anaphora Resolution – What Helps in, *Pre-Proceedings of the International Conference on Linguistic Evidence*.

17 Sobha, L. and Patnaik, B.N. (2000), Vasisth: An Anaphora Resolution System For Indian Languages, *International Conference on Artificial and Computational Intelligence for Decision, Control and Automation in Engineering and Industrial Applications ACIDCA*.

18 Agarwal, S., Srivastava, M., Agarwal, P. and Sanyal, R. (2007), Anaphora resolution in Hindi documents, in *Proceedings of IEEE NLP-KE-2007*, pp.452-458.

19 Vishnuprasad, T.M. and Sanyal, R. (2007), Coreference resolution using hybrid approach, *Proceedings of International Conference in Universal Digital Libraries (ICUDL)*.

20 Hofmann, *op.cit.*

21 Tejaswi, T., Parai, G., Borah, P., Shah, S., Sanyal, S., (2008), SCORES: Summarizer using Combination and Reduction of Extracted Sequences, accepted for publication in *International Journal of Reasoning-based Intelligent Systems*, Science Direct, Elsevier.

22 Marcu, D. (1997), From Discourse Structures to Text Summaries, In The *Proceedings of the ACL'97/EACL'97 Workshop on Intelligent Scalable Text Summarization*, pp.82-88.

23 Jade, G., Vibhu, M., Jaime, C. and Mark, K. (2004), Multi document summarization

by sentence extraction, *Proceedings of the NAACL-ANLP Workshop on Automatic summarization*, **4**.

24 Columbia Newsblaster, *newsblaster.cs.columbia.edu*

25 Intellexer Summarizer, *http://summarizer.intellexer.com/*

26 IBM many aspects document summarization tool,.*http://www.alphaworks.ibm.com/tech/manyaspects*

27 AGROVOC Thesaurus, *www.fao.org/agrovoc/*

28 AGRIS/CARIS, *www.fao.org/AGRIS/*

29 Jean, D., Myriam, C., Hubert, E. and Ching, Y.S. (2001), Extraction of text areas in printed document images, *Proceedings of the ACM Symposium on Document engineering*, pp.157-165.

30 Vishnuprasad, *op.cit.*

31 Marcu, *op.cit.*

32 Diane, J.L. (1996), Cue Phrase Classification Using Machine Learning, *Journal of Artificial Intelligence Research*, **5**, pp.53-94.

33 Marcel, G. (2006), Coding semantics of handwritten annotation, *International Journal of Metadata, Semantics and Ontologies*, **1**, pp.216-223.

Chapter 15

Adaptable Records: Making Heritage Information Accessible to All

Liddy Nevile[1]

[1]*Department of Computer Sciences*
La Trobe University, Australia
liddy@sunriseresearch.org

Abstract

Heritage maintenance imposes obligations on record creators and heritage conservators to ensure that all means available are used to ensure that heritage records are effective in the future, as well as that the content preserved provides an adequate record, for the circumstances and for the context. Given the inability to predict the facilities that will be available in the future, it is imperative that such records are as flexible as possible in anticipation of a wide range of user agents being deployed to access them. Such accessibility is already advocated for current users of heritage records – often in the form of adaptability for people with disabilities. Inclusive design, then, is a fundamental requirement of all heritage work both for immediate and future welfare. Quality processes are essential for the production of inclusive resources (and services) to satisfy these adaptability needs.

Keywords: Heritage Information, Preservation and Access, Inclusive Resources.

15.1 Introduction

In this paper, the requirements for inclusive digital resources are considered through the lens of making resources accessible immediately to everyone.

By law in many countries, public resources are required to be available to all equally, including not discriminating against those who cannot access text, or sounds, or visuals because of disabilities.

It is not easy to ascertain the needs of an individual for a number of reasons. Many people have mild disabilities that minimally impact their daily activities and as these become more significant, they learn to adapt to them and perhaps to adjust what they choose to do. That is, many people do not think of themselves as having disabilities but have adapted behaviours that may inhibit their use of resources that otherwise would enrich their lives. (This is proving a problem with aging communities in Europe as European governments increasingly depend on information being online.)

Many resource providers assume they can anticipate their audience and often they even attempt to provide for several different audiences but it is difficult to determine the needs of others, their individual challenges, and how they may choose to accommodate their difficulties with essential adaptations. It is even more difficult to predict their preferences, small adaptations that make activity more pleasant and inclusive.

What matters to an individual user is whether, or not, they can access a resource. What matters to a publisher of resources is whether, or not, the audience for their resource will be able to access it. The challenge is to satisfy both needs.

15.2 Identifying Accessibility Needs

Recently an Englishman flew a small plane from the UK to Australia[1]. The only way in which it was obvious that this man had special needs was offered in a photograph of him in August 2007 showing his white cane. His particular needs are not visible: many blind people use technologies that allow them access to an amazing range of resources, tolerating many in a very inferior form from that accessed by others. Some blind people read Braille: for them 'cutting and pasting' and other activities associated with visual reading/writing can be important, so even printed Braille is not sufficient for their needs. Most blind people never learn to read Braille.

In 2003, Microsoft Research discovered, somewhat unexpectedly, that in the USA, among working-age people (18 to 64), due to a range of mild to severe difficulties and impairments:

- 38% (64.2 million) of working-age adults are likely to benefit from the use of accessible technology due to mild difficulties and impairments.
- 22% (37.2 million) of working-age adults are very likely to benefit from the use of accessible technology due to severe difficulties and impairments.
- 40% (67.6 million) of working-age adults are not likely to benefit due to no or minimal difficulties or impairments[2].

There is every reason to assume these are reasonably indicative figures for people living with good access to good health care but in other countries, the situation can be expected to be far worse.

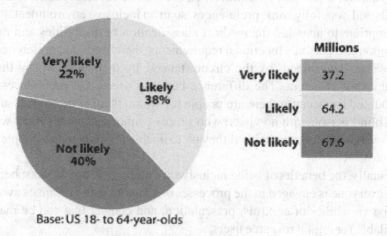

Base: US 18- to 64-year-olds

Fig. 15.1: The likelihood of difficulties with Web content for people with varying disabilities in the US[3].

(Source: Study commissioned by Microsoft, conducted by Forrester Research, Inc., 2003.)

15.3 Being Inclusive

Many communities try to cater for people with disabilities but they do not always do this in an 'inclusive' way. There is a difference between an environment with special accommodations for some people and one in which everyone can participate according to their needs and preferences. The latter is more 'inclusive' than the former.

It is asserted that lack of inclusiveness often occurs naturally when people with disabilities are classified by their disabilities, rather than included in a community of individuals who operate equally according to their particular needs and preferences.

In Europe there is an even more open view of disabilities in the digital age: people use different devices in different context and many of these make for problems with access to digital information and resources[4]. This can be the result of having, say, a mobile device to access directions while driving a car. In this case, the driver should be using their eyes for the road and so they need a device that does not require vision for control. Such a driver is 'eyes-busy' and, like a blind person, has needs that include non-visual controls and resource output.

Whatever a person's disabilities, all that can be accommodated is their needs and hopefully some preferences, so in an inclusive environment, it is appropriate to abandon the medical classification of disabilities and turn attention to a person's functional requirements, their needs and preferences. These are determined by the circumstances, by their purpose, by their disabilities, et cetera. The difference between needs and preferences is accounted for because there are people for whom there is no choice, such as a blind person with no vision who simply cannot see and a person who can see but tires unacceptably if they try to do this for more than a couple of minutes.

Finally, the benefits of being inclusive are numerous, not the least being that everyone is engaged in the processes of adaptation and becomes aware of the variability of controls, presentation, and content that can be made available for digital resource users.

15.4 Accessibility Accommodations

Accessibility accommodations have generally been determined according to either the lowest common denominator of needs or, in many cases, by website publishers who guesstimate their audiences and provide several alternative versions of the site for them.

It is extremely difficult to predict the audience for any resource that has value as this can change from time to time but even more because it is almost impossible to predict what needs and preferences a user will have.

The pilot (mentioned above) cannot see but knowing that does not make it easy to determine in what form he wants to receive information: it's not possible to tell from that information alone if he reads Braille, if he can read it while flying, or even what standard of Braille he reads. So providing him with Braille could be the perfect solution or leave him in a continued state of lack of access to the information he needs. In other words, his functional requirements are needed to inform the choice of presentation and, in the end, his medical condition is irrelevant and the same requirements can be relevant to people for other reasons. This is defined to be an inclusive approach to the determination of the user's needs as well as the most efficient.

Not only is it not possible to attribute a complete set of requirements to a blind person, it is often not easy to even predict if a blind person will want to use the resource. There are many examples in universities, of students studying courses in situations where inappropriate assumptions have been made about who will undertake what related vocation upon completion of their course. It is now not unusual to find health workers who have disabilities, such as blind masseurs, or a blind medical journalist, who studies medicine to gain a better understanding of the field.

15.5 Accessibility from the Core Web Founders

The World Wide Web Consortium (W3C)[5] found that the introduction of the graphical user interface to the Web was at once a blessing to the millions of people who could now manipulate resources with little technical expertise but alienated many of the blind people, and people with other disabilities. These people had become dependent upon computer technology for their work and even their learning and entertainment.

In response to this problem, the W3C has collaborated with many others to define guidelines for the use of Web technologies to alleviate the problem. W3C looked at what was needed in the way of software to produce Web content, and to view or interact with it and guidelines for producing Web content. They also worked on their own development strategies to ensure that in the future, all their work was vetted for accessibility before it was released.

W3C is a technical specifications body that undertook some special work in the area of what they called 'technology and society' and it was within this field that the accessibility work fitted. The choice of activities and the way of doing them has, to a large extent, been very similar to their work in other domains however. As time has gone on, W3C's need to make their work operational has led to even the accessibility work favouring an approach that might otherwise be thought to be very closely related to the field of computer science. The guidelines have been assumed to operate as specifications in many countries that have relied on them to set their local standards and so the newer versions of the guidelines have had to be re-written more as specifications, which is the sort of work W3C usually does.

While such specifications are very useful, they are not able to support every possible use case. It has been argued that the W3C Web Content Accessibility Guidelines (WCAG)[6] in particular, are flawed. It can easily be shown that there are examples of user needs that are not supported by them[7], and because even if a resource does not satisfy the so-called specifications, the resource might nevertheless be very useful for an individual[8].

While W3C's work is respected for the way in which it has managed to provide guidelines, and the extent to which compliant resources would be useful to many people with disabilities, there has not been sufficient implementation of them for this to make a substantial difference. It is estimated that about 3% of what might be thought of as important resources are accessible to, well, nearly everyone. In the DRD study of 1000 university websites in the UK, this was the case[9], and universities are required to be concerned about accessibility so it may be lower in other cases.

In summary, it is not sufficient to provide specifications, or guidelines, and expect that the Web will become accessible.

15.6 Inclusive Server Systems

The Inclusive Learning Exchange (TILE)[10] at the University of Toronto provides a good example of how resources might be adapted to an individual's needs and preferences by a service. In this case, TILE maintains a profile of the user's needs and preferences, a PNP, and a description of the accessibility characteristics of a resource, a DRD. When a user attempts to access a resource, the components for that resource that match the user's current PNP are assembled for presentation to the user. A user may, at any time, change their profile so even while a resource is being used, captions might be added to it to make it more accessible if a user finds they cannot hear the dialogue, for instance.

TILE is able to adapt resources because the resources are created on demand, from a set of components that include many, often redundant, forms so that an image can be immediately supplemented by a description, captions can be added to video, Braille can be generated, etc.

The learner's profile is not considered a profile of the person but of their functional needs and preferences. The potential range of needs and preferences is anticipated in so much as the many formats are developed when the resource is made (in the case of TILE), but the components are not locked into any particular presentation of the resource. By having atomic elements to use as these components, the developers enable flexible mixing and matching of components, and in many cases can reuse components in a range of complete resources.

The example offered by TILE is of a system that is primarily user-centered, constantly adaptable, and built on two matched profiles, one of the user's selected needs and preferences and the other on the resource's relevant characteristics. For example, someone driving a car while learning from a pod-cast might want descriptions of all images in just the same way as a blind student. The choice of auditory over visual components entered in the student profile is matched to the resource's access mode in the description of the resource's characteristics. The access mode of interest is not the format of the resource but the sensory mode that will be required to use the intellectual content of the resource. Fortunately, text encoded according to the W3C Guidelines can be rendered as small or large text, printed, read aloud by software, or even converted to Braille.

Some resources, of course, have more and less important content so it is useful to be able to distinguish between content that is a major component of the intellectual content of the resource. For example, some text in an illustrated story would be considered essential while the illustrations may be required to make sense of the story or just be ornamental, and any accompanying advertising could perhaps be considered ornamental.

15.7 AccessForAll Profiles

To support this approach being developed by the AccessForAll work, attention has been on the metadata that describes the needs and preferences of users and the matching metadata that describes the accessibility characteristics of resources, to be matched to the user profiles.

As has been made clear, such profiles are not profiles of people but rather of functional requirements that people might choose to use. As it is common for people's requirements to change as their context changes, a single person may refer to one or more such profiles at different times. They might even refer to some that are made publicly available, some specially made for them, and still want to make changes on-the-fly. Similarly, people might share profiles, a good example being people who use a particular lecture theatre and so equally want large text for their presentations. The first set of profiles was for purely digital resources, and comprised a pair. These were published by the IMS Global Learning Consortium in 2005[11].

Before the first pair were finished at the ISO level, several other pairs of profiles have been commenced. These include a pair for resources that are a mix of digital materials and physical or human components, a pair for the accessibility of events and places, and others to do with language and cultural considerations that are relevant to adaptation of resources[12]. It is anticipated the pattern will continue.

15.8 AccessForAll for Digital Resources

For the matching of digital resources to users' needs and preferences, a structured set of requirements with a defined range of values was required. This precision, while often not necessary, was essential in the case of accessibility for people who are dependent on assistive technologies. Such devices are not usually mainstream market devices, and so it has always been important to make sure the manufacturers can accommodate the proposed standards. In fact, many assistive technologies are now becoming more mainstream. For example, dictation is being used for voice input by people not familiar with computers or busy using their hands at a check-out, and screen readers by 'early adopting' people using mobile telephones to access the Web and so not having sufficient screen 'real estate' to display larger resources.

The relevant aspects of personal needs and preferences for digital resources were considered to be of three kinds:

- Display: how resources are to be presented and structured,
- Control: how resources are to be controlled and operated, and
- Content: the available supplementary or alternative resources.

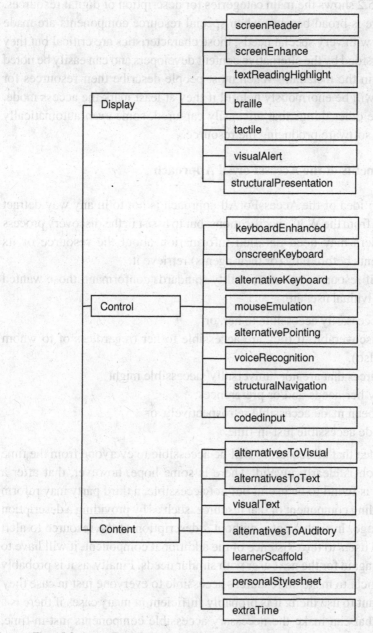

Fig. 15.2: AccessForAll structure and vocabulary (image from AccessForAll Specifications[13])

Fig. 15.2 shows the main categories for description of digital resources. The range is broad because when special resource components are made for users with very special needs, those characteristics are critical but they are understood by the alternative content developers and can easily be noted by them in the metadata. When most people describe their resources for users, it will be enormously helpful if they at least mark the access mode. There are other things that are easily captured, some even automatically from the software producing the resource.

15.9 Benefits of the AccessForAll Approach

The main idea of the AccessForAll approach is not to in any way detract attention from the W3C specifications, but to assist in the discovery process when users may need detailed information about the resource or its components before they (or their agents) retrieve it.

Even if resources are accessibility standards conformant, those wanted by an individual user are:

- not necessarily accessible to her, or
- not discoverable if they are accessible to her (regardless of to whom else also).

Resources that are not 'universally' accessible might

- satisfy her needs and/or preferences;
- have been made accessible retrospectively, or
- be made accessible just-in-time.

The idea that all resources will be accessible to everyone from the time of creation is clearly invalid. There is some hope, however, that after a resource is found to be useful but not accessible, a third party may reform an offending component of that resource, such as by providing a description of an image. In such a case, without a description of the resource to alert potential users to the existence of the additional component, it will have to be made again for the next user with similar needs. Finally, as it is probably not practical to make all resources accessible to everyone just in case they might want to use them, it is probably sufficient in many cases if there is a service that can make the necessary accessible components just-in-time. By having descriptions of resources and components, publishers will benefit as much as the individuals who expect to use the resources.

In Australia in January 2008, of 28 universities and similar institutions that produce alternate format resources or components, none were found to have published descriptions of those new resources that could be discovered by others. It is hoped that a new project will be undertaken to change this as soon as possible. The most commonly needed information is about the presentation (or display) of the resource: whether it needs to be seen, or perhaps listened to, or touched, to be used. In fact, it turns out that knowing what components there are and if they are visual, textual, olfactory, auditory or textual, accounts probably for most of the things most people want to know. These are all to do with sensory interaction with the resource, and textual fits because it can be adapted to a range of sensory forms.

To be able to fully match resources to users' needs and preferences, it is necessary to know the display, control and content characteristics of the resources. Even in cases where such matching is not to be done automatically, it is possible to make it easier for users to find what they want and can use if this information is available.

Basic digital resource descriptions (DRD) metadata includes:

- Access Mode: vision, hearing, touch, text
- Access Mode Usage: informative or ornamental
- Display: amenability of a resource to transformation of the display
- Control: how the method of control is flexible
- Alternatives: any known alternatives and, where appropriate
- Components: any parts that make up this resource (a sound file, an image, etc.) or a composite resource of which it is a part
- Hazards: any dangerous characteristics
- Support tools: electronic tools associated with the resource (calculator, dictionary, etc.).

A DRD for alternative components also includes:

- Identity of the original resource
- Type: kind of alternative
- Extent: extent of coverage of original resource

In order to make sure that the task of adding the metadata is not onerous, the most important information is recommended for most resources, and for others, only the detailed information where experts know what that is and why it matters. Authoring tools can help with this process at least by prompting the author, if not by actually supplying some of the information.

Preferably, the information is available about the individual components of the resource. If a resource contains an image and a user cannot see that image, they might want simply to replace it with a description of the image but still have access to the rest of the resource. As the Web becomes more flexible and users take more control over how they access resources, this is becoming more important.

15.10 Distributed Accessibility Provision

The initial effort for AccessForAll metadata to help in the discovery of accessible resources for individuals has been undertaken in closed environments where there is some control over the range of components and their availability. The approach will have greater value, it is assumed, when it is distributed across the Web. If someone has bothered to make a Braille version of a famous poem, its existence should be discoverable by everyone using resources related to that poem. For this to be possible, it may be necessary for resources to be described not only at the individual item level but also, according to the entities of the Functional Requirements for Bibliographic Records (FRBR)[14], probably at the level of the expression and manifestation[15].

The idea here is that if a resource is about the poem manifested as an image of text on parchment, but someone has bothered to make an electronic Braille version of the poem, that alternative to the image should be discoverable. This will mean searching by subject as well as by form but currently resources are not described appropriately. What is needed is a way to search for an alternative expression of the original work, not just another item. There is some hope this will be at least partially addressed as part of the new GLIMER work led by OCLC[16].

15.11 Accessibility for Heritage Resources

Digital versions of heritage resources can and should be accessible to everyone. For this to be possible, the resources need to be developed according to the W3C guidelines and described in metadata according to the

AccessForAll standard. If care is taken to work this way, the long term benefits should more than justify the effort as it will also promote, as best we currently know how, the adaptability of the resources that will be necessary as user agents change over time.

15.12 Conclusion

There is experience distilled in the W3C Web accessibility work that demonstrates the best specifications for inclusive resource development in a world of widely varying user requirements. Conformant resources, coupled with clear descriptions of the resources, will be discoverable and useful to individuals and users who can expect to find what they need with far greater satisfaction than is currently possible.

References

1 *http://informationmike.spaces.live.com/blog/cns!C767E1E33BA24175!413.entry*

2 *http://www.microsoft.com/enable/research/workingage.aspx*

3 *http://www.microsoft.com/enable/images/research/figure3.gif*

4 European Commission Report Number *DG INFSO/B2 COCOMO4*, p.14

5 *http://www.W3C*

6 Chisholm, W., Vanderheiden, G. and Jacobs, I. (1999), Web Content Accessibility Guidelines Version 1.0. Online at *http://www.w3.org/TR/WAI-WEBCONTENT/*

7 Disability Rights Commission (2004), The Web Access and Inclusion for Disabled People A formal investigation conducted by the Disability Rights Commission. London: TSO ISBN 0 11 703287 5. Online at *http://www.drc.gov.uk/publicationsandreports/2.pdf*

8 Nevile, L. and J.Treviranus, J. (2006), Interoperability for Individual Learner Centred Accessibility for Web-based Educational Systems, in IEEE TCLT's *Journal of Educational Technology & Society*, **9** (4), Online at *http://www.ifets.info/issues.php?id=33*

9 Disability Rights Commission, *op.cit.*

10 The Inclusive Learning Exchange, *http://www.barrierfree.ca/tile/*

11 Heath, A., Nevile. L. and Treviranus, J. (Eds.) (2005), Individualized Adaptability and Accessibility in E-learning, Education and Training Part 1: Framework (draft online at *http://jtc1sc36.org/doc/36N1024.pdf*); Individualized Adaptability and Accessibility in E-learning, Education and Training Part 2: AccessForAll Personal Needs and Preferences Statement, (draft online at *http://jtc1sc36.org/doc/36N1025.pdf*) and Individualized Adaptability and Accessibility in E-learning, Education and Training Part 3: AccessForAll Digital Resource Description, (draft online at *http://jtc1sc36.org/doc/36N1026.pdf*).

12 *ISO/IEC JTC1 SC36, http://jtc1sc36.org/*

13 IMS Learner Information Package Accessibility for LIP and IMS AccessForAll Meta-data Specification. Both online at *http://www.imsglobal.org/accessibility/*

14 Functional Requirements for Bibliographic Records Final Report, Online at *http:// www.ifla.org/VII/s13/frbr/frbr.pdf*

15 Morozumi, A., *et al.* (2006), Using FRBR for the Selection and Adaptation of Accessible Resources, for *Dublin Core Metadata Conference*, Mexico.

16 Weibel, S. (2008), A Glimir of the Future, online at *http://weibel-lines.typepad.com/weibelines/2008/02/a-glimir-of-the.html*

Chapter 16

An African Perspective on Digital Preservation

Hussein Suleman[1]

[1]Department of Computer Science
University of Cape Town, South Africa
hussein@cs.uct.ac.za

Abstract

The preservation of culture, language and history is recognised as being of crucial importance for future and current generations. Africa, especially, has the unique problem of needing to archive many collections of crucial significance to the world, yet without the skills or funds that often are utilised in this pursuit. The Bleek and Lloyd collection, that documents Bushman culture, and the DISA collection, that documents the South African liberation struggle, are examples of such projects. In both cases, and in other similar projects, there is a growing need for approaches to digital preservation, tools and techniques that better suit the needs and environment of developing countries. Some very specific solutions have emerged to solve problems related to Internet bandwidth and information accessibility, and these will be discussed, but these problems are only recently being acknowledged. Current digitisation efforts still outstrip efforts to organise information. Future technical solutions will therefore need to be found to maintain the pace of preservation as well as ensure ongoing access to all the peoples of the world.

Keywords: Africa, Digital Preservation, Developing World, Curation, Dissemination.

16.1 Introduction and Motivation for Preservation

Digital preservation is motivated by different factors in different parts of the world. UNESCO states in its charter on preservation of digital heritage that access to heritage is one of the motivators for preservation and further stresses that cultural heritage should be made accessible to all the people of the world[1].

In the global north-west (Europe and USA) there have been numerous projects related to different aspects of preservation. PREMIS develops metadata to support preservation[2]. PLANETS focuses on preservation planning and tools to support it[3]. CASPAR is about a European infrastructure for preservation based on the Open Archival Information System model[4]. Trustworthiness and auditing of repositories is the central theme for yet other efforts[5]. These are among some of the key issues for heritage preservation. However, there are other very specific and practical concerns that affect developing countries but not the northern counterparts.

Africa, in particular, is made up almost solely of developing countries. While these are fairly heterogeneous, there are some problems and solutions that transcend country borders to create a shared context for heritage preservation activities. In this context, a prime motivator for heritage preservation is the large number of significant collections that are of great value and in need of curation and dissemination. Unlike the LOCKSS focus on dark archives and more recent work on automated migration[6], heritage preservation in these cases focuses more closely on archiving and access. A number of example collections are presented along with the motivation for preservation in each case.

The Mapungubwe Collection[7-8] is a collection of archaeological artefacts from the northern parts of South Africa that indicate the existence of a sophisticated culture in the region during the Iron Age. According to researchers, the community in this area included the notions of class and evidence indicates that there were artisans and craftspeople within the community. While the civilization did not flourish beyond the 1300s, it is now recognized as the earliest advanced civilization in Southern Africa. This find was made during the Apartheid era of South African history and the information was intentionally kept from people because it was evidence that Black South Africans were not descendant from savages. Thus, it is vitally important that this collection be preserved and made accessible to people to correct the misinformation of the past.

The Timbuktu Manuscripts[9] are a collection of approximately 700000 documents found in Mali that document science and medicine as studied and practiced in the local community around the year 1300. This is a significant piece of evidence of a modern written knowledge system in Africa before European colonization. As such, the manuscripts are currently being physically and digitally preserved.

The Kirby Collection[10] contains African musical instruments from the early 1900s in South Africa. This provides a useful non-textual insight into local cultures. Many instruments that form part of this collection are already obsolete.

Digital Imaging South Africa at the University of Kwazulu-Natal[11] has as its flagship project a collection of magazines and newspapers that document the struggle for liberation in South Africa. This collection forms as alternative source of information on historical events. Unlike the previous examples, this collection is completely digitized and available online with browse and search interfaces.

The Bleek and Lloyd archive[12] includes artefacts and documents related to Bushman culture in the south-west parts of Africa. The Bushman groups are recognized as being among the oldest cultures in the world, so whatever is known about their culture needs to be preserved. A large part of this culture was transmitted orally, and there are few storytellers in modern 21st century society, hence the urgency to document the culture. The Bleek and Lloyd collection includes notebooks with transcriptions of stories and dictionaries as well as annotated drawings, all of which serve at the very least as a guide to the rock art in the region.

Finally, there are numerous new collections being created within institutional repositories and digital archives in public institutions and institutions of higher learning. While the need to preserve at-risk information is paramount, the new knowledge that is being created on an ongoing basis must be part of any digital preservation strategy.

16.2 Why an African Perspective

An African perspective on preservation ought not to be different from other perspectives. However, digital preservation is often discussed in terms of technology, infrastructure and practices in the global north-west. Africa is largely composed of developing nations and thus has particular problems, the solutions to which can potentially influence global practices. The following are examples of issues that need to be considered in the African context.

16.2.1 Artefact Deterioration

Some documents and storage media (e.g., in the Timbuktu Manuscripts) are rapidly deteriorating and oral history (e.g., in the Bushman cultures) is no longer being maintained in modern society. As a result, there is an urgent need to preserve information about ancient cultures which would otherwise be lost. There was no written language in many parts of Africa. Early researchers, like Wilhelm Bleek, transcribed oral histories to paper but these documents are themselves in danger of deterioration.

16.2.2 Rewriting History

We now know that there were significant ancient civilizations in many parts of Africa. Up until recent times, this information was suppressed by colonial governments to maintain intellectual superiority over local people. Part of the process of rebuilding a post-colonial world includes educating people about the important contributions of every culture – for this the untainted history must be restored. Unfortunately, in many instances there is little evidence of this history left and preservation of what is left is therefore more critical.

16.2.3 Skills and Education

Archivists in African institutions are arguably not as technically skilled as their counterparts in other parts of the world. The availability of computer systems in some parts of the continent has the effect that curators of information do not receive sufficient training in electronic systems. Digital media is not the norm for many forms of communication and information storage.

The level of education of the general population in many African countries also is a problem. The number of literate individuals, as well as the number of individuals with access to a computer and the Internet is lower than elsewhere in the world. This creates a challenge for digital preservation both in terms of collection building, especially for end-user submissions, and dissemination. Novel solutions are needed for both these problems to make digital archives effective.

16.2.4 Funding

Typically, there is little funding for digital preservation, and heritage preservation in general, because of other priorities in many countries. Many preservation projects receive funding from external international agencies (e.g., Mellon Foundation, Ford Foundation) but there are sometimes restrictions placed by the agencies that limit who the data may be shared with.

In general, there is a need to do more with fewer resources –sharing and reuse of resources are critical parts of any solution.

16.2.5 Internet Bandwidth (Digital Divide)

The digital divide is still a major hindrance. In many parts of Africa there is little access to computers and the Internet. In those parts where there is Internet access, the resources, such as bandwidth, are severely limited or extremely expensive. As of December 2007, only 4.7% of Africans have access to the Internet, which is well below every other continent[13].

Some digital preservation systems, such as LOCKSS, have questionable applicability. In the case of LOCKSS, a group of sites collaboratively maintain the integrity of collections. LOCKSS, however, does not cater for unstable and irregular bandwidth availability – its algorithms will not make the most efficient use of bandwidth and may exacerbate problems at sites with poor bandwidth.

All online archives need to make use of bandwidth in a way that is both minimal and cognizant of the differences among sites.

16.2.6 Why not a Global Perspective

Africa is not special in terms of the problems that affect digital preservation or preservation of heritage. Some communities in other developing countries face many of the same problems and many communities face some of the same problems. However, most communities, be they developing world or not, can benefit from the solution to these problems – e.g., greater efficiency, increased robustness of systems, lower costs.

16.3 Techniques and Solutions

The following techniques and solutions have been adopted in African projects to preserve heritage, in an attempt to deal with the identified problems.

16.3.1 Lightweight Systems

In order to build a lightweight system, simplicity is a key criterion. If the systems and processes are easy to implement, they will be easy to maintain and migrate in future when other systems are put into place.

XML can be used as an underlying data storage mechanism. While this creates some inefficiencies in accessing data collections – as opposed to databases – there are numerous advantages. These include that XML is human-readable, structured and can be stored in flat files which do not require software intermediaries.

Archives should be minimalist to reduce the overhead of maintaining systems. In many cases, metadata is being managed in spreadsheets as this is a simple technique which does not require that data capturers are re-trained and there is no need for a metadata repository until the data needs to be made discoverable.

Static collections of digital objects are easier to preserve than dynamically-managed or mediated objects because only the data needs to be preserved and not the service[14]. The files can simply be copied and archived. In contrast, a service that mediates access to digital objects must be preserved along with the manifestations of the digital objects.

Repositories can be made multi-purpose so that a single installation of the core software systems can be shared across multiple conceptual repositories. This serves as an enabler of collection development where the hardware, software and human resources are shared among collections. This approach is sometimes frowned upon but works well where resources are limited and archiving software (e.g., Dspace) allows for distinct sub-divisions within the collections.

Skills also can be shared, thus creating less work within a community. Communities of practice in the same geographical area have resulted in training and support networks in repository management, especially from the Open Access perspective.

16.3.2 Bandwidth

Collections can be made accessible over different media. Greenstone supports the creation of CD-ROM versions of its collections[15]. In additions, collections can be shared over a network or on removable media such as USB drives. These approaches reduce the need for bandwidth or eliminate it altogether. In addition, preserving the bits in such cases is a matter of copying files rather than invoking software services – the former can be accomplished using any backup and archiving tools.

In order to minimize bandwidth, client-side services can be created that run within the end-user's Web browser e.g., using Asynchronous JavaScript and XML (AJAX). Such services can perform a wide range of useful tasks, with only minimal interaction with the server instead of loading of new pages for each request. Services could be invoked off a local device, thus operating without any form of Internet connection.

16.3.3 Case Study: Bleek and Lloyd Collection

The Bleek and Lloyd collection includes a set of books and drawings documenting the near-extinct culture of the *xam* and *kun* Bushman groups of Southern Africa. They are widely acknowledged as descendents of the first people on earth and elements of their culture are of interest to researchers and scholars.

The notebooks that this collection revolves around were produced by Wilhelm Bleek, Lucy Lloyd and others in the late 1800s in Cape Town. They were the result of interviews with prisoners from the local prison, who belonged to various Bushman groups. These stories and other pieces of information were transcribed into over 14000 pages of text (see Fig. 16.1) with the original text in many cases juxtaposed with translations thereof. Thus, the notebooks serve as a Rosetta stone of the Bushman language and culture. Accompanying the notebooks are a collections of approximately 800 annotated drawings that, for example, can help to explain the meaning of Bushman art, particularly rock art.

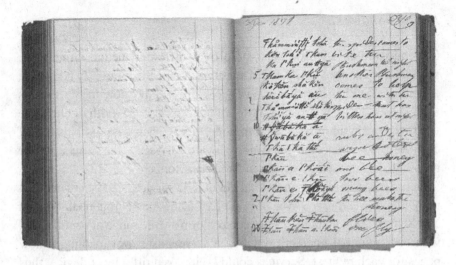

Fig. 16.1: Sample page from Bleek and Lloyd notebook.

This collection has been placed by UNESCO on its Memory of the World register and it is jointly curated by a group that includes the University of Cape Town, National Library of South Africa, Iziko-South African Museum and the University of South Africa. Digitization of the collection was funded by the Mellon Foundation and De Beers and this effort was led by the Michaelis School of Fine Arts at the University of Cape Town.

After digitization, the digital objects and metadata were to be assembled into a system that would allow the greatest possible access. In particular, the following were deemed as requirements:

- The collection needed to be accessible from a wide range of storage devices: over the Web, off a CD-ROM drive, off a local or network drive, etc.
- The collection needed to be accessible irrespective of the hardware and software platform (Mac/MS-Windows/Linux/etc.).
- The system needed to be usable with minimum end-user barriers (such as requiring software installation).
- The system needed to comply with standards wherever possible.

All metadata was first created and edited in Microsoft Excel, and thereafter converted to XML

The first software solution considered was Greenstone, as it is the only digital library toolkit with a CD-ROM distribution option. Unfortunately, Greenstone requires software to be installed on the target computer and it does not work on all platforms. The second software option considered was to create an XML Stylesheet Language Transformation (XSLT) stylesheet to convert the source XML files into PDF using the XSL Formatting Objects (XSL-FO) standard. This worked well for small subsets of the collections as PDF documents have a built-in search facility and the digital objects could be embedded in browsable pages. However, as the collection size was increased, the PDF files became unmanageable and most PDF viewers would slow down drastically because of the size of the files. Thus, this option too was not feasible.

The technology decided upon was a static XHTML website. The XML metadata was translated into XHTML using XSLT stylesheets. One stumbling block with this approach was that of scalability and this was suitably resolved using a combination of the following techniques[16]:

- The 16000 XHTML documents were split into batches to avoid generating all of them at once. The XSLT engine would consume memory proportional to the number of documents being generated, so this technique placed a bound on the resources required when generating the website.
- Non-trivial XSLT stylesheets using large XML source documents resulted in very slow XPath query resolution. To resolve this, indices and keys were used to speed up XPath queries – in a manner very similar to database indices.
- XSLT does not support queries that cross document boundaries so all the data had to appear in a single XML document.
- To create browseable listings of objects within the collection, it was necessary to group items logically according to various criteria (like author). Grouping is not common in XSLT but the Muenchian Method[17] allows one to efficiently group items by exploiting indices and the semantics of XSLT set operations.

The other major problem was that static websites cannot offer users services such as search engines. This was resolved by using an AJAX-based query system[18]. As in any typical information retrieval system, there are a set of inverted indices – these are created immediately after the XHTML files are generated and stored along with them. Then, when the

XHTML pages are viewed, a small AJAX application (see Fig. 16.2) allows the end-user to search using the pre-generated inverted files, without any server-side dynamic operations. This system works identically, therefore equally well, if the collection is distributed on CD-ROM, is on the Web or is on a local drive.

Fig. 16.2: Search engine interface in Bleek and Lloyd collection.

16.4 Future Challenges

The preservation of heritage collections is faced with many peculiar problems in developing countries. However, experience with current projects indicates that most of these problems can be resolved with appropriate and innovative use of new technologies.

One of the remaining challenges is how to scale the preservation effort itself. Few collections have been curated to date, usually at institutions with some capacity or funding. However, the techniques and tools need to be reusable so that heritage collection curation is as simple as the development of Open Access collections.

The tools for heritage collection management are still somewhat of a hurdle. Greenstone is a popular and well-developed tool so this could possibly be extended to cater for collections with special requirements. Alternatively, special tools could be developed or adapted to manage metadata and digital objects such that they can fulfill the needs of curators and users in Africa who may submit to the collections.

16.5 Conclusions

Digital preservation of heritage is an ongoing activity in Africa, with much interest but not enough capacity or resources. African projects typically highlight the special needs of developing countries and the innovative solutions that must be put into place. With such solutions, it is indeed possible to digitize and disseminate heritage collections, but this is not necessarily a repeatable process. Some effort is still needed to create tools and processes that exploit emerging technology, resulting in simple solutions that work across a wide range of contexts.

References

1 UNESCO (2003), Charter on the Preservation of the Digital Heritage, Place: UNESCO, *http://portal.unesco.org/ci/en/files/13367/10700115911Charter_en.pdf/ Charter_en.pdf* (Accessed 16 March 2008).

2 Caplan, P. and Guenther, R. (2005), Practical Preservation: the PREMIS Experience, *Library Trends*, **54**(1), *http://www.loc.gov/standards/premis/caplan_guenther-librarytrends.pdf* (Accessed 16 March 2008).

3 Becker, C., Kolar, G, Küng, J., and Rauber, A. (2007), Preserving Interactive Multimedia Art: A Case Study in Preservation Planning, In *Proceedings of Tenth International Conference on Asian Digital Libraries, ICADL 2007*, Hanoi, Vietnam, 10-13 December, *http://publik.tuwien.ac.at/files/pub-inf_5204.pdf* (Accessed 16 March 2008).

4 Giaretta, D. (2006), CASPAR and a European Infrastructure for Digital Preservation, *ERCIM News*, **66**, *http://www.ercim.org/publication/Ercim_News/enw66/giaretta.html* (Accessed 16 March 2008).

5 OCLC (2007), Trustworthy Repositories Audit & Certification: Criteria and Checklist, Place: OCLC, *http://www.crl.edu/PDF/trac.pdf* (Accessed 16 March 2008).

6 Rosenthal, D.S.H., Lipkis, T., Robertson, T. S., and Morabito, S. (2005), Transparent Format Migration of Preserved Web Content, *D-Lib Magazine*, **11**(1),

http://www.dlib.org/dlib/january05/rosenthal/01rosenthal.html (Accessed 16 March 2008).

7 SouthAfrica.info. (2008), Mapungubwe: SA's lost city of gold, *http://www.safrica.info/ ess_info/sa_glance/history/mapungubwe.htm* (Accessed 16 March 2008).

8 Huffman, T.N. (2000), Mapungubwe and the Origins of the Zimbabwe Culture, pp.14-29, *Goodwin Series*, **8**, African Naissance: The Limpopo Valley 1000 Years Ago.

9 Minicka, M. (2006), Safegaurding Africa's Literary Heritage : Timbuktu rare manuscriptsproject, In *Proceedings LIASA WCHELIG Winter Colloquium: Collaboration for success*, Cape Town, South Africa, *http://eprints.rclis.org/ archive/00006729/* (Accessed 16 March 2008).

10 University of Cape Town (2007), The Percival R. Kirby Collection of musical instruments, *http://web.uct.ac.za/depts/sacm/kirby.html* (Accessed on 16 March 2008).

11 Pickover, M. and Peters, D. (2002), DISA: An African Perspective on Digital Technology, *Innovation*, **24**.

12 Skotnes, P. (2007), Claim to the Country: *The Archive of Wilhelm Bleek and Lucy Lloyd*, Auckland Park: Jacana, p.388.

13 Internet World Stats (2007), World Internet Users, *http://www.internetworldstats.com/ stats.htm* (Accessed 16 March 2008).

14 de Lusenet, Y. (2002), Preservation of digital heritage, Draft discussion paper prepared for UNESCO, European Commission on Preservation and Access, Place: UNESCO, *http://www.knaw.nl/ecpa/PUBL/unesco.html* (Accessed 16 March 2008).

15 Witten, I. and Bainbridge, D. (2003), *How to Build a Digital Library*, San Francisco: Morgan Kauffman, p.518.

16 Suleman, H. (2007), Digital Libraries Without Databases: The Bleek and Lloyd Collection, pp.392-403, In *Proceedings of Research and Advanced Technology for Digital Libraries, 11th European Conference (ECDL 2007)*, Budapest, Hungary, 16-19 September, edited by Kovacs, L., Norbert F. and Meghini, C., *http://pubs.cs.uct.ac.za/archive/00000433/01/ecdl_2007_dlwd.pdf* (Accessed 16 March 2008).

17 Tennison, J. (2007), Using the Muenchian Method, *http://www.jenitennison.com/xslt/ grouping/muenchian.html* (Accessed 16 March 2008).

18 Suleman, H. (2007), in-Browser Digital Library Services, pp.462-465, In *Proceedings of Research and Advanced Technology for Digital Libraries, 11th European Conference (ECDL 2007)*, Budapest, Hungary, 16-19 September, edited by Kovacs, L., Norbert F. and Meghini, C., *http://pubs.cs.uct.ac.za/archive/00000434/ 01/ecdl_2007_ajax.pdf* (Accessed 16 March 2008).

Chapter 17

nestor and kopal — Co-operative Approaches to Digital Long-term Preservation in Germany

Thomas Wollschläger[1]

[1]*German National Library*
Information Technology
Adickesallee 1,
D-60322, Frankfurt am Main, Germany
t.wollschlaeger@d-nb.de

Abstract

The changing publication culture towards the electronic publication in Networks changes considerably the profile of libraries that are responsible for preserving the cultural heritage of a nation. The long-term accessibility of all digital resources of lasting value must be preserved, despite the changing conditions arising from rapid technological development. In Germany, the project nestor - Network of Expertise in Long-Term Storage and Long-Term availability has the aim to secure the preservation of digital resources in Germany and to work with others internationally to secure the global digital memory and knowledge base. One of the major national projects to actually implement a productive long-term archival system has been the project 'kopal' (Co-operative Development of a Long-term Digital Information Archive). It had the mission to practically prove and implement a co-operatively build and used long-term preservation system for digital publications. Kopal is now being transferred into a lasting institutional archive by the former project partners.

Keywords: Digital Long-Term Preservation, Archival Storage, Preservation Model, Migration, Bit-stream Preservation.

17.1 Introduction and Long-term Preservation Challenges

To maintain a responsible care for their digital collections that have been grown considerably over the past year, universities, libraries and other memory institutions need suitable and consistent archives for the electronic materials. The existing archives in most cases do not, however, fulfill the demands to be truly reliable and lasting solutions. The considerations of the German National Library (DNB) for its digital long-term archive focussed on the needs first, to preserve the binary data and second, to ensure long- term access.

No existing data carrier is lasting forever or even long enough. The first CD-ROM's are becoming unreadable already now, and for complex materials (e.g., multimedia applications) the loss of single bits might become fatal. Therefore, the archive should be able to conduct regular bit-stream preservation (data carrier migrations). Recent experiences with the fragile integrity of certain document servers also indicate that the long-term archive should rely on multiple copies of the archived content in physically separated places. Also, the fast technology changes progressionally hinder the access to older file formats. Many formats already exist and constantly new ones are being developed, whereas current formats diminish or become obsolete. Additionally, there exist complex dependencies between those formats and various software and hardware environments. Any long-term archive should be able to allow constant format migrations (regular conversions) as well as emulations (re-enacting of needed systems).

What are the advantages or disadvantages of these strategies? During migration, older file formats are converted into more recent formats early enough, as long as they are still readable. That is being done continuously and means to preserve the integrity and availability of the digital resource in spite of a changing environment. There is, however, the risk of possible – but maybe undetected – loss of information (parts) during automatically performed migration routines. The more complex the source format, the more imminent will become the chance that after long migration chains (over the years) some features may be lost or no longer executable. But migration is, on the other hand, the ideal approach for large amounts of data and will be the most reasonable procedure for the more static data (e.g., text and unmoving pictures).

During emulation, a special program (the emulator) tries to re-enact an older system environment onto a present system environment (e.g., the DOS emulation on Windows platforms). The goal is to be able to execute programs and process data that originally were intended for another, historical system on a recent system. That can be very extensive and presupposes a very exact definition of hardware and software requirements. The advantage of emulations, however, is to be most suitable for complex formats (e.g., multimedia applications) to keep the features of that formats usable as long as possible. That means, both strategies have advantages and disadvantages. Therefore, an archive system whose task is to provide long-term preservation as well as long-term access of digital resources should be able to use a combination of both strategies.

17.2 The nestor Project

When defining the scope of long-term preservation in Germany that should be adopted by memory institutions several years ago, the foremost area of activities was identified as the necessary community build-up. It was abundantly clear that no institution can address long-term preservation alone and on its own. Challenges and tasks, expertise and experiences had to be co-ordinated and bundled. Experts needed a forum for discussion and exchange, and guidelines for the community were to be developed. A second area of activities that came into focus – but which would have to follow the mentioned first steps – was a precise and individual build-up of the actual archives in the memory and heritage institutions. Major institutions were thought to develop long-term preservation model projects and solutions for the present archive materials, along with use cases, re-usable strategies and service models. In that area, too, co-operation was thought to encourage wherever possible.

All these factors led to the foundation of the nestor project[1]. Nestor stands for "Network of expertise in Digital long-term preservation". Its major goals are to establish a centre of competence in Germany in digital long-term preservation (or, digital curation); to provide an information platform for all activities in German speaking countries (Germany, Austria, Switzerland), to form liaisons with international developments or projects and to provide an expert's database. Whereas the first approaches of the

German Research Foundation (DFG) lay way back to 1995, finally in 2002 the constitution of an initial group in the Federal Ministry of Education and Research of Germany (BMBF) took place. In July 2003, the actual nestor project was started, along with six partner institutions. They represented the broad field of cooperation that nestor was to address: science, libraries, archives, museums, data centers and training centers. The project formed a sub-project of the larger BMBF-project "New Services Standardisation, Metadata". Already in the end of 2004, the nestor Information platform with experts' profile database, news, newsletter, etc. was released to the public. In mid-2006, the 2nd project phase has been started that will run until 2009.

The nestor activities centre on several important areas. These areas are mainly training, research, certification, tools/workflow and current awareness. Some examples may give a short glimpse on the subjects of those activities:

- *Training* – nestor Spring/Winter School, cooperation with training centers, seminars of the Bundesarchiv, collaboration in DPE
- *Research* – standardised delivery of electronic objects to the archive (Ingest), grid technology and long term preservation, collaboration in EU-projects, e.g. PLANETS, CASPAR, PARSE
- *Certification* – Catalogue of Criteria for Trusted Repositories; Catalogue of Criteria for PIs, collaboration with DIN and ISO
- *Tools/Workflow* – co-operation with kopal, exemplary IIPC web Archiving
- *Current Awareness* – "What's New in Digital Preservation" from PADI/ DPC

Currently, in nestor about 30 institutions are involved in conducting of and/or participating in those activities, and they form six special workgroups for addressing the most important tasks. One clear result of the nestor work so far, is the obvious benefit of co-operation in all areas and the necessity of broadening these co-operations. Another nestor activity is the publication of research results on long-term preservation subjects and providing them to the heritage community. Within the scope of the project, nestor concludes contracts with universities and science/research institutions to conduct special studies in that area. The Fig. 17.1 gives an example of those publications (all of which are freely available via the nestor homepage).

Fig. 17.1: Some examples of recent nestor publications on long-term preservation subjects.

Parallel to the already running nestor project, the first real projects to implement working long-term preservation archives were set up in Germany. One of the first of those projects was the national initiative kopal.

17.3 kopal System Background and Principles

"Kopal" is the German acronym for the Co-operative Development of a Long-Term Digital Information Archive. The goal of the kopal project was to develop a technological and organizational solution to ensure the long-term availability of electronic publications. The project was funded by the German Federal Ministry of Education and Research for a three-year period, from 2004 to 2007, for a total volume of funding of over four million Euros. The core of the project is the IBM Digital Information Archiving System (DIAS) solution, developed originally for the National Library of the Netherlands[2]. Using the functions of that base system, the transparent integration into existing library systems and the re-usability by memory institutions has played a critical role. Following the project phase, the resulting archive system is now being integrated into the running environment of the participating libraries.

In the implementation of the kopal system, international standards for long-term archiving and metadata have been adopted to guarantee both sustainability and the ability to advance the system in the future. As part of the project, massive amounts of digital materials of all types from two partner organizations, the German National Library and the Goettingen State and University Library, have been deposited. These materials range from digital documents like electronic theses and dissertations, electronic journals and digitized collections in the form of PDF, TIFF, or TeX files to complex objects like images of CD-ROM's and digital videos.

The participation of IBM Germany as a development partner was to enable the professional customization of the software components. IBM is also providing long-term support. The technical operation of the long-term archive is located at the Gesellschaft fuer wissenschaftliche Datenverarbeitung mbH Goettingen (GWDG). Also the archive itself is located at the GWDG site in Goettingen. Objects are being transferred into the system by secure Internet connections. The GWDG has a vast experience in safe and secure data hosting and bit-stream preservation. GWDG stores the data in two copies at their main site and in two additional copies at a physically different place in Goettingen. Furthermore, in due time, a third institution in Munich will receive an additional copy of each object for added security. Thus, the kopal project can fall back on distributed data storage if needed. Additionally, the logical structure of kopal adheres to several important principles, namely universality, reusability and flexibility.

The project was aimed to build a universally usable archival system in which long-term availability is supported through migration and emulation. There are no limitations within kopal regarding the types of material which can be imported into the archive (text, images, audio, video) and possible data formats. Although the kopal system still has a limited total capacity at the moment, the size of the individual archive object per definitionem is unlimited. Each of the partners who acts as a full client of the system, opens its own secure account on the central storage system. He is completely free when it comes to the selection of, and setting of rules for, the import of its collected objects. Also, no party can access the contents of another client's account.

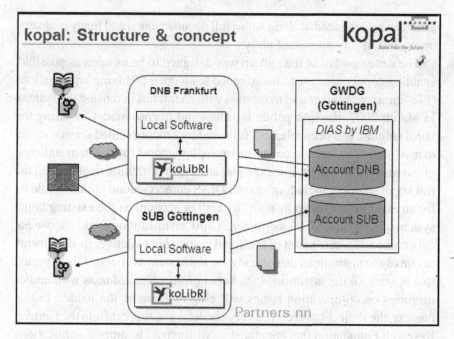

kopal: Structure & concept

kopal

DNB Frankfurt

Local Software

koLibRI

SUB Göttingen

Local Software

koLibRI

GWDG
(Göttingen)

DIAS by IBM

Account DNB

Account SUB

Partners nn

Fig. 17.2: Kopal system architecture with remote access of the clients to their accounts.

Reuse of kopal by other institutions that need long-term archiving is expressly desired. From its inception, the kopal solution has been geared towards a number of different needs. In order to guarantee reusability, established standards are applied. The transfer of objects into a digital archive via standardised formats, paths and interfaces has been a key requirement in this context. The kopal project has therefore devised the "Universal Object Format" for this purpose, which enables digital objects to be archived with (technical) metadata and exchanged between institutions and systems[3].

The DIAS software is also being enhanced with flexible modules. DIAS is based on IBM's standard software components. GNL and Goettingen State and University Library have built software products onto the DIAS core which have been published as the "kopal Library for Retrieval and Ingest" (koLibRI) under an Open Source Software license[4]. These kopal tools primarily support the import of objects into the archive and the access to the archived objects. To the end of the project, the kopal consortium has released the fully developed and tested 1.0 version of these koLibRI tools.

They can be downloaded along with a full documentation and freely evaluated or re-used by any interested party.

The development of the system was designed to be as open as possible, enabling cooperative use to be extended to all other archiving organisations (like libraries, archives and museums) with an interest in reusing the system. In March 2007, the first public business and license model for using the kopal solution had been released, followed by a more detailed service model in mid-2007. That release covers an exemplary model for a certain audience of interested institutions. For example, an (large) institution might install the full kopal solution, including an own DIAS core. A second option would be for an institution to open its own "locker" or account on the existing kopal system of DNB and SUB Goettingen. Third, an institution could choose not to become a separate client of the kopal system but to deliver its documents to one of the institutions that already use the system as clients. It is expected that at least all the institutions the kopal project has had tests with and/or meetings on co-operation issues will closely examine the model. In this context, the project has received very encouraging support from the German Research Foundation that has stated its willingness to support applications from institutions that want to long-term archive their scientific digital publications with kopal.

17.4 Preservation Process by kopal

In effect, the following preservation strategy shall be executable by the kopal system. On the one hand, it is possible to migrate the object (e.g., a certain document) with a precise identifier (the German National Library uses the urn:nbn system as Persistent Identifiers[5]) into a certain new format. One can also even migrate all objects of (or, more exactly, all files within all objects that contain) a certain – obsolete - format into a specified new format (e.g. from TIFF to PNG). In fact, the migration of objects with TIFF images into objects with PNG images has been prototypically executed during the project time of kopal as a proof of concept. In addition to the migration of objects, the implementation of emulation view paths will take place. Because of the complex structure of emulators and emulation processes, the basis for emulation paths will be implemented as a second step during the course of 2008.

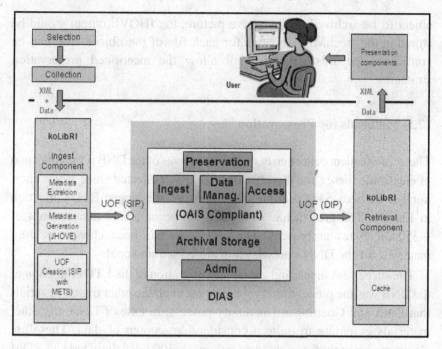

Fig. 17.3: Outline of the kopal archive system.
The inner core refers to the OAIS model.
The koLibRI software handles the creation of the archive objects and their retrieval.

The basis for the execution of migration and/or emulation processes are technical metadata. In kopal, the technical metadata are stored in METS[6] containers that are being packed into one transport unit, together with the actual object, before ingesting into the archive. The METS container includes technical metadata according to the LMER standard (Long-term Preservation Metadata for Electronic Resources)[7].

The creation of these metadata consists of two process steps: First, extracting technical metadata as they are delivered with the digital object itself; second, generating additional technical metadata by using appropriate tools. When the metadata format of the delivered publication contains, for example, information on file ID, format, character set, file size, creation application etc, these data are being integrated into the METS file of the archival object. In addition to the extracted metadata, in the second step the tool JHOVE[8] (JSTOR/Harvard Object Validation Environment) is being used to generate additional technical metadata for each file of the object to be archived. In the above picture, the JHOVE output would be stored in the "techMD" sections for each file of the object. One can be confident that this structure will allow the mentioned preservation strategies.

17.5 Materials for Preservation

The most excellent collection of digital documents of the DNB is the collection of electronic theses and dissertations (ETD's), collected since 1997. Their number exceeds 55.000 at present and forms the largest ETD collection in Europe. The growth has resulted in an accumulated data amount of ~ 350 Gigabytes at present. The collection has been chosen as pilot materials for the DNB's preservation efforts within kopal.

The successful ingest and exemplary migration of the ETD collection of the DNB was the precondition for the ingest of all the other digital materials that DNB and Goettingen University possess. In case of DNB, the other materials cumulate to quite a considerable amount of data. These are electronic journals & serials (data volume: ~ 300 GB), digitized CD-ROM images (~ 56.000 GB), and several collections of digitized materials. That includes the *Exil Press Digital* (~ 150 GB), some external digital collections, digitized books from the German Book & Scripture Museum (~ 5.000 GB, for starters) and born-digital and digitized audio from the German Music Archive (~ 544.000 GB). It should be mentioned that the carrier-based digital collections have been digitized not nearly complete by now; in fact, that process will take several years. Also, the music data will be only ingested over a period of several years at least. But already now, the kopal system has been designed to be able to store more than the readily available data volume. An impression of the relationship between the potential materials that will be ingested into kopal, and the present capacity, is shown in the Fig. 17.4.

17.6 Web Archiving in kopal

The new legal deposit law in Germany by using the term "media works in virtual forms" expressively covers representations in public networks.

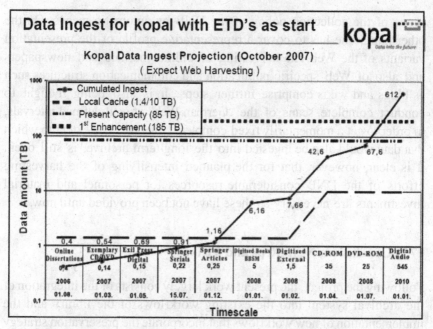

Fig. 17.4: Planned data ingest for the kopal system. The solid line indicates the possibly ingestible amount of data to ingest during the next years (logarithmic graph).

Because for this type of media the task to ensure long-term preservation and availability is valid as well, in kopal Internet contents that have been collected by Web harvesting will be archived in the future, too.

Prior to the release of the new deposit law, the German National Library tested certain possible automated harvesting methods and storage options. Especially promising seemed to be the WARC format of the IIPC that has been submitted as an ISO standard[9]. Within pilot projects with the European Internet Archive, its crawling method has been evaluated. When selecting that method, the crawl results will be ingested into the long-term archive as .arc files. The development of suitable retrieval mechanisms for those objects is, however, still a desired feature at the moment.

The next steps will, regarding the past experiences, concentrate on static Web pages, especially on the servers and publications of scientific, cultural and governmental institutions and organizations. On the one hand, there is the goal to identify and archive relevant materials in the scope of the collection policy of the DNB by automatic means. On the other hand, one has to cover a representative profile of the presentation variants of the Web.The harvesting of online journals and newspapers and also of Web specific publication and communication structures such as blogs and wikis comprise further steps. It is also being thought to conduct complete scans of the "German Web" at well-defined intervals, in order to get a momentarily fixed complete coverage. The extent to which that data would also be ingested into the long-term archive, is still open. It is clear, however, that for the planned intensifying of the harvesting efforts of the DNB considerable resources for personnel and material investments are necessary as these have not been provided until now.

17.7 Conclusion, Next Steps and Vision

Following the project, the present work largely consists of the integration of the archival system into the existing workflows of the library and the implementation of new workflows that incorporate the preservation strategy for the digital materials right from the delivery by the publishers. Since kopal does not provide an end-user access or a direct ingest from the outside (as can be observed in Fig. 17.1, kopal supports and/or provides interfaces to the collection/acquisition side and to the user services of the library), these components – the user interface and the placing of the materials to be ingested at the disposal of the kopal tools – have to be provided by the appropriate departments of the DNB. Of course, these departments, the IT department and the kopal team are working closely together to set up suitable interfaces and workflows.

Other steps next to be taken include a reliable scalability of the system, an improved performance and a better user support. An example might illustrate a resulting task. In face of rising data volumes and large single objects (e.g. digitized DVD-ROM images with more than 8 GB each), it is very important to guarantee a sufficient performance of the system. When an end-user clicks on a link within the search result displayed in the online catalogue of the DNB, the retrieval of the archived document from the kopal system starts. But, in case of very large objects, it might take several minutes to get the object via the Internet onto the screen. To prevent users from multiple clicking or simply walking away, fast Internet connections have to be provided for, and suitable access systems have to be implemented that facilitate an appropriate user support (e.g., including messages on the needed retrieval time).

The other major working package includes the implementation of a functioning Preservation Planning mechanism. Since the reference to precise file formats is an essential component of any migration or emulation mechanism, the best support for the kopal – and any other long-term preservation effort – would be the successful setup of a functioning international File Format Registry. Several international efforts, in some of which DNB is participating, are currently under way to cover that area but, unfortunately, none of those registries is equipped with re-usable machine interfaces for automated requests. While these efforts are under way, kopal has to prove the performance of migration of large data volumes as well as the successful implementation of emulation mechanisms.

Finally, all memory institutions have to broaden their information, support & encouragement of digital content producers towards a more well-founded format and preservation awareness. Also, other memory institutions should be encouraged to adapt to long-term preservation solutions in order to protect, preserve and make available the digital cultural heritage of our times for future generations.

References

1 Nestor homepage, *http://www.langzeitarchivierung.de/index.php?newlang=eng*

2 *http://www.kb.nl/dnp/e-depot/dm/dias-en.html*

3 *http://kopal.langzeitarchivierung.de/index_objektspezifikation.php.en*

4 *http://kopal.langzeitarchivierung.de/index_koLibRI.php.en*

5 *http://www.persistent-identifier.de/?lang=en*

6 Metadata Encoding & Transmission Standard, *http://www.loc.gov/standards/mets/*

7 *http://www.ddb.de/eng/standards/lmer/lmer.htm*

8 JSTOR/Harvard Object Validation Environment (JHOVE), *http://hul.harvard.edu/jhove/*

9 *http://netpreserve.org/*

Chapter 18

Preserving the Past — Towards the Digitization of German Cultural Heritage

Thomas Stäcker[1]

[1]*Leiter Abteilung Alte Drucke, Digitalisierung*
Herzog August Bibliothek
Postfach 1364 - D-38299
Wolfenbuettel, Germany
staecker@hab.de

Abstract

This paper outlines the major digitization projects for German cultural heritage regarding rare book digitization. An overview of digitization projects is given and more specifically the digitization activities at the Herzog August Library in Wolfenbüttel. Issues of long-term preservation, accessibility and dissemination of digital resources are discussed.

Keywords: Mass Digitization of Rare Books, Cooperative Internet Projects, Digital Preservation, Durable Linking, Dissemination of Metadata, German Cultural Heritage.

18.1 Introduction and Digitization Activities in Germany

The past few years saw important developments in the digitization of cultural heritage materials in Germany. Many rare books, have been digitized and placed on the internet, freely accessible for everyone. Serious efforts are undertaken to develop strategies to digitise the entire German cultural heritage and make it available through internet within the next decade. Digital initiatives of the European Community have been paralleled by national undertakings. The German Distributed National Library (AG SDD)[1], for example, agreed on a memorandum aimed at coordinating activities according to the focus and national responsibilities of the libraries involved. As a result the Munich State Library undertook to concentrate on projects relating to the 16th, the Herzog August Library in Wolfenbüttel on projects relating to the 17th and the Göttingen State Library on those relating to the 18th century. The task is, however, immense. A first calculation showed more than 2 million editions containing half a billion pages to be scanned, not taking into account materials from museums or archives. However, it is estimated that complete digitisation can be accomplished within the next decade.

Above all it is the German Research Foundation, which financed various digitisation projects since 1996. Their first program 'Distributed Digital Library' (1997) intended to explore the field and develop prototypes and best practice procedures. As a result, a series of digital collections came into existence, which were only loosely connected to one another and were characterized by divergent digitization standards and metadata. The establishment of two digital competence centres at Göttingen and Munich States Libraries did not help much. These centres focused on their own projects, but failed to establish standardized metadata and collaboration project. A study carried out in 2004 by Manfred Thaller[2] from Cologne University showed that most users did not even know to what extent digital resources pertinent to their field of research were available and were highly surprised to hear how much had already been digitized. One of the major complaints was that a central access point is missing for digital scholarly resources in Germany. As a consequence the German Research Foundation financed a project aimed at implementing a central portal for digitized books called *zvdd* (central inventory of digitized imprints)[3]. Its aim is to collect data from the various projects and convert them into a given format in order to include them in a central database. This turned out to be more difficult than expected because of the diversity of data and some of the more sophisticated data could not be converted up to this day. Yet, the portal succeeded in developing recommendations for standards at the collection, bibliographic and structural data level, an important step for further developments. Whether the portal will succeed to play a leading role as a central portal and access point for digitized rare books after funding runs out cannot be foreseen. Currently it is about to be migrated to the States- and University Library at Göttingen. European activities become more and more relevant in Germany, too. Especially Europeana[4] the new European search engine launched in November 2008 could bring a breakthrough for finding European cultural material on the web.

The German Research Foundation launched a new program in 2006 dedicated to the mass digitization of rare books, above all from the German- speaking areas, in order to stimulate content production. First, all books contained in the national cataloguing databases of the so called VD 16[5] and VD 17[6] comprising 350.000 titles of the 16th and 17th century are due to be digitized. Four mass digitization projects started in Dresden, Halle, Munich and Wolfenbüttel in 2007. Their aim is to digitize selected holdings, to improve the interoperability and integration of metadata, and to provide best practices for further mass digitization projects. Accordingly various methods and strategies are pursued. While Wolfenbüttel (Germanic languages, see below) and Dresden (technical literature[7]) attempt to combine the aspect of mass digitization with a subject related approach to establish a defined corpus of imprints addressing a specific research community, Halle favoured to digitize a particular provenance (collection Ponickau[8]). The most ambitious project is the one of the Bavarian States Library in Munich. Munich plans to digitize all of its books from the 16th century contained in the VD 16 within the next two years[9]. This means that about 60,000 imprints of the German speaking area from the 16th century will be available on the web within very short time. To achieve this Munich cooperates with Treventus[10] a company which developed a scan robot specially designed for the purposes of rare book digitization and which is capable of scanning up to 800 pages per hour. Unlike the other projects Munich does not supply any structural metadata or applies any selection criteria in its digitization process. All of these projects will provide models for further activities.

Important for the initiative is an agreement between these and other projects to establish a joint set of metadata in order to allow for the aggregation of metadata in portals. The development of various portals and digital libraries has also shown that the diversity of services, browsers and viewers to navigate through the digitized material grew more complex. While in digital library A, the forward arrow is green and at the bottom, the same function can be found with library B at the top in blue. Images are displayed in various forms and sizes, functions and designs are varying considerably. Although particular features may be welcome in one environment they are apt to confuse the user switching between different resources. To counteract this diversification and provide the user with a unified access to the resources the four projects mentioned above in collaboration with the university library in Göttingen (representing *zvdd*) and the Berlin State Library created the so-called DFG Viewer designed by and located at the State and University Library at Dresden[11]. The group adopted the METS[12]/MODS[13] model originally developed by the Library of Congress and designed an application profile for its own purposes. The DFG Viewer works on the basis of a common interface, a URL is transmitted to the Viewer which in turn harvests the data in XML format provided by the institution. The Viewer can be addressed by using the following URL pattern: *http://dfg-viewer.de/v1/?set[mets]= http://your-library.de/mets.xml*

For example, to view an item from the Wolfenbüttel Digital Library the following URL can be used: *http://dfg-viewer.de/v1/?set[mets] = http://dbs.hab.de/dfgnavi/get_navi.php?dir=drucke/6-1-geom*[14]

The digital archive responds to this request with a METS file having a MODS container with bibliographic metadata and at least a list of URLs each representing an image of the digitised imprint or manuscript, as can been seen in Fig. 18.1.

The interface of the Viewer also supports OAI compliant requests and responses, such as: *http://dfg-viewer.de/v1/?set[mets] = http://dbs.hab.de/ oai/?verb=GetRecord&metadataPrefix=METS&identifier=oai:diglib.hab. de:ppn_539984248*[15]

Three of the mass digitization projects in Dresden, Halle and Wolfenbüttel have already implemented both the Viewer-METS and the OAI METS interface. The advantage of this kind of implementation lies in its not interfering with local viewers, that means, each digital library may have its own web presentation and viewing software, but can offer its users to either select a more sophisticated and specialized local view or to use the unified DFG-Viewer they may be more accustomed to. The partners agreed, however, that all links of the VD17 database should take the user to the DFG Viewer first. Wolfenbüttel has already implemented this feature[16].

Hopefully the increasing number of institutions with OAI interfaces delivering the METS format will pave the way to a greater harmonization of metadata and enable harvesters to retrieve more specialized data than Dublin Core. Other institutions are about to follow (e.g. the university library of

```xml
<?xml version="1.0" encoding="UTF-8" ?>
- <mets:mets xmlns:xsi="http://www.w3.org/2001/XMLSchema-instance" xmlns:mets="http://www.loc.gov/METS/"
    xmlns:mods="http://www.loc.gov/mods/v3" xmlns:xs="http://www.w3.org/2001/XMLSchema"
    xmlns:xlink="http://www.w3.org/1999/xlink" xmlns:pdd="http://zvdd.gdz-cms.de/" xmlns:dc="http://purl.org/dc/elements/1.1/"
    xsi:schemaLocation="http://www.loc.gov/METS/ http://www.loc.gov/mets/mets.xsd">
  + <mets:metsHdr>
  - <mets:dmdSec ID="ppn_517662418">
    - <mets:mdWrap MDTYPE="MODS">
      - <mets:xmlData>
          <!-- MODS bibliographische Metadaten -->
        - <mods:mods>
          - <mods:titleInfo>
              <mods:title>Projet D'Une Nouvelle Mechanique. Avec Un Examen de l'opinion de M. Borelli, sur les propriétez des
                Poids suspendus par des Cordes. Avec Un Examen de l'opinion de M. Borelli, sur les propriétez des Poids
                suspendus par des Cordes</mods:title>
            </mods:titleInfo>
          - <mods:name type="personal">
              <mods:namePart type="family">Varignon</mods:namePart>
              <mods:namePart type="given">Pierre</mods:namePart>
            + <mods:role>
              <mods:displayForm>Varignon, Pierre</mods:displayForm>
            </mods:name>
          - <mods:originInfo>
            - <mods:place>
                <mods:placeTerm type="text">Paris</mods:placeTerm>
              </mods:place>
              <mods:publisher>Martin</mods:publisher>
              <mods:dateIssued keyDate="yes" encoding="w3cdtf">1687</mods:dateIssued>
            </mods:originInfo>
            <mods:identifier type="purl">http://diglib.hab.de/drucke/6-1-geom/start.htm</mods:identifier>
          </mods:mods>
        </mets:xmlData>
      </mets:mdWrap>
    </mets:dmdSec>
  + <mets:amdSec ID="amd_drucke_6-1-geom">
  - <mets:fileSec ID="fs_drucke_6-1-geom">
    - <mets:fileGrp USE="DEFAULT">
      - <mets:file ID="drucke_6-1-geom_00001" MIMETYPE="image/jpeg">
          <mets:FLocat xlink:href="http://diglib.hab.de/drucke/6-1-geom/00001.jpg" LOCTYPE="URL"/>
        </mets:file>
      - <mets:file ID="drucke_6-1-geom_00002" MIMETYPE="image/jpeg">
          <mets:FLocat xlink:href="http://diglib.hab.de/drucke/6-1-geom/00002.jpg" LOCTYPE="URL"/>
        </mets:file>
      - <mets:file ID="drucke_6-1-geom_00003" MIMETYPE="image/jpeg">
          <mets:FLocat xlink:href="http://diglib.hab.de/drucke/6-1-geom/00003.jpg" LOCTYPE="URL"/>
        </mets:file>
      - <mets:file ID="drucke_6-1-geom_00004" MIMETYPE="image/jpeg">
          <mets:FLocat xlink:href="http://diglib.hab.de/drucke/6-1-geom/00004.jpg" LOCTYPE="URL"/>
```

Fig. 18.1: Detail of METS file.

Heidelberg has already set up an interface), because the German Research Foundation as one of the leading sponsors in the field will prescribe this interface in its digitization recommendations[17]. Further developments of the Viewer will follow. It is planned that the Viewer should display structural metadata as well. The mass digitization projects have already endorsed a list of shared terms[18], but development of the representation in METS is still in progress.

Another topic of current interest and discussion is the issue of the standardization of metadata for collections. Standards such as DC CD[19] have not been generally accepted in Germany, yet. The big union catalogues being the backbones for the delivery of bibliographic metadata paid little attention to the collection level in the past. However, recent activities, such as *Michael Plus*[20], which is funded by the European Community and aims at recording all digital collections irrespective of their material, is a promising initiative and may change the scene. With the increasing number of digitization projects the demand is growing for better access to and survey of collections available on the web.

Whereas digital image collecting is making good progress the growth of full text corpora is rather slow. The main reason is that it is still expensive to create textual digital content, because texts have to be copied by hand. OCR software is not available to reliably transcribe texts from the early modern period, whereby reliable means that recognition rates should be higher than 99,5%. To encode full texts and prepare scholarly electronic editions TEI[21] is the most popular standard in Germany. It is also used for the description of medieval manuscripts.

It is not only the public sector which promotes digital conversion of rare books or cultural heritage material, Google's library scan plan is also active in the field[22]. Recently Google has announced the Bavarian State Library has joined their project as 13th library. It is the first one from Germany and the fifth European library to sign with Google; the others are Oxford University, the University Complutense of Madrid, the National Library of Catalonia (Barcelona) and the University of Ghent[23]. The aim is to scan over a million pages within the next 5 or 6 years. Up to today comparatively few digital items from mediaeval times and the early modern period are available via Google Books (2,500 hits for the years 500-1500; 3,000 hits for 1501-1700; 49,000 hits for 1701-1800 and finally 1,400,000 hits for 1801-1900[24]). This may be due to Google's OCR failing to achieve reasonably good results with texts from the early modern period and to the company being interested mainly in full text and not images so as to enhance their index.

While the digitization of rare book materials has made considerable progress, the digital conversion of materials from museums or archives is still in its infancy. An exception is the *Bildarchiv Foto Marburg* portal[25], which contains about 1.7 million records related to works of art or photographs. The archives in Germany do not have any larger digitization initiatives or comparable portal, yet, although there are some major players like the Federal Archive (Bundesarchiv)[26].

18.2 Digitization at the Herzog August Library

Before continuing about current activities at the Herzog August Library in Wolfenbüttel, it may be appropriate to give a brief background of this institute. Wolfenbüttel, a town of 60,000 inhabitants, situated approximately 200 km West of Berlin. The library was founded in 1572 and flourished in the 17th century under its patron duke August the younger who acceded to the Duchy in 1634. During his lifetime he collected about 135,000 books, making it one of the largest libraries of his time. Today, the library owns 450,000 rare imprints from the period before 1850, amongst them 3,000 medieval manuscripts, 3,500 incunabula and 80,000 imprints from the 16th century. With more than 150,000 imprints from the 17th century, it is by far the largest collection of imprints from the 17th century in Germany. Unlike other countries, Germany has no historical national library; the German National Library was not founded until 1912. The consortium of the distributed national library in Germany was founded to compensate for this by designating individual collections with important holdings printed before 1913 to serve as national repositories for certain centuries. As a member of the so-called distributed national library the Herzog August Library is responsible for collecting German books of the 17th century.

The library functions as a research centre for the European medieval and early modern period running a grant program with up to 50 post-graduate and 25 doctoral grants a year, a conference program with about 30 events a year, a cultural program with exhibitions, concerts and lectures, and its own publication program. The library is open for use to the general public and is financed by the State of Lower Saxony. At present there are 150 staff members on board.

In view of its exceptional holdings the Herzog August Library provides best conditions to play a leading role in the digitization of rare books of the medieval and early modern period. The library has been engaged in various projects in the course of the past years, to enhance access to source material by making digitized manuscripts and imprints online available, indexing the structural information they contain. Some full-text scholarly editions are provided, too, digitised according to TEI.

Criteria for selecting imprints to be digitised are relevance for research, rarity and uniqueness as well as preservation reasons. 4,000 editions with more than 600,000 pages have been digitized and placed online in the past decade[27]. Another 2,000 editions with more than half a million pages will be scanned within the years 2008 and 2009 in our mass digitization project *dünnhaupt digital*[28]. As mentioned, the library pursues a policy of compiling digital corpora by subject related criteria. It addresses scholarly communities and collaborates with them so as to establish digital collections of high relevance. The library resorts to broadly accepted bibliographies, databases or card catalogues for the selection of pertinent works in projects which include larger numbers of titles, because selecting works is time-consuming and requires expensive intellectual work.

The project *dünnhaupt digital* relies on the bibliography of Gerhard Dünnhaupt, a renowned scholar who compiled a canonical bibliography of works of some 200 central German Baroque authors and their works. The project shows that the Wolfenbüttel digital library is able to create as many digital reproductions in the past two years as were previously created in eight years, and this process can be accelerated considerably. The library provides structural metadata for the digital facsimile editions allowing the user to easily navigate through the sequence of images. Captions, annotations, illustrations, printer's devices and the like are indexed. The overall aim is to provide added value to the digitized copies. For example, nobody would use a digital copy of a dictionary of 1,000 pages without having at least alphabetical access[29].

Because digitization should serve conservational purposes as well, it is our conviction that preservation of the original can only be achieved when usability of the digital copy is as good as or even better than the original. The user should be encouraged to draw on the copy and as a result of this the original will probably be used less and suffer less mechanical damage due to handling. A digital copy may be easier and faster to handle than its original. As a point in case may serve the thumbnail view in our Navigator, which can show 50 pages per screen.

Projects complying with this policy are Festival Culture Online[30], Decentral Digital Incunabula Collection[31], Leibnizressourcen digital - digitization of scientific, technical and medical literature read by Leibniz[32] - or Archaeological Finds in the Early Modern Period. Some of the projects offer even more. The Festival Culture Online project not only provides structural metadata, but also sophisticated search facilities. A thesaurus[33] was designed for this project allowing to search metadata of both the English partner project and the Wolfenbüttel one. Iconographic information was indexed by means of the classification scheme Iconclass . Notations can be browsed by an Iconclass[34] browser[35] which was designed by Arkyves[36], another project partner located in the Netherlands.

The collaboration with these partners provides a good example of how projects can interact on the web and may benefit from each another. There is no need to have all resources at one place. The Warwick metadata and digital images of the British Library are available at the British Library web site and are referenced only by the Wolfenbüttel database. The Wolfenbüttel Iconclass metadata were sent to the Netherlands, while the browser implemented in the Netherlands was included in the Wolfenbüttel web presentation within a frame. Wolfenbüttel agreed that its Iconclass metadata may also be used in other environments by Arkyves and in turn was allowed to use Arkyves Iconclass browser for free. As can be seen, the internet opens up entirely new cooperation scenarios for scholarly projects.

Collaboration is regarded as a key concept for internet based scholarly projects in Wolfenbüttel. It can be divided into quantitative and qualitative cooperation. Qualitative cooperation means one of the partners contributes a qualitative new feature to the project such as the Iconclass browser. Quantitative cooperation means the partners aggregate metadata of the same kind such as the Warwick and Wolfenbüttel projects which put their metadata together.

An example of quantitative cooperation is the project Decentral Digital Incunabula Collection. It was carried out by the City and University Library at Cologne and the Herzog August Library and undertook to digitize 1300 incunabula - books printed before 1500, counting amongst the most precious cultural materials. The incunabula were indexed and presented on a joint web site at Cologne. This was the first project in Germany attempting to digitize larger numbers of incunabula, demanding high technical skill and intellectual expertise. Two current similar projects are carried out at the university library at Darmstadt and at the Bavarian states library.

Another quantitative collaboration project is the *Virtuelles Kupferstich kabinett*[37], carried out by the Herzog Anton Ulrich Museum in nearby Braunschweig and the Herzog August Library. 32,000 prints (woodcuts, copper engravings, etchings, etc.) dating from the mid-15th century to 1800 are digitized and described in detail. Formal descriptions of the prints based on international standards are entered into a database and linked with their digitised images; the database is freely available online. About 5,000 of the prints, mostly anonymous works for which suitable descriptive metadata are not available are further indexed by Foto Marburg using Iconclass notations. Special about this project is the cooperation between a museum and a library. Both institutes keep holdings which once belonged to the former ducal collections and are now divided between them. The project is not only one of the most comprehensive in the field, but also offers an opportunity to virtually reconstruct (part of) the former ducal collection and shows how different kinds of institutions can cooperate in that they make use of each others competences.

An example of a qualitative cooperation is a joint project with the Berlin Brandenburgische Akademie der Wissenschaften called *Leibnizressourcen digital*. The Academy in Berlin presents a digital edition of scientific, medical and technical writings of Gottfried Wilhelm Leibniz (1646-1716), the famous German philosopher, mathematician, scientist and former librarian at the Herzog August Library[38]. Leibniz cites works of other mostly contemporary authors in this edition. The Herzog August Library digitized more than 400 works Leibniz refers to in this project and the Academy linked them with Leibniz's citations. When a reader clicks on a quote in the digital edition he is presented with the citation in the digital copy. The link takes him to the page of the book Leibniz quotes. Vice versa Wolfenbüttel implemented in its Navigator[39] a button called 'citations', which allows for an internet search for sites containing links to the Wolfenbüttel imprint. Consequently even if one does not know there is a Leibniz edition the link contained in the Leibniz edition can be found by means of this function. The project shows how resources of various kinds can be connected through the internet and how research may benefit from these new developments.

Other similar projects can be found at the website of the Herzog August Library[40]. It may be added that all reproductions of complete books ordered by users of the library are placed online, too. The digital library grows steadily according to the user's demand in that way.

As a matter of course, digitization not only raises issues of selection or project design, but also of access, storage and preservation. In the beginning it was often underestimated how many organisational problems involving the interaction of different operational sections would evoke. Focus was on production, not on the workflow of selection, production, creation of metadata and indexing. Reproduction problems are solved with high end scanners and cameras by now. Standards for digitization and workflows are established. Even rare, precious and fragile materials can be scanned carefully thanks to book cradles and other handling techniques. Rare books require special treatment. Unbinding the books or other violent measures like opening them at an 180° angle cannot be done without harming those precious objects. The Herzog August Library has therefore developed a special book cradle, called book reflector in a public-private partnership. This allows scanning a book not only at just a comfortable 45° angle, but also at high speed (see Fig. 18.2)[41].

Various cameras are in use depending on the size and kind of material. The library owns 6 Nikon DX2s with 12 Mio pixels., 2 Kodak DCS with 16 Mio pixels, a Kodak Scan Back Pro with 16 Mio pixel and a Senar 54M with 22Mio pixel. The latter is suited for scanning even oversized books or maps at high resolution. Resolution must be 300 dpi minimum according to international recommendations. As a result a Nikon DX2 having a matrix of 4000 × 3000 pixels can only be used for books with a maximum height of 34 cm[i]. All pictures are taken in RGB colour, while some older pictures are still in greyscale or monochrome. These latter images are replaced by new ones, because they do not comply with modern standards asking for colour reproductions. The monitors of the operators are colour calibrated to ensure good results. The digitization of objects that cannot be scanned on these conditions will be postponed until

---

[i] According to the formula: 4000 / 300 = 13,3 inch * 2,54 = 34 cm

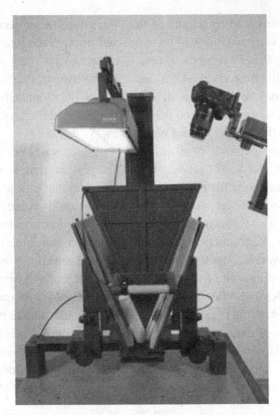

Fig. 18.2: Wolfenbüttel book reflector.

suitable techniques are available. For this reason much manuscript material is digitised in the past, because digital camera techniques did not meet the higher standards for these materials.

As mentioned before, unlike production of digital facsimiles full text production is still difficult since there is no reliable OCR software available. Nonetheless the library has initiated a few minor pilot projects to provide full text transcriptions of works dating from the early modern period. Some selected texts such as Daniel Georg Morhof's *Polyhistor* (1688)[42] or entries in early modern dictionaries were copied by hand and encoded according to TEI. Although the comprehensive production of full text transcriptions is not yet possible the library engages itself in digital edition projects. It not only promotes research in mediaeval and early modern history, but also offers a platform to publish electronic editions. An electronic issue of

Dasypodius' famous dictionary *Latinogermanicum* (1535) edited by Jonathan West is published recently[43]. An edition of Lipsius' *De Bibliothecis*[44], one of the key texts of European library history from the 17th century, is in preparation. It is planned to improve full text search facilities by implementing the native open source XML database eXist[45], which will allow entering XML encoded texts into the digital library.

Three versions can be distinguished for presenting digitised texts on the internet. Most texts are displayed as digital facsimile with bibliographic and structural metadata added. Less common are texts represented as digital facsimiles with a transcription provided. The most advanced representation is a digital edition which may include an introduction, translation and commentary. It is obvious that transition from one stage to another is flexible and that there may be transcriptions providing an introduction, but no commentary or other additions. Unlike printed editions it is possible to present digital editions as work in progress, starting with a digital facsimile to be followed by a transcription, translation, commentary, or even assign various tasks to different persons or institutions. Accordingly, it should be possible to put the digital facsimile online at one location and add the transcription at another. It is believed that the web will change editorial practices fundamentally.

18.3 Long-term Preservation, Permanent Linking, Accessibility and Dissemination of Digital Resources

Since other contributions in this volume treat the question of long-term preservation in a more general view, the following paragraphs discuss long-term archiving at the Herzog August Library only. It is a common and frustrating experience at times resources are not available or have completely disappeared from the web. Some loss of information is not very harmful and not everything is worth preserving. However, it is the library's task to select and store relevant digital cultural resources and to beware of losses which result from negligence or disregard. But how to certify permanent availability of digital resources in an archive and on the internet? Meaning in-terms of, durability and persistence of both the resources itself and the link to it.

Digital images are stored in TIFF uncompressed at Wolfenbüttel, an archive format which has been widely adopted and can be read by almost every image software. Other archive formats may also be used in the future, such as PNG or JPEG2000. Full texts are stored in XML or, if there is no other way to preserve the layout, in PDF/A. Each digital image is on average 23 MB. The archival fileserver[ii] contains 13,437,886 MB (ca. 14 TB) of data at present, which are stored on RAID-Arrays with 88 hard discs which have a capacity between 400 and 750 GB. The calculated increase is 7 TB each year. Backups are stored on magnetic tape (LTO3) in an automated process using a tape library. Over ten years ago in 1997 the library started with CD's as archival media, but quickly realized this was not a good strategy. First, CDs turned out not to be as durable as expected – reading errors occurred when changing CD players, some sectors were corrupted – secondly, in view of thousands of CDs too much time and money was needed to migrate data on new media such as DVD.

The current digital preservation policy is to keep everything in a state of flux. With this decision the former policy was brushed aside of focusing on the preservation of the carrier rather than the information itself, because digital information is not related to its material carrier. Contrary to other media, such as paper or film, digital media can be copied and distributed without any loss of information. This is why the prime consideration about the preservation of the carrier, the substrate, is not its durability, but its function to store and copy information as conveniently as possible. The carrier is no longer an object of preservational, but of operational or functional concern. The strategy is to permanently copy data rather than to consider the durability of CD, DVD, magnetic tape or hard discs. In order to allow easy and convenient copying it is important to keep the infrastructure simple. The more complex the ways data are organized, the more sophisticated the archival systems, the more difficult becomes securing the flux of data. Changes of operating or file systems may affect storage software. Firms' bankruptcy, lack of support or disinterest may prove harmful. In general, the more one has to rely on particular software, the riskier archive storage becomes and it seems more recommendable to store data in transparent form or at least to take care of standardized interfaces. Data are simply organized in a directory structure here. Each item is stored in a directory

---

[ii] Windows 2003 Server (DELL PE 2850); RAID-Arrays (EonStor A24U, 2*easyRAIDQ16+, 2*easyRAIDS16); in addition a TapeLibrary (Adic Scalar i500).

bearing the name of the shelf mark, containing images and metadata in XML. It turned out advantageous to use human readable shelf marks instead of numbers to name the directories, because each item can be easily accessed even if the software does not work.

This is neither an innovative nor - from a technical angle - an elegant solution and in terms of performance even debatable. But it serves its purpose best, namely to store data in a simple system relying on merely a few functional conditions such as the directory system and ASCII 7-Bit for the naming. It has proved to be very reliable and stable for almost 10 years, whereas the management software has changed several times. Two parallel directory trees are set up. One contains the master files, the other the derivative JPEG files for the internet. This allows easy conversion and copying of data from the master tree to the internet.

Accessibility is not only secured by reliable storage, but also by persistent linking and cataloguing. As regards the latter, it must be stressed that it is crucial to provide sufficient metadata, at least at bibliographic level. Each digital edition is catalogued in the library's OPAC and in the central union catalogue with a URL or URN at the bottom of the record's entry (title description), which takes the user directly to the digital copy. As said above, broken links are a common and frustrating experience on the web. Missing access is annoying, but a broken link may mean a broken connection to other pieces of information. Interrupting a chain of links may disrupt a network of knowledge. The importance of persistent linking is often underestimated. Only stable links in connection with XML based standards allow reliable collaboration and scholarly networks between various partners. The network itself and not only the items that are connected by it needs to be preserved. It is a new matter of concern that a link can be a valuable thing, and especially heritage institutions such as libraries have to take care about the persistence not only of the digital objects as such, but also of their interconnection. The means of providing persistent or permanent links are manifold, but all rely more or less on the same principle, namely connecting a durable und unalterable name to a resource or a location of this resource. The concepts of PURL, URN, Handle, DOI or ARK (Archival Resource Key) all function in this way. The Herzog August Library began to establish persistent URLs (PURL) in the late 90's. Although this form of persistent linking may appear odd today, it still works smoothly[46]. The PURL is redirected to a new location, and despite the *start.htm* at the end of the string an HTML file no longer exists. Five years ago it was first replaced by a Perl, later by a PHP script.

Even if one objects to this form of URL (today we would not use a file suffix such as *htm*) the link has been valid for almost 10 years by now - a pretty long time measured by digital life cycles – and the library will continue to secure its validity. In addition, a particular declaration published on the website of the library, guarantees this longevity. Persistence and longevity of digital resources is not only a technical issue of storage procedures or file and metadata formats. Persistence in the digital age is above all an organisational issue. Someone is responsible for re-directing mechanisms and supply of uniform identifiers. Ideally it should be an organisation in the public sector financed by the state in order to ensure independent free access to cultural heritage, and to allow the collection and preservation of cultural objects irrespective of their market value. Without public institutions, institutions which are controlled by public organisations or greater communities in charge of maintaining links or providing re-directing services, no persistent linking is possible.

One of the great challenges in a network environment is the ability to exchange or disseminate metadata in XML. Already a variety of standards is endorsed by the respective communities allowing exchanging and aggregating metadata or searching distributed resources but not all digital libraries support them, yet. Currently one of the most important and comparatively widely used standards is OAI-PMH[47] and the Wolfenbüttel digital library has implemented an OAI interface[48], Dublin Core is mandatory, and the MODS and METS format is supported. Further metadata formats will be added to the interface in the near future such as TEI-P5/MASTER for manuscript descriptions or *Museumdat*[49], a format for providing core data from museum holdings[50]. OAI or other dissemination formats play a decisive role in aggregating higher quality data. For example, the new search engine *Europeana* (see above) will harvest data from OAI data repositories, another well known portal of that kind is OAIster[51]. Besides OAI a digital library should support alerting services like RSS or Atom and the Wolfenbüttel digital library has implemented a RSS 2.0 interface to inform their users about recent publications[52].

18.4 Conclusion

Converting our cultural heritage into a digital form will not only preserve it for future generations, but will also open up new scholarly approaches and co-operation scenarios, which we do not foresee in full detail and scope, yet. Free access independent of time and place will stimulate research and allow work with materials which were formerly nearly inaccessible. Joint ventures and Web 2.0 techniques will intensify this process of international cooperation and will improve research conditions worldwide. In order to reach at such a goal internationally agreed strategies on preservation and durable access are indispensable. It requires hardware and software solutions, international standards for data archival and metadata, agreements on persistent linking and quoting digital resources, on dissemination standards, and last but not the least, it requires cultural heritage institutions willing to take charge of preserving the analogue past for the digital future.

References

1 Arbeitsgemeinschaft Sammlung Deutscher Drucke: *http://www.ag-sdd.de/eng/index.htm*

2 Thaller, Manfred (2005), Retrospektive Digitalisierung von Bibliotheksbeständen – Evaluierungsbericht über einen Förderschwerpunkt der DFG. Universität Köln, *http://ww.dfg.de/forschungsfoerderung/wissenschaftliche_infrastruktur/lis/ download/ retro_digitalisierung_eval_050406.pdf*

3 Zentrales Verzeichnis Digitaler Drucke: *http://www.zvdd.de*

4 *http://www.europeana.eu*

5 *http://www.vd16.de*

6 *http://www.vd17.de*

7 *http://digital.slub-dresden.de/en/sammlungen/kollektionen/projekt-quellen-zur-technikgeschichte-1617-jh-2*

8 *http://digitale.bibliothek.uni-halle.de/content/overview*

9 *http://www.bsb-muenchen.de/Digitalisierung_der_im_deutsch.1841.0.html*

10 *http://www.treventus.com/index_en.html*

11 *http://www.dfg-viewer.de*

12 *http://www.loc.gov/standards/mets*

13 *http://www.loc.gov/standards/mods/*

14 For reasons of better readability the request URL is put in plain text. If applied, the URL which is to be passed to the Viewer must be URL-encoded: *http://dfg-viewer.de/v1/?set[mets]=http%3A%2F%2Fdbs.hab.de%2Fdfgnavi%2Fget_navi.php%3Fdir%3Ddrucke%2F6-1-geom*

15 URL encoded: *http://dfg-viewer.de/v1/?set[mets]=http%3A%2F%2Fdbs.hab.de%2Foai%2F%3Fverb%3DGetRecord%26metadataPrefix%3Dmets%26identifier%3Doai%3Adiglib.hab.de%3Appn_539984248*

16 The URL in this record takes the user immediately to the *DFG Viewer*: *http://gso.gbv.de/DB=1.28/SET=5/TTL=2/COLMODE=1/CMD?ACT=SRCHA&IKT=1016&SRT=YOP&TRM=vdn+23%3A320244N*

17 *http://www.dfg.de/forschungsfoerderung/formulare/download/12_151.pdf*

18 *http://dfg-viewer.de/profil-der-strukturdaten/*

19 *http://www.ukoln.ac.uk/metadata/dcmi/collection-application-profile/2004-08-20/*

20 *http://www.michael-culture.org/en/home*

21 *http://www.tei-c.org*

22 *http://books.google.com/*

23 *http://www.libraryjournal.com/article/CA6431810.html*

24 Google Books , *op.cit.* Checked 22nd March 2008.

25 *http://www.fotomarburg.de/index_html?set_language=en*

26 *http://www.bundesarchiv.de/*

27 *http://www.hab.de/bibliothek/wdb/index-e.htm*

28 *http://diglib.hab.de/?link=017*

29 Cf. Basilius Faber: *http://diglib.hab.de/drucke/kb-11-2f/start.htm*

30 *http://www.hab.de/bibliothek/wdb/festkultur/index-e.htm*

31 *http://www.hab.de/forschung/projekte/incunabula-e.htm*

32 *http://diglib.hab.de/?link=011*

33 *http://www.hab.de/bibliothek/wdb/festkultur/fb-thesa.htm*

34 *http://www.iconclass.nl/*

35 *http://dbs.hab.de/barock/iconclass.htm*

36 *http://www.arkyves.com/*

37 *http://www.hab.de/forschung/projekte/kupferstichkabinett-e.htm*

38 *http://leibnizviii.bbaw.de/*

39 *http://diglib.hab.de/drucke/34-5-phys-2f/start.htm*

40 *http://www.hab.de/bibliothek/wdb/projekte.htm*

41 *http://www.hab.de/bibliothek/rw/buchspiegel/index-e.htm*

42 *http://diglib.hab.de/drucke/ea-490/transcript-roh.htm*

43 *http://diglib.hab.de/edoc/ed000008/start.htm*

44 *http://diglib.hab.de/edoc/ed000001/start.htm*

45 *http://exist.sourceforge.net/*

46 *http://diglib.hab.de/*

47 *http://www.openarchives.org/*

48 *http://dbs.hab.de/oai*

49 *http://www.museumdat.org/index.php?ln=en&t=home*

50 Cf. The experimental interface for the virtual printroom project at *http://dbs.hab.de/ grafik/museumdat/*

51 *http://www.oaister.org/*

52 *http://dbs.hab.de/rss/*

Chapter 19

Establishing Trust in Digital Repositories

Bruce Ambacher[1]

[1]*College of Information Studies*
University of Maryland, College Park, USA
bambache@umd.edu

Abstract

Creators and potential depositors of digital heritage materials cannot always physically examine a "bricks and mortar" repository in the same way previous cultural heritage creators and depositors could examine traditional repositories. This has raised issues regarding how one can determine the suitability of a digital repository for their digital information. This chapter will trace the development of international standards for establishing and operating digital repositories that have assumed or been assigned the digital preservation mission for specified data. It traces this development over more than two decades from the earliest theoretical discussions and lamentations over the loss of digital heritage, through early discussions, the development of the Open Archival Information System Reference Model international standard and supporting ingest standards, to the current efforts to develop a repository audit and certification system as an international standard.

Keywords: Digital Repositories, OAIS Reference Model, Trustworthy Digital Repository Standard, Audit and Certification Standard.

19.1 Introduction

Imagine it is 1958. You are a prolific author with an extended career. You are looking for an appropriate repository for your papers. Your papers consist of typed and hand-written manuscripts, correspondence, business related documents, printed materials, photographs, maps and assorted awards and memorabilia. How will you determine where to deposit your papers? What criteria will you use to make your decision?

You could begin by asking others where they deposited their papers. You could ask them what criteria they used to select that repository. You could visit those repositories to determine whether they meet your criteria, whether they had an appropriate building that met current requirements in terms of environment, shelving, and security. You could ask whether they had appropriate staff to process and provide access to your collection. You could examine the repository's budget and endowment. You could determine how many staff were employed and in what capacities. You could examine similar collections they had processed and determine the quality of the processing and the associated finding aids.

In sum there would be tangible ways to assure yourself that your papers had a reasonable chance of being appropriately preserved in a repository of your choice.

Now let us imagine that same process occurring today. There will be several differences. First, the physical nature of your "papers" will be different. Your collection will be predominantly digital in origin, form and storage. Your correspondence will be created on word processing software and/or received and sent in an email utility. Your correspondence and email will be controlled by automated indexing systems. Your "printed material" also will be digital or printed from digital sources. Even your photographs and maps will be digital. Some of your records will reflect your participation in Second Life. Only the memorabilia may still be in the same format.

You may begin the search for an appropriate repository in the same way and with the same basic questions. The answers, however, will be different. Your search will be less concrete and it may be more difficult to select the appropriate repository. The "right" repository may not be an imposing "brick and mortar" edifice. It may be a computer center. Or it may appear to be nothing more than a webpage that acts as a portal to the digital world in which storage is virtual and your data is moving around the grid taking physical form only when a user requests a copy of specific information.

What criteria can you use to determine if that web portal, computer system or digital data center is what it says it is? Will you know if the digital repository it represents can provide the environment, care and handling your collection should receive? Or, will you learn that it is the digital equivalent of the Wizard of Oz standing behind the curtain speaking into a megaphone to appear bigger than life?

Consider how much easier your search would be if an international standard existed that signified a digital repository was a trusted digital repository, one that had been audited and certified to be in compliance with applicable national and international requirements and standards for identifying, accessioning, storing, and providing access to your data. And what if that trusted digital repository was able to display a seal signifying such status on its website, building, finding aids and other documentation?

Current efforts to develop audit and certification criteria are seeking to do just that. The goal is a process that reassures donors, curators, and users that a digital repository can maintain digital collections properly. It is clear that standards must play an even larger role than in the past to achieve that confidence in the digital repository and in the digital holdings.

This chapter will provide both some historical perspective on building digital trust and information on what is currently being done to develop digital audit and certification standards.

19.2 Views on Digital Preservation

Worldwide there is a lack of confidence in the ability of archivists and librarians to manage digital data. Those professions are seen as slow to embrace digital data preservation. While librarians embraced digital access to information through search engines and automated indices before archivists did, both have been cautious regarding digital data acquisition and preservation. The professions have spent far too much time studying the issues, far too much time on grant-funded pilot projects, far too much time developing redundant best practices, and far too little time developing recommended standards. The professions may have been waiting for someone else to solve the problems, for someone else to provide an out-of-the-box solution.

The producers of digital data, however, were not able to wait for the archival and library professions to develop the perfect solution that will guarantee that digital data will be available any time in the future in a usable form. The producers recognized the value of their data to their designated communities. They recognized that others required access to the data. They filled the void and created in-house repositories and discipline data centers staffed by discipline specialists who acquired digital data preservation and dissemination skills. They coined new discipline titles such as digital curator and cultural heritage information professional to denote both the broader mix of duties and the specialized focus on data of broad value and utility, and to avoid using the traditional titles associated with archives and libraries.

The physical location of these repositories within or strongly affiliated with the creator's discipline means that the data creators, producers or custodians play a larger role with digital data than they did with similar analog information. The location of the new repositories also means that they focus more on serving their designated communities, providing less assistance to other users than similar repositories located in traditional archives and libraries.

19.3 Early Efforts at Digital Preservation

Some would mark the beginning of the quest for digital data preservation standards with the pioneering work of the United States National Archives and Records Administration (NARA). In 1939 it was the first national archives to declare punch cards as records. Four years later it broadened the definition of records to include "other documentary materials, regardless of physical form or characteristics." In the mid-1960s its staff began to explore digital data acquisition and in April 1970 accessioned their first digital records[1]. As every archivist knows, accessioning records is inevitably the first step toward long-term preservation. In this same timeframe digital data was acquired by the Interuniversity Consortium for Political and Social Research (ICPSR) at the University of Michigan and the National Archives of Canada. These early preservation efforts focused on maintaining and providing the data in a hardware and software independent format that could be used in any contemporary computer.

Others would mark the beginning of the search for digital data preservation standards with the work of the Committee on Records that began its 1985 Report with the dire warning that "The United States is in danger of losing its memory"[2]. The Report brought the issues before Congress and a broader public.

Still others can point to significant research in the early 1990s into the archival nature of digital records funded by various national and international sources. Two significant studies that should be mentioned here are the study of the functional requirements for authentic digital records at the University of Pittsburgh and the recordkeeping study at the University of British Columbia that had a major influence on the later development of the DoD 5015.2 Standard[3].

19.4 Preserving Digital Information

In one sense the historical development of digital trust, as exemplified by the movement to develop audit and certification criteria, is brief. Many trace the actual roots of the search for international standards to the establishment of the Task Force on Archiving of Digital Information by the Commission on Preservation and Access and the Research Libraries Group (RLG) in December 1994. Their charge to the Task Force was to investigate how to ensure "continued access indefinitely into the future of records stored in digital electronic form"[4]. In *Preserving Digital Information*, the final report issued in May 1996, the task force envisioned the establishment of national systems of digital archives charged with providing long-term storage and access to the digital materials they collect and charged with responsibility for rescuing at-risk culturally significant digital information. A clear goal of certification was to reduce the impact of technology's marketplace forces on digital preservation[5].

The task force popularized the concepts of ensuring the integrity of digital information through clear presentations of the content, provenance, and context of the information and ensuring the content through means to ensure its fixity and reference or through a persistent identifier. The task force placed the initial burden for these aspects on the creator and ultimately on the repository[6]. User confidence in the digital information would come from the internal procedures of the repository as it adhered to established and regulated practices and demonstrated to auditors that its practices and structure qualified that repository to be classified as a "certified" digital archives. As with most repositories, the critical infrastructure and financial stability required for that repository to continue to exist would be invisible to most creators and users. Every aspect of the repository's operations, from appraisal and selection through accession, storage, and preservation, would demonstrate that commitment to long-term preservation and access. Significant attention to changing formats, building migration paths for preserved digital information as needed, incorporating standards, engineering preservation and access systems, and managing costs and finances to ensure longevity were considered hallmarks of a trusted repository[7].

The nine recommendations in the report, broken into three general headings of pilot projects, needed structure support, and development of best practices, set an aggressive agenda for every institution concerned about digital preservation and seeking a reasonable solution, a prescribed set of norms and standards. The recommendations included sharing case study examples, developing audit and certification criteria, developing security criteria to ensure the authenticity and integrity of the digital objects, disaster recovery measures, approaches to sustainability, and development of digital preservation models[8].

19.5 The Reference Model for an Open Archival Information System

Two initiatives that built on the *Preserving Digital Information* report would have significant impacts on furthering digital preservation efforts and broadening professional understanding of the challenges. The first was the Reference Model for an Open Archival Information Systems (OAIS), developed as an ISO standard by the Mission Operations and Information Management Systems working group of the Consultative Committee for Space Data Systems (CCSDS). CCSDS is a voluntary organization of member space agencies formed in 1982 to address data system problems to ensure data could be exchanged and available for the long term. Data collected on more than 300 space missions have been shared using CCSDS developed standards.

CCSDS began work on OAIS in 1995. In an October 1995 seminar CCSDS opened the process to all interested institutions and individuals worldwide. The majority of the actual standard development work was led by staff and contractors at NASA's Goddard Space Flight Center, supported by a core of volunteers. The core working group included space scientists, information technology specialists, space collections curators and one archivist. The U.S. National Archives and Records Administration (NARA) hosted twenty of the twenty-four multi-day workshops held in the U.S. to develop the OAIS. Opportunities for others to help shape the standard came through posted minutes of the workshops, published draft updates to the model, and participation in reviews at the CCSDS semi-annual meetings.

Preserving Digital Information was a formative factor in the CCSDS effort to understand the roles of authenticity, fixity, provenance, and context as aspects of a trusted digital object[9]. Additional input was obtained at two open workshops held at NARA. ISO, CCSDS, the Johns Hopkins University Applied Physics Laboratory, NASA, NARA and RLG co-sponsored the Digital Archives Directions (DADS) workshop in June 1998. All of the sponsors had a strong interest in the digital information arena. Speakers addressed the current issues on many digital preservation topics including digital archiving, digital preservation, and efforts to provide solutions for numerous data formats such as office automation, geospatial information systems, exchange metadata, data authentication and persistent identifiers[10].

NARA, NASA and ISO also hosted the *Archival Workshop on Ingest, Identification and Certification Standards (AWIICS)* in October 1999[11]. AWIICS included current status reports on the draft OAIS and previewed the growing focus on standards for audit and certification. One of the three tracks at the AWIICS meeting focused on certification. As discussion leader for that focus group I introduced four approaches to certification: individual certification such as the programs for becoming a Certified Archivist or a Certified Records Manager, program certification such as the Historical Manuscript Commission's Approval or the Museum Assessment Program of the American Association of Museums, process certification such as the ISO 9000 suite or DoD 5015.2-STD, and data certification focusing on persistence of data content and information security standards such as Public Key Certification. Participants agreed to a layered concept of certification that incorporated aspects of all four processes. The certification focus group developed a preliminary checklist that became one of the major sources for the preliminary work on *Trusted Repositories: Audit and Certification*[12].

As the OAIS reference model neared completion in 2000 digital preservation staff from institutions such as the Joint Information Systems Committee of the United Kingdom System for Higher and Further Education (JISC) and the Kroninklijke Bibliotheek (KB) participated in the working sessions to enhance the preservation focus. Extensive comment and responsive modifications came from the call for, and resolution of, comments from scores of interested parties in 2001. The model gained ISO status in 2002 as ISO 14721.

One aspect of the OAIS Reference Model that often is overlooked is Section 1.5, (Road Map for Development of Related Standards). This section included an item "standard(s) for accreditation of archives," reflecting this long-standing demand for a standard against which repositories of digital information may be audited and on which an international accreditation and certification process may be based. *Trusted Repositories Audit and Certification* represented the first comprehensive effort to implement this need.

The OAIS Reference Model became a standard just as digital preservation was becoming a "must do" part of the mission of numerous repositories. These new digital preservationists, looking for guiding principles and/or best practices, quickly saw OAIS as the high level model it was, one that would allow them latitude in integrating its requirements into their already extant mission statements and operating programs. Others saw OAIS as a 'recipe" for establishing a digital repository with its six major activities to be implemented – ingest, archival storage, dissemination, preservation planning, data management, and administration. Some, however, lamented that OAIS was too high level to serve as an Information Technology blueprint or systems development template; something the standard's creators specifically avoided. OAIS has had one of the quickest and most widespread adoptions of any ISO standard.

19.6 Developing a Trustworthy Digital Repository Standard

The second initiative to build from *Preserving Digital Information*, was the RLG-OCLC task force that worked from 2000 into 2002 to produce *Trusted Digital Repositories: Attributes and Responsibilities*. Their goal was to "reach consensus on the characteristics and responsibilities of trusted digital repositories for large-scale, heterogeneous collections held by cultural organizations"[13]. The task force defined a "trusted repository" as one "whose mission is to provide reliable, long-term access to managed digital resources to its designated community, now and in the future"[14]. The report recommended development of a certification process that "would dictate criteria that must be met and would employ mechanisms for assessment and measurement." Certification, over the long term, could provide a tool for determining which repositories are "trusted" and are capable of maintaining reliable data over time[15].

The report laid out seven challenges focusing on developing a framework to support certification; identifying the attributes of digital materials to be preserved; developing models for networks, services, and persistent identifiers; and developing strategies for trusted repositories, access mechanisms, and appropriate metadata[16-17]. Crucial attributes of a Trusted Digital repository included complying with OAIS, accepting administrative responsibility for long-term digital preservation, providing financial sustainability, developing appropriate technological and procedural suitability, providing system security and maintaining procedural accountability[18].

The task force report devoted chapter 4 to certification of trusted digital repositories. Building from the AWIICS workshop report the document described two viable models currently in use for certification: an audit model for government digital records repositories and a standards model underlying such activities as preservation quality microfilm and interlibrary lending. The report also recommended the layered approach developed in AWIICS and urged development of "a framework and process to support the certification of digital repositories"[19].

RLG and OCLC issued *Trusted Digital Repositories* in May 2002. Early in 2003 RLG partnered with NARA to build on the momentum and interest in developing audit and certification criteria. They established a new task force to develop an audit and certification checklist. With representatives from several major repositories in the U.S. and Europe (RLG, NARA, Library of Congress, KB, Harvard, Stanford, Cornell, the Internet Archive, NASA and the University of London Computing Center), and with several experienced OAIS developers, the task force spent two and a half years developing a draft set of criteria, *Checklist for the Certification of Trusted Digital Repositories*. The draft checklist was available for public review and comment from August 2005 through January 2006. Like the earlier projects cited here, this was a "top-down" view developed by working experts who also were knowledgeable about the technical issues, e.g., an insider's view. OAIS was the obvious starting point for this effort. The working group faced several scoping questions such as: how to get repositories to seek and undergo certification audit, determining which repositories should be either subject to or eligible for certification, and whether there should be different levels of certification or a "one size fits all" approach[20].

In January 2006 the working group began the process of adjudicating comments. It also examined parallel work coming from the Center for Research Libraries, the German Network of Expertise in Long-Term Storage of Digital Resources (nestor) project, and audit work conducted by the

Digital Curation Centre (DCC). In the revised report the working group clustered the audit and certification criteria into three major categories: organizational infrastructure, data object management, and the technology infrastructure. A fourth focus, designated community and the intended uses of information, is embedded in and developed throughout the three main categories.

Part A, Organizational Infrastructure, contains twenty-two criteria focusing on whether the repository has the appropriate controls and safeguards in place including a clear mission statement, the appropriate structure and staffing, a plan of succession for its holdings, financial sustainability and the necessary contracts, licenses and agreements in place to ensure its longevity.

Part B, Data Object Management, is the major category and its forty-four criteria address the repository functions, processes, and procedures, focusing on the life cycle of data from the repository's perspective – ingest, creation of the archival information package including persistent identifiers and metadata development, archival storage, preservation planning, and access management.

Part C, Technology Infrastructure and Security, is a set of activities and responsibilities that are shared between the archival staff and the information technology staff. These activities are covered by only twelve criteria, reflecting the overlap with well-established Information Technology and Security standards that should be incorporated into a repository's operations[21].

19.7 Testing the Approach

During the August 2005 – January 2006 public comment period for the RLG-NARA draft report some of the working group participated with others in conducting a test of the audit procedures. The Center for Research Libraries (CRL) was awarded a grant from the Andrew Mellon Foundation to develop processes and activities required to audit and certify digital archives developed by the cultural heritage community[22]. CRL, joined by RLG and DCC, implemented the audits utilizing the perspective of "users" and of those with a fiduciary and management perspective. They worked to determine what information must be produced by the audit and certification process to both achieve a high level of confidence that the repository could do what it proclaimed it would do and to provide information to interested administrators such as a university provost or a legislator that the repository met all required criteria. The project audited three types of digital archives – two e-journal depositories utilizing different storage and access protocols and a data archive.

The CRL audit tests were the first effort that merged the audit and certification activities discussed before with parallel efforts by the nestor Working Group on Trusted Repository Certification and the Digital Curation Centre. It did so by developing and circulating a cross-walk between TRAC, nestor requirements, and the DCC and DigitalPreservationEurope (DPE) *Digital Repository Audit Method Based on Risk Assessment (DRAMBORA)*, then in draft and issued in February 2007[23]. This cross-walk has been quite helpful to the ongoing standard development effort.

Since 2003 Germany has pursued both a "soft" and a "hard" approach to certification for developing trusted repositories. In the soft approach, adherence to certain criteria is encouraged rather than required; repositories are "coached" into compliance. The hard approach establishes strict requirements that can be met by only a small minority of digital repositories, earning them the highest level of trust. The German Initiative for Networked Information (DINI) seeks to improve interoperability among German institutions of higher education and to provide a vehicle for those institutions to "raise the visibility, recognition, and importance of the digital repository" within its institution. Digital repositories meeting certain levels of standards can earn a DINI certificate that denotes the level of trustworthiness (bronze, silver, gold). The DINI initiative focuses largely on electronic publishing including theses, dissertations, monographs, e-journals, preprints, and scanned materials. DINI certified repositories report that the process caused their funding authorities to reflect more on their mission, philosophy, and funding needs[24-25].

The nestor certificate, based on its *Catalogue of Criteria for Trusted Digital Long-term Repositories*, strives for a "hard certification" that documents the trustworthiness of the digital repositories. Its reach extends beyond the universities and includes national and state libraries and archives, museums, and data centers. The nestor criteria utilize a three step approach that begins with orientation to the recommendations, best practices and standards to be audited, through self-evaluation to demonstrate qualification, and concludes with the actual audit and certification by outside experts. The goal is to establish a network of trusted repositories for Germany, reinforced by a network of experts in long-term storage[26-27]. The working group developing nestor have advanced their goals through sharing information, making expertise available, encouraging communication, and developing relevant reports. While working within an environment of laws, guidelines, and goals specific to Germany, nestor also is working cooperatively with other, similar national and international groups to develop a common set of audit and certification criteria, supplemented by specific national requirements.

19.8 Incorporating Risk Analysis

The third piece of the cross-walk was the *Digital Repository Audit Method Based on Risk Assessment (DRAMBORA),* released in draft version 1.0 by the Digital Curation Centre and DigitalPreservationEurope (DPE) in February 2007. Staff at the University of Glasgow and the National Archives of Netherlands developed *DRAMBORA* for the DCC and DPE. DRAMBORA is a risk based assessment tool in which repositories assess themselves against the baseline criteria contained in TRAC and the nestor working group, supplemented with aspects from international information standards with the primary focus on the risk involved in non-compliance or minimal compliance. DRAMBORA represents six stages of development and assessment: identifying the organizational context; documenting the applicable policy and regulatory framework; identifying core activities, the assets involved and the responsible parties; identifying risks; assessing those risks; and then managing those risks.

DRAMBORA places the digital information object at the center of the effort. It seeks to have each repository "determine whether the repository has made every effort to avoid and contain the risks that might impede its ability to receive, curate and provide access to authentic, and contextually, syntactically, and semantically understandable digital information"[28]. DRAMBORA does not establish a single, fixed benchmark that each repository must meet or exceed. Rather, it encourages each repository to assess itself based on its goals which may be both specific and subjective. A comprehensive sense of context, objectives and specific assessments are then used by each repository to develop its own list of risks, their attributes, responsible parties, and proposals to avoid or mitigate those risks. This approach recognizes that in the digital world not all repositories have acquisition, preservation and access as their core mission, that the placement and responsibilities of digital repositories varies, and that not all digital repositories are assigned full responsibility for all aspects of the archival life cycle[29].

Between April 2006 and January 2007, the Digital Curation Centre conducted five pilot audits to determine an optimal methodology and to evaluate the applicability and robustness of the TRAC and nestor guidelines and the DRAMBORA approach. The biggest weakness in those guidelines was the lack of metrics such as policy statements, laws, regulations and guidelines to which the repository adheres; procedures manuals; operating procedures; records of actions taken; staffing patterns; and disaster plans; to measure the extent and effectiveness of compliance[30]. For each audited risk there is both a Risk Probability Score of 1 to 6 and a Risk Impact Score of 0 to 6. These are accompanied by a formal risk description that identifies the risk, the owner, the issues, the probability, the probable impact and the mitigation steps in place or planned. Collectively these formal descriptions represent an overview of the risks facing the repository, the responsible parties, the resources needed, and the actions required to mitigate those risks[31].

19.9 Developing the Standard for Audit and Certification of Trustworthy Digital Repositories

The next chapter in this quest – an international standard of certification criteria for digital repositories and - is the focus of the current international working group under the auspices of the Consultative Committee for Space Data Systems. CCSDS members initially created a "Birds of a Feather" interest group within the Mission Operations and Information Management Systems sector of CCSDS, the same component of CCSDS responsible for developing the Reference Model for Open Archival Information Systems. This allowed the interested parties to organize a wiki and establish a project description, timeline and draft charter. Subsequently the CCDSD Management group reviewed these documents and formally established the working group[32].

The timeline is ambitious and has experienced some slippage. In March 2008 the group delivered a marked up version of the TRAC text to satisfy the deadline for a Deliverable: Draft certification document that serves as a

CCSDS White Book Version 0. The October 2008 deadline for a Version 1 White Book was not met. Instead several members of the working group met during the October 2008 CCSDS meeting in Berlin, Germany, to discuss the progress to date and enumerate the outstanding issues. They adjusted the time table, and began preliminary planning for a meeting in Washington, DC early in 2009.

Under CCSDS procedures a version 1.0 White Book should be a nearly finalized version suitable for broad review within CCSDS. When it is produced CCSDS provides for a review and formal comment period. The working group then reviews and adjudicates the comments and edits the document as needed. The resulting product is a CCSDS Red Book, a final draft forwarded to ISO Technical Committee 20/Subcommittee 13 for international review. That version will enter the ISO review process and become the basis for an ISO Audit and Certification Standard. The current timetable projects that process to be completed by October 2009[33].

The working group also will produce a "Requirements for Bodies Providing Audit and Certification of Digital Repositories" - "Requirements for Auditors" for short. This requirements set will be modeled on ISO 17006 and prepared along similar lines. During the development phase early in 2009 the requirements tested by conducting a set of test audits based on the draft requirements. The working group, which includes several members who participated in the earlier text audits, found those tests to be "somewhat superficial" and not as rigorous as they could have been. The guiding principles for this set of test audits includes keeping the results confidential in order to assure cooperation from the participating archives. They also use "nearby" repositories where "auditors" can assist with the preparatory "self-audit" that precede the audit[34].

The main focus of the CCSDS working group is the detailed examination of TRAC. Working with a core of the earlier TRAC working group, supplemented by staff from interested digital repositories and CCSDS members, the group, which numbers almost 100 participants and observers, is examining each of TRAC's audit criteria to confirm its applicability and universality. Each remaining criteria has been reformatted to state the requirement in a mandatory structure. Each requirement then is supported by Supporting Text, Examples, and Discussion. This has resulted in the elimination of some TRAC criteria, consolidation of other criteria, the division of still other criteria into two or more requirements, and additional cross-references between criteria[35].

The bulk of the work is done through weekly web chats that mix voice and text. This follows individual review of the online working document and the posting of questions, comments and suggestions for change within the online document and shared with all participants. Between six and twelve people participate in each weekly web chat. The bulk of the time has been devoted to Section B, Digital Object Management, which contains the core archival functions of ingest, storage, preservation, and dissemination.

An international standard establishing certification criteria that can be audited to ensure digital repositories that claim a mission of long-term preservation of and access to cultural heritage data can fulfill that mission will be adopted. This will lead to the audit and certification of repositories. This, in turn, will provide digital data creators and donors a means to gain confidence in the repository they choose. On July 16, 2009, the working group forwarded a draft Standard for Audit and Certification of a Trustworthy Digital Repository to the CCSDS Technical Editor. The editor creates the CCSDS Red Book version of the draft standard. The Red Book will simultaneously circulate in the CCSDS community and the ISO community for review and comment. The timeframe expected was to be from early fall 2009 through spring 2010. At that time the working group was to adjudicate the comments and create the final version of the standard. The text of the draft standard can be viewed at[36]:

Several critical major issues of importance to the digital cultural heritage, however, will not be answered by this standard. The standard will not determine the best long-term solution for long-term preservation. The debate over migration or emulation will continue. This standard will not determine whether the path to long-term preservation lies with shared solutions that focus more on current access than long-term preservation or with some future solution developed by the information technology sector. Nor will this standard establish how much metadata is required and whether preservation metadata is required to understand digital information over the long-term. Likewise the standard will not address whether digital cultural heritage data would be better preserved and accessed through preservation in a broad, unaffiliated set of repositories such as traditional information has been housed or in a tight network of a small set of national and international data centers.

Finally, this standard will not address copyright and intellectual property rights in this age of distributed information, reinforced by "click and copy." Those are issues to be addressed by other international working groups and other international standards.

19.10 Conclusion

Until an international standard for audit and certification is adopted and released the digital cultural heritage community has developed several very good examples of archival institutions with a long pedigree in acquiring, managing, preserving and providing access to digital data. Those repositories are leading the way. They are conducting self audits and posting results so other institutions can benefit from their experience. Other, more broadly based cultural institutions and discipline based repositories are helping develop new approaches and best practices.

For decades we have seen digital cultural heritage professionals cope with the long-term preservation of digital information. They have been weaving a "safety net" to ensure long-term preservation of the digital information for which they have responsibility. The safety net is virtually complete. Laws and regulations represent one set of threads in the net. Standards and best practices represent another set of threads. Interdisciplinary cooperation is another set. Once we more thoroughly interweave archival principles, practices, and experience we will have a very strong and extensive safety net to assure digital data producers that data archives can be trusted to accession, preserve and provide access to digital data over the long-term.

References

1 Ambacher, Bruce I. (ed) (2003), *Thirty Years of Electronic Records*, Lanham, MD, Scarecrow Press, See Chronology, pp.ix-xii.

2 Committee on Records (1985), *Report*, Washington, DC.

3 Conrad, Mark (2003), Early Intervention: The NHPRC's Electronic Records Program, in Bruce I. Ambacher (ed.) *Thirty Years of Electronic Records*, Lanham, MD, Scarecrow Press, pp.167-186.

4 Commission on Preservation and Access and the Research Libraries Group (1996), *Preserving Digital Information,Report of the Task Force on Archiving Digital Information*, p.iii

5 *ibid.*, p.iii.

6 *ibid.*, pp.11-19

7 *ibid.*, pp.21-39.

8 *ibid.*, pp.40-44.

9 Sections 2.2.2 of the OAIS at *http://public.ccsds.org/publications/archieve/650x0b1.pdf*

10 Information about the Digital Archives Directions workshop, including presented papers, is available at: *http://nost.gsfc.nasa.gov/isoas/dads/*

11 Information about the Archival Workshop on Ingest, Identification, and Certification Standards, including presented papers and recommendations, is available at: *http://nost.gsfc.nasa.gov/isoas/awiics/nssdc.gsfc.nasa.gov/nssdc_news/sept98/01_j_garrett_0998.html*

12 Archival Workshop on Ingest, Identification, and Certification Standards (AWIICS) (1998), *Certification (Best Practices) Checklist*, available at: *ssdoo.gsfc.nasa.gov/nost/isoas/awiics/CertifBase.ppt*, The Certification group at the AWIICS workshop recommended that "accreditation of archives is important and should be pursued, but that it can only be accomplished when best practices are in place." Since the OAIS Reference Model was only in draft at the time, certification activities were delayed until the Reference Model was ready for ISO standardization; Donald Sawyer and Jerry Winkler, "Digital Archive Directions Workshop Extremely Successful," *NOST Hosts Archiving Workshop,* **14**(4) (September).

13 RLG-OCLC Working Group on Digital Archive Attributes (2002), *Trusted Digital Repositories: Attributes and Responsibilities*, p.i

14 *ibid.*, p.i, 5, 37.

15 *ibid.*, pp.38-39.

16 *ibid.*

17 Dale, Robin (2005), Making Certification Real: Developing Methodology for Evaluating Repository Trustworthiness, *RLG DigiNews*, **9**(5) (October 15).

18 RLG-OCLC Working Group on Digital Archive Attributes (2002), *Trusted Digital Repositories: Attributes and Responsibilities*, pp.13-15.

19 *ibid.*, pp. 32-35

20 RLG -NARA (2005), Taskforce on Digital Repository Certification: Audit *Checklist for*

Certifying Digital Repositories, (July), passim, For a view of a preservation perspective developed from a systems perspective see: David Rosenthal, *et al.*, Requirements for Digital Preservation systems: A Bottom-up Approach, *D-Lib Magazine*, **11**(11) (November).

21 RLG-NARA Taskforce on Digital Repository Certification (2007), *Trustworthy Repositories Audit and Certification: Criteria and Checklist,* (February), passim.

22 Details of the grant, the audits, and the results are available at: *http://www.crl.edu/content.asp?l1=13&l2=58&l3=142*

23 Digital Curation Centre and DigitalPreservationEurope (2007), *Digital Repository Audit Method Based on Risk Assessment,* Release Version 1.0.

24 Dobratz, Susanne and Schoger, Astrid (2005), Digital Repository Certification: A Report from Germany, *RLG DigiNews*, **9**(5), (October 5).

25 Dobratz, Susanne and Scholze, Frank (2006), DINI Institutional Repository Certification and Beyond, *Library Hi Tech*, **24**(4), pp.583-594.

26 Nestor Working Group (2006), *Catalogue of Criteria for Trusted Digital Repositories*, Version 1.

27 Dobratz, Susanne, Schoger, Astrid and Strathmann, Stefan (2007), The nestor Catalogue of Criteria for Trusted Digital Repository Evaluation and Certification, *Journal of Digital Information*, **8**(2).

28 Digital Curation Centre and DigitalPreservationEurope (DPE) (2007), *Digital Repository Audit Method Based on Risk Assessment* (DRAMBORA), released in draft version 1.0 in February, p.11.

29 *ibid.,* pp.16-17.

30 *ibid.,* pp.23-31.

31 *ibid.,* passim.

32 An overview of the progress can be seen at: *http://wiki.digitalrepositoryauditand certification.org/bin/view/Main/WebHome*

33 The projected timeline is available at: *http://wiki.digitalrepositoryauditandcertification.org/ bin/view/Main/WorkSchedule*

34 Minutes of the MOIMS Trusted Repository committee meeting (2008), CCSDS meeting, Berlin, Germany, October 14, available at: *http://wiki.digitalrepositoryaudit andcertification.org/bin/view/Main/FaceToFaceMeeting20081014.*

35 The working document is available at: *http://wiki.digitalrepositoryauditand certification.org/bin/view/Main/ReqtsWithTemplate.*

36 *http://wiki.digitalrepositoryauditandcertification.org/pub/Main/MetricsWorkingDocument FollowingFaceToFace/AuditCertificationTDR-MB-20090716-final.doc.*

Chapter 20

Issues of Scale and Storage in Digital Preservation

Richard Wright[1]
[1]*BBC Research & Innovation*
BBC Future Media & Technology
BC3D6 Broadcast Centre, 201 Wood Lane
London W12 7TP UK
richard.wright@bbc.co.uk

Abstract

The reliability of the computer systems that underlie digital repositories is a basic issue in long-term preservation. Errors and failures in systems and storage puts preserved material at risk – of becoming 'unpreserved'! The information technology industry has impressive statistics, used to convince us all that we can indeed rely upon mass storage: mean times between failure of hard drives of over one hundred years; file read failures (from disc) on the order of one in 10 to the seventeenth power. However large datasets, including the massive files originating from audiovisual content, make these figures less impressive. Failure of systems and storage is a reality that large digital archives (petabytes of storage, thousands of disc drives, millions of read cycles per day) will have to manage. This paper will set out the principal strategies and measures available to archive managers for coping with system and storage failures.

Keywords: Digital Preservation, Long-term Preservation, System and Storage Failures, Technology Obsolescence.

20.1 Introduction and Significance of Storage

As storage costs continue to drop by roughly 50% every 18 months, there are two effects:

- *Storage looks free (but isn't)*: the cost of storage devices becomes negligible[i], but power, space, cooling, management and replaced costs remain significant.
- *Storage is abundant*: much more storage is used

The following figure shows how hard drive storage has increased over the last 25 years[1].

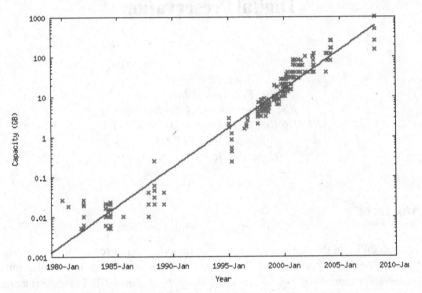

Fig. 20.1: Increase in the hard drive storage capacity over the years.

The largest available size (for a desktop computer) has increased from 5 MB to one terabyte – a factor of 200 thousand (which is about 18 doublings in about 25 years, so very close to doubling every 18 months).

The 'growth of risk' is of course much larger: a factor of 200 000 in disc size, times the increase in the usage of discs (about 10 000 over the same period)[2].

This "growth of storage" also divides into two effects:

- the number of storage units (globally, and used by any given institution) increases

---

[i] 'Storage is free' is a dangerous statement to make – if storage is free then keeping multiple copies is free and hence there is no cost in reducing risk – you can do LOCKSS for free.

- the amount of data stored on each unit also increases

The increase in storage units (devices) means that statistics on failure rates that were once seen as 'safe' are now appreciable risks. An advertised Mean Time Between Failure of 1000 years looks very safe to a person buying a new hard drive (though it will be obsolete in 5 years). Schroeder and Gibson[3] give results on a survey of major datacenters holding 100000 discs, and found annual failure rates ranging from one to 13 %, averaging around 3% - far higher than an MTBF of 1000 years.

This failure rate means that owners of 1000 of those same hard drives will need systems (e.g. big RAID6 arrays) and processes (e.g. continual hot- swapping and rebuilding) to ensure these failures are managed.

The increase in storage units results in more and more users being responsible for, or dependent upon, storage systems that have thousands of individual storage devices (hard drives, optical discs, data tapes). The increase in the amount of data stored on each device makes the failure of each device more significant in terms of the volume of data potentially lost. A 3.5" floppy disc with 1.4 megabytes (MB) of data represented a few dozen files. A 650 MB CD could hold 500 times more data: thousands of files, or one hour of audio. A USB-attached terabyte hard drive is 700 000 times bigger than a floppy, and 1400 times bigger than a CD. It could, for example, hold the entire contents of an institution's audio collection (such as several years' work by many people, collecting oral history recordings).

20.2 Storage Costs

Digital data requires storage, and that storage must be managed (maintenance; digital preservation). This section considers the cost of maintained storage, looking at costs of a *service* rather than of a storage device or *product*. A product is essentially some hardware and some software, with a purchase price – but beyond that are the human costs around the storage system, with its staffing and maintenance that make the total system 'trusted', and give it any hope of permanence. We compare managed storage and with the raw costs of digital storage devices and the costs of shelf-based storage. This section concludes with a recommendation for the implementation of repository functionality in an off-line (tapes on shelves) rather than online (everything on servers) environment.

One of the first organisation to offer a 'trusted digital repository' service is the OCLC = Online Computer Library Center in the USA[ii]. The OCLC Digital Archive[iii] is a commercial proposition, and uses the digital library standards (OAIS, METS[iv])

The OCLC service is an unlikely 'maintained storage' solution for digital audiovisual collections, because of the relatively high costs. According to the 2002 figures quoted by Chapman[v], OCLC was charging US$15.00/GB per year (at the best rate, for a terabyte or more of storage). Further, that charge is for secure digital storage, NOT for what Chapman refers to as "the capability to render intellectual content accurately, regardless of technology changes over time"[vi].

The problem is: shelf storage had an annual cost in 2002 of about US$10 per shelf foot (for storage with full environmental control). At 10 videotapes per foot, one hour each at Digibeta quality (80 Mb/s), the storage is 400 GB for $4 (for the shelf) plus $40 for the tape itself, meaning about $0.10 per GB! The difference is a factor of 150. [This comparison is simplistic, because the tapes will last longer than one year, and so it is unfair to put the full $40 digibeta tape cost against the first year. But after five to ten years the tape will have to be migrated, and that cost has not been included in the figure of $0.10 per GB. The two effects offset each other, though on balance the figure $0.10 per GB is at the high end of estimates for shelf-based storage of videotape.]

Some further information on managed storage costs is given in the recent paper "The Digital Black Hole" by Jonas Palm of the Swedish National Archives[4]. Managed storage requires staff as well as equipment, and staff can be a major part of the total cost. Palm quotes a Microsoft source on information management costs (primarily from the text world, where 1 TB of data represents roughly 250 million pages). In the financial world 1 TB of data requires one system manager, and other costs add up to US$300k per terabyte. In other sectors this drops to one system

---

[ii] www.oclc.org

[iii] www.digitalarchive.oclc.org/

[iv] Digital Repositories and related standards are fully covered in PrestoSpace D13.4 Digital Repositories Explained, submitted for project and reviewer approval in January 2007.

[v] jodi.tamu.edu/Articles/v04/i02/Chapman/

[vi] jodi.tamu.edu/Articles/v04/i02/Chapman/p.4

manager per 10 TB, and for 'aggregators' like Google where data management is very automated, it drops again to one manager per 100TB. Personal communication[vii] with the Sun "Honeycomb" storage management project[viii] also indicated a 'bottleneck at around 10 TB', with 'negative economies of scale' – meaning costs increased more rapidly as storage increased – for storage volumes greater than 10 TB.

These cost comparisons are summarised in the following table. The first row, 2002 costs, shows that managed storage is 150 times the price of storage of videotape on shelves, as discussed above[5]. The middle column is for storage on hard drives of the cheapest sort – just the cost of the drives and nothing more.

As shown in the successive rows of the table, cost in the middle column drops dramatically. This drop is the storage variant of Moore's Law[6]: storage capacity (for the same cost) doubling every 24 months. This drop has been steady for about 40 years. Prospects for the next 10 years are covered in another PrestoSpace publication: "Ten-year Forecast of Storage Evolution"[ix].

Table 20.1: Estimates of annual audiovisual storage costs.

Cost for one GB for one year	Analogue on shelves	Digital media (offline)	Managed storage (online)
2002 (reported)	$0.10	$4	$15 = 7 + 8
2006 (estimate)	$0.11	$1	$9 = 7 + 2
2010 (estimate)	$0.12	$0.25	$7.50 = 7 + 0.50
2020 (estimate)	$0.15	$0.02	$7= 7 + 0

The managed storage figures quoted by Palm indicate that around US$30k per terabyte, meaning US$30 per gigabyte, was the "going rate" in 2005. These figures are higher that the Chapman figures, because they refer to

---

[vii] Personal conversation with Mike Davis, Honeycomb senior project manager, Sun Honeycomb have participated in PrestoSpace STAG (Storage Technology Advisory Group) events.
[viii] research.sun.com/minds/2005-0628/
[ix] www.prestospace.org/project/deliverables/D12-5.pdf

the IT industry in general rather than OCLC's service for archive storage. But the difference between the Chapman and the Palm figures does not matter. What matters is:

- the figures are in rough agreement ($30 and $15 per gigabyte)
- the real issue is what happens to storage costs in the future.

Table 20.1 starts with the Chapman figure of $15/GB/yr, and looks at what happens as Moore's Law applies to the raw storage part of that figure. We assume that about half the cost in the Chapman / Palm data represents staff and facilities[x], not storage devices themselves. These costs do not drop, but neither do they rise. Small improvements in IT management technology offset inflation, and basically IT systems cost now what they did 20 years ago – but the amount of storage in the systems (for that same price) has grown by the storage variant of Moore's Law[7], storage capacity (for the same cost) doubling every 24 months.

As seen in the right-hand side of the table, raw storage costs drop by Moore's Law, and all that is left, eventually, is the rest of the cost: management, maintenance, facilities. The table shows managed storage costs levelling off, not dropping as in the middle column. The numbers in the right-hand column could be off by a factor of two, but the general conclusion is that managed storage will NOT continue to reduce in cost. There will be little reduction after 2010, with cost stablising at US$5 to US$10 per GB per year.

The first column, shelf costs, increases only as general inflation increases – which in most areas that are using digital repositories is quite low. The middle column follows Moore's law and shows storage becoming practically free – but only for raw storage devices, not managed servers.

The implications are very plain:

- archives will continue to find a managed service unaffordable, if by

---

[x] This cost breakdown is deduced from the "one staff member per ten terabytes" statement quoted by Chapman. If storage costs around $100k per $300k for 10 TB, and includes one full-time staff member, then it is reasonable to conclude that about half the cost is for the member of staff and for all associated infrastructure.

managed service one means a fully online system of mass storage (server-based storage; mass storage);

- letting materials sit as they are on shelves is untenable, as digitisation is required for preservation – certainly for audio and video materials;
- what's left is the middle column: use of raw storage media, which offers digital storage and low cost.

The problem with raw storage media is that it simply can't be trusted – for durations as short as three years much less the indefinite future. Raw media has NONE of the attributes of a trusted repository. Material just dumped onto storage media is very much at risk. The media is prone to failure, there is no inherent way to find anything, and the files themselves if they can be found and read (as data) will become obsolete and unplayable – and possibly unidentifiable and, effectively, lost.

The need, and really the only hope for the huge amounts of digital storage required by audiovisual archives, is to combine the physical storage approach of the middle column of Table 20.1 – offline storage – with the functionality associated with the highest levels of service from online trusted digital repositories. Clearly what is needed are trusted offline repositories, with the security of the online repositories of the right-hand column of Table 20.1, at costs closer to the centre column.

20.3 Cost Modeling

We will present an approach to risk that combines the dimensions of cost, risk (uncertainty) and value (benefits). This model builds upon and extends work on cost modeling by both the digital library and audiovisual communities. Early on in the development of digital libraries there was the fundamental work on preservation strategies by Beagrie and Greenstein[8], Hendley[9], Granger, Russell and Weinberger[10] – and eventually something about the audiovisual sector from EU·PRESTO project[11]. The state of the art was brought together, and specifically labelled 'life cycle', in the important paper of Shenton[12].

Since then, there have been entire projects and conferences devoted to life-cycle models and costs. At a conference organised by the Digital Preservation Coalition and the Digital Curation Centre[13] there were reports from the LIFE[14] and eSPIDA[15] projects, both specifically about costs, though the eSPIDA work was more generally concerned with a formal method for including intangible benefits (value) in business cases. More pertinent to the present paper, it also specifically introduced the issue of uncertainty into the modeling process.

Specific digital library and digital preservation cost models reported at the 2005 DPC/DCC conference included work from Cornell University, TNA in the UK, and the Koninklijke Bibliotheek in the Netherlands as well as two papers arising from PrestoSpace[16]. In all these models and studies, and for digital library technology in general, little is said about storage (except in the PrestoSpace work). Digital libraries assume that storage will be there (somewhere), and will work and continue to work. In estimating Total Cost of Ownership (TCO), the complexity of the models just mentioned is devoted to digital library processes, not storage devices (or their management). In digital library/repository TCO models, storage cost is generally modeled as a single number per year, and the model simply 'adds up' those numbers.

20.4 Cost-of-Risk Modeling

Estimation of cost involves uncertainties. Some uncertainties can be represented as variances in cost estimates (uncertainty about how much costs may vary from the predicted value), but a whole range of uncertainties are related to things that may or may not happen, and should be formally identified as risks[17].

A risk is the likelihood of an incident along with the business consequences (positive or negative)[18].

Examples of possible incidents include:
- Technical obsolescence, e.g. formats and players
- Hardware failures, e.g. digital storage systems
- Loss of staff, e.g. skilled transfer operators
- Insufficient budget, e.g. digitisation too expensive
- Accidental loss, e.g. human error during QC
- Stakeholder changes, e.g. preservation no longer a priority
- Underestimation of resources or effort
- Fire, flood, meteors …

Traditional risk modeling (and its use in project management) looks at lists of such incidents, and their attendant likelihoods (assessing likelihood may have the largest uncertainty of the whole process!) as contained in a risk register, and then proceeds to predict the consequences – the impact – of each item.

Possible consequences for preservation from the above list of incidents would include:

- Corruption or loss of audiovisual content
- Interruption to services
- Inefficiencies and increased costs
- Corner cutting and increased risks
- Failure to meet legal obligations
- Loss of reputation or loss of customers

A more comprehensive approach to the whole issue of uncertainty in preservation is to include the concept of value (benefit). The work of eSPIDA has already been mentioned.

The combination of uncertainty, cost and benefits forms a three-way interaction, as shown in the Fig. 20.2. The key point about this approach is that it is as applicable to the whole issue of business-case planning, not just to the more narrow issues of risk analysis and cost modeling[19].

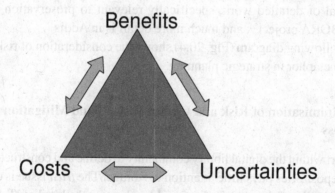

Fig. 20.2: Issues in preservation modeling process: A three way interaction

A typical preservation scenario, which can be optimized by use of the cost-of-risk approach, is given in the Fig. 20.3:

This integrated approach to cost, risk and value allows all the factors affecting preservation planning, funding and management to be considered in one set of interactions, rather than being taken separately.

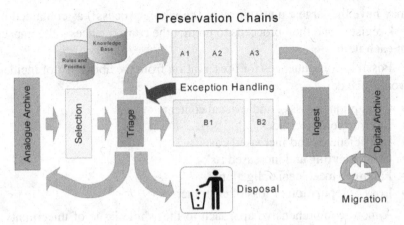

Fig. 20.3: A typical preservation scenario.

For quantitative modeling, all three factors need to be converted to a common unit of measurement. As cost and benefits are already commonly thought of in financial terms, the task is then to also express the uncertainties in monetary units: the cost-of-risk.

Full details require a much longer presentation. There has already been a great deal of detailed work, specifically relevant to preservation, in the DRAMBORA project[20], and much more detail is in Addis[21].

The following diagram (Fig. 20.4) shows the consideration of risk as the central metaphor in strategic planning.

20.5 Minimisation of Risk and Cost of Risk — and Mitigation of Loss

The effort within the digital library community to define and construct trusted digital repositories pays little attention to storage. The *trust* issue is defined and examined mainly at the institutional level, not at the level of IT systems and certainly not at the level of individual device or file failures. Yet the *only* physical reality of the content of a trusted digital repository lies in its files, sitting on its storage. The 'atomic level' of success or failure of a repository is the success or failure of an attempt to read individual files. Such success or failure is clearly fundamental to the concept of trust for the whole repository.

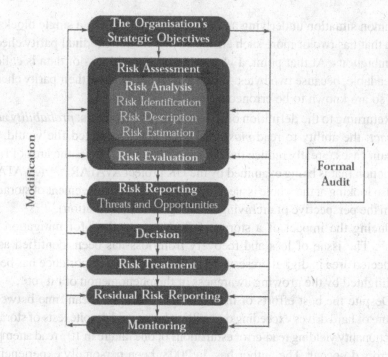

Fig. 20.4: Consideration of risk as the central metaphor in strategic planning.

Effort of the storage area of the IT industry is entirely focused on reducing the likelihood of read errors (device failure or file read error). There is no concept, within standard IT systems, of a partially-recoverable file. If the inevitable low-level errors cannot be corrected by the built-in error detection and correction technology, the read fails and the file fails to open. There is nothing that the ordinary user can do at this point, and even the all-powerful system manager can only look at backups to see if there is another copy of exactly the same file. There is technology to attempt to read corrupted files or failed hard drives, but such technology falls in the category of *heroic measures*: sending the file or drive to an external company that will attempt a recovery using proprietary technology, at a substantial price[22].

Physically, a file with a read error is not an all-or-nothing situation. There will still be a stream of data (somewhere in the *stack* of operations between the user and the hardware) which is likely to be mainly correct, and is also likely to even have indications of which bytes are incorrect (because of lateral parity errors). For simple error detection and correction schemes, a common situation underlying an inability to read a file is a single block of data that has two or more such errors, so that the longitudinal parity check is ambiguous. At that point, a whole file of many blocks of data is called unreadable, because two bytes – at known locations – fail their parity check and so are known to be erroneous.

Returning to the definition of risk as having two factors: *probability* and *impact*: the ability to read *most* of the data in a corrupted file would, in certain cases, greatly reduce the *impact* of the error. This is the area of risk reduction that is being examined by the UK project AVATAR[23, 24]. (AVATAR is also looking at the whole issue of optimization and management of storage, from the perspective of archiving and long-term preservation).

Reducing the impact of a storage failure is a method for mitigation of loss[25]. The issue of loss and recovery from loss has been identified as a neglected area in digital preservation thinking, but its importance has been highlighted by the growing awareness of the phenomenon of bit rot[26].

Despite the best efforts of the IT industry, despite mean time between failure of hard drives exceeding one million hours, and despite tests of storage functionality yielding read-error estimations of one failure in 10^{17} read attempts – errors do occur. The author has, in 2008, been personally experiencing one file read failure per month – and in each case these are total failures, with no possibility of mitigation (beyond the commercial route of heroic measures).

20.6 Redundancy and Risk

Standard practice for reducing risk of loss is to have another copy. The use of second (or higher) copies is a method of reducing impact: a file read error or a device failure has much less impact if recourse can be made to a backup copy or system.

At a more sophisticated level, arrays of hard drives are used to gain the benefits of redundancy at lower cost. RAID[xi] technology achieves protection for the loss of one of N drives in a set of N+1 – so the net cost is N+1 drives, rather than the 2N that would be required by simple redundancy.

[xi] RAID: Redundant Array of Inexpensive Discs – an efficient method of achieving device-level redundancy, *en.wikipedia.org/wiki/Redundant_array_of_independent_disks*

RAID has now advanced (e.g. RAID6) to the point where multiple disks can fail without data loss, which means data can still be accessed safely whilst individual disks are being replaced and live rebuilding takes place.

This allows disk systems to be built that are resilient to hardware failures, human errors and data read errors. For large data centers, the problem is shifted from risk of loss from device failure to having the right support processes to 'feed' large systems with a constant supply of new drives and have the people in place to do so.

At the same time as redundancy is added to storage systems to reduce risk, redundancy is being taken out of the files stored on those systems, as a way to save space. Compression, lossless or lossy, is based on the innate redundancy (entropy) of the original data. When the redundancy is removed from a file, a complex transformation has to be applied to the resulting data in order to transform it back to the original (or close to the original, in the case of lossy compression).

20.7 To Encode or Not to Encode

The process of compressing (encoding) a file has profound consequences for attempts to mitigate against loss. A consequence of removal of redundancy is that the remaining data is all very significant – because a compression process is entirely an attempt to eliminate insignificant data. If one byte of the resultant file is then damaged, that byte is then very likely to be used involved in computations (the decoding or decompressing process) that will affect many other bytes. Encoding a file severely affects the ability to use corrupted data as a method of reducing the impact of error.

As an example: an uncompressed audio .WAV file is simply a header followed by a sequence of numbers – one number per sample of the desired audio waveform. If the audio is sampled at 44.1 kHz (the rate used on CDs), each sample represents about 23 micro-seconds of data. Losing one byte of data results in one bad sample, but there is no spread to any of the rest of the data.

Hence an uncompressed audio file can be perfectly usable despite loss of one byte. Indeed, experiments have shown that a .WAV file with 0.4% errors is almost undistinguishable from the original, whereas an MP3 file with the same level of errors either will not open at all, or will have errors affecting most of the audio, and rendering it unusable.

The same logic applies to video, images – and even to text if represented as a sequence of characters (with embedded mark-up, as in the old days of 'printer control characters' as escape sequences within a text 'stream').

An extensive study of the consequences of byte-level errors on different file types, compressed and uncompressed, was recently presented by Heydegger[27]. His results include the following data for image files; in each case exactly one byte had been changed:

- a 10 MB TIFF = .000 01% errors (meaning just that one byte affected)
- a lossless JP2 had 17%[xii] errors for a saving of 27% in storage
- a lossy JPEG had 2.1% for a saving of 62% in storage[xii]

As an example of the affect of data loss on imager files, here are two examples: a BMP (uncompressed) and a GIF (compressed). Each had one byte in 4k changed – meaning 3 bytes total for the GIF, and 12 for the BMP.

Not quite ready for retirement:
Steamboat Willie, 1928
Used without permission

BMP with one error every 4K bytes   GIF file with one error every 4K bytes.

Fig. 20.5: Affect of data loss on imager file.

From the above results, it is evident that removing redundancy increases impact, the "cost of error". The compression increases the proportional damage caused by an unrecoverable read error. However

---

[xii] Is this really 17% for a saving of 27% storage? – that's a pretty crap trade off.

if there is no mechanism for using files despite read errors, then it is of no practical significance whether a one-byte error causes major damage, or only very local and very minor damage. If the file can't be read in either case, the error-magnification factor caused by compression is hidden.

If less-than-perfect files can be passed back to the user, or to a file restoration application, then the increase in 'cost of error' caused by compression can be legitimately compared with the decrease in cost of storage[xiii].

An unsolved issue in preservation strategy is whether it is better (lower 'cost of risk' for the same or less total risk) to use lossless compression and then make multiple copies (externalized redundancy) as a way to reduce the impact of storage errors – or to avoid compression and exploit the internal redundancy of the files. The problem at present is that there is little or no technology (within conventional storage systems, or conventional digital repositories) to support the second option.

The question of which strategy to take depends on more than just the ability of file systems to return files with partial errors. A holistic approach to risk management means dealing with disaster recovery (fire, flood, theft etc.), human error (accidental corruption, deletion, miscataloging etc.), and technology obsolescence (formats, software, devices etc.). All present powerful drivers for multiple copies in multiple places using multiple technical solutions. If an offsite copy of uncompressed video is created to address DR, then lossless compression may allow two offsite copies for the same cost. Three copies in three places may well be enough to reduce the risk of loss due to individual storage failures to a level where no further measures are needed beyond those of conventional storage systems, e.g. RAID.

However, until file reading systems are willing and able to return files despite errors, and include media-specific reconstruction techniques to 'fill in' where errors are known to exist, there will be no effective way to exploit file-error recovery as a method to mitigate against loss. This prevents a whole class of 'cost of risk' strategies from being used to complement conventional techniques.

[xiii] I don't think it's completely true. As device costs (disks or tapes) may become negligible, but TCO for storage (inc. maintenance, upgrade, power, space, people etc.) certainly won't – see intro section.

The frustration for audiovisual archivists is that digital technology has taken us one step forward, and now is taking us two steps back. The ability of analogue videotape recorders to cope with loss of data (dropout) was limited, and black lines would appear in the resultant images. Digital tape recorders had much better built-in compensation: the *concealment* option would allow a missing line to be replaced by a neighbouring line, and expensive machines could even replace entire frames with an adjacent (in time) frame. Now file-based digital technology has no ability to cope with loss, beyond the 'external redundancy' option of multiple copies.

One could accept that files are, and will remain, 'all or nothing' entities – you either get everything in them or you lose the lot. The strategy then becomes one of splitting assets, e.g. a video sequence, into multiple files and then implementing safety measures at the 'application' level. For example, an audiovisual program could be split into separate files for shots, scenes, frames, regions of interest, audio, video or many other ways. The most important parts would then be assigned to one or more storage systems with appropriate levels of reliability – avoiding the 'all eggs in one basket' problem. The advantage here is that how to 'split' an asset into pieces can be done based on an understanding of what the asset is – something that a file system or storage device will never have. The downside is increased technology and management costs – a violation of the 'simplest is best' principle.

We hope that current work in preservation theory and methodology, with use of file description metadata , will support and encourage the ability of storage systems to return less-than-perfect files in a usable fashion.

Examples of work with relevance to file description include Planets (file characterization) and Shaman:

- MPEG-21 DIDL = Digital Item Declaration Language[28]
- XCEL, XCDL = eXtensible Characterisation Languages[29-30]
- Shaman = multivalent approach[31]

20.7 Conclusions

Comprehensive and integrated planning for preservation can be accomplished through use of a three-factor model, based on costs, benefits and uncertainties. The cost-of-risk concept allows all three factors to be quantified on a common, monetary scale.

Reduction of the cost-of-risk, and the best chance for mitigation of loss, is by always taking the simplest option – beginning with not compressing the data.

Storing only uncompressed data would appear to add cost rather than reduce it – but storage costs are typically a small part of a preservation project or strategy (labour is always the dominant cost), and storage cost is dropping by 50% every 18 months.

The full benefit of uncompressed files (in terms of mitigation of loss and consequent reduction of impact) will remain irrelevant unless and until the storage industry and digital repository architects produce systems that allow access to less-than-perfect files.

Acknowledgements

This paper is based on a paper written by myself, Ant Miller (BBC) and Matthew Addis (ITI, Southampton University), published in the proceedings of iPRES2008 *www.bl.uk/ipres2008*, and also on work supported by the EC-funded PrestoSpace project.

References

1 Hankwang (2008), *http://en.wikipedia time.png*

2 Computer World (2008), Seagate ships one-billionth hard drive, *http://www.computerworld.com/action/article.do?command=viewArticleBasic&taxonomyName = storage&articleId=9079718&taxonomyId=19&intsrc=kc_top*

3 Schroeder, Bi and Gibson, G.A. (2007), Disk failures in the real world: What does an MTTF of 1,000,000 hours mean to you? 5th USENIX Conference on File and Storage Technologies, Feb 2007, *www.usenix.org/event/fast07/tech/schroeder/schroeder_html*

4 Palm, J. (2006), The Digital Black Hole, *www.tape-online.net/docs/ Palm_Black_Hole.pdf*

5 Chapman, S. (2003), Counting the Costs of Digital Preservation: Is Repository Storage Affordable? *Journal of Digital Information*, 4(2), Article No. 178, 2003-05-07.

6 Moore's Law, *http://en.wikipedia's_law*

7   *ibid.*

8   Beagrie, N & Greenstein, D. (1998), A strategic policy framework for creating and preserving digital collections, *British Library Research and Innovation Report 107*, London: British Library, *www.ukoln.ac.uk/services/elib/papers/supporting/pdf/framework.pdf*

9   Hendley, T. (1998), Comparison of methods and costs of digital preservation, *British Library, Research and Innovation Report*, 106, *www.ukoln.ac.uk/services/elib/papers/tavistock/hendley/hendley.html*

10 Granger, Russell and Weinberger (2000), *Cost models and cost elements for digital preservation CEDARS project*, *www.leeds.ac.uk/cedars/colman/costElementsOfDP.doc*

11 Wright, R. (2002), Broadcast archives: preserving the future, *PRESTO project*, *http://presto.joanneum.ac.at/Public/ICHIM%20PRESTO%2028_05_01.pdf*

12 Shenton, H. (2003), *Life Cycle Collection Management LIBER Quarterly*, **13**(3/4).

13 DPC/DCC (2005), *Workshop on Cost Models for preserving digital assets*, *www.dpconline.org/graphics/events/050726workshop.html*

14 LIFE: Life Cycle Information for E-Literature, *www.life.ac.uk/*

15 eSPIDA: (costs, benefits and uncertainties in project proposals), *www.gla.ac.uk/espida/*

16 PrestoSpace, *www.prestospace.eu, http://digitalpreservation.ssl.co.uk/index.html*

17 Risk definition and risk management, *JISC: www.jiscinfonet.ac.uk/InfoKits/risk-management/*, PRINCE2, *www.ogc.gov.uk/methods_prince_2.asp*

18 Addis, M (2008a) Cost Models and Business Cases (for Audiovisual Curation and Preservation) *presentation at HATII-TAPE Audiovisual Preservation Course*, Univ of Edinburgh, May 2008, *www.hatii.arts.gla.ac.uk/news/tape.html*

19 Wright, R. (2007), *Annual Report on Preservation Issues, www.prestospace.org/project/deliverables/D22-8.pdf*

20 DRAMBORA (2008), *www.repositoryaudit.eu/*

21 Addis (2008a), *op.cit.*

22 Recovery Tool Box, *http://www.recoverytoolbox.com/*, This company is just one of many offering tools that *may* be able to repair a corrupted file.

23 AVATAR-m: *http://www.it-innovation.soton.ac.uk/projects/avatar-m/*

24 Addis, M., *et al.*, (2008b) Sustainable Archiving and Storage Management of Audiovisual Digital Assets; to be *presented at IBC 2008*, September, Amsterdam.

25 Knight, S. (2007), Manager Innovation Centre and Programme Architect National Digital Heritage Archive, NLNZ, Remarks 'from the floor' on the significance of efforts to mitigate against loss, at the SUN PASIG meeting, Nov 2007, Paris, *http://sun-pasig.org/ nov07_presentations.html*

26 Bit Rot: *http://en.wikipedia*

27 Heydegger, V. (2008), Analysing the Impact of File Formats on Data Integrity, *Proceedings of Archiving 2008*, Bern, Switzerland, June 24-27; pp.50-55.

28 File Description methodologies, DIDL: *http://xml.coverpages.org/mpeg21-didl.html*, XCEL, XCDL: see Becker, 2008 and Thaller, 2008

29 Becker, C., *et al.* (2008), A generic XML language for characterising objects to support digital preservation, *Proceedings of the 2008 ACM symposium on Applied computing*, Fortaleaza, Brazil, pp.402-406, *http://portal.acm.org/citation.cfm?id=1363786&jmp=indexterms&coll=GUIDE&dl=GUIDE*

30 Thaller, M. (2008), Characterisation (Planets presentation), *http://www.planets-project.eu/docs/presentations/manfred_thaller.pdf*

31 Watry, P. (2007), Digital Preservation Theory and Application: Transcontinental Persistent Archives Testbed Activity, *International Journal of Digital Curation*, 2-2, *www.ijdc.net/ijdc/article/viewArticle/43/0*

Index

3D, 157, 158, 160, 161, 164, 165, 166, 168
  Digital, 155, 164, 165, 166, 167, 168
  Data cataloguing, 164
  Model, 157, 165, 166
  optical scanner, 157, 158, 159
  Scanning, 158
  vision, 157

access systems, 319, 346
Accessibility, 282, 284, 285, 286, 292, 293, 294, 333, 335
accuracy, 188, 189, 190, 192, 196, 201, 202
adaptability, 281, 293, 294
Africa, 295, 296, 297, 298, 299, 301, 302, 305, 306
African musical instruments, 297
Agent based Systems, 21
AGORA, 169, 174, 176, 177, 181, 182, 185
AJAX, 301, 303
algorithm, 166, 167, 190, 199, 200
Alignment
  point cloud, 158, 159, 162, 164
ambiguities, 184
ancient cultures, 298

Anglo-American Cataloguing Rule (AACR2), 53
Annotating, 211, 212
annotations, 169, 176
APIs
  apply ontologies, 60
  handles all transactions, 60
  Joseki and Jena, 60
  lexica management, 60
  metamodeling, 60
  modularisation, 60
  multiple functionalities, 60
  ontology evolution, 60
  querying, 60
  retrieve ontology, 60
  store ontology, 60
application domain, 80
approaches, 68, 89, 91, 93, 94, 97, 100, 105
approximate algorithm, 104
archaeological artefacts, 296
archaeologists, 157, 161
architecture, 52, 53, 61, 207
archival life cycle, 353
Archival Resource Key, 335
archived articles, 143
archives, 157, 308, 309, 310, 311, 314, 344, 345, 347, 350, 351,

354, 356, 357, 361, 366, 367,
378
archivists, 343
Archivists, 298
Artefact Deterioration, 298
artifacts, 155, 157, 160, 165, 166,
167
  reproduce digitally, 157
Artificial Intelligence, 2, 19, 279
arts, 139, 143
artwork retrieval, 80
ASI, 22
Asian Language, 152
Atom, 336
ATOS Scanner, 158
audit and certification, 341, 343,
345, 346, 347, 349, 350, 351,
355, 356
  criteria, 342, 343, 345, 346, 348,
349, 350, 351, 352, 353, 354,
355
  developing recommended
standards, 343
  Trusted Digital Repositories,
348
automated
  approaches, 235
  classification, 235
  migration, 296
automatic
  annotation, 205
  extraction, 261, 262, 263, 264,
265, 268, 269, 270, 271, 272,
274, 275, 276, 277, 278, 279
  metadata, 261
  image retrieval, 170, 181
  indexing, 171, 261, 262, 271
  tagging, 207

training approach, 4, 7, 8

bandwidth, 295, 299, 301
Bangla, 128, 134
Bayes classifiers, 94
Bayesian Networks, 24, 38
benchmarks, 126
Bengali corpus, 151
bibliographic
  catalog, 51, 60
  cataloging records, 53
  metadata, 322, 324, 326, 333,
335
binary search models, 187
bi-tri grams, 148, 149, 150
Bleek and Lloyd archive, 297
blobworld representation, 93
BMBF, 310
bookmarks, 60
Braille, 282, 284, 287, 292
browser, 146, 329
building recognizers, 119
Bushman culture, 295, 297
BVH project, 172

CAD, 157, 160, 165, 167
  CAM, 165
CASPAR, 296, 305, 310
cataloging
  rule, 51, 55, 56, 58
  standard, 51, 53, 55, 56, 58
cell image retrieval, 226, 237
certification, 310
CESR, 169, 170, 173, 175, 176,
178, 180, 181, 183
change
  components, 12
  management, 13

character
  classes, 120, 121, 126
  encoding schemes, 142
  recognition, 178, 182
  segmentation, 121, 125, 126,
    132
classical
  library, 52, 53, 59
  systems, 53
classification
  ontologies, 61
  scheme, 52
clinicians, 218, 219
clustering, 122, 129, 205, 213
  techniques, 129
collaboration, 310
  platform, 206
collaborative learning, 206
collection
  development, 52, 300
  management, 52, 53
Colon Classification, 53
color correlogram, 39, 46, 50, 99,
    225
color descriptors, 110
color feature descriptors, 74
  CEILAB, 74
  RGB, 74
color histograms, 92, 225
Committee for Space Data
  Systems, 346, 353
communication, 298, 318, 365
  IE, 137, 138, 139, 140, 141, 142,
    150
  IR, 137, 138, 139, 140, 141, 142,
    148, 150, 151
  QA, 140
computation, 79, 82, 84

Computer Graphics, 165
concept mapping, 97
conceptualisation, 2, 7
consonant, 126
content, 5, 6, 67, 68, 69, 70, 73,
    76, 77, 79, 80, 81, 83, 84, 86,
    87, 88
  based image retrieval, 67, 68,
    70, 80, 86, 87, 88
  based retrieval, 225, 226, 237,
    239, 240
  based search, 205, 224, 225
content management system, 206
  learning, 205
  web mining, 205
context sensitive, 205
contextual advertising, 47
copyright, 264, 274, 276, 356
copyrighted material, 145
coreference, 268, 271
  resolution technique, 271
Corel datasets, 112
corpora, 137, 138, 140, 141, 142,
    146, 151
corpus, 169, 175, 183, 186
  acquisition, 138, 142
  annotation, 150, 151
  cleaner, 146
  postprocessor, 146
  shareable, 145
Criteria for Trusted Repositories,
    310
Cross Language Evaluation Forum
  (CLEF), 141
Cross-Lingual Information Access
  and Retrieval (CLIA/ CLIR),
    151

cultural heritage, 90, 117, 120, 133, 155, 156, 268, 296, 307, 319, 321
  German, 321
  image retrieval techniques, 91, 101
  inventory, 90

Data Harvesting Agent, 59
data interchange, 59
data modeling, 217
DC element, 264, 265, 268, 270, 272, 273, 274, 275
Decision trees, 232
Description Logic, 25, 63
descriptive metadata, 330
descriptors, 90, 92, 101, 106, 107
  MPEG, 90, 106, 107, 110, 113, 118
  Scale Invariant Feature Transforms (SIFT), 106
detectors, 76, 77, 78, 79, 81
developing countries, 295, 296, 299, 304, 305
  infrastructure, 296, 297
Developing extensions to ontology representation languages, 17
developing nations, 297
  practices, 297
  technology, 297, 303, 305
Dewey Decimal Classification (DDC), 53
DFG Viewer, 324, 338
diagnostic workstation, 219
DICOM, 218, 219, 220, 221, 236
diffusion
  distance, 106, 108, 109
  kernel, 109, 110, 111, 113

  maps, 105, 108, 109, 113
digital
  access, 343
  access to information, 343
  cultural heritage, 355, 356
  future, 337
  libraries, 53
  Long-term Repositories, 351
digital archives, 345, 351
  in public institutions, 297
  institutions of higher learning, 297
Digital Curation Centre (DCC)., 350
digital data, 164, 165
  preservation standards, 344
  preserving, 345, 346, 348, 356
  providing access, 343, 356

digital heritage library, 24
  architecture, 22, 27, 30, 33, 34, 35, 36, 37, 38, 45
  coordination agent, 35
  Directory Agents, 36
  media agents, 36, 38, 39
  ontology agents, 35, 38
  repository agents, 35, 36, 38
  user interface agents, 36
digital heritage material, 321, 326
digital image cytometry, 226
digital imaging, 297
digital information, 284, 307, 311, 334, 341, 345, 347, 348, 352, 355, 356
Digital Information Archiving System (DIAS), 311
Digital initiatives, 321

digital library, 101, 119, 121, 123, 175, 202, 205, 206, 207, 208, 210, 211, 214, 215, 263
searching, 212
services, 53
systems, 54, 55, 61, 187
toolkit, 303
digital long-term archive, 308, 314, 318
digital media, 261, 274, 298, 334
digital objects, 300, 302, 303, 305, 315
digital preservation, 295, 305, 334, 343, 344, 358, 363, 368, 372, 378, 379
digital repositories, 341, 348, 349, 351, 353, 354, 355
Digital Repository Audit Method, 352, 358
digital resources, 264, 281, 288, 290, 321, 322, 333, 336, 337, 348
Dissemination, 321, 333
digital trust, 343, 345
building, 342, 343, 345
digital watermarking, 166
digitization, 53, 155, 219, 271, 273, 275, 302, 321, 322, 323, 324, 326, 327, 328, 329, 331
efforts, 295
projects, 171, 173, 175, 178, 181, 343, 346, 349, 354
digitized
items, 261
manuscripts, 328
material, 323
texts, 179
Dimension Reduction, 226

dimensionality, 72, 89, 91, 96, 102, 103, 104, 105, 109, 110, 113, 117, 118, 196, 197, 198, 221, 225, 226, 228, 238
problems, 102
reduction techniques, 102, 104
DIN, 310
DINI, 351, 358
certificate, 351
DISA collection, 295
disabilities, 281, 282, 283, 284, 285, 286
discrete features, 122
disseminating information, 22

dissemination formats, 336
distributed engineering environment, 165
diverse media, 261
document
acquisition, 142
categorization, 151, 176, 262
clustering, 262
corpus, 139, 146
images, 119, 124, 129, 130, 135
representation, 191
structure, 182
DoE corpus, 137, 138, 139, 140, 144, 146, 147
DOI, 335
domain centric knowledge, 223
domain ontology, 22, 33, 44, 181
DPC, 310, 368, 378
DRAMBORA, 351, 352, 353, 358
DSpace, 61
Dublin Core, 60, 184, 261, 263, 277, 324, 336

standards, 263, 264
dynamic fonts, 144
dynamic time warping, 122, 129, 133

EAD, 184
Efficient Indexing, 130
eigenimages, 93
eigenvectors, 109
electronic materials, 308
electronic publication, 307
elements, 4, 5, 24, 35, 55, 75, 104, 170, 179, 182, 183, 192, 194, 201, 211, 212, 213, 262, 263, 264, 277, 287, 301, 378
features, 5, 24, 30, 31, 32, 34, 37, 38, 41, 43, 44, 45, 46, 48, 67, 68, 69, 70, 72, 75, 76, 77, 78, 79, 80, 81, 84, 87, 89, 90, 91, 92, 93, 94, 95, 96, 97, 98, 99, 100, 101, 102, 105, 106, 107, 108, 112, 113, 118, 122, 129, 130, 132, 144, 157, 166, 193, 215, 222, 225, 226, 227, 229, 231, 234, 237, 241, 261, 264, 265, 272, 273, 276, 308, 309, 323
relationship, 4, 5, 27, 54, 55, 76, 77, 78, 80, 92, 96, 104, 196, 222, 226, 228, 231, 240, 267, 268, 272, 316
empirical research, 139, 141
emulations, 308, 309
Encoding, 137, 170, 174, 182, 319, 373
ETD collection, 316
European
colonization, 297

Community, 321, 326
digital library project, 68
languages, 12, 17, 43, 49, 54, 60, 119, 120, 121, 122, 123, 124, 125, 126, 127, 128, 129, 132, 137, 138, 139, 141, 142, 149, 170, 181, 183, 190, 191, 201, 202, 217, 266, 267, 268, 272, 275, 277, 323
renaissance, 169
event-based environments, 113
evolution strategies, 13
excavated, 156, 167
experimental validation, 139
Extraction, 1, 2, 7, 16, 18, 19
extraction tasks, 3
Co-reference Task, 3
recognition tasks, 24
Template Element Task, 3
Template Relation Task, 3

factors, 10, 28, 82, 144, 231, 295, 309, 369, 370, 372, 377
related to the ontology life cycle, 10
Feature
based similarity, 98
extraction, 71, 73, 81, 98, 105, 122, 225, 226, 235
extraction methods, 105
hypotheses, 78
selection, 105
Transformation, 196, 197
file formats, 158, 308
fine feature detectors, 76
Flexible Image Retrieval Engine, 234

formats, 59, 107, 138, 142, 172,
217, 264, 273, 287, 308, 309,
312, 313, 319, 334, 336, 345,
347, 368, 375
FRBR, 292, 294
funding, 62, 165, 299, 304, 311,
322, 351, 369
Fused Deposition Modeling, 155
fusion, 89, 95, 96, 109, 115, 211
Fusion of Visual and Textual
keywords, 107
fusion schemes, 95
fuzzy color histogram, 67, 74, 88

Gabor filters, 225, 226
Gabor texture filters, 93
Gallica, 172, 178, 185
geometrical model, 156, 167
Germany, 19, 49, 172, 307, 309,
310, 311, 312, 316, 321, 322,
326, 327, 330, 351, 354, 358
global digital memory, 307
glyph, 122, 125, 126, 128, 142, 144
graphical catalogue, 165

handwritten manuscripts, 129
handwritten material, 120
harvesting, 59, 172, 317, 318
hash based search, 132
Heritage, 21, 33, 38, 39, 40, 41, 42,
44, 45, 47, 117, 155, 156, 167,
261, 264, 281, 292, 305, 306,
379
artifacts, 22, 45
collections, 22, 23, 35, 36, 304,
305
documents, 188, 262, 274, 275
information, 22, 33, 262, 344

preservation, 296, 299
records, 281
resources, 21, 22, 292
high-level semantic, 68, 70, 80, 84,
91
based Image Retrieval, 70
historical handwriting, 122
historical handwritten
manuscripts, 129
HMM, 121
Hole Filling, 159
HSV color space, 93
HTML, 142, 143, 144, 146, 263,
336
Human-centered, 99
humanities, 156, 170, 175, 177, 180
images and text, 112, 176, 262
IMS Global Learning Consortium,
288
Inclusive
Learning Exchange, 286, 293
resources, 281
Incorporating linguistics, 17
indexing, 23, 33, 34, 35, 36, 40, 50,
67, 70, 71, 92, 93, 97, 98, 99,
103, 104, 130, 149, 165, 174,
176, 178, 180, 188, 189, 205,
207, 210, 211, 212, 215, 223,
224, 225, 226, 229, 235, 237,
238, 240, 328, 331, 342
Indian Languages, 43, 119, 138,
266, 278
Indian scripts, 40, 119, 121, 122,
123, 124, 126, 127, 132, 144
Indian sub-continent, 138
Indic OCRs, 123
Inductive Logic Programming, 6
inflations, 126

information
  accessibility, 295
  context- specific, 51
  intelligent mechanism, 51
  keywords, 89
  retrieval algorithms, 190
  retrieval system, 188
  retrieval systems, 189
  Retrieval Techniques, 187
  storage, 51, 298
Information Extraction, 1, 2, 6, 18,
  97, 137, 138, 139, 141, 207, 211
information management costs, 364
information retrieval, 49, 52, 86,
  91, 92, 93, 96, 97, 100, 110,
  118, 141, 152, 188, 189, 190,
  191, 192, 217, 222, 234, 241,
  242, 262, 264, 265, 266, 268,
  271, 277, 303
ingesting, 315
institutional repositories, 297
integrated queries, 229, 230
integration
  classical and digital library, 52,
    53, 54, 55
Intellexer Summarizer, 269, 279
intelligent dissemination, 53
intelligent search, 205, 213, 215
intentional knowledge, 17
interaction, 4, 11, 30, 35, 69, 84,
  177, 206, 217, 224, 228, 233,
  234, 291, 301, 331, 369
Interactive frameworks, 99
Interface Evaluation, 217, 233
international standards, 312, 330,
  337, 341, 345, 356
interoperability, 8, 29, 33, 47, 58,
  61, 323, 351

Intinno, 205, 206, 207, 214, 215
inverted files, 93, 304
IPR, 274
ISCII, 144, 146, 152
ISO, 113, 241, 288, 294, 310, 346,
  347, 348, 354, 355, 357
  Audit and Certification
    Standard, 341, 354
issues
  African context, 297
JeromeDL, 61, 63
JHOVE, 316, 319

keyblock, 94, 114
Kirby Collection, 306
knowledge, 1, 2, 3, 4, 5, 6, 7, 8, 9,
  10, 11, 12, 13, 14, 16, 17, 23, 24,
  25, 28, 29, 30, 31, 32, 34, 35, 36,
  39, 41, 42, 43, 48, 52, 53, 54, 55,
  61, 76, 77, 78, 81, 86, 94, 137,
  141, 162, 174, 175, 179, 181,
  191, 223, 297, 307, 335
knowledge engineering approach, 3,
  4, 7
Knowledge Management, 19, 62,
  240
knowledge resources, 25
  lexicons, 4, 182, 272
  rule set, 4
  templates, 3, 4, 223
kopal, 307, 310, 311, 312, 313,
  314, 315, 316, 317, 318, 319
kopal Library for Retrieval and
  Ingest" (koLibRI), 313

LabelMe, 110, 111, 112, 118
language engineering community,
  137

language independent techniques, 261

language inputs, 201, 202

language models, 127, 133, 187, 201, 202, 266

language researchers, 145

layout analysis, 121, 124, 132, 176, 185

layout recognition, 124, 125

learning algorithms, 12, 231, 269

Learning Management System, 205

learning material, 206, 208

legacy application, 52
    for library management, 53

legacy library information systems, 58

libraries, 24, 25, 35, 39, 51, 52, 53, 60, 61, 87, 90, 119, 165, 169, 172, 173, 178, 180, 215, 263, 277, 307, 308, 310, 311, 314, 322, 323, 327, 335, 336, 344, 351, 367, 368

library automation, 52

library classification schemes, 60

Library of Congress Classification, 53

library resources, 52, 53, 55, 60
    Crawling, 60, 137
    manageability issues, 60
    network infrastructure, 60

library science, 52, 170

library systems, 311

Lightweight Systems, 300

Linear Discriminant Analysis, 227

linguistic
    dependencies, 262

Multi-annotation, 184

locality sensitive hashing, 122, 129, 130, 132

LOCKSS, 296, 299, 362

long term
    access, 309, 348
    archiving, 312, 313
    availability, 312
    preservation, 307, 309, 310, 311, 315, 317, 319, 321, 333, 344, 345, 355, 356, 361, 372
    storage, 307, 345, 349, 352

longevity, 336, 346, 350

low-level
    description, 4, 33, 35, 47, 48, 51, 52, 55, 59, 100, 101, 105, 108, 117, 173, 175, 178, 211, 223, 228, 239, 265, 268, 269, 270, 272, 275, 286, 287, 290, 292, 326, 335, 353, 376
    image, 69, 80, 93, 112
    visual, 67, 69, 70, 91

machine learning, 67, 70, 100, 105, 215, 269, 272

Magnetic Resonance Imaging, 218

Maintaining an ontology, 10

managed storage, 363, 364, 365, 366

manpower-intensive method, 142

manuscripts, 134, 169, 174, 176, 184, 298, 324, 332, 336

mapping, 58, 60, 69, 72, 80, 91, 97, 105, 109, 122, 178
    between real-world applications and multimedia entities, 222

Mapungubwe Collection, 296

MARC21, 59, 61

MarcOnt Initiative, 63
matrix elements, 193, 194
Maximization algorithm, 199
measures
  of accuracy, 189, 190
  of similarity, 187
measuring document similarity,
  189, 192, 193, 201
media works
  in virtual forms, 316
medical image
  formats, 217, 220
  Management, 218
  retrieval, 228, 234, 235
  searching, 235
medical imaging, 218, 226
Memory of the World, 302
Merging, 158
Message Understanding
  Conferences, 2, 141
metadata
  formats, 336
  standards, 91
  Techniques, 261
metric spaces, 104, 118
METS, 315, 324, 325, 326, 336
migration, 308, 312, 314, 315, 316,
  319, 345, 355
MILOS software, 110
Modality Fusion Techniques, 89, 95
Modern Images, 180
MODS, 324; 336
M-OWL, 21, 30, 43
MPEG, 29, 33, 35, 48, 49, 86, 376
MRI, 218, 223, 229
multicolored objects, 92
multidimensional
  indexing scheme, 104

scaling, 203, 238
multi-document summarization,
  269
Multi-feature Indexing, 70
multilingual, 101, 137, 138, 266,
  269, 275
  search engine, 101
multilingualism, 181
MultiMatch, 101, 102, 117
multimedia
  Concept Recognition, 31
  conceptual framework, 33, 90
  Construction, 30
  Content Description Interface,
    90, 118
  datasets, 104, 238
  element, 94
  evidential reasoning system, 24,
    31, 32, 33
  indexing, 99
  ontology, 24, 27, 28, 31, 35, 36,
    45, 46, 47, 49
  ontology learning module, 30
  retrieval, 49, 68, 96, 97, 101,
    103
  retrieval applications, 89, 105
  search and retrieval, 98, 104,
    105, 219
  signals, 99
Multimedia web Ontology
  Language (MOWL), 24
multimodal
  approach, 89, 94
  based image retrieval, 105
  emotion recognition, 99
  Image Presentation, 109
  Image Representation, 92, 107
  Image Retrieval, 106

keyword, 110, 111
  representation, 113
  vector representation, 89, 94
multi-modality, 108, 235
Multiparameter indexing, 205
multiple interfaces, 234
multi-word indexing units, 149
musical instruments, 306
mythological entities, 170, 181

named entity
  identification, 151
  recognition, 191, 266, 277, 278
NARA, 344, 346, 347, 349, 350,
  357, 358
natural language, 2, 6, 60, 139,
  188, 189, 190, 193, 196, 222,
  262, 266, 269
  Processing, 138, 267
  processing techniques, 196
navigation tool, 235
nestor, 307, 309, 310, 311, 349,
  351, 352, 353, 358
  certificate, 351
Network Semantic Search Agent, 60
neural network architecture, 103
news corpora, 138, 141, 142
  for IR/IE Research, 141
Non-contact digitizing system, 155
non-linear techniques, 105

OAI
  interfaces, 324
  PMH, 336
  protocols, 178, 183
OAIS, 315, 341, 346, 347, 348,
  349, 357, 364
OAIster, 336

object management, 350
object ontology, 70, 80
Object- oriented Systems Model
  (OSM, 5
object property, 58
Observation Model, 24, 31, 32, 33,
  34, 35, 38, 39, 40, 41, 42
Obtaining an ontology, 10
OCLC, 305, 348, 349, 357, 364,
  366
OCR, 40, 98, 116, 119, 120, 121,
  123, 124, 125, 126, 129, 132,
  134, 143, 170, 174, 177, 181,
  326, 332
  algorithm, 124
  software, 120
old documents, 176
ontology, 1, 7, 10, 11, 12, 13, 16,
  18, 19
  based system, 81
  bibliographic purposes, 61
  driven Information Extraction
    Systems, 7
  Evolution, 12
  for Multimedia, 24
  integration, 12, 36
  Learning and Population, 11
  library resources, 53
  management infrastructure, 51
  Management Module, 10, 16
OntoSyphon, 6, 19
OPAC, 335
Open Archival Information System
  model, 296
  Reference Model, 341
Open Language Archives
  Community (OLAC), 263
open source

course material, 208
material, 206
solution, 60
optical character recognizers, 119
organizational infrastructure, 350
OWL-DL, 54, 55
    sound and decidable reasoning,
    54

PACS, 217, 218, 219, 220, 236
PADI, 310
palm leaf manuscripts, 120
PARSE, 310
persistent linking, 335, 336, 337
personalized recommendation, 205,
    215
perspective, 297, 300
phrases, 6, 148, 149, 150, 268, 272,
    273
PLANETS, 296, 310
PLSA, 198, 200, 202, 266, 268
Point Cloud Processing, 158
polygonization, 159
polysemy, 193, 196, 198
Portable Font Resource (PFR)
    technology, 144
portals, 22, 45, 47, 323
post-colonial world, 298
post-coordination algorithms, 235
posterior probability, 32, 96
post-processors, 127
Precision, 112, 190, 233, 234
PREMIS, 296, 305
preprocessing, 16, 144, 187, 190,
    191, 197, 201
preservation
    Planning mechanism, 319
preservation of

heritage, 167, 299, 304
preservation of culture, 295
preserved, 228, 281, 296, 297, 300,
    307, 335, 342, 345, 348, 355,
    361
Preserving Digital Information, 345
Principal component analysis, 227
Probabilistic Ontology Model
    (POM), 13
probabilistic technique, 104
probabilities, 29, 32, 39, 95, 96,
    122, 199
profiles, 287, 288
proposed image retrieval system
    minimum bounding rectangle
        (MBR), 72
    R-trees, 72, 84, 117
    Self-organizing Relevance
        Feedback, 72
    Structure SOM, 71
Proposed Image Retrieval System,
    70
Prototyping, 155, 157, 160, 168
Provenance, 263, 276
public resources, 282
PURL, 335
QBE, 223
QBIC, 68, 86, 93, 116, 225
    system, 237, 240
Qualified Dublin Core (QDC),
    263
qualitative cooperation, 329, 330
query
    concepts, 70, 80
    Formulation, 114
    languages, 217
    processing, 35, 36
    Refinement, 231

query by picture example, 68, 69
Question Answering, 140, 268

radiological imaging, 218
radiologists, 218, 219
RAID, 219, 334, 372, 373, 375
RAID6 arrays, 363
ranking, 32, 38, 121, 214, 230, 235,
    268, 269
Rapid Prototyping, 160
rare book materials, 327
Raw multimedia information, 222
recall, 6, 39, 84, 111, 112, 190,
    193, 195, 233
Recognition Free Matching, 129
reference model, 261, 262, 347
relevance, 50, 69, 70, 71, 72, 73,
    84, 87, 88, 91, 93, 97, 101, 117,
    122, 139, 140, 150, 151, 152,
    181, 189, 223, 229, 231, 232,
    234, 241, 328, 376
relevance feedback, 67, 68, 69, 72,
    74, 88, 115, 217
relevant resources, 206
Renaissance books, 169, 172, 182
repository, 33, 34, 38, 53, 59, 60,
    183, 208, 222, 262, 263, 270,
    271, 277, 300, 341, 342, 343,
    345, 348, 349, 350, 351, 352,
    353, 355, 363, 364, 367, 368,
    370, 377
Research Issues, 116, 164
Research Libraries Group (RLG),
    345, 347, 348, 349, 350, 357,
    358
resolution, 155, 166, 191, 201, 218,
    219, 221, 226, 266, 267, 268,
    269, 271, 278, 303, 331, 347

Resource Identifier, 263, 275
Resource Ontology, 51, 55, 64
resource providers, 282
retrieval
    effectiveness, 152
    performance, 83, 232, 233
    system, 67, 68, 70, 84, 86, 101,
        188, 229, 233, 240, 242
RETRO, 174, 181, 182
reverse annotation, 122, 134
Reverse Engineering, 155, 157
Rewriting History, 298
Rights Holder, 263, 276
Rights Management, 263, 274
RIS (Radiology Information
    System), 218
RIS Communicator, 219
risk analysis, 352, 369
RSS, 336
Rule Generation Module (RGM), 9,
    13, 16

sample queries, 139, 140, 150
scalability, 10, 36, 62, 189, 303,
    318
scanning, 72, 155, 158, 165, 167,
    323, 331
sculptors, 157
sculptures, 155, 156, 157, 164, 165,
    166, 167, 271
Search Agent
    Communication, 61
    Network Semantic, 60
Searching and browsing, 60, 240
    based queries, 60
    simple queries, 60
security, 312, 342, 346, 347, 349,
    367

segmentation, 98, 106, 121, 122, 124, 169, 176, 271
segmentation algorithms, 124
segmented characters, 124
self audits, 356
semantic
  analyzer, 76, 77, 78, 79, 80, 81
  applications, 62
  approach, 68
  capturing, 89
  concepts, 91
  content, 80
  description of the resources, 51
  descriptions, 59, 100
  digital library, 52
  enabled digital library, 52
  features, 77
  information, 68, 83, 90, 139, 186, 269
  library services, 51
  models, 194
  Reasoning Approach, 81
  technology, 51, 52, 53, 54, 55, 58
  technology applications, 58
  template, 70, 80
Semantic Analysis, 67, 77, 111, 187, 196, 197, 198, 203, 266, 267
  Latent, 111
  probabilistic latent, 189
semantic analysis of images, 84
  coarse level, 77
  contextual knowledge, 77
  semantic analyzer, 77
  semantic resoning, 78
semantic indexing method, 189
  probabilistic latent, 189

Semantic Web, 36, 49, 61
  application, 62
  Challenges, 62
  Technology, 63
semi-automatic bootstrapping approach, 6
semi-fine feature detectors, 77
Service Oriented Architecture, 24
Shape Feature Descriptors, 75
similarity analysis, 170, 181
similarity measure matrix, 227
similarity measures, 17, 83, 84, 193, 213
SIMILE, 61, 63
Simple Dublin Core (SDC), 263
Simple Object Oriented Protocol (SOAP), 37
  XML Messages, 37
Singular Value Decomposition (SVD), 197, 227
sketch tool, 235
Skills and Education, 298
SOAP, 37, 55, 61
software agent, 51, 54, 55
  artificial agent, 55
solution architecture, 51
solutions, 23, 61, 97, 175, 184, 295, 296, 297, 298, 300, 305, 308, 309, 319, 337, 347, 355, 375
sophisticated indexing, 215
source-link components, 12
South Africa, 297, 302, 306
South African, 295, 296, 302
South Asia, 137, 138
South Asian languages, 138
Spatial Event Cube (SEC), 104
speech recognition, 121

SQL, 223
standard databases, 126
Standards for digitization, 331
Static collections, 300
static data, 308
statistical
  Analysis, 137, 146
  information, 126
  mapping, 122
  problem, 92
  tool, 146
stemming, 107, 191, 192
stop word removal, 191
stop words, 16, 191, 194, 201, 265
storage
  costs, 361, 365, 366, 377
  Problem, 165
Stratasys FDM, 160
structural information, 262, 264,
  265, 271, 272, 273, 276, 277,
  328
structural metadata, 323, 326, 328,
  329, 333
structure analysis, 169, 174, 176
Subject Ontology, 60
supervised learning, 69, 100, 241
support vector machines (SVM), 94
surface fitting, 159
synonymy, 193, 196
system and storage failures, 361
System Architecture, 9

Tag Augmentation, 213
tagging, 181, 183, 184
Target Documents, 175
technique
  semantics-preserving image
    compression, 93

text information retrieval, 96
Technology Development for
  Indian Languages, 138
Technology Infrastructure, 350
TEI, 170, 183, 184, 328, 332, 336
  consortium, 184
term-document matrix, 92, 110,
  192, 193, 194, 197, 199, 201,
  202
term-matching retrieval, 92
terracotta art, 164
text annotations, 89, 90, 91, 92, 96
text based
  queries, 228
text corpus, 137, 141
Text Retrieval Conference
  (TREC), 141
text search engines, 119
textual access methods, 232
textual heritage information, 262
textual information, 25, 70, 80, 92,
  138, 222, 233, 234, 241
textual semantic access, 217
Texture Feature Descriptors, 74
thesaurus, 94, 104, 169, 179, 180,
  181
thumbnail images, 165
TILE, 286, 287
Timbuktu, 296, 298, 306
tokenization, 191
toolkit, 118, 145, 146, 303
tools/workflow, 310
Topic tracking, 151
transcriptions, 171, 181, 297, 332,
  333
triangulated data, 159, 160
triangulation, 159
trusted digital repository, 343

UNESCO, 296, 302, 305, 306
Unicode, 127, 142, 144, 264, 275
uniform identifiers, 336
union catalogues, 326
Universal Object Format, 313
unstructured data, 196
URL, 47, 48, 50, 237, 238, 239,
   240, 263, 275, 324, 335, 336,
   338
URN, 335
User Interface, 36, 39
user network
   FOAF metadata, 60

vector space models, 187, 196, 197
ViewFinder, 229, 230
Virage, 116, 237
Virtual Humanistic Libraries, 169,
   171
virtual museum, 22, 47
virtual reality environments, 157
visual
   concepts, 99
   content of images, 70
   Description Tools, 90
   feature descriptors, 27, 81
   features, 70
   keyword-image matrix, 107
   keywords, 94
   layout, 143
   synonyms, 94
Visual C++, 145

Visual Keyword Construction, 106
visualization, 238
vowel, 126
VRA, 90, 113
   Core, 90, 113

W3C, 24, 25, 48, 50, 285, 286, 287,
   290, 292, 293
web
   Archiving, 316
   based architecture, 219
   Content Accessibility
      Guidelines, 286
   image retrieval, 80, 115
   mining techniques, 215
   Services, 37, 50
   Services Architecture (WSA), 37
websites, 143, 178, 208, 210, 215,
   286, 303
Weighted Multi- dimensional
   scaling (WMDS), 227
wikipedia, 208, 210, 212, 215, 372,
   377, 379
word spotting, 119, 123, 129, 132,
   134, 174
WorldNet, 114
written knowledge system in
   Africa, 297

XML, 37, 40, 170, 183, 210, 300,
   301, 302, 303, 324, 333, 334,
   335, 336, 379